IGNATIUS OF LOYOLA

HIS PERSONALITY

AND

SPIRITUAL HERITAGE

1556–1956

Series II. Modern Scholarly Studies about the Jesuits, in English Translations

No. 1.   Joseph de Guibert, S.J. *The Jesuits: Their Spiritual Doctrine and Practice. A Historical Study.* Translated by W. J. Young, S.J. 1964 and 1972, 717 pages.

No. 2.   *Ignatius of Loyola: His Personality and Spiritual Heritage, 1556-1956. Studies on the 400th Anniversary of His Death,* By F. Wulf, S.J. (Ed.), Hugo Rahner, S.J., Karl Rahner, S.J., and others. 1977, 318 pages.

IGNATIUS OF LOYOLA
HIS PERSONALITY
AND
SPIRITUAL HERITAGE
1556-1956

Studies on the 400th Anniversary of His Death

by

Friedrich Wulf, S.J.

Hugo Rahner, S.J.

Hubert Becher, S.J.

Hans Wolter, S.J.

Josef Stierli, S.J.

Adolf Haas, S.J.

Heinrich Bacht, S.J.

Lambert Classen, S.J.

Karl Rahner, S.J.

Edited by Friedrich Wulf, S.J.

THE INSTITUTE OF JESUIT SOURCES

St. Louis, 1977

This book is an authorized translation of
Ignatius von Loyola: seine geistliche Gestalt und
sein Vermächtnis (1556-1956). Friedrich Wulf, S.J.,
Editor. Würzburg: Echter-Verlag, 1956.

IMPRIMI POTEST: Very Reverend Leo F. Weber, S.J.
                    Provincial of the Missouri Province
                    September 8, 1976

IMPRIMATUR: Most Reverend Charles R. Koester
                    Vicar General of St. Louis
                    September 16, 1976

© 1977   The Institute of Jesuit Sources
         Fusz Memorial, St. Louis University
         3700 West Pine Blvd.
         St. Louis, Missouri 63108

To the memory of

REVEREND EDWARD V. MONAGHAN, S.J.

1879–1922

through the generosity of his brother

MR. JAMES L. MONAGHAN

1867–1963

to whom the Institute of Jesuit Sources

owes its financial foundation

CONTENTS

PART I. ST. IGNATIUS' PERSONALITY

PART II. ST. IGNATIUS' SPIRITUALITY

EDITOR'S FOREWORD

This present symposium of studies on the personality and spiritual heritage of St. Ignatius of Loyola first appeared in Germany in 1956, as a volume of commemorative essays on the occasion of the four-hundredth anniversary of the saint's death. To prepare for a fitting celebration of this anniversary, Father Friedrich Wulf, S.J., the editor in chief of the well-known periodical on the spiritual life, *Geist und Leben*, wrote to many German Jesuit scholars who had shown themselves active in studying the life and work of Ignatius. He invited them to contribute essays to go into the anniversary volume. The result was this collection of studies respectively from Fathers Bacht, Becher, Classen, Haas, Hugo Rahner, Karl Rahner, Stierli, Wolter, and Wulf. The book was published by Echter-Verlag, Würzburg, with the title: *Ignatius von Loyola: seine geistliche Gestalt und sein Vermächtnis* (1556-1956).

The Institute of Jesuit Sources is now happy to make these essays available in English. They are manifestly studies in depth which were carried out with precision of statement, careful documentation, and soundly based reflection. Many of them have already exerted important influence on Ignatian investigations during the past two decades since they first appeared.

The work of translating them into English was begun already in the early 1960's by a group of American Jesuit scholastics in the theologate of Innsbruck, Austria. Unfortunately, the pressure of other work has made it impossible to complete the editing and publication until now. The book which has at last appeared is the result of great labor generously expended by a long list of Jesuits to whom recognition and sincere gratitude are now expressed: G. Richard Dimler, Peter J. Esseff, Thomas N. Gallagher, Hugo J. Gerleman, Morton J. Hill, James F. McAndrews, James E. O'Hearn, James M. Quigley, Louis W. Roberts, Harold E. Weidman, Robert Williams, and others too whose names, if all were to be added, would make this list unduly long. The names of the translators are respectively given on the first page of each Study.

But special thanks are due to Father Friedrich Wulf, the editor of the original German volume, and to his publisher, Echter-Verlag, for the help they continuously gave and the patience they showed when the many delays were encountered.

George E. Ganss, S.J.
Director and General Editor
The Institute of Jesuit Sources

Heinrich Bacht, S.J., is professor of Fundamental Theology in the theologate Sankt Georgen, Frankfurt-am-Main. He is a specialist in early monasticism.

Hubert Becher, S.J., is a specialist in the history of Germany. He was Rector of Aloisiuskolleg in Bonn-Bad-Godesberg. Later he was an associate editor, at Munich, of the periodical *Stimmen der Zeit.* He died in 1964.

Lambert Classen, S.J., was a professor of Metaphysics in the former theologate at Valkenburg, Holland, a rector of the Canisiuskolleg in Berlin, and spiritual director in the seminary at Hildesheim. He died in 1966.

Adolf Haas, S.J., is professor of Biology and Natural Philosophy in the Jesuit Faculty of Philosophy at Munich. He was associate editor of a German translation of St. Ignatius' *Spiritual Diary* (1961), and also the author of a translation of and commentary on the *Spiritual Exercises* (1967).

Hugo Rahner, S.J., was for many years professor of Church History in the University of Innsbruck, Austria, and also the Rector of the University for a time. He has published numerous books, articles, and reviews on St. Ignatius of Loyola. He died in 1968.

Karl Rahner, S.J., was professor of Dogmatic Theology in the University of Innsbruck and later in the University of Münster in Westfalen. He is presently Honorary Professor of Theological Investigations in the Universities of Munich and Innsbruck. He has published many studies on Ignatius and Ignatian spirituality.

Joseph Stierli, S.J., formerly provincial of the Vice-Province of Switzerland, is director of the retreat house at Schönbrunn, Switzerland.

Hans Wolter, S.J., is professor of Church History in the philosophate and theologate, Sankt Georgen, in Frankfurt-am-Main. He is also Honorary Professor of Church History in the University of Frankfurt-am-Main.

Friedrich Wulf, S.J., received his doctorate in ancient and medieval history. For many years he has been living in Munich as the editor in chief of the periodical on the spiritual life, *Geist und Leben.* He has also been an associate editor of two series of books, "Studien zur Theologie des Geistlichen Lebens," and "Geist und Leben. Studien zur Verwirklichung des christlichen Lebens."

PART I

ST. IGNATIUS' PERSONALITY

INTRODUCTION

by FRIEDRICH WULF, S.J.

Editor of the German book
Office of Geist und Leben
Munich, 1956

THE EXTRINSIC motivation for the composition of this book was
the celebration of the four-hundredth anniversary of the death, on
July 31, 1556, of St. Ignatius of Loyola, the founder of the Society
of Jesus. The authors who contributed their scholarly essays toward
its production wished to proclaim their love for and express their
gratitude toward the man whose school they attended and to whose
work their lives are also dedicated. It was designed to be a *Festschrift*,
a tribute to their father. Yet it has finally become something with a
much broader scope. Even though the single contributions could not
be closely coordinated with one another, and even though much is
still lacking that the subtitle might lead one to expect to find in it,
the book is still unified. Not only does it present a good insight into
what matters are the object of Ignatian research today; but, above
all, it brings to light the point of view from which the members of the
order today look upon their founder and his spiritual teaching.

This view of Ignatius is not only more profound and comprehensive than that of the past, but it also differs in important points from
the image of Ignatius and Ignatian spirituality that is current outside
Catholicism, and also within it. This is not a mere accident. The
time is ripe for a correction of that image. Since the primary sources
for the life of the saint and his own writings have been collected and
published in a critical edition in the Monumenta Historica Societatis
Jesu, Ignatian research has received a powerful impetus. Both the
baroque exuberance of the Catholic image of Ignatius and the erro-
neous and distorted picture of him that had its origins in Protestant and
rationalistic polemics against the Jesuits have had to give way in the
light of scientifically conducted historical research. Indeed, it has
become impossible for anyone to deny any longer the true greatness
of this man. Yet the essential core of his nature, his divine secret,
has still remained hidden from most men. The application neither of

psychological nor of purely ethical categories succeeded in making Ignatius completely comprehensible. The view "from below" required a complementary view "from above."

It was only the decades after the First World War that gradually introduced a shift in the approach. People began to open themselves to emotional values, to the mysteries of life and of the human soul that are not immediately comprehensible to reason — in more or less conscious opposition to the rationalism of the nineteenth century. In the area of religion and the Church, this showed itself in a strong inclination to mystery, to the efficacy of prayer, and to mysticism. It is no wonder that this side of Ignatian spirituality also was given stronger emphasis and that special attention was paid to those of his writings that reveal him to have been a divinely favored mystic, especially the *Autobiography* which he himself dictated and his *Spiritual Diary*. From that time on there has been an unbroken chain of inquiries that seek to feel their way to a more profound knowledge of his mystical union with God, of his visions and consolations. Viewed from this basic aspect, the fundamental theological principles of his spiritual doctrine became more intelligible than before: the transcendent position of the Divine Majesty, the continuation of the redemptive activity of Christ, the view of history as a universal salvational event, and of Christian perfection as ever greater service. New light also fell on the saint's relationship to the world, his attitude toward creatures, his asceticism, his prayer, the favored position that obedience receives in his thought. There was an ever clearer recognition of the range of Ignatian spirituality, of the reciprocal correlation of the pairs of opposites found therein. It was stressed that the individual activity of the person, so emphatically demanded by Ignatius, is not for its own sake, but is intended to awaken in one a readiness to receive the call of grace; man must "depart from all self-will" so that he can "enter into God." Just as in Ignatian thought — as in a contemplative spirituality — "asceticism" and "mysticism" match each other, explain, preserve, and complement each other, there is a similar complementarity between the explanation of the function of conscience and the demand for "obedience of the understanding," between the indication that one's inner experience is the way to recognition of the will of God and that calm sobriety which seems to subordinate everything to the intellect and to logical thought.

That is the recent picture of Ignatius. It is again based on the sources and seeks to suppress nothing. It abounds in apparent opposites and thus is frequently subject to misunderstanding; and yet it has an amazing intrinsic unity, based on the supernatural. Its depths are open only to the man of faith. One of the most intimate companions of the saint named the attitude that of a *contemplativus in actione*, a contemplative in action, in the redemptive work of Christ, in a loving " being-there " for one's brother. Today we again consider this to be the summation of Ignatian spirituality. Perhaps it is only in our day that we have regained the ability to see the whole Ignatius without excluding anything and without the overemphasis on certain aspects that was customary in past centuries. We have gained a certain distance from the Enlightenment with its stress on the rational and the ethical; we also have a better understanding of the dangers that threaten genuine Christian spirituality when there is a one-sided emphasis on grace and mysticism. Therefore, we can again risk facing the wide range of an Ignatius, the *coincidentia oppositorum* (correspondence of opposites) that is found in him. We even believe that his spiritual doctrine has long been insufficiently absorbed and assimilated into theology and traditional spirituality, and that thus its hour has really not yet arrived. Ignatius has a mission to our age.

This last was also the intention of the authors who worked together to produce this book. We have first of all attempted to make the man Ignatius live by looking at the natural and supernatural foundations of his character, to sketch a comprehensive picture of him, to work out an idea of his personality and of his spiritual character. How did he operate, what impression did he make upon others, what influence did he have upon them, what was their opinion of him ? Another purpose was to put his teaching on the spiritual life in its proper place in the history of the Church's tradition, to indicate its " metahistorical " connexions which have value far beyond their own historical circumstances, in order to make clear how completely Ignatius drew the materials of his life from the rich tradition that is alive in the Church, how completely he was a man of the Church. Only when this is clear does it follow that we have an obligation to listen to him and to hand his teaching on to others. He signifies a call to us from God. Our final concern was to present the key to his teaching, "seeking God in all things" (realized by Ignatius himself right up to the heights of a trinitarian and soteriological mysticism). This point is the core of Ignatian spirituality. The most important contributions are therefore dedicated to this question: In what way does Ignatius seek to apprehend the will of God for this individual, for his life as a whole or in a particular situation ? What role is played in this by one's interior experiences, the discernment of spirits ? How can his method, which appears in this specific form for the first time, be justified theologically ? To some extent this is new territory that is being explored. Not all of this has been rounded off to the last detail; many matters still remain open and await further development. Yet even so, it has at least been made clear what fullness, what riches, what yet undiscovered treasures are to be found in Ignatius.

May this modest labor be a new beginning; may it stimulate others and be a call to them to undertake their own study of these questions. That would be the best thanks that we could render to Ignatius. Then the purpose of the celebration of the four-hundredth anniversary of his death would be accomplished.

IGNATIUS AS A SPIRITUAL GUIDE

Friedrich Wulf

JUVARE ANIMAS, to aid souls! This phrase often passed across the lips of Ignatius, the great renewer, the founder, one can even say, of the modern apostolate. This phrase is not merely the summation of the external spiritual goal that he would like to imprint ever more deeply in the hearts of the men of his order. It is even more a testimony to that spiritual road, rich in grace, that he walked upon in the school of God, in the school of Christ the Lord. It lays bare the interior of his heart, pierced and transformed by the call of God. It expresses the essence of his spirituality. This is no denial of the unique position that devotion to the Divine Majesty and to the Triune God held in the life of his soul. Just as the love of God and love of neighbour form one commandment, so for Ignatius "the greater service of God our Lord" and "the service of souls" flow directly into one another.[1] Pope Paul III, in the bull *Regimini militantis* (September 27, 1540), rightly designates these two goals, expressed together in one breath, as the very heart of the new order.[2]

For this reason, it is no wonder that, in the first drafts of the religious rule as well as in the definitive Constitutions, reverence, praise, and service of God are repeatedly spoken of alongside the help of souls and the well-being of one's neighbour as being the criterion of a Jesuit's genuine orientation and of every endeavour in the Society of Jesus.[3] Now if God has called a man to the service and care of souls in such a

---

Study 1 was translated from the German by Louis W. Roberts.

1 *Cons*, [603]. For a LIST OF THE ABBREVIATIONS used throughout these footnotes, such as *Cons*, ConsMHSJ, *Autobiog*, see page **294** below.
2 "...quas [sc. Constitutiones] ad... Jesu Christi Domini nostri gloriam ac proximi utilitatem conformes esse judicaverint..." *Regimini militantis Ecclesiae* (1540), [9], in *Cons*MHSJ, I, 31.
3 The Formula of the Institute, *Regimini militantis Ecclesiae* (1540), [3], and *Exposcit debitum* (1550), [3], in *Cons*MHSJ, I, 26, 375.

unique and, one could almost say, exclusive manner, then he has certainly not done so without considering the individual and distinctive qualities which this man has brought along for use in the apostolate. It is normal for God to consider the natural powers of man when bestowing his graces and vocations, and he then normally expects these to complement one another. Thus Ignatius the counselor of souls is the product of nature and grace, of divine vocation and human co-operation working together. His unique apostolic charism lies neither in teaching and preaching, nor in missionary work, nor even in organization (for which he is so often rightly praised), but rather in the immediate person to person direction of souls. Ignatius is the great spiritual guide, one of the most outstanding the Church has had in the course of her history.

Servant of All Men

"God, to whom all things, even our inmost hearts, are known, knows what desires for the salvation and progress of souls he has given to me."[4] The whole of Ignatius is contained in this seemingly casual sentence from a polite letter of refusal to a pious lady of high nobility. This is not rhetorical embellishment, not courtly epistolary style, but a faithful expression of his religious convictions. Ignatius is firmly convinced: God himself has intended men to be his life's work. Even in his final years —during the dictation of his memoirs to Father Gonçalves da Câmara —he still knows exactly how all this came to be. At the beginning of his religious journey, in Manresa, and during his first stay in Barcelona, he often sought out religiously interested and spiritually experienced men in order to converse with them about God and about questions of the interior life.[5] Many things urged him to this: the new realizations that filled him and stimulated him, the almost bewildering array of visions and consolations, the perceptions

---

4 Letter of January 14, 1549, to Jacqueline de Croy, marchioness of Bergen (near Antwerp), in *EppIgn*, II, 303. [An English translation of the whole letter is found in Hugo Rahner, *St. Ignatius Loyola: Letters to Women*, trans. from the German by Kathleen Pond and S. A. H. Weetman (New York: Herder and Herder, 1960), pp. 159-160. This will be cited henceforth as *Letters to Women*. Editor.]

5 "At that time there were many days when he was very eager to speak of spiritual things and to find persons who were open to them." *Autobiog, 34;* cf. 21, 22, 37. [References to Ignatius' *Autobiography* are given according to the numbers of paragraphs. It is printed in *FN*, 1, 354-507; and in *Obras completas de san Ignacio de Loyola*, ed. Candido de Dalmases, "Biblioteca de autores cristianos" (Madrid, 1963), pp. 84-159. There is also an English translation, in which the same numbering of paragraphs has been kept, *St. Ignatius' Own Story*, trans. by W. J. Young (Chicago, 1956).]

of the different spirits which moved his soul back and forth, the transformation by grace of his thought and feeling, the interior difficulties.[6] As yet he was little experienced in spiritual affairs and consequently sought out people of similar inclinations, from whom he hoped to draw help and counsel.[7] Experience soon taught him that only a limited few had genuine spiritual experience at their disposal and that none could aid him in his difficulties.[8] It was not long before he gave up these spiritual dialogues, insofar as he had undertaken them for the elucidation of his own soul and for the sake of his own spiritual progress.[9] God alone remained his real teacher.[10] From the very beginning his spiritual odyssey was marked with mystical favors.

But this is worthy of note: alongside this initial divine guidance, which withdrew Ignatius from the companionship of men, was still another force, apparently opposed to this divine guidance, which roused in him a desire to be with men. Hardly had his heart begun to turn toward God — during his convalescence in the Castle of Loyola — than " he used the time in which he spoke with household acquaintances only for divine things, and thereby brought them spiritual aid."[11] Here we observe for the first time his eagerness and his ability " to aid souls." In Manresa it was no different than in Loyola. Despite his great love of solitude, of long prayer and stiff penance — " he prayed daily seven hours on his knees, got up at midnight and

---

6. *Autobiog*, 19-37.

7 Ibid., 20, 21, 27.

8 He succeeded in overcoming his scruples only through the intervention of God's grace (ibid., 22-27). As a final comment on the first year after his conversion, he says: " But neither in Barcelona nor in Manresa, in all the time that he was there, was he able to find persons who would help him as he desired; only that woman in Manresa . . . who told him that she had asked God that Jesus Christ might appear to him: she alone seemed to him to have entered rather deeply into spiritual matters " (37). Ribadeneyra had heard much the same thing from Ignatius (*FN*, II, 327-328); Nadal also (*MonNad*, IV, 645).

9 " Thus, after he left Barcelona, he lost completely that anxious urge to seek out persons interested in things of the spirit " (*Autobiog*, 37). This is not absolutely accurate. As late as 1535, we find Ignatius spending a week in profound conversations on mystical matters with the Carthusian Juan de Castro in the monastery of Val de Cristo near Segorbe (*FN*, I, 468, 486).

10 " During this period God dealt with him as a teacher deals with a child he is instructing. Now, whether this was because of his inexperience and slowness in understanding, or because he did not have anyone to teach him . . . he has always been of the opinion that God was dealing with him in this manner. Before having any doubt about this, he would consider that he was insulting His Divine Majesty " (*Autobiog*, 27).

11 Ibid., 11.

continued performing all the other . . . exercises of piety [high Mass, Vespers, Compline] " (no. 23) — one finds him continuously in conversation with some friendly persons, " who thought very highly of him and wished to converse with him . . . . because he spoke with such ardor and displayed such a strong determination to make progress in the service of God " (no. 21). " In addition to the seven hours of prayers," Ignatius says later when recalling that time, " he put himself to aiding some souls who sought him in questions of the spiritual life " (no. 26). From then on spiritual conversations become a permanent feature of his life. He became such a master at spiritual dialogue that this, more than anything else, stands out as the hallmark of his apostolic labor. The impulse came not only from the outside, from the men who desired his teaching, but also from his own self, from that flood of grace which compelled him to share it. " One day his reason was suddenly lifted out of itself, and it was as if he was allowed to view the most Holy Trinity under the form of three organ keys. This was accompanied by so many tears and sighs that he could not control himself . . . . this lasted until dinner time. And even after dinner he could speak of nothing else but the most Holy Trinity and indeed in ever different and new comparisons and with great inner joy and consolation " (no. 28).

His first apostolic experiences wrought a decided change in Ignatius' previous manner of living. " After he had once experienced God's rich consolation and had observed the fruit he achieved in their souls through his relationship with men, he ceased the austerities he had practiced earlier; he once again cut his nails and hair " (no. 29). From this point on his consideration for men and their salvation determined his life and action; he develops into a systematic apostle. The thought of aiding souls is an unbroken thread running through the remainder of the pilgrim's recollections. He began writing down his inner experiences, for he believed that " they could also be of use for other men " (no. 99). If he was invited to table, " he listened to what was said and tried to draw from this a few thoughts which could provide him a starting point for speaking about God " (no. 42). The purpose of his journey to Jerusalem was " to aid souls " (no. 45); and, when this purpose was frustrated, " he became ever more convinced that he should study for some time, in order to be able to aid souls " (no. 50). The thought of aiding souls had so conquered his heart that even while studying he sought opportunity " at the same time to devote himself more conveniently to the spiritual life and also to be of use to souls " (no. 54). Everywhere he went in the succeeding years — in Alcalá, Salamanca, and Paris — he began gathering about himself religiously open men, to introduce them, in small groups or individually, to a more perfect life and to give them the Spiritual

Exercises (no. 57). When this activity was forbidden to him by the ecclesiastical authorities — as in Alcalá and Salamanca — he felt entirely helpless and no longer knew what he should do; for "it seemed to him that every door was barred against his bringing effective aid to souls" (nos. 63, 70). No hostility and no annoyance erased his conviction that "he must aid souls, and for this purpose he must continue studying and obtain some companions of like purpose" (no. 71).

In the later review of his life he does not remember his studies as the principal content of these years of preparation (we read actually very little in his biography about his studies although he had devoted himself so intensely to them), but he recalls that he had dedicated himself to the salvation of souls. At all the important milestones in his life's journey the first thing of which he speaks, in almost stereotyped phrases, is his work for the salvation of souls. In the prison of Salamanca "people constantly came to visit him; and the pilgrim continued his usual activity, inasmuch as he spoke about God and other religious topics" (no. 67). "After he returned from Flanders for the first time, he began to devote himself to religious conversations more intensely than before. At practically the same time he gave the Spiritual Exercises to three men" (no. 77). On the occasion of a visit to Loyola — the first after his conversion — "he spoke with many people who came to visit him in the hospital about the things of God and, with His grace, had considerable success" (no. 88). "In Venice at that time he was busy giving the Spiritual Exercises and engaging himself in other religious conversations" (no. 92). "After returning to Rome, he occupied himself in aiding souls, and he gave the Spiritual Exercises to several persons at the same time" (no. 98).

Ignatius views his life with an impressively logical consistency. Everything in it can be summed up in this one thought of aiding souls. One might think that he perceives a certain narrowness of spirit in such a way of life, underlined as it is by the sober, almost indifferent style of the report. But behind the clumsy words of this taciturn man one must feel his burning heart; one must illustrate these words with scenes from his life. Only then do they become alive and display the richness of the breadth of a magnanimous soul, and speak of all the cares, labors, and joys that bound Ignatius to men in a most personal manner. His life is souls, with all the misery and happiness they conceal within themselves; for their sake no journey is too long and no work too difficult. He himself recedes completely into the background.

There was a fellow student of the Parisian period who had wasted the money Ignatius had given him for safekeeping. He was now sick in Rouen and had no one to care for him. "By means of a letter from him, the pilgrim learned of his sickness and a desire came over him to

11

leave Paris in order to visit him and help him. At the same time, considering his friend's condition, he thought that he could persuade him to give up the world and devote himself entirely to the service of God."[12] He had already given him the Exercises.[13] In order to prevail upon God by means of a special sacrifice and so make his petition more urgent, he covered the 150 kilometers from Paris to Rouen in a three-day march, barefoot and without eating anything. When one of his first companions had serious doubts about his vocation and was hesitant to make his final vows, Ignatius fasted three days and prayed until the individual had overcome the temptation.[14] He did this not merely once, but rather this was his custom.[15]

It is moving how, although he himself was sick and overtaxed with work, he departed from Rome at the beginning of November, 1552, in order to seek the duchess Juana Colonna [de Aragón], who was dwelling in Neapolitan territory, and to persuade her to be reconciled with her husband, Ascanio, with whom she was embroiled in marital strife. " On the morning of the day set for departure the rain poured down in torrents. Polanco suggested to Ignatius that it was perhaps more advisable to delay the departure till the following day so that the heavy downpour might not damage his health. But our father replied: ' We leave immediately. For thirty years I have not allowed myself to be delayed by water or by wind or by any other unpleasantness of weather from beginning at the determined hour a work planned for the service of God our Lord.' And so they departed on time."[16]

It is also delightful to see — Ribadeneyra calls it *pulcherrimum spectaculum*, an amusing drama — how Ignatius accompanied through the streets of Rome the elegant courtesans, whom he had brought away from their questionable trade, in order to conduct them to the House of St. Martha built for that purpose or to a lady of high Roman society acquainted with him. When someone would remonstrate with him that such conversions were not lasting and so were not worth the labor he applied to them, he would answer: " And if with all my trouble and care I could persuade only one single person to refrain from sin for one night for the sake of my Lord Jesus Christ, then I would stop at nothing that for this time at least she might not offend God — even if I knew that she would afterwards fall back into her old vice."[17]

---

12 Ibid., 79.
13 Ibid., 77.
14 *FN*, I, 651, [210]; *SdeSI*, I, 345, [21].
15 *De ratione S. Ign. in gubernando*, ch. 3, no. 9, in *SdeSI*, I, 451.
16 *FN*, II, 414; *Letters to Women*, 139-140.
17 Ribadeneyra, *De Actis*, [44], in *SdeSI*, I, 355-356.

It is scarcely believable how many thousands of details the saint concerned himself with in order to be able to help souls, the errands he ran, the time he sacrificed, the annoyances he endured. One need only cast a glance at his huge correspondence. There are two nobles in the retinue of Charles V who are enemies. They have gone so far as to strike and slap each other. The whole affair threatens to become more than a mere scandal. Ignatius is aware that the two are setting their salvation in jeopardy; such affairs of honor normally had a tragic end. This is reason enough for him to intervene and explore every possibility of reconciling the fighting cocks with each other.[18] There is an unhappy Dominican priest who, because of some misdemeanor, had been sentenced to three years in prison and had already done eight or nine years of strict penance. Now he wishes to be rehabilitated so that he can resume his priestly functions. As so often happens, he asks Ignatius to intercede for him with the papal curia. After he is convinced that the case merits a good word, he brings all his authority to bear in his behalf. He does it for the sake of this man's soul; for, as he writes to his noble benefactress, Margaret of Austria, who is to intercede with the pope on Ignatius' behalf: " Among all spiritual works, one of the most beautiful and most merciful is to console a soul in extreme distress and despair. Thus I cannot do otherwise than support his cause, and I humbly beg Your Excellency for help for the soul of this father."[19]

In his concern for the salvation of souls, Ignatius knows no distinction of rank, no human respect, and no artificial deference. Thus, although not yet a priest himself, he ventures with a holy audacity to write a long letter to one of the leaders of the Venetian reform circle, the Theatine Father Carafa, who was later to mount the papal throne in 1555 as Paul IV — certainly a very humble letter, yet completely frank. In it he submitted several proposals as to how Carafa himself and the community founded by him could better serve the honor of God and the salvation of souls. It was not worldly prudence that led Ignatius to such an action. For he could have foreseen what actually happened; that is, that Carafa took offense at the letter and observed only the criticism in it. Ignatius was after all the younger man and of lower rank. But Ignatius had not thought of that. On the contrary, he was so filled with his holy task that the only thought before his mind was that of the greater service of God and the help of souls. He had thought that these priests of Venice, so eager for

---

18 Letters 115 and 116 in *EppIgn*, I, 363-366. Letter 115 is also on pp. 89-90 of *Letters of St. Ignatius of Loyola*, Selected and Translated by W. J. Young (Chicago, 1959), hereafter abbreviated *LettersIgn*.

19 *EppIgn*, I, 271-273; *Letters to Women*, 80-81.

13

reform, would understand him since he had observed a truly Christ-like spirit among them. It sounds almost like Franciscan simplicity when one reads sentences like the following: " When I consider that our life in eternal blessedness. . . .consists in an interior and genuine love of God, our Creator and Lord, and obliges us all to a genuine, unfeigned, and honest love in the Lord,. . . . I have thought that I should write you this letter, dispensing with the usual formalities. . . . For one can readily expect of someone who leaves the world and disregards its temporal honors and dignities, that he has no desire to be honored and flattered by high-sounding words. . . . With this intention and in readiness to serve all whom I know to be servants of my Lord, I would like to speak in all simplicity and love, just as if I were addressing my own soul. . .and I thought that I should write you the following, as simple people are accustomed to do toward their superiors when they can advise them or be useful to them in regard to some point in the service of God our Lord, whenever there is a danger that those superiors might not seize a direct or indirect opportunity [for this service of God]."[20] There follow very concrete suggestions which require a good deal of humility in one who will willingly listen to them.

When it is necessary, when a man is in danger of losing his eternal salvation, Ignatius can become very insistent and will, so to speak, pull out all the stops. A Spanish secular priest, Francisco de Miranda, offered the order a house as a foundation for a college. The business dragged on for several years. In the meantime Francisco lived in Rome, leading a disgraceful life. His health was weak, and one had to consider the possibility of an early end. Daily, Ignatius had two holy Masses offered for his conversion,[21] but the desired success did not appear. Then Polanco, the saint's secretary, had to sit down and write a letter of entreaty in which polite reserve no longer finds a place. " Dear Sir, it is not the time for anyone who has regard for your Grace to masquerade before you. Do not consider anyone a friend or servant, but rather the chief enemy of your soul, who wastes your time with flattery, especially with such flatteries as keep you in your sins. Your Grace has need of penance, and no slight penance at that. This

20 *EppIgn*, I, 114-118, *LettersIgn*, 28-31; also in Hugo Rahner, *Ignatius von Loyola. Geistliche Briefe* (" Menschen der Kirche in Zeugnis und Urkunde." 3rd ed. Einsiedeln, 1956), pp. 72-77, hereafter cited as *Geistliche Briefe*. [Wulf refers to this book whenever it contains a German translation of the letter in question. We will also do this, even when an English translation exists, because Rahner has provided brief but very useful preliminary comments that will be helpful to anyone who wishes to study the matter more deeply and reads German.]
21 *EppIgn*, VII, 544.

demands not only a separation from sin, and sorrow for it, but also an offering of satisfaction to God." What follows is a fiery sermon on hell. And then another plea: " I beg you by the love of Christ and by the blood which He has shed for your soul . . . . May your Grace forgive me for speaking so bluntly. But my love compels me to speak. I do not want my conscience to accuse me of not having fulfilled my duty as a man who wishes with his whole heart to serve your Grace and who longs for your salvation."[22]

Polanco knows his father and master. Even in his choice of words he has expressed that which moved the heart of Ignatius. He must often enough have heard Ignatius use the expression, " service." " With the intention and in readiness to serve all whom I know to be servants of my Lord," he had written to Carafa and then closed with the characteristic phrase, " in the sincere desire to be of service to all the servants of God our Lord."[23] In almost the same words he writes to the Benedictine nun Teresa Rejadella of the convent of Santa Clara at Barcelona: " Now I am indeed certain of this, that for many years the Divine Majesty has given me the burning desire, without my being worthy of it, to do anything I can for any person, whether man or woman, who walks in the path of His good will and pleasure. By the same token I would wish to be of service to all who labor in the service of God."[24] Likewise to Juana de Aragón: " That active longing which his unspeakable goodness has aroused within me moves me to be of service to Your Excellency and to encourage you to all perfection."[25] With an exclusiveness such as men can tolerate only in saints, in all his relations with others he considers only the help of souls, so that he can say of himself that during all his years of study he engaged in many conversations, but never in a worldly one.[26] When, after a ten-year separation, he again takes up correspondence with his blood brother Martin García, the lord of the Castle of Loyola, his only motive is " that my letters may somehow contribute to the service and praise of God our Lord and may bring aid to my relatives according to the flesh, so that we may also be related according to the spirit and at the same time may help each other in those things which are of everlasting value." With an audacity without parallel, he betrays his inmost heart when he adds, " For in this life I am able to love any person only insofar as he is thereby helped in serving and glorifying God our Lord."[27]

22 Ibid., IX, 309-310; *LettersIgn*, pp. 397-398.
23 *EppIgn*, I, 118; *Geistliche Briefe*, p. 77.
24 *EppIgn*, l, 100; *Geistliche Briefe*, p. 79; *LettersIgn*, 19.
25 *EppIgn*, IV, 506; *Letters to Women*, p. 141.
26 *EppIgn*, I, 80; *Geistliche Briefe*, pp. 68-69; *LettersIgn*, p. 7.
27 Ibid.

One should not misunderstand such sentences as the above as though Ignatius no longer knew warm human love. But what meaning is there for him in a love that does not include the eternal salvation of the other ? He desires a greater love and a more selfless love than the man who has only natural motives for his love. Therefore he continues in the letter to his brother: " Urgently and more than urgently, if one can say that, I desire that there may grow in you and in our relatives and friends a great and true love and constancy in the service and praise of God our Lord. Then I will be able to love and serve you more and more." Service in the salvation of souls is the determining factor in all his decisions. For example, whether one should accept the office of palace confessor or not, the sole basis of the decision lies in the greater advantage for souls. " The security [of your own conscience] does not seem to me to be relevant to the case. If, according to our vocation, we should seek nothing but to be secure, and if we had to neglect some good in order to remain far from danger, we should no longer live among our neighbors and converse with them."[28] The same consideration is valid in the question as to whether one should speak or not speak to others about his personal experience of grace. " One must sometimes bridle the desire to speak of the grace of God our Lord; at other times we should relate more about it than our inner desire urges us to; for in this matter it is our neighbor's advantage rather than our own desires that we must consider."[29] Ignatius can rightly say of himself — and it sounds the theme of his entire life: " To serve the servants of my Lord, that is my pride and that is my glory."[30]

Father in Christ

Ignatius was endowed with a true genius for pastoral labors that fully matched the intensity of his apostolic ardor. His completely spiritual personality impressed all who came into personal contact with him. Even the mere sight of his figure and countenance could grip men and effect an interior change in them. In the process of beatification Father Filippo Aupolino relates: " When I entered the Society, I found Ignatius in possession of such a reputation for sanctity, not only among the people, but also among ourselves, that every time he went out the people on the street crowded together to see him pass by.... Serious men in high positions came in large numbers, drawn by his sanctity, to make his acquaintance and to be able to speak with

---

28 *EppIgn*, IV, 627; *Geistliche Briefe*, p. 239; *LettersIgn*, p. 284.
29 *EppIgn*, I, 106; *Geistliche Briefe*, p. 86; *LettersIgn*, p. 23.
30 *EppIgn*, I, 81; *Geitsliche Briefe*, p. 67; *LettersIgn*, p. 7.

him. It is also worthy of note that he seldom spoke to anyone without turning his thoughts to a better life and inflaming him to strive for a perfect life. He knew how to console harassed and despairing men with astonishing ease, and just the sight of him brought them joy."[31] What struck everyone who knew him was his seriousness, which was coupled with mildness and kindness.[32] He spoke little;[33] but his words were measured, clear, precise, penetrating, and of great weight.[34] "As far as I can remember, I have not said or promised anything during the past eleven or twelve years that I have later regretted,"[35] he once confessed when a careless promise had escaped his lips. "He spoke in such a manner that it became evident that God himself had given him great certainty that he should do it," Gonçalves da Câmara relates about the conversation in which Ignatius informed him that he had now decided to dictate his memoirs.[36] The same father recalls the "persuasive power of some expressions" on the listener, a power he could scarcely imitate when transmitting them to paper.[37] "The manner in which Father Ignatius tells his story is the same he uses in all situations; that is, with such clarity that he makes the entire past present to the listener."[38] Toward all men, even those closest to him, he maintained an extreme reserve. He remained always the *noble caballero*,[39] a noble, knightly man of breeding, joining dignity and reverence for the other. "Never," he wrote to one of his first companions, "do I allow myself a complete lack of caution, whether in spiritual conversations or in other more indifferent or even intimate conversations."[40] This caused others to feel in him a certain superior or even special quality so that, compared to Ignatius, Blessed Juan de Ávila seemed a child in the presence of a giant.[41]

Despite this evident reserve — and here begins the secret of his

---

31 *SdeSI*, II, 476-477.

32 Ribadeneyra, *Vita Ignatii Loyolae*, V, ch. 7, in *FN*, IV, 822; see also *FN*, II, 413.

33 No. 227, in *FN*, I, 659.

34 Nos. 99, 227 in *FN*, I, 585-586, 659.

35 *FN*, II, 327.

36 Foreword of Gonçalves da Câmara to *Autobiog*, in *FN*, I, 357.

37 Ibid., no. 3, in *FN*, I, 361.

38 Ibid., no. 3, in *FN*, I, 359.

39 This is an expression used by Ignatius himself (in the *Directory* to the *Spiritual Exercises* dictated by him, in *DirSpEx*, p. 96) as the reverse of the expression *perverso caballero* — a wicked knight — in the Contemplation on the Kingdom of Christ (*SpEx*, [94]).

40 *EppIgn*, XII, 630; *Geistliche Briefe*, pp. 103-104; *LettersIgn*, p. 130.

41 *SdeSI*, II, 836, 855.

personality — nearly everyone who knew him closely felt irresistibly drawn to him. "Our father," wrote Pedro de Ribadeneyra, "possessed to a high degree the art of winning the affection and trust of those who associated with him, and thus of leading them to God."[42] What opened the hearts of men to him was first and foremost his great amiability,[43] which never became familiarity, to be sure, but always preserved a measured dignity.[44] "One can say of our father," notes Gonçalves da Câmara in his diary, which is based on daily observation from close at hand, "that he is the most well-bred and courteous man in the world; he was born that way."[45] "His inclination to love appears to be constantly growing, so much so that he seems to be entirely love. For this reason he is so universally loved by all that there is no one in the Society [of Jesus] who does not cherish a great love for him or who does not consider himself loved by him."[46]

And now the unique characteristic — for a saint: Ignatius wanted to be loved by those he directed and so avoided anything that could alienate his friends and followers. This went so far that he preferred to send another person to impart any unavoidable reprimand.[47] He did not do this for selfish reasons, from vanity and to capture the favor of men. Rather he was so closely united to God and so responsive to his call that he sought an affectionate relationship with another not for itself but for the "greater service" of the neighbor; that is, to be of greater aid to him in his spiritual progress.[48] Such an inner awareness is almost frightening: an awareness that thinks over everything, illuminates it, and puts it all to use for one goal alone — the

---

42 Ibid., I, 461.

43 "La grande afabilidad" (no. 88, in *FN*, I, 580).

44 "But with all this he displayed toward everyone a measured dignity (*a gravidade devida*) . . . so that one can say that he was friendly to everyone and familiar with no one" (no. 89, *ibid.*).

45 "Mas cortes y comedido hombre" (no. 290, *ibid.*, 697).

46 Luis Gonçalves de Câmara, *Memoriale*, no. 86, in *FN*, I, 579.—". . . some of the first fathers wrote, from their long experience, that he [Ignatius] was compounded of love and kindness" (Danielo Bartoli, *De vita et instituto S. Ignatii*, III, 41). [There is an old translation of this into English: Father Daniel Bartoli, *The Life and Institute of St. Ignatius de Loyola*, trans. by the author of "Life in Mexico"— Mme. Calderon de la Barca, nee Fanny Macleod — (New York, 1855). It is translated from the Italian original, and the division into chapters is so different from that of the Latin version used by Wulf (Lugdini, 1665) that it is virtually impossible to locate the page on which the passage in question is to be found. Therefore we will follow him and give only the page numbers of that Latin edition, in this case, p. 273. Editor.]

47 *Memoriale*, no. 88, in *FN*, I, 580.

48 *MonNad*, IV, 662-663; Bartoli, *De vita et instituto*, p. 266.

honor of God and the salvation of souls. In the case of an ordinary human being every bit of spontaneity and all authenticity in his relations with others would be destroyed. In the case of Ignatius this was not so. His love for others was humanly genuine, but it always proceeded from an all-pervading love of God. This was clear to anyone who once heard him speak.

Ignatius was a master of spiritual conversation. When Nadal, one of the most intimate companions of the saint, later spoke on the subject to his fellow religious, his heart beat faster and one could have believed that he saw his " father " still alive before him. In direct, personal conversation " Ignatius was wonderful," he says. " As he was enflamed with love for his neighbor and was outstanding in regard to the discernment of spirits and moral prudence, he so adapted himself to those with whom he conversed by the brevity and kindness of his words and caused them to be so well-disposed toward him that he evoked amazing movements of soul in them. He had such insight into them that he almost seemed to enter into their mind and heart. He spoke in such a manner that no one could withstand his words. Furthermore, a mysterious, divine power and light appeared to shine forth from his countenance, which much enkindled the love of spiritual things in those who looked upon him."[49] This was no exaggeration. We have a sufficient number of other witnesses who confirm the words of Nadal, often quite impressively.

Isabel Roser, the great benefactress of the poor pilgrim and student of Barcelona, once related her first meeting with Ignatius to Ribadeneyra. She had noticed him sitting among the children on the altar steps in order to hear the sermon, and she had invited him to dinner. " He spoke after the dinner about God, about the virtues, and about eternal life in such a wonderful manner that all present felt themselves inspired to a life of piety."[50] Gonçalves da Câmara can still remember how the saint, at the time of an account of conscience, gave him advice to help him overcome a certain fault and on this occasion also told him some things about his former life: " He spoke to me in a manner that gave me great consolation so that I could no longer hold back the tears."[51] Several novices who had become weak in their vocation had the same experience. A single colloquy with

---

49 *MonNad*, IV, 662. The radiance on the face of Ignatius is attested by many; for example, by Philip Neri (*SdeSI*, II, 425-426, 428, 488, 491, 499, 559, 1010), by Isabel Roser (Ribadeneyra, *Vita Ignatii*, 1, 10, in *FN*, IV, 145), and others.
50 Ribadeneyra, *Vita Ignatii*, I, 10, in *FN*, IV, 145-146. Cf. *EppIgn*, I, 83, n. 2; *SdeSI*, I, 733-734.
51 *Autobiog*, 1*, in *FN*, I, 356.

19

Ignatius was enough to free them from their despondency.[52]   The word of the religious founder, her spiritual counsellor and confessor, had such penetrating influence on Margaret of Austria, otherwise a very proud woman and easily angered, that she yielded to Tivoli in a dispute between that city and the town of Castel Sant' Angelo, which belonged to her.   Polanco could write someone: "Madama [this was the name the Romans gave to the emperor's daughter] makes no difficulty at all about whatever Master Ignatius considers just and honorable."[53]   Finally, we have the touching letter of a small girl of thirteen, a maid of honor to the duchess Colonna, Juana de Aragôn. Ignatius had met the girl at the beginning of her stay at Rome and had probably spoken to her about God.   She tells him: "Of all the advice you gave me in earlier days, I have not forgotten one word. For truly, one cannot forget your words."[54]

It is no wonder then if men tried to receive a word from him. A conversation with him remained unforgettable; his letters were read again and again and preserved as something precious.[55]   In his correspondence one repeatedly comes across sentences like this: "I sincerely beseech Your Paternity not to forget to show me your accustomed

---

52 Examples of this are given in Anton Huonder, *Ignatius von Loyola, Beiträge zu seinem Charakterbild*, ed. Balthasar Wilhelm (Köln, 1932), pp. 147-148.

53 *EppIgn*, II, 240; *Letters to Women*, p. 84.

54 *EppMixt*, I, 18; *Letters to Women*, p. 149.

55 On March 31, 1540, Francis Xavier wrote to Ignatius from Bologna: "I received your letters on Easter day... and they brought with them so much joy and consolation — God alone knows how much.   Since I believe that in this life we shall see each other only through letters, and in the other life face to face with many embraces, there remains in the short period of life left to us only the glimpses of each other we will receive by means of frequent letters" (*EppXav*, I, 29 30).   [For various reasons, the writings of St. Francis are preserved in such diverse languages that it requires considerable linguistic knowledge to make use of the critical edition in the *MHSJ*.   All his writings, in easily readable Spanish, are printed in *Cartas y Escritos de San Francisco Xavier*, ed. Felix Zubillaga ("Biblioteca de Autores Cristianos." Madrid: La Editorial Católica, 1953).   This letter is on p. 57-59.   An English translation of the whole letter is in Henry James Coleridge, *The Life and Letters of St. Francis Favier* (2 vols. London: Burns Oates & Washbourne, 1921), I, 60-62; most of it also in James Brodrick, *Saint Francis Xavier* (New York: The Wicklow Press, 1952), p. 79-80].   A similar thought is expressed in a letter of January 29, 1552, from Cochin: "God knows how much your letter consoled my soul; and among the other holy words and consolations in it, I read the last ones, which said: 'Entirely yours, without being able to forget you at any time.   Ignatius...   As I read them with tears, so now I am writing with tears...'" (*EppXav*, II, 286-287). [*CartasXav*, 421; Coleridge, *Xavier*, 365; Brodrick, *Xavier*, p. 459].   The famous Letter on Obedience to the Province of Protugal "was received in Coimbra and in all of Portugal with real enthusiasm," as Hugo Rahner says (*Geistliche Briefe*, p. 243).

favor by sending me a few lines so that I may not be deprived of the consolation that my soul receives from you."[56]   The reliance which his fellow religious and externs placed on the word of their " dearly beloved Father in Christ " is almost unlimited.[57]   One cannot read without emotion the letter of a devout woman who owed her conversion and change of heart to the companions of the saint, and therefore would gladly have followed her " true father and lord " in personal obedience.   Despite Ignatius' denial of this request, she did not let her trust in him waver: " Whoever begs for something with great trust does not cease making his request again and again, even when he receives a flat refusal.   That is what I also am doing, dearest Father and Lord.   It is true that I have written you several times.   Today I hold your answer in my hands — but it cannot take away my confidence in your love.   Just the opposite: your refusal has only made the flames of my desire burn more fiercely.   My devout confidence has simply grown so much in me that it is with me as it once was with Christ the Lord: when the crowd pressed in on him from all sides, he still felt clearly that someone had touched with faith the outer hem of his garment.   So, dearly beloved Father and Lord, would I have you feel how I touch the hem of your garment."[58]

Just wherein lies the secret of this man, who exercised such an influence on other men ?   Upon what did these people base such trust that they were almost blindly devoted to him ?   First of all, it was the certain knowledge that they were here dealing with a man of God in whose words, therefore, the voice of God spoke to them.   " I have no other wish than to obey and to do what seems good to Your Paternity, " Sister Teresa Rejadella, who had experienced his spiritual help to a great degree, writes to him.   " I place my trust in the fact that God our Lord lets you know what it is most profitable to do."[59] Ignatius was in fact a man of few thoughts, and these were wholly directed to the supernatural.   He could think only those thoughts that came from God and were directed toward Him.   His soul was filled with only one thing: the service of the Divine Majesty, Christ the Lord, and the salvation of souls.   Even from a consideration of his somewhat rare correspondence with royal ladies, a correspondence demanding much tact and prudence, Hugo Rahner makes the

56 *EppMixt*, II, 466; *Letters to Women*, p. 240.
57 " My Father," " My Father in Christ," " My true Father," " My much loved Father " are salutations that appear frequently in letters to Ignatius, not only in those from the members of the order but also from many who were not members.   The members of the order usually called him " our Father " when speaking among themselves.
58 *EppIgn*, XII, 377; *Letters to Women*, p. 309.
59 *EppMixt*, II, 379; *Letters to Women*, pp. 364-365.

judgment: "that even here Ignatius remained entirely a man of the spirit, who speaks to these ladies only of the things of the other world, or who calls them to serve the only work on earth that seems to him great or important — the help of souls."[60]

When a father once complained to him that he was hindered in his practice of the presence of God because he was frequently called to the parlor, Ignatius gave him this answer: "When anyone comes to you for help or for spiritual consolation, you should receive him with special love. Make your prayer beforehand or in the intervals. . . . But at the time let all your thoughts and words be directed to bringing him spiritual help." And he makes the characteristic addition: Should people come merely for a pleasant chat, you should direct the conversation to spiritual things You will thereby cause some to find an excuse to leave. You will arouse interest in the others and bring them closer to God — they are the ones we are interested in.[61] Ignatius himself spoke about God and eternity in such a way that he made their reality almost visible. One felt that everything he said was based on personal experience. Very seldom in Christian tradition has anyone spoken and written so deeply and clearly as he did about the movement of the various "spirits" in the soul, about the influence of Satan and, in opposition to that, about the manner of divine consolation.[62] When he instructed or advised anyone, one obtained the impression from the sureness of his words that he had perceived what he said in a supernatural light and was therefore speaking almost immediately in God's name.[63]

Alongside his completely supernatural attitude, there was something else that won for Ignatius the affection and trust of men. Ignatius took very seriously anyone who came to him, whether of high or low degree, and no less the small and weak. If he required of the fathers that they consider in the other not his position or his external appearance, but the image of God and the soul purchased by the blood of Christ,[64] this was a foregone conclusion for Ignatius himself. The requirement of the *Spiritual Exercises*, [22], that one must be more ready to interpret the words of one's neighbor favorably than to condemn them, was followed by him to an unusual degree. In the

60 *Letters to Women*, p. 37.

61 *Responsio Manarei ad Lancicii postulata*, no. 17, in *SdeSI*, I, 515-516; *FN*, I, III, 430-431.

62 Confer, for example, one of Ignatius' most important letters of spiritual advice, that to the Benedictine Sister Teresa Rejadella of June 18, 1536 (*EppIgn*, I, 99-107; *Geistliche Briefe*, 79-87; *Letters to Women*, pp. 331-335).

63 *Autobiog*, 1*, in *FN*, I, 357; *Epistola P. Lainii*, no. 60, ibid., 141.

64 *EppIgn*, XII, 252; *SdeSI*, I, 490.

same line of thought, he could say of himself, " I have a great longing to express myself as submissively and humbly as possible to all men."[65] Despite his great reserve, he immediately made contact with everyone. He would listen as attentively as if they were discussing his own personal affairs and as if he were there for that person alone.[66] " Our father," says Nadal, " met everyone whom he wished to help " along the way to God " with a tangible and gently glowing love so that he quickly conquered his heart and spirit."[67] He once wrote to Doña Leonor Mascarenhas, who occupied a high position at the royal court of Valladolid and Madrid and who was very close to him: " You have asked me to write you my opinion and to advise you as to what you should do now. I will inform you of the impression I have, in the presence of the Divine Majesty, just as I feel it in my innermost soul and as if I were in the place of Your Grace."[68] Especially when he had to say something unpleasant, he imagined that he was saying it to himself.

In everything that he did for those whom he had won for God and whom he directed, he had " his whole heart in it." " Everyone knows," Polanco wrote to the superior at Palermo, " that it is part of his character to push forward most intensively everything that he takes in hand."[69] He remained often astonishingly devoted to anyone whom he had met in God. After a decade and a half he is still writing to a recluse whom he had come to know during his years of study in Salamanca as a God-fearing woman and with whom he may have had several spiritual conversations: " In truth, I could never imagine that I would ever lose the picture of the true and genuine love which I cherish in the Lord for your soul. No, you are ever present before me in spirit."[70] He preserved this loyalty especially when a tragedy overcame those entrusted to him. When Margaret of Austria had to leave Rome at the command of the pope, there was not the slightest change in Ignatius' attitude toward her. He expressly let her know: " Your Excellencies. . .have left Rome. Yet the wish has not left my soul, and never will as long as I live and God gives me his help, that the sovereign goodness of God may direct all the affairs of Your Excellencies and allow them to prosper."[71] It was only after his death that many realized just how much of a father he had been. Cardinal Otto

65 *EppIgn*, I, 187; *Letters to Women*, pp. 275-276.
66 *Memoriale*, no. 202, in *FN*, I, 648-649.
67 *MonNad*, IV, 662.
68 *EppIgn*, XI, 416; *Letters to Women*, p. 430.
69 Ibid., II, 384; *Letters to Women*, p. 447.
70 Ibid., I, 172; *Letters to Women*, p. 370.
71 Ibid., III, 146; *Letters to Women*, p. 85.

Truchsess wrote from Waldburg to the Jesuits at Rome, expressing the emotions felt at that time by the friends of Ignatius, " He was a refuge and harbor for us in all our moments of uncertainty."[72] And even years later he was still so much alive to Pedro de Ribadeneyra that he could say, " The remembrance of him is enough to make the weak strong."[73]

Master of Spiritual Direction

Nevertheless, Ignatius was not from the start a master at handling men nor a perfect spiritual guide. He had to pay dearly for his education. His first companions all left him in the lurch, and the direction of women brought him not a few vexations. One will scarcely go wrong if he says that at the beginning he pursued his goal in too direct a manner, unbothered by the human and religious preconditioning of those under his care. Since he always spoke with great ardor and urgency of the " one thing necessary," he could certainly awaken enthusiasm; but he also could demand too much of the weak and call them to ideals to which they were not equal, at least not yet. In this respect he had much to learn, and he did it thoroughly. He had already changed his tactics when he was dealing with Francis Xavier. He did not win over the ambitious and high-spirited Basque master only by his never-wearying patience and his ever-constant love. He also sought to win his sympathies by means of quite ordinary things, by little favors and financial support. He spoke favorably of him before others and brought him pupils.[74]

Learning from his success, he reconsidered his previous behavior and thereby arrived at new knowledge of how one has to handle men in order to win them for God. Because of his organizational talent and his completely practical spirit, there grew out of this something like a system, which he reduced to an easily remembered formula for its practical application by his followers. He often said that one must proceed in the same manner as the Devil, who comes in through a man's door in order to lead him out by his own. One must therefore accommodate himself to men, to their character, their temperament, in order to dispose them for the word of God and the things of the

---

72 *SdeSI*, II, 39-40.

73 *MonRib*, I, 598.

74 Nos. 6-9, In *EppXav*, I, 9 ff.; *CartasXav*, 50-52; *PolChron*, I, 48-49. *Georg* Schurhammer, *Franz Xaver: Sein Leben und seine Zeit* (Freiburg, 1955), Vol. I, 146, 148-149, 161-162, 165-167. [An English translation now exists: G. Schurhammer, S.J., *Francis Xavier: His Life, His Times*, Volume 1, *Europe*, 1506-1541. Translated by M. Joseph Costelloe, S.J. (Rome: The Jesuit Historical Institute, 1973). See pp. 155-159. Editor].

Lord.[75] As a result of all this he came to know the men whom he
wished to help. He interested himself in simply everything that
filled and motivated their everyday lives — even the number of fleas
that annoyed a man during the night, as he once playfully said.[76]
He tried to ascertain " under what circumstances a man lived or had
lived earlier, what disposition he had, what temperament — whether he
was choleric, phlegmatic, sanguine, or melancholic — what had been
his earlier occupations, and what he was doing now."[77] He wanted to
know what was happening in his soul: whether he was moved by spirits
and by which ones; what inspirations, desires, and consolations he
experienced; whether he was tempted and how he reacted to the
temptation. On the other hand, he warned that one should not desire
to probe into men's personal secrets[78]— their sins, for example — or to
speak about them unless the man himself should provide one with the
opportunity.[79]

In addition, Ignatius' own personal experience induced him always
to keep in mind, during the course of spiritual direction, the concrete
human being with his natural tendencies, his difficulties, and his needs.
First of all there was his own illness. God had sent this to him, he
believed, in order that he might not overburden men and that he might
have understanding for the greater or lesser measure of their strength.[80]
Again and again he urged prudent moderation in one's religious aspirations; true virtue, he said, lies in the middle between tepidity and
excessive zeal. One of his longest and most important letters is devoted
mainly to this question.[81]

Even more than weakness of the body, he feared the sicknesses
of the soul: scrupulosity, depression, and persistent temptations.
He knew from his own experience how they could cast doubt on

75 *EppIgn*, I, 179-180; *Geistliche Briefe*, pp. 108-109; ibid., p. 513; *Responsio P.
  Manarei*, no. 20, in *SdeSI*, I, 517; *FN*, III, 432; *MonNad*, IV, 662; Ribadeneyra,
  Vita Ignatii, V, ch. 11, no. 83, in *FN*, IV, 893; Bartoli, *De vita et instituto*,
  III, 37, p. 266.
76 Da Câmara, *Memoriale*, no. 87, in *FN*, I, 580; *SdeSI*, I, 491.
77 *MonNad*, IV, 662-663.
78 *SpEx*, [17]: " It helps very much if the one who is giving the Exercises, without seeking to search out or know the personal thoughts or sins of the exercitant, is carefully informed about the various movements and thoughts that
  the different spirits cause within him."
79 *MonNad*, IV, 662: " Nec ad ejus vitia veniendum, nisi ipse det ansam, quam
  placide apprehendere possimus."
80 *De Vita Ignatii*, ch. 3, in *PolChron*, I, 24; *FN*, II, 532-533; Ribadeneyra, *Vita
  Ignatii*, V, ch. 8, no. 110, in *FN*, IV, 831.
81 Letter to the Scholastics at Coimbra, in *EppIgn*, I, 495-510; *Geistliche Briefe*,
  pp. 143-158; *LettersIgn*, pp. 120-130.

everything and how even the best will was lamed by them.[82]   Consequently, he treated those afflicted by them with extreme consideration.   Ribadeneyra later wrote: " It is unbelievable what consideration and patience he showed to everyone whom he saw to be under the pressure of a temptation or under the influence of a strong passion. In such cases he avoided any rebuke and said nothing until he perceived that the storm and the crisis had passed, that the sick man once more had possession of his reason, and had repented.   Then the man was full of shame for what he had done and for the sorrow he had caused the father.   Finally, full of grateful reverence, the man could recognize the skillful tact, more divine than human, that the father had shown him."[83]

It is more than likely that Ribadeneyra has himself in mind. For it is well known that Ignatius had taken a very special liking to him — the noble madcap had entered the order at the age of fifteen and a half — and overlooked many of his faults.   Out of a grateful heart, he has therefore set down in his confessions a touching memorial to his father: " What shall I say, O my God, of the kindness and gentleness with which this holy man treated me, while he forgot my bad moods, the worry and care I caused him, and remembered only the tears which I cost him and especially the blood that you have shed for me !   You, my God, had animated the blessed father, your true servant, with your own dispositions; you had endowed him with that tenderness, that fatherly love, with which you forgive those who have turned their hearts from you, with which you forget the sins they have committed, in order to cover them with the cloak of mercy, without reproaching them at all, with turning yourself away from them.   In such a way did this angelic physician treat the spiritual sicknesses of his children, retaining in his heart not even a bitter remembrance of them."[84]   These are not merely the extravagant words that one gladly dedicates to the departed dead; what Ribadeneyra here prayerfully confesses is in accord with reality.   Ignatius had often admonished his followers to receive tempted and oppressed souls in love and patience.   " Depressed and tempted persons we must meet with a special love," he writes in an instruction to Broët and Salmerón, " for their sake prolonging conversations and generally appearing pleasant and happy so as to be of service to them in leading them to the

---

82 *Autobiog*, 22-25, in *FN*, I, 392-399; *De Vita Ignatii*, ch. 3, *PolChron*, I, 21-22; *FN*, II, 530-531.

83 Ribadeneyra, *De ratione gubernandi*, ch. 3, no. 8, in *FN*, III, 617; *SdeSI*, I, 450-451.

84 *MonRib*, I, 41.

contrary humor for their greater edification and consolation."[85] " Whoever associates with men in order to help them must act as an
experienced doctor does, who never shows fear or disgust no matter
how serious and repulsive the wounds he sees may appear to be. He
must endure patiently and gently the weaknesses and moods of the
sick person and should not see in him merely the descendant of Adam
and the fragile vessel but the image of God that has been purchased
with the blood of Christ."[86]

From such consideration for concrete human nature and its
weaknesses and for the actual situation of the individual, there ripened
in Ignatius that universally admired discretion characteristic of him,
which prudently weighed distinction of one case from another and
which constituted the high point of his great ability in the direction of
souls. It had grown up in him only through painful experience. He
then held to it all the more passionately. He considered this the
decisive point in all spiritual direction. "Innocence and sanctity,"
he once said to Ribadeneyra, "are in themselves of more value than
all else; if however they are not joined to prudence and skill in dealing
with men, they are lacking something and are not sufficient for the
direction of others. Outstanding prudence with moderate virtue is
often worth more in the direction of others than great sanctity with
less prudence; for the privileges which God grants His saints are not
easily reduced to a system of rules. That is to say, God is able to and
often does endow his friends and elect with unusual graces which,
because of their very unusualness, cannot be measured by ordinary
standards."[87]

Such a statement, pronounced by a saint who had personal
knowledge of the unspeakable riches of sanctity, shows true greatness.
It reveals to what extent Ignatius, with his own wishes and ideals,
had retreated behind the call of God to help souls. A true zeal filled
him when there was question of preserving and ensuring the well-being
and rights of the individual and the diversity of the ways to salvation.
He reproved superiors and confessors who, in matters of the spiritual
life, wanted to judge everyone according to their own experience and
clung tenaciously to what they had recognized as good for themselves.
On the contrary, everyone has his own gift.[88] On this point he himself was extremely conscientious. When he gave Favre the Exercises

85 *EppIgn*, I, 180; *Geistliche Briefe*, p. 190.
86 Ribadeneyra, *De ratione gubernandi*, ch. 5, no. 12, in *FN*, III, 628; *SdeSI*,
   I, 463.
87 Ribadeneyra, *Vita Ignatii*, V, ch. 10; no. 156, in *FN*, IV, 871.
88 *FN*, III, 635-636; *SdeSI*, I, 470 (no. 12). Ribadeneyra, *Vita Ignatii*, V, ch.
   10, no. 135, in *FN*, IV, 855. Bartoli, *De vita et instituto*, III, 37, p. 267.

during the time in Paris — it was during a very hard winter — he found out one day that this man " had eaten nothing for six days, slept on the pieces of wood they had brought him to make fire with, and made his meditation in a yard filled with snow. He said to him: ' I am convinced that you have not sinned in this; just the opposite, you have earned great merit. I will return in an hour and tell you what you should do.' He then went to pray in a nearby church. His own inclination was to allow Favre to fast as long as he himself had once done. But after he had prayed, he did not dare agree despite his own inclination. He went back, built him a fire, and told him to eat."[89]

It was well known, and even a topic of discussion, that Ignatius often treated different men differently in regard to the same question. He stressed again and again that one and the same good was not the best thing for everyone and in every situation. He himself had ample acquaintance with the gift of copious tears and knew how to treasure it; but he also knew that one may not request it unconditionally. For " it is neither necessary nor good for everyone."[90] How much one should pray, even in a religious order,[91] what mortifications he may take upon himself,[92] all this is not to be determined by fixed rules but must be decided anew in each case. He handled the question " the cloister or the world " with what was, in that historical period, an absolutely astonishing freedom. On one side, his fixed conviction was this: " To follow the counsels of Christ and to long for a life of devotion is something so praiseworthy that any opposition to it is in no way to be allowed."[93] Nevertheless, in the individual case, he can advise against the choice of the religious life, even when the desire and longing for perfection are present. For example, the sister of one of the fathers had decided to leave the world. Her vocation did not seem to him to be secure because of her vacillation, and so he writes of her, " Angelica should rather not shut herself up in the cloister." The reason he gives is very interesting — remember that this was written in the sixteenth century: " It is also possible to live securely in the world, each according to his personal circumstances, although life in the cloister is in itself more secure."[94] He made similar judgments in other cases also at a time when many an

---

89 Da Câmara, *Memoriale*, 305, in *FN*, I, 704-705.
90 *EppIgn*, V, 714; *Geistliche Briefe*, p. 262; *LettersIgn*, p. 312.
91 *Cons*, [582, 343].
92 Ibid., [300, 582].
93 *EppIgn*, IV, 93.
94 Ibid., 279; *Letters to Women*, p. 406.

overzealous director would already have hurried the person into entering a religious order.[95]

On the other hand, when he believes that someone is called by God and is capable of great things, he does not shrink from directly demanding of the person that he give himself to God in a life of the counsels — as in the case of his confessor in Paris, Emmanuel Miona, whom he openly besieged to make the full course of the Exercises.[96] Ignatius treated everyone according to his capabilities and powers and with consideration of the concrete situation.[97] Just a few days before his death he writes to a young scholastic, who had turned to him in a moment of spiritual distress, that there are two ways of fighting sensuality. The first is that of repressing the sensuality with the help of reason and of light from God. " The second consists in giving up recreation and things otherwise lawful, out of longing for mortification and the cross. . . . This second way is not suitable for all persons nor at all times. On the contrary, it is sometimes more meritorious (in order to preserve one's strength in the service of God for the long run) to accord some honest recreation to the senses instead of repressing them. From this you may conclude that the first way of resisting is fitting for you but not the second, even though you have the intention of walking in the way that is most perfect and most pleasing to God."[98]

" To heal sicknesses that outwardly appeared the same, he often used quite different methods — even on many occasions contrasting or conflicting ones. He handled one man with circumspection and kindness, another with unrelenting harshness."[99] " To heal a large wound one applies a different salve at the beginning than one uses later on or when it is almost healed," Ignatius writes to his brother.[100] But on the other hand it was said of him, " To beginners in the religious life he gave milk, to those further advanced solid food."[101] What was meant by solid food we learn from several examples. Nicolás Bobadilla, one of the first companions, once asked the saint for permission

---

95 Hugo Rahner treats individual cases in *Letters to Women*: Leonor Mascarenhas, pp. 427-433; Isabel de Vega, pp. 460-464; Helena Fantuzzi, pp. 214-216. In contrast with the general opinion of his time, Ignatius thought that the " third state " of remaining single could be a true Christian vocation (*ibid.*, p. 216).

96 *EppIgn*, I, 112-113; *LettersIgn*, pp. 27-28.

97 Ribadeneyra, *De ratione gubernandi*, ch. 4, in *FN*, III, 620; *SdeSI*, I, 454.

98 *EppIgn*, XII, 151-152; *Geistliche Briefe*, p. 324.

99 Ribadeneyra, *De actis Ignatii*, no. 98, in *FN*, II, 387; *SdeSI*, I, 386. Da Câmara, *Memoriale*, no. 86, in *FN*, I, 579.

100 *EppIgn*, I, 79; *Geistliche Briefe*, pp. 67-68; *LettersIgn*, p. 6.

101 Da Câmara, *Memoriale*, no. 105, in *FN*, I, 588.

to exchange his extremely small room for a larger one. Ignatius, who knew his virtue, sent a reply that he should share his room with two other fathers.[102] " He scarcely ever spoke a friendly word to Polanco, who for nine years was his secretary and his chief aid. . . . On several occasions he gave such terrible rebuffs to Nadal that he wept bitterly. . . . In the last year before his death he treated Laynez [to whom the Society owed more than it did to any other man] so harshly that this man himself admitted to me that he was often very depressed because of this treatment and turned to God our Lord with the question, ' O Lord, what have I done against the Society that this saint treats me this way ? ' "[103] Ribadeneyra can give no other answer to this than that Ignatius wished to test those who had grown strong in virtue, " so that they might march forward with great strides in the way of perfection."[104] To be sure, he adds that his example is more to be admired than imitated.[105] When one took the occasion to consider the fact that the saint treated one man in one way and another in a different way, and that from time to time he handled the same man in a completely different manner according to the circumstances, it eventually became clear that his silence, his gentleness, or even his severity had been completely relevant to the situation.[106] " The success always proved that the medicine he applied was the better and more suitable for the person concerned."[107]

To his much admired gift of discretion, always knowing exactly what was more serviceable for the spiritual advancement of each person, Ignatius united in his guidance of souls great clarity and precision. Not only did he speak slowly, deliberately, with sureness of purpose, without digression, always emphasizing the main points;[108] but he also wrote simply (even a little clumsily) and clearly, often dividing the matter with one, two, three.[109] That was not just simply his style. Rather he did it in order to be of more help to souls, in order to make himself as understandable as possible. One need only glance at the many corrections and deletions in the drafts of letters

---

102 Ibid., 292, in *FN*, I, 698-699.
103 Ribadeneyra, *De ratione gubernandi*, ch. 4, in *FN*, III, 620-621; *SdeSI*, I, 454-455.
104 Ibid., " para que corriesen á rienda suelta á la perfeción;" literally, " that they might race to perfection with loosened reins."
105 Ibid., ". . . estos exemplos . . . mas son admirables que ymitables . . ."
106 Da Câmara, *Memoriale*, no. 105, in *FN*, I, 588.
107 Bartoli, *De vita et instituto*, III, 37, p. 266.
108 Da Câmara, *Memoriale*, no. 379, in *FN*, I, 732. *Responsio P. Manarei*, no. 11, in *FN*, III, 428-429; *SdeSI*, I, 513. *Autobiog*, 3*, in *FN*, I, 358.
109 Examples in *Geistliche Briefe*, letters nos. 3, 4, 6, 12, 15, 17, 21, 30, 39, 40b, 44; respectively in *LettersIgn*, pp. 13, 28, 24, 439, 72, 93, 111, 212, 260 and 261, 274, 298.

remaining to us to know how much he had reflected upon every point of advice he gave to others. From his awareness that, " the uncertain guide understands little and helps less,"[110] he strove after clarity and precision in his direction and his answers, though always leaving the ultimate decision to the other person.[111]

Particularly in his relationship with women he united the precision of direction demanded by them with great sobriety and distance, revealing his capacity for sympathetic understanding in his approach to difficulties without giving in to an exaggerated feminine longing to be directed in all details. An excellent example of how Ignatius thought and acted in this is a letter to Sister Teresa Rejadella: " You ask that I should write in detail what the Lord has given me to say, that I should express my opinion clearly and definitely. All right, I will therefore say what I consider before the Lord to be right; and I will say it very clearly and plainly, with complete good will. If here and there my words seem to you to be sharp, the harshness is directed more against the Enemy who is trying to confuse yon than against you personally."[112] And then comes this refreshingly direct way of unraveling and clarifying a tangle of thoughts, feelings, and temptations: " Make no fuss about bad, nasty, or sensual thoughts...; a great deal is gained by simply not giving too much attention to the whole business...if only my soul loves God our Lord alone and conforms herself to His Divine Majesty. Once the soul is thus conformed to Him, she herself works on the body and makes it subordinate to the divine will whether it wants to or not." This conformity with the will of God is one of his favorite themes in treating with women, whose frequently varying difficulties were tied to preconditions which could no longer be reached by rational means. He writes to a soul in distress: I therefore think " Your Grace must conform your own will entirely to the will of Christ our Lord and give itself over completely into his hands.... If you do this, then I have no doubt that almost all your sufferings will cease."[113]

Ignatius was just as clear and persistent toward his own sons, if it was a matter of winning them over from established opinions and inclinations that were opposed to the religious ideal of the order. Here also he adapted himself completely to the individuality of each one.

110 *EppIgn*, I, 108; *Geistliche Briefe*, p. 89; *LettersIgn*, p. 24.
111 For example, on one occasion he gives a piece of advice; but then he adds: " In any case, it is better that Isabel should herself choose one solution or the other " (*EppIgn*, XII, 216).
112 Ibid., I, 101; the next quotation is from ibid., 109; *Geistliche Briefe*, pp. 79-80, and 90; *LettersIgn*, pp. 19, 25.
113 Ibid., VI, 161-162; *Letters to Women*, p. 409.

Inimitable is the way in which he took the spiritually sensitive Francis Borgia in hand; with what simultaneous tact and persistence he knew how to detach him from his excessive longing for contemplation and penance.[114] Completely different again was the union of affectionate brotherly love and inflexibility during the dispute with Simâo Rodrigues, the provincial of the Portuguese Province of the order.[115] It was almost always the case that he arrived at his purpose without having injured anyone. On the contrary, he made the ties that bound men to him much stronger by the clear and unequivocal manner in which he treated them. For everyone recognized what union with God and love motivated his actions.

And there is still one final characteristic of Ignatius' guidance of souls: the appeal to magnanimity, to nobility of mind — sometimes an explicit appeal, but usually unspoken though underlying everything he says. This appeal finds impressive expression in a letter to Juana de Aragón, in which the duchess is urged to yield in her dispute with her husband. " This would be a deed of special strength and greatness of soul," it says, " as accords with Your Excellency's noble blood and magnanimous heart. By this you could show that you are no longer afraid of anything, not even of the danger of death — a thing of which ordinary men stand in fear. On the contrary, so many cautions and safeguards are not for the truly great."[116] " Although Ignatius possessed prudence to an unusual degree, he did not care for over-prudent people because it was his opinion that they seldom accomplish anything worthwhile in the service of God."[117] He had indeed bridled his own love of holy madness for the sake of serving souls, but it had left its brand deep within him and the hidden embers continued to have their effect.[118] He therefore quickly took a liking to men in whom he discovered the same love, as in the case of Philip Neri. He preferred even less holy passions to all too even characters, who had no particular difficulties and could therefore adapt themselves easily to anything. The former seemed to him more able to be aroused to great things; he treasured more highly virtues that had been won by struggle because they transformed the soul more deeply.[119] He desired therefore that one should be especially willing to undertake

---

114 *Geistliche Briefe*, nos. 16, 25, 29; *LettersIgn*, pp. 83, 179, 194 and 195.

115 Ibid., no. 60, I-VIIb. *LettersIgn* contains all but IV and VIIa: pp. 254, 300, 296, 302, 326, 402.

116 *EppIgn*, IV, 507; *Letters to Women*, p. 142.

117 Ribadeneyra, *Vita Ignatii*, V, ch. 11, no. 195, in *FN*, IV, 898.

118 " Santas locuras:" *EppIgn*, I, 507; Da Câmara, *Memoriale*, no. 219, in *FN*, I, 656; *Epistola P. Lainii*, no. 60, ibid., 141.

119 *Responsio Manarei*, no. 14, in *SdeSI*, I, 514, and *FN*, III, 430; Ribadeneyra,

the direction of capable, though difficult men; that one should lead them with understanding and kindness, but also with firmness, to win control over themselves so that they can be ready for the call of God's grace.[120]

Whenever Ignatius considered that a man would be receptive to the call, he spoke to him without reserve of the perfect following of Christ — it made no difference to him whether he was dealing with religious or laymen. Thus he wrote to his friend, Juan de Vega, vice-roy of Sicily, on the occasion of the death of his wife and son: " May God daily increase in Your Highness what he is aiming at by such means; that is, the growth of love for Himself and for all perfection. This will increase the more, the less one concerns himself for anything created."[121] Ignatius often had to write letters of consolation. He understood the human heart, but his was never a cheap consolation that restricted itself to the emotions. The saint always sought to use the opportunity to make the person more mature and detached, according to each one's interior preparation. His consolation came from that Spirit who is called the Spirit of consolation, who introduces into all truth. " God does not will that we here below be able to rest ourselves or lay ourselves comfortably down to sleep with our self-love," he writes to a noble lady. " Therefore He takes care to purify his elect, not only by giving them a longing for heaven, but also by means of earthly trials."[122]

A particularly skillful device he used in his direction consisted in suggesting to men something great and good, as though they already possessed it, so that they felt that it was personally addressed to them and that they felt powerfully motivated to follow the call of their spiritual father. Here are a few samples from his letters: " I am in the sight of His Divine Majesty completely convinced that Your Highness, though the sister in the flesh of Father Francisco [Borgia], desires much more to be his sister in that spirit which does not look to personal satisfaction and consolation, but always looks only to that which serves the more effective help of souls and which touches the service and praise of God our Creator and Lord." Or, " Since I am certain that Your Grace wishes only that which is more pleasing to God our Lord. . . ." And again, " In all things you aim directly at the greater honor of God our Lord. . . ."[123] What noble-spirited person

Vita Ignatii, V, c. 10, no. 136, in *FN*, IV, 857; Bartoli, *De vita et instituto,* IV, 12, p. 319.
120 *SdeSI,* I, 437, nos. 80-82.
121 *EppIgn,* III, 64; *Geistliche Briefe,* p. 197; *LettersIgn,* 218.
122 *EppIgn,* VI, 223-224; *Letters to Women,* p. 194.
123 *EppIgn,* V, 369; VIII, 655; I, 357; *Letters to Women,* pp. 125, 217, 425.

could withstand such trust and such a personal call ? No wonder then if one senses in many letters to the saintly director of souls, an echo of the great enthusiasm his words had aroused. Those who were guided by Ignatius not only retained something of his spirit of noble idealism, directed to the accomplishment of great things; often enough they even spoke his language: of " longing for great things even unto death," of " service of the Divine Majesty," and of the " deliverance of souls."[124] The world of their father had become their own.

This rounds off the picture of this great and unique director of souls. Gentleness, patience, and moderation on the one hand, and the constant drive towards the more perfect on the other — these counterbalanced each other in his character. He saw just as clearly the limitations of those entrusted to him as he saw their possibilities. With prudent discretion he at one time gave more consideration to one aspect, at another time to the other aspect, always thinking of the greater spiritual advancement of the individual. If one includes the fact that he united respect for the individuality and freedom of those guided by him to the clarity and firmness of his direction, it then becomes clear that Ignatius, the spiritual guide, cannot be described in one word. He was rather a man of astonishing breadth, who bound the apparent contradictions in the depth of his soul together into a mysterious unity.

Guide to Perfection

If one seeks to advance further into this depth and learn its secret, then one meets with Ignatius the saint and overhears him in conversation with such as desire to walk in the way of perfection. We thus enter the inner sanctuary of his direction of souls. Though he was himself *theodidaktos*, taught by God, having matured in solitude with God,[125] Ignatius strongly believed — and he spoke here from rich experience — that anyone who earnestly aspired to perfection must have a confessor and spiritual director; for " it is a serious danger in spiritual things to run on without the bridle of prudent counsel and wise discernment."[126] In religious life there is added obedience. The

---

124 Sister Teresa Rejadella says: "... thus it is a very great necessity for me to keep the longing for higher things until I die " (*EppMixt*, II, 288; *Letters to Women*, p. 360). The secretary of Margaret of Austria writes of her: " Madame would die a hundred times in the service of God and the king ... She has the courage and the strength of will for it " (*Letters to Women*, p. 75). The Ignatian terminology appears most clearly in the letters of Isabel Roser (in *Letters to Women*, pp. 278-295).
125 *MonNad*, IV, 645.
126 *EppIgn*, IV, 676, no. 14; *Geistliche Briefe*, p. 250; *LettersIgn*, p. 291. This is in the midst of the famous Letter on Obedience.

superior is at the same time the spiritual director. / Consequently the Constitutions demand that all be open to their superiors and spiritual directors, and that they confide to them all that moves their soul, their inclinations and difficulties, to what they feel themselves driven and in what they are tempted, their consolations and desolations, in order that they may be better directed not only in external matters but more especially in their spiritual journey.127) They should submit to their counsel and advice the amount of time they give to prayer and what they do for penance.128 " We may not," says Ignatius, " keep our temptations secret, nor such inspirations and thoughts which seem good to us; but we should reveal them to the confessor or superior because the evil spirit often changes himself into an angel of light. In all other affairs we should also act according to the advice and judgment of our spiritual fathers rather than according to our own opinion, and we should always be suspicious of our own judgment."129 " I should not at all desire to be my own master, but I must surrender myself to Him who created me and to him who directs and rules me in the place of God. In his hands I should be as soft wax in the hands of the sculptor."130

With this in mind, one understands why Ignatius wanted so much to know that spiritual conversation would be cultivated. " Try to get close to the pupils in spiritual friendship,"131 he advised the first Jesuits to go to Germany; and even the theologians of the order to the Council of Trent were advised to take time, in addition to their chief work, for spiritual conversation and religious instruction.132 Under certain conditions a spiritual conversation is of more importance for the advancement of the soul than prayer.133 If however no one is near at hand from whom one may expect spiritual help, then spiritual correspondence can also be useful and fitting.134 Everything which the concept of *pater spiritualis* had originaly meant in the Church, already in ancient monasticism, is once more brought to life in Ignatius.

It could possibly be cause for some surprise that Ignatius, at a time when individual personality was beginning to be more and more valued, revived once again the teaching of monastic tradition about

127 On the obligation of the account of conscience: *Exam*, [92]; *Cons*, [263], [424], [551]; Avisos, no. 9; (*Cartas*, II, 477).
128 On the frequency of Holy Communion, *EppIgn*, XII, 218; on prayer, ibid., III, 509; on penance, ibid., I, 506-507.
129 Avisos, no. 9; *Cartas de san Ignacio de Loyola*, II, 47.
130 From the " Testament " of St. Ignatius, no. 7, in *FN*, I, 595.
131 *EppIgn*, XII, 243, no. 5; *Geistliche Briefe*, p. 193.
132 *EppIgn*, I, 386-387; *Geistliche Briefe*, pp. 129-130; *LettersIgn*, p. 95.
133 *EppIgn*, 11, 234, in a letter to Francis Borgia; *LettersIgn*, pp. 179-182.
134 In advice given to Teresa Rejadella, ibid., I, 106-107.

obedience in its most powerful form. The comparisons with the
" corpse " and with the " stick in the old man's hand " are well known.
But one must leave this sort of obedience in the context in which it
has traditionally stood; one must see it as an essential element of
spiritual, not primarily external, direction. For Ignatius, in a certain
contrast to the mystical tradition of the more contemplative
monasticism, the most important aim of this direction was to discover
the concrete will of God and to bring it to completion. This is actually
a distinguishing characteristic of his spiritual direction: by means of
obedience and indifference to liberate men from themselves and to
direct them to the inner movements of the soul, to the gentle workings
of grace and the guidance of the Holy Spirit.

It is not therefore just a pious way of speaking, which one no
longer gives much thought to, when the saint so often mentions the
workings of grace and recalls to men's minds its inestimable value.
Many of his letters begin with the same words: " May the supreme
grace and eternal love of Christ our Lord visit you with his most holy
gifts and spiritual graces."[135] "Without the divine gifts of grace,"
we read another time, " all our thoughts, words, and actions are quite
tepid and slack, worth little or nothing. We must therefore at all
times reach for these gifts with much strength and eagerness or at
least have the desire to possess them. For with these gifts we are
endowed with such skill in all our actions that whatever we do is well
advised and pleasing to His Divine Majesty."[136] For the souls under
his direction, Ignatius can wish for nothing better than these gifts of
grace. " May it please God our Lord ever to multiply in you His
graces so that you may advance in the greater service and praise of
God from what is very good to what is still better."[137] " I cherish the
hope that these graces may ever be increased in your blessed soul by
our Lord. For a good means to receive new graces consists in using
well the graces one has already received."[138] In a letter to Francis
Borgia, he states more precisely just what gifts of grace he has in
mind: " I mean those that are not immediately obtainable through our
own power when we wish, but are solely the free gift of Him who gives
and has the power to give every good thing. To these belong. . .ardent
faith, hope, love, joy, spiritual peace, tears, deep consolation, exaltation of
spirit, divine touches and illuminations, and all other inner experiences

---

135 " santisimos dones y gracias espirituales;" another opening to his letters runs:
" The eternal grace and love of Christ our Lord be ever with us as a gracious
assistance."
136 *EppIgn*, II, 260.
137 Ibid., 258-259; *Letters to Women*, p. 452.
138 Ibid., I, 319; *Letters to Women*, p. 423.

and perceptions which accompany such graces. ... Each one of these most holy graces must be preferred to any exterior acts [he is thinking especially of exterior mortification] which are good only so long as they are ordered to the attainment, at least partial, of these gifts."[139]

As a director of souls, therefore, Ignatius is primarily concerned with leading those entrusted to him to a spiritual experience, to the experience of precisely these gifts of grace. The person should receive an inner sense for the workings of God's grace. The saint expresses to a mother his wishes for her son in this way: "May it please God our Lord to grant him His grace in order that he may attain a deep knowledge of himself and may feel in the depths of his soul the presence of His Divine Majesty. For if a man is a prisoner of the divine love and grace, then he is a free man regarding all created things of this world."[140] Similarly in another letter: "I feel that I am in no way free of the duty of offering urgent and continuous prayers to God our Lord for all Your Grace's affairs. And this as one who has a great longing before His Divine Majesty to see in you a constant increase of God's gifts. Such an increase is accompanied by an inner light and a constantly growing sensitivity for spiritual and eternal things so that the intensity of the longing for corporal and earthly things becomes ever weaker."[141] Or: "Divine grace must have already done great and powerful work in your soul, giving you the feeling for and love of the eternal things that you have."[142]

It goes without saying that Ignatius is not primarily concerned with mere feelings. "Feeling" means for him a higher "perceiving" and "knowing" and a "feeling of being led onward," as well as a "tasting," based on peace, joy, and consolation.[143] In such a spiritual experience it is not merely a question of the simple perception of the *presence* of God, of the beauty and sublimity of the eternal things; but rather of the inner consciousness of a *direction*, of the perception of the divine *guidance*. According to Ignatius the ultimate and proper meaning of the divine gifts of grace that move the soul lies in the fact that one is enabled to learn from them the will of God, His concrete will for the particular person. Thus we find desires and petitions like

---

139 Ibid., II, 236; *Geistliche Briefe*, p. 164; *LettersIgn*, p. 181.
140 Ibid., I, 92; *Letters to Women*, p. 183.
141 Ibid., III, 121; *Letters to Women*, p. 456.
142 Ibid., VI, 710; *Letters to Women*, p. 386.
143 Thus, in the closing words of the letters of 1556, the word "knowing" often stands in place of "feeling": *EppIgn*, XI, 334, 338; XII, 148, 200, 350, 351. See Henri Pinard de la Boullaye, "Sentir, sentimiento, y sentido, dans le style de saint Ignace," *AHSJ*, XXV (1956), 416-430.

the following: " May it please God to grant us all who still remain
here below the fulness of His grace in order that we may always feel
His most holy will within us and fulfil it perfectly."[144] " May the
supreme and infinite goodness of God grant us all the fulness of his
grace so that we may know his will and accomplish it."[145]

Ignatius has made sufficiently clear how this " perception " and
" feeling " of God's will proceeds. First of all, the person must take
care that the thoughts (and images), "which are brought to mind by
the corrupt part of ourselves or by the Evil One and strive to lead us
to think of disturbing, vain, or evil things," be suppressed as far as
possible by meditative prayer. " The more such thoughts recede or
die away, the more do good thoughts and holy impulses come. We
must give them a clear field, opening wide the gates of our soul."[146]
In these good thoughts and holy impulses, Ignatius believes, God works
for *this* soul and announces His will to it. Thus he warns: " Try
always to preserve your soul in internal peace and quiet readiness for
the time when our Lord will work in you." " Rather seek the Lord
of all things himself, I mean the holiest gifts of his grace; for example,
an illumination or tears. ..." The operation of God in a soul is shown
by the fact that it is driven or drawn now one way, now the other.
The soul should therefore not pursue its own thoughts, however exalted
they may be, but should give its attention to that which moves and
takes place within it. " Take counsel with your spirit [and pay
attention to] where it drives you."[147] " He sees and knows what is
most beneficial to each individual and, as the all-knowing One, shows
each his way. To find this way, with the grace of God, it is a great
help to examine the situation in various manners so that [finally] each
may travel on *that* way which is for the individual the clearest, the
happiest, and the most blessed in this life — directed totally to eternal
life — whereby the soul is completely infused with the holiest gifts of
grace."[148]

Here we stand at the summit of Ignatian spiritual direction. He
who can take it, who shows himself ready, who has a noble and magnanimous heart — this man is led by the saint to find his own personal
way, the way in which the grace of God wishes to lead him, the way
of perfect union with God in all he does, in all circumstances and

---

144. *EppIgn*, III, 220-221; *Letters to Women*, p. 438.
145 Ibid., XI, 334.
146 Ibid., II, 234; *Geistliche Briefe*, p. 162; *LettersIgn*, p. 179.
147 " Consule spiritum, ad quem ipse potissimum te moveat ac impellat " (*EppIgn*,
    XII, 679; *LettersIgn*, pp. 441-442).
148 Ibid., II, 236; *Geistliche Briefe*, p. 164; *LettersIgn*, p. 181.

whatever happens. It is not a way without its dangers. It is open to the possibility of many dangers. The self-seeking and indolence of a quietistic mysticism, wilfulness, vanity, and pride can accompany it. It was not by chance that Ignatius was suspected of the error of the Alumbrados. Safety measures have to be built into it. The primary ones Ignatius recognizes are mortification, indifference, obedience, humility, and the willing endurance of trials and suffering. As sublime as his directions are where it is a question of awakening the internal senses of the soul and of sharpening them that they may perceive where the grace of God is leading them, just so simple and sober and almost offensive do his basic ascetical demands sound. But both belong together and one presupposes the other. If one divorces them, he makes of Ignatius either an illuminist, speaking as a false mystic, or an ascetic of mind and will, who arouses a man to individual activity and leaves the grace of God out of consideration. One only does him justice when he brings out the purpose and direction of his asceticism. That asceticism is one which makes possible and safe the way on which inner grace is leading.

According to Ignatius self-love and disordered passions are the chief hindrance to union with God, to " finding God in all things." One must therefore struggle against them. This takes place first of all in interior mortification, self-denial, which consequently plays such a large role for him. His biographers report he had no other words so often in his mouth as " Vince te ipsum ! " (" Conquer yourself ! ").[149] In the sentence of the *Exercises*, [189], " One will make progress in proportion to the extent that he goes out from his self-love,"[150] he joins together practically everything that seems to him important for a proper election and for the perfect following of Christ. " The mortified man," he was accustomed to say, " who has conquered his passions, finds what he seeks in prayer much more easily than the unmortified and imperfect man."[151] " For this reason," adds Ribadeneyra, " our blessed father attached so much importance to mortification and preferred it to a prayer that did not aim at self-mortification and thereby at union of one's self with God." " For a truly mortified man

149 Ribadeneyra, *Vita Ignatii*, V, ch. 10, no. 137, in *FN*, IV, 857; Bartoli, *De vita et instituto*, IV, 12, p. 318.

150 *SpEx*, [189]; the relationship between abnegation and the vision of God is expressed beautifully in one of his letters: "... for when men go out of themselves and enter into their Creator and Lord, they are filled with inner recollection, attention, and consolation; and they experience how our eternal Good exists in all creatures"; to Francis Borgia, *EppIgn*, I, 339; *Geistliche Briefe*, p. 124; *LettersIgn*, p. 84.

151 *SdeSI*, I, 471; *FN*, III, 636.

a quarter of an hour is sufficient to attain union with God," Gonçalves da Câmara heard him say.[152]

Ignatius also viewed obedience primarily as a school of mortification, of the denial of self-will. Only when one knows the high purpose that he had in view in all his spiritual direction, the conformity of the human will with the will of God, will one be able to understand his obedience of the intellect. How perfectly he wished this to be practised is shown by the following directive, which stems from Ignatius himself: " Everyone shall be ready to give a practice sermon [in the refectory], no matter whether in Greek, Hebrew, Latin, German, or any other language; and, even though he understand not one word of the language in question, he should nevertheless, in case it be so ordered, without hesitation or dispute climb into the pulpit in the belief that obedience signifies nothing other than availability [for any service] and mortification of one's own will. And should he be able to say no more than two or three words about the subject on which he has been directed to preach, he shall speak them, or, in case he is unable even to do that, say, ' I am ready to say whatever is pleasing to you.' And he shall not descend from the pulpit until he shall have received permission to do so."[153]

That this did not remain a mere refectory exercise is made clear by the following incident. About the year 1548, when plans were being made for the foundation of a college at Messina in Sicily, Ignatius proposed several questions to the members of the community of the professed house in Rome. They were to answer them after three or four days of prayer and mature consideration. The questions dealt with the complete readiness to do and accept everything that Ignatius wished of them regarding the foundation of the college. We still possess some of the answers. This is the one given by St. Peter Canisius: " After mature consideration of the questions that Master Ignatius, my reverend father in Christ and superior, has proposed for my response, I declare first of all that, with the help of God, I am drawn with completely equal force to both sides — whether he now orders me to remain here forever or sends me to Sicily, India, or anywhere else. Furthermore, if I should go to Sicily, I declare without reservation that I will undertake with great joy any duty, whether that of cook, gardener, porter, student, or teacher, with complete indifference to any field of knowledge whatever, even if it be unknown to me. And from today on, that is from February 5, I make a completely unconditional vow that I will in the future never undertake

152 *SdeSI*, I, 471, no. 13; ibid., 367, no. 64; *FN*, III, 636.
153 *Constitutones Societatis Jesu, latine et hispanice* (Matriti, 1892), Appendix XIII, p. 341. The statement is also quoted in Huonder, *Ignatius*, p. 205.

anything that could be to my advantage, whether it concerns my place of residence, sphere of duty, or anything else, in matters of this sort submitting myself once and for all to the care of my father in Christ who is my superior. To him I yield the direction of my soul and of my body, to him I entirely subject even my understanding and my will, to him I humbly offer them and recommend them to him, full of trust in Jesus Christ our Lord."[154] A scholastic from Augsburg, Jakob Speg, writes in a similar vein: "I am ready with the help of God gladly to carry out everything that has been mentioned — to say yes, to say no, to remain indifferent, just as seems good and pleasing to Your Paternity. And I offer once more the vows of poverty, chastity, and obedience to my superior."[155]

Ignatius must have been very satisfied with such answers. They were wholly in accord with his ideal. For him the point of primary importance was that there be effective and repeated *exercise* of indifference, of obedience, of the denial of self-will. He was convinced that a virtue put into actual *practice*, even just one time, was worth more than a thousand abstract resolutions because the soul is transformed in her depths only by exercise. For this reason exercise plays such a large role in his direction of souls. It was his wish that anyone who wanted to follow the call of Christ in the Society of Jesus should be tested by being subjected to various exercises: to make the Spiritual Exercises, to serve in a hospital, to beg alms, to do lowly and humbling work.[156] A good deal of the novitiate formation was built on this. In comparison with this the life of prayer became of strikingly secondary importance Thus it could happen, for example, that someone at his entrance into the order might not be required to make the Exercises but would be put right away to some work or other: to study, to preach, or even — especially if it were a case of a learned and important man — to work in the kitchen, where he would be subordinate to a lay brother.[157] The reprimands that Ignatius meted out and the penances that he imposed, which were often extraordinarily severe, were intended for that same end.[158] The individual should be exercised in willing acceptance of blame, in bearing humiliations and

154 Otto Braunsberger, *B. P. Canisii epistulae et acta* (8 vols. Freiburg, 1896-1923, I, 263).

155 *EppIgn*, I, 709; two other answers are found ibid., XII, 485-486.

156 See Joseph de Guibert, S.J., *The Jesuits: Their Spiritual Doctrine and Practice* (Chicago, 1964), hereafter cited as *DeGuiJes*, pp. 80-81, 94-95, 102-104.

157 Thus, for example, Father Juan (Johannes) Rubies did not make the Exercises when he entered the Society, but had to undergo the test of serving in the kitchen for twenty-two days (ibid., p. 82).

158 Examples are given in Huonder, *Ignatius*, pp. 101-104.

privations, loneliness and desolation. These exercises would help him learn detachment from things, from men, and especially from himself, and lead him to place his trust ever more entirely in God.

With the same end in mind if suffering came to men, the saint would always use the opportunity to point out to them the meaning of suffering for the greater service of God. For example, he once wrote to a sick woman: " I can actually feel no sadness [about this sickness], because I consider that all illnesses and the losses of our material goods often come from the hand of God our Lord. They teach us greater self-knowledge and take from us our partiality toward created things. They make us realize how short this earthly life actually is, and they prepare us for the other life that lasts forever. . . . I know that a servant of God can come out of an illness part theologian, made such in order now to direct and order his life to the glorification and service of God our Lord."[159] He writes in a similar vein to Alexis Fontana, the secretary of Charles V, who had lost his position when Philip II ascended the throne and who tried in vain to win the favor of the new king. Ignatius did not console him with empty words, but boldly indicated the chance that God was offering him in this loss: " One must express his thanks to the Divine and Supreme Goodness no less sincerely for the loss of a thing one has sought than one would do upon obtaining the same. The satisfaction and peace which Your Grace experiences in this case are a clear sign that God is endowing Your Grace with the resolve and a sincere longing for his greater service."[160] Whenever counselling one in distress and difficulties, Ignatius always indicates first the necessity and duty of exercising genuine virtue before he gives concrete suggestions. " I perceive that God our Lord visits you with difficulties. With this he gives you a good opportunity for practising the virtues which he, in his divine goodness, has granted you and for giving evidence that they are solid virtues."[161]

Once the hard school of indifference — of liberation from creatures, of continual mortification — was presupposed, Ignatius showed a sublime and amazing liberality toward those whom he directed. He not only allowed their abilities ample opportunity for development but also, to a great extent, allowed them to follow their inclinations.[162] Still greater, however, was the respect he had for their freedom and independence in the spiritual realm. Just as he appealed to his own

---

159 *EppIgn*, I, 84-85; *Letters to Women*, p. 265.
160 Ibid., XI, 190.
161 Ibid., II, 374; *Letters to Women*, p. 355.
162 Da Câmara, *Memoriale*, no. 117, in *FN*, I, 596.

conscience when important decisions were to be made,[163] so also should one experienced in spiritual matters follow the inclination of his own conscience. In his opinion, the sole determining factor in making a particular practical choice should be "spiritual advancement," which consists in this, "that the soul grow in virtue — especially in love, humility, self-abandonment, and mercy."[164] Thus, for example, Ignatius recognizes no particular devotions: "prayer, examination of conscience, holy Mass, and the sacraments, that is all."[165]

Whether an individual should take up some such devotion is to be decided according to the spiritual "profit" that he experiences from it. So Ignatius can write to his sister Magdalena, ". . . it will give me great joy in our Lord if you will occasionally send me news in our Lord of the spiritual progress which you perceive in yourself [from praying a rosary enriched with many indulgences], to the greater honor of his Divine Majesty."[166]

Whether someone should go to Holy Communion depends on whether the reception of it benefits the soul. Accordingly, in a concrete case he decides, "If you know from experience that this food of the soul strengthens you and gives you great peace and makes you persevering and more zealous to serve God ever better, to praise and glorify Him, then frequent communion is without doubt permissible for you; and it will be [even] better for you to communicate daily."[167] Despite the stir that such advice aroused at that period, despite the displeasure of many priests and the protests of spiritual authorities,[168] Ignatius did not allow himself to be diverted from recommending even to laymen, "Go often to confession and receive Holy Communion as often as you can."[169] As a "completely valid witness" for the correctness of his advice, "the judgment of his own conscience" is in itself enough for him.[170] To be sure, he always insisted that "a high esteem of all the gifts of grace that come from His kindness and generosity" must go hand in hand with a growing "contempt of self";[171] and "the inner feeling, of which we become conscious, neces-

163 *EppIgn*, II, 494 (mirando á lo que mi consciencia me obliga); ibid., IV, 627 (porque de una vez yo satishaga en esta parte á my conscientia).
164 *EppIgn*, XII, 218; *Geistliche Briefe*, p. 114; *LettersIgn*, p. 58.
165 Paul Dudon, *S. Ignace de Loyola. Lettres spirituelles* (Paris, 1933), p. 10.
166 *EppIgn*, I, 171; *Letters to Women*, p. 119.
167 *EppIgn*, I, 276; *Letters to Women*, p. 339.
168 See H. Pinard de la Boullaye, *Saint Ignace de Loyola, Directeur d'âmes* (Paris, 1946), p. XXXVII; also Huonder, *Ignatius*, pp. 311-312.
169 *EppIgn*, I, 170; *Letters to Women*, p. 119.
170 Ibid., 276; *Letters to Women*, p. 339.
171 Ibid., X, 7; *Letters to Women*, p. 477.

sarily signifies that we conform ourselves to His Commandments, the precepts of the Church, and obedience to our superiors."[172] But once all this is presupposed, he can say with unequalled daring, recalling the saying of Augustine: " Everything is allowed you in the Lord — apart from obvious mortal sin and with the exception of that which you might consider as such — if you judge that thereby your soul experiences greater help and is more powerfully urged on to the love of its Creator and Lord."[173] " The soul that passionately longs to serve its Creator and Lord puts into service every means that is possible for it."[174]

Just as Ignatius himself was a man of great universality, so also is his teaching on the direction of souls. Asceticism and mysticism, obedience and freedom, indifference to creatures and a broad use of them are all combined by him into a unity. The boldness of his direction and teaching did not spring from himself. " God treated him as a teacher instructs a child."[175] He allowed him to pass through all the stages of spiritual experience in order that he might be able to help others, as Polanco once said.[176] Everyone who knew him, his sons especially, knew that there was no other among them who understood the direction of souls as he did. That which Ribadeneyra reports was the opinion of all: " However much Master Favre (so Master Laynez once said to me) is experienced in spiritual things, as we know and as one can see in his letters and in his book, in comparison to our father, in the art of directing souls he stands as a boy in comparison to a very wise man."[177] Ignatius was not only a man of great zeal for the honor of God and the salvation of souls. He was also a unique spiritual guide.

172 Ibid., I, 105; *Letters to Women*, p. 334.
173 Ibid., 275-276; *Letters to Women*, p. 339.
174 Ibid., 170; *Letters to Women*, p. 119.
175 *Autobiog*, 27, in *FN*, 1, 400.
176 " Quia vero tentatum per omnia Ignatium esse oportebat, qui alios multos in variis tentationibus pro officii sui ratione erat aliquando sublevaturus ": *PolChron*, 1, 21 (*Vita*, ch. III), in *FN*, II, 527, no. 18.
177 Ribadeneyra, *De actis Ignatii*, no. 86, in *FN*, II, 279; *SdeSI*, I, 380.

IGNATIUS OF LOYOLA AND
PHILIP NERI

Hugo Rahner

THEY WERE CANONIZED together on the same day, March 12, 1622.
Yet their lives were so utterly different that one is continually tempted,
in comparing these two men of God, to survey once again that magni-
ficently broad expanse within which the one common ideal of Christian
sanctity can be realized.[1] The founder of the Jesuit Order and the
originator of the Roman Oratory — at first glance they have such
opposite temperaments; and their ideals of religious life, or more
precisely the realization of these ideals in the Church and in history,
differ so much that a comparison may at first appear almost artificial.
Or it might again bring to life some of that ill feeling of curial politics
that existed between the Professed House at the Gesù and the Oratory
at Vallicella during the years of preparation for the canonization.[2]
The repercussions of this were still at work during the baroque period
when the following question was discussed with scholarly seriousness:
whether Ignatius at one time had actually urged " Pippo buono "
to enter the Society of Jesus and had to suffer a cheerful rebuff; or
whether it was not that Philip had sought admittance, but Ignatius
seriously and politely said no.[3] With this in mind, one can imagine

---

Study 2 was translated by James F. McAndrews, S.J.

1 For the life of St. Philip Neri we have used the best biography that has
appeared so far: Louis Ponelle and Louis Bordet, *Saint Philippe Néri et la
societé romaine de son temps*: 1515-1595 (Paris, 1929). Throughout this
article [only], this work will be cited as Ponelle. [English translation by Ralph
Francis Kerr, *St. Philip Neri and the Roman Society of His Times* (London:
Sheed and Ward, 1932). In the references to Ponelle, the page number in
the English translation will be added in brackets to the page number of the
French original].

2 Ponelle, 520, [571]. On disagreements as early as the generalate of St. Francis
Borgia, see *ibid.*, 264, [313]; 58, [105].

3 Ibid., 54-55, [102-103]; also Pietro Tacchi Venturi, *Storia*, Vol. II, Pt. 1,
pp. 300-304.

how Ignatius, "the small Spaniard who limps slightly and has such cheerful eyes,"[4] and Philip, the joyous one, looked down on this un-glorified Rome of their sons with the smiles that were characteristic of both on earth. Just by imagining this we begin to perceive that these two saints, despite all the contrasts, already belonged together in their earthly life and resembled each other in a common depth of soul.

They met in Rome, most probably already in that terrible winter of famine, 1538-1539, when the companions of Ignatius gathered the sick and the poor in the Casa Frangipani and then distributed them among the city's hospitals.[5] At that time Philip became acquainted with Ignatius and Francis Xavier; and even after many years he will read out loud with glowing enthusiasm Xavier's letters from India during his evening spiritual hour at San Girolamo della Carità, the origin of the Oratory.[6] During all the years that Ignatius was in Rome (1537-1556), Philip, who blessed the same Roman soil during the sixty years (1534-1595) of his pastoral labors, remained united in reverential love with the Spanish Master at the Church of Santa Maria della Strada. He often acknowledged that it was really Ignatius who had first introduced him to "interior prayer"[7] and that he had seen on the face of Ignatius a mysterious glow — indeed, he later thought, no painting could reproduce that radiance.[8] Philip's un-erringly sharp sense for spiritual things consequently saw more in Ignatius than the external appearance; and precisely at these concealed depths is he the same as Master Ignatius and therefore comparable. Let us attempt to comprehend in a concise outline this similarity hidden under the dissimilarity of their human and Christian individuality.

The Man

Philip Neri arrived in Rome four years before Ignatius, most probably toward the end of 1533. He was a young man of eighteen, without the same experience of sin as the elegant officer, Iñigo de Loyola, yet impelled by the force of his "conversion" to a flaming and exclusive love for the things of God. For Philip this meant first of all a passionate love of poverty, that daring rejection of all apparently prudent safeguards to insure one's day-to-day existence. For Iñigo de Loyola, from the time of his departure from home and family

---

4 *FN*, II, 637.
5 Schurhammer, *Franz Xaver*, I, 427-428, 481; Schurhammer, trans. Costelloe, *Francis Xavier*, I, 446-447, 501.
6 *EppXav*, I, 17*; II, 571-572; Ponelle, 163-164, [210-211].
7 *Acta Sanctorum*, July 7, p. 532, no. 588.
8 *SdeSI*, II, 425-426, 491; I, 513; *FN*, III, 447, 428.

(1522), through all his years of study, up to and inclusive of the happy hermitage at Vicenza, this was also the essence of the evangelical imitation of Christ.

Philip also was living in his "hermitage" in the Piazza San Eustachio in the autumn of 1537 when Ignatius arrived in Rome. From there he tried to study theology at the Sapienza; and perhaps he heard a few lectures of Ignatius' two companions, Favre and Laynez, who began lecturing there in 1537. Since he also heard theological lectures in the cloister at San Agostino, he may well have listened to the Lenten sermons of the famous Agostino Mainardi which enflamed the first attack in Rome against the Parisian Masters of Ignatius.

Here we can already catch a glimpse of the profound contrast between Philip and Ignatius. From the time of his unsuccessful pilgrimage to Jerusalem, the Spaniard was motivated by a single idea: To help souls, study is imperative. For years he sits on the school bench, and the battle between dry metaphysics and mystical fervor is always decided in favor of reason. Philip soon put his books aside. At the same time that Iñigo is laboring with iron-willed determination to earn his Master's diploma (1535), Philip confesses, "I have never studied much and I have not been able to learn much, for I was occupied with prayer and other spiritual exercises."[9]

Philip felt the same powerful forces that impelled Ignatius, the impulse to love of God and to solitary prayer. But Philip surrendered himself to this force with mystical abandonment; Ignatius yields to it only temporarily and always under the highest degree of self-control. While studying in Paris, Ignatius occasionally sought compensation for this in a stuccoed cave on Montmartre[10] or in the austere psalmody of the Carthusian monks. During the same period this force draws Philip to the sweet solitude of the Roman Campagna's half-ruined catacombs and to the solemn Vespers at the stational churches. Then he steps out from the dark haunts of his prayer into the light of the narrow Roman streets, just as Ignatius marched into these same Roman streets after the mystical enlightenment at La Storta, in order to feel out calmly and soberly the terrain for the thoughtful and prudent reform of the Church.

With Philip everything is gifted improvisation; he questions only his loving heart. He sauntered by the merchants' stalls, becoming God's holy vagabond. He sought to win over the young Florentine merchants and the Roman street urchins with such great charm (*con*

9 Ponelle, 34, [82].
10 *SdeSI*, I, 524; *FN*, III, 438, no. 38.

tanto bel modo)[11] that no one can resist him. He was miles apart from
that cautious, almost pedantic seriousness that characterized the band
of Parisian Masters as they sat together at night, early in 1539, discussing how they wanted to form themselves into a religious family
so that they might organize their pastoral work at Rome and in the
world.

The solemn, serious Spaniard and the cheerful Pippo have fundamentally the same goal: once again to make Rome the Holy City.
This was the Rome in which, ever since it had been sacked, so much
of the new and good was stirring and yet, according to the sober
judgment of Ignatius, was " sterile and barren soil, overgrown with
evil fruits."[12] After sixteen years of hard work he will still write, " We
reap some fruit here, even though Rome is what it is."[13]

In the way in which they begin and carry on their work of reform,
the two apostles of Rome are as different as can be imagined. Ignatius
gives the Spiritual Exercises to humanists and cardinals; his learned
companions teach at the Sapienza, and they carefully apportion their
sermons to the most frequented churches of the city.[14] Philip, however, who is not yet a priest (he does not accept ordination until
1551), remains in the streets; and his pastoral work is already characterized by an inimitable " homely friendliness " (*familiarità e domes-
ticezza*)[15] that wins to him all hearts, even of popes and cardinals.

In the years before his arrival at Rome, the life of Ignatius had
been a progressively greater denial of all the ascetical peculiarities
that had remained with him since the time of his conversion and the
days at Manresa. It was a long way from the pilgrim's sackcloth to
the " devotion to ordinary dress " which, in his mature years, he called
a characteristic of genuine spiritualization.[16] It was also a long way
from his own " holy follies " to the first draft of the plan for the new
order in which the companions at the Casa Frangipani dismissed with
astonishing audacity everything that up to then had been considered
as characteristic of asceticism, " fasting, disciplines, nakedness of head
and feet, colored garments."[17] So daring was it that the cardinals
commanded that these phrases be omitted in the bull founding the
order. There seemed no longer to be any mystical individualism in

11 Ponelle, 88, [136].
12 *EppIgn*, I, 138, 143.
13 Ibid., VII, 256.
14 Schurhammer, *Franz Xaver*, I, 397-398, 407-408; Schurhammer, trans. Cos
   telloe, *Francis Xavier*, I, 415-417, 425-426.
15 Ponelle, 524, [574].
16 *FN*, I, 609.
17 *Cons*MHSJ, I, p. 20, 30.

Ignatius, nothing of that which characterized a Philip. Philip's bio-grapher is right in saying, " Ignatius based the future of his order on a denial of the eccentricities of the mystical life and on a rigorous subordination of the individual to the common goal."[18]

Now we understand more clearly why the meetings between Ignatius and Philip during these years could have only this result, that each of the two men recognized more exactly and distinctly his individuality and his own vocation. Philip was genuinely impressed by the Spanish Master's new religious foundation; and according to a tradition which is indeed not completely verifiable, he led some of his young men to follow Ignatius.[19] However, he himself (and this is certainly the correct interpretation of what is found in the sources) could only answer Ignatius' tactful invitation to join the new com-munity with a cheerful no. If later the general of the Jesuits, Mutius Vitelleschi, referred to Philip's statement that he had wanted to enter the Society of Jesus, but that Ignatius had declined to accept him, these words of Pippo buono were probably one of those jests with which he covered the depths of his humility "in that graciously playful manner of his " (*da quel modo graziosamente scherzevole*), says Pietro Tacchi Venturi in this regard.[20] Ignatius equals Philip in this sublime humor; from that particular meeting, which both separated and united them, comes that humorous comparison: Philip is like a bell in a church tower —its ringing summons everyone to enter the church, but it remains outside.[21] No, this Pippo was neither made nor called to be a son of Ignatius; and the most profound reason for this lay simply in his unrestrained nature, in his " humor " (in the most radical sense of that ancient word), and in his heart that would never let itself be bound.

But we need not delay at this point where the apostolic paths of the two great men of the Roman Reform diverge. There are blessedly vast regions within these two saints where they walk together as friends, and depths in which they are astonishingly alike. Yet there is always a difference. Ignatius never allowed what one might call his " philippian " tendencies to break loose; but Philip's unrestrained heart might throb, rejoice, and weep in blissful unconcern in order to accomplish in everything exactly the same thing that Ignatius strove for with strict self-control and restraint of his emotions: to love

---

18 Ponelle, 51, [99].
19 Ibid., 54, [102]; Schurhammer, *Franz-Xaver*, I, 489, fn. 4; Schurhammer, trans. Costelloe, *Francis Xavier*, I, 509, fn. 156.
20 Tacchi Venturi, *Storia*, Vol. II, Pt. I, p. 303.
21 Ponelle, 54, [102]; *Acta Sanctorum*, May 6, p. 525.

everything in God and in everything to love God alone. By comparing Ignatius with the much less complicated nature of Philip, we shall come to understand the depths of his nature which otherwise shyly keep themselves hidden.

To begin with, the contrasts are already almost irreconcilable when we observe the two men in their relationships with others. Ignatius is reserved, the enemy of idle gossip, always under control and always somewhat formal. He acknowledges this about himself (herein surveying the great distance between his interior disposition and his exterior behavior), " Whoever measures my love merely by how much of it I manifest outwardly will deceive himself greatly."[22] Philip is loquacious, merry, good-naturedly gruff, apt and witty. Occasionally he can cuff his penitents and box the ears of his young friends with the humorous remark, " That was not for you, but for the devil in you."[23] No one can resist his radiant charm, and one can think of this rare human being only as " devoutly vivacious " (to borrow a phrase from Goethe).[24]

This inimitable charm of his, which always maintains its genuine Florentine character, is the secret of his pastoral work. But it was precisely this Pippo buono who saw on the face of Ignatius the reflection of an equally inimitable joy; and thus, with a kinship of spirit, he perceived something that was alive within himself. In fact, when we listen to the other men who lived with Ignatius, we hear — from the Portuguese diary, for example, which Luís Gonçalves da Câmara kept during the last years of Ignatius' life — that the general of the order, who was usually looked upon with a timid respect, " was inclined so strongly to love that he was almost love incarnate; and for that reason was so loved by everyone in the entire order that each felt himself, so to speak, to be especially loved by him."[25] " When he welcomed any visitor, he showed him such a cheerful joy that it appeared as if he wanted to take him into the center of his soul."[26] That was exactly the experience of the young people who met in Pippo's small cell at San Girolamo and whom he delighted with the first strains of his Oratorian music, which later became so famous.

This music, which Philip with the instinct of a divine virtuoso placed at the service of his pastoral work and which at first sight makes him appear so immeasurably distant from Ignatius and the ideal of his

---

22 *FN*, I, 588.
23 Ponelle, 91, [138].
24 Goethe, *Italienische Reise* [Journey through Italy], Naples, May 26, 1787.
25 *SdeSI*, I, 423; *FN*, I, 579, no. 86.
26 *FN*, I, 637; *Letters to Women*, p. 414.

order, actually brings these two souls close together in the depths of their natures.[27] Ignatius had already made a strict renunciation of any cultivation of liturgical music in the first draft of the rules of his order in 1539, even though he clearly perceives the pastoral and ascetical significance of music: "All the members in sacred orders . . . are obliged to recite the Office according to the Church's rite, but not in choir, that they may not be withdrawn from the offices of charity, to which we have totally devoted ourselves. These members, therefore, should employ neither organs nor ceremonies with liturgical song in their Masses and other ceremonies; for we have found in our experience that these practices, which praiseworthily embellish the divine worship of other clerics and priests, and which have been devised to arouse and move the minds of men in accordance with the nature of the hymns and sacred mysteries, have hindered us in no small measure"[28] from the offices of charity to which we have devoted ourselves "according to the pattern of our vocation." Yet he had in the depths of his soul the same mystical sense for music that Philip had. This statement from his mystical diary could be one of Philip's sayings: "At Mass many tears. And all this with such a deep sense of the words heard interiorly that it was a likeness to or a remembrance of celestial speech or music."[29] Often he went into the little church of San Giuseppe della Pigna to hear the singing of Vespers.[30] During the Paschal Season the Austrian Father Peter Schorich had to sing for him privately one of his Allelujuas.[31] Luis Gonçalves da Câmara notes in his diary: "What most stimulated him to exaltation in prayer was music — singing about the things of God, like Vespers, solemn Masses, and similar services. So great was this stimulation that he once confessed to me that, upon entering a church in which the Divine Office was being sung, he immediately felt 'transported outside himself' (*se trasportava totalmente de sy mesmo*). And that not only helped his soul, he said, but also his bodily health. Thus it happened that when he was sick or felt out of sorts (*estava com grande fastio*), nothing comforted him more than a pious song sung to him by one of his fellow Jesuits. Of course he never permitted anyone to come to him expressly for this purpose, not even from the German College where there were so many

---

27 C. A. Kneller, "Das Oratorium des heiligen Philipp Neri und das musikalische Oratorium," in *Zeitschrift für katholische Theologie*, XLI (1917), pp. 246-282.
28 First Sketch of the Institute of the Society of Jesus, in *Cons*MHSJ, I, p. 19.
29 *SpDiary*, May 12, 1544, [224]; *Cons*MHSJ, I, p. 137.
30 *FN*, II, 337.
31 *LittQuad*, IV, 328-329; J. Brodrick, *St. Peter Canisius*, (London, 1935; reprinted Chicago, 1962), p. 277.

good singers. It was only a few times that Father des Freux visited him and played a little on the clavichord for him as he sat in his room in rather low spirits, or that a very modest and virtuous lay brother sang him one of the many pious songs he knew by heart."[32]

Another common quality of the sublime humanity of the two saints is their bond with nature, in which they find the divine. From the small balcony of his room Ignatius looks up at the same stars shining in the Roman sky that Philip gazes at from the loggia he had had built at the Vallicella for that purpose.[33] The thought of the only one of Philip's sonnets that still survives expresses what was also in the soul of the star-drunk Ignatius: "What prison holds the soul back so that it cannot depart from here below, and so finally tread the stars under foot and live in God and die to itself?"

> Qual prigion la ritien ch'indi parire
> non possa, e al fin coi piedi calcar le stelle
> e viver sempr' in dio e a se morire?[34]

With the same heartbeat, these two men lost in God love the colorful everyday life of the Roman streets and of their sinful inhabitants: Philip, in the laughter of the noisy young men about him; Ignatius, even in the turmoil of the streets, when he sees three men walking together and immediately feels his heart glowing with love for the Trinity.[35] Even today it is still impossible to walk through the streets of the old city without remembering both of them: Pippo, who every day hurried along from the Vallicella to San Girolamo with a swarm of happy youths behind him; Ignatius, as he gave his catechetical street sermons to boys at the Zecca, in the Campo dei Fiori, or next to the Rotunda.

The recollections of the old people who still recall those days during the canonical process for Ignatius' beatification are priceless. They show us a truly "philippian" Ignatius. One of them remembers how Don Ignazio had playfully pulled his ear; another, how Ignatius gave him a fatherly hug (*mi faceva carezze come a putti*); a third, how he remained calm even when street boys threw apples at him.[36] The Ignatius who could cheer up a disconsolate soul with a gay Basque dance[37] was of like nature with the Philip who danced a true *grotesque*

---

32 *FN, I*, 636-637.

33 *SdeSI*, I, 523; *FN*, 376-377; Schurhammer, *Franz Xaver*, I, 462; Schurhammer, trans. Costelloe, *Francis Xavier*, I, 482.

34 Ponelle, 525, [575].

35 *SpDiary*, February 19, 1544, [55]; *Cons*MHSJ, I, p. 101.

36 *SdeSI*, II, 825, 828, 831.

37 Mikolaj Lenczycky (Nicolaus Lancicius), *Opuscula spiritualia* (Antwerp, 1650), II, 639; Schurhammer, *Franz Xaver*, I, 397, fn. 5; Schurhammer, trans. Costelloe, *Francis Xavier*, I, 415, fn. 55.

even before cardinals and who called upon a lay brother, who was waiting table for him, to amuse his distinguished guests with a country dance.[38]

Because they were truly saints, both were truly men. Therefore they were filled with that divine cheerfulness which is the sign of the authenticity of Christian seriousness. In Philip it was a Florentine humor, effervescent, sometimes wrathful or whimsical. In Ignatius it was a quiet superiority which, at the beginning of his conversion to God, often arose from a sort of discriminating disdain toward others. At any rate, this is one of the most significant pieces of information given us by Pedro de Ribadeneyra: " The Father, at the beginning of his conversion to God, often felt himself tempted to break out laughing at the sight of certain people. He drove this laughter away with blows of the scourge; in fact, he used just as many blows when he had scarcely smiled at someone else."[39] But the diary of Luís Gonçalves da Câmara still reports this same inclination in 1555; and he indicates how Ignatius — in an ascetical manner, one could say — has transformed this smiling at others into a happy smile at the blessings or virtues of the one who provoked him to laughter.[40] One sees that the cheerfulness of Ignatius has a different quality than Pippo's has. It is, as it were, more acquired, more conscious, more phlegmatic. However, it is a characteristic of the mature Ignatius; it is that " cheerful and religious joyousness, prudent and measured " (*alegria e facilidade religiosa, gravidade e prudencia*) which, according to the Portuguese witness Da Câmara, Ignatius wished to see in his sons.[41] Thus it was that no one enjoyed a well-aimed joke or a comical situation more than Ignatius himself; such occurrences were always " a feast " (*grande festa*) for him.[42]

The Mystic

We would fail to understand both saints if we were to compare them only with regard to their natural charm as human beings. Both are mystics, and the mighty intervention of the divine within the bounds of their humanity destroys all ordinary standards of measurement. Things happen in their lives which we no longer understand. In a man who has emptied himself before God, the " membrane " that marks his natural psychological limits has become,

---

38 Ponelle, 93, [141]; 373, [423-424].
39 Ribadeneyra, *Vita Ignatii*, V, ch. 10, no. 155, in *FN*, IV, 868-871.
40 *FN*, I, 542.
41 *FN*, I, 642.
42 *FN*, I, 643, 656, 701, 703, 713; Schurhammer, *Franz Xaver*, I, 470; Schurhammer, trans. Costelloe, *Francis Xavier*, I, 490.

as it were, so thin that, when the divine touches that part of the soul, purely spiritual phenomena and parapsychological phenomena are so confusingly similar that they can be distinguished only through a discernment of spirits which, in the last analysis, only the mystic himself has at his disposal. This is the basis for the astonishing fact that both Philip and Ignatius, who received the highest mystical graces, were filled with a lively, often frankly pointed distrust of such occurrences in themselves and in others. Delusion is the rule, genuine mysticism the exception: that is Philip's definitive judgment.[43] This conclusion had been forced upon him by his own experience in the case of the deluded mystic, Orsola Benincasa;[44] just as Ignatius had learned it from dealing with the stigmatic woman from Bologna or with the Spanish Magdalena de la Cruz.[45] The practical rules for the direction of souls that both saints articulated above all for the guidance of pious women are in complete agreement.[46] Both had a wonderfully sharp sense for distinguishing the divine and the diabolical in the borderline areas in the depths of the soul.

All the more remarkable is it then that, in examining the agreement of the mystical experiences of both saints, we thereby establish just as clearly the dissimilarities between them. For the dissimilarity in their reactions stems from the differences in their natural dispositions and thus also from the differences in their vocations within the limitless range of possible actualizations of Christian existence. Let us try to point out a few of these mystical phenomena.

Philip Neri is a mystic of modern times in whom there once more comes to life all that we are otherwise accustomed to read about only in the lives of the fathers of the desert who sought their ideal in " folly for the sake of Christ."[47] He is " a mystical-ascetic figure of the highest perfection, clothed in the garments of a harlequin out of love for God."[48] Right from the days when he first received mystical graces, it was as if he had been thrown off the track of all that is merely natural to man: the touch of the divine, the inner fire, divine love, the heart-searing abandonment to the eternal, all appeared to him to demand that he turn everything naturally human upside down, that he laugh heartily at all that is merely rational, and that this

---

43 Ponelle, 530-531, [580].
44 Ibid., 85-87, [133-134].
45 *FN*, I, 645-646, 719; *SdeSI*, I, 407; *FN*, II, 328-329. B. Wilhelm, " Die Stigmatisierte von Bologna," ZAM, V, (1930), pp. 176-178; Huonder, *Ignatius*, pp. 298-299; *Letters to Women*, pp. 25-26.
46 Ponelle, 527, [577]; *Letters to Women*, pp. 12, 14, 20-22.
47 S.Hilpisch, " Die Torheit um Christi Willen," ZAM, VI (1931), pp. 121-131.
48 J. Schmitz in *Lexicon fur Theologie und Kirche*, VIII (1936), p. 232.

folly of his should be just the thing that would provide a living example and visible proof that the divine is always completely different from the apparently normal.

This harlequin of the Roman streets was an enigmatic human being. He really enjoyed being considered mad; he allowed himself excesses that people forgave only in Pippo; he used words that shocked even the saintly Cardinal Borromeo; he made silly jokes that sounded stupid and yet were intended merely to conceal the extremely sensitive shyness of his love for God. He covered over his joyful but fearful awe before the mystery of the Mass by cheerful chatter and playing with birds and puppies in the sacristy. When visitors came to him in his small cell at Vallicella to hear some sublime words from the mouth of the man of God he could hide behind an almost rude grumpiness and say, " Would you like me to strike a pose and spit out pious words ? "[49] He expresses his awe-struck love for God, his confidences and his profound insight into the mysteries of grace in a paradox that seems capricious but is in truth rather frightening: "If I regain my health ", he once said on his sickbed, " then I want to make a vow always to offend God. For I anticipate that his goodness will give me the grace never to offend him."[50] " I promise God that I will never, on my own part, do anything good; that is, I despair of myself, but I entrust myself to God."[51] Truly, this fool is lost in God, and he lives out what he sang in his sonnet; he treads on all the stars of rationality, for he is already dead and lives now only in God. Therefore, one might say, he has lost the feeling of any distance between himself and God. His prayer is a constant " putting pressure on God "; and he can say to Jesus, " The wound in your side is large; but if you do not order me to stop, I will make it even larger !"[52] To disregard being disregarded (*spernere se sperni*)— no one has lived out this ultimate folly of one irretrievably lost in the divine more than this Pippo buono who conceals with his foolish laughter the terrible force that threatens to blow him apart.[53]

Now let us place next to this harlequin of God the Ignatius of the Roman years, who walks through the streets quietly and with

49 Ponelle, 96, [143].
50 Ibid., 529, [579].
51 Ibid., 529, n. 7, [579, no. 9].
52 Ibid., 529, [579]; 531, [582].
53 The motto made famous in Goethe's interpretation (*Italienische Reise*, Unterwegs [traveling], June 4-6, 1787): *Spernere mundum, spernere neminem, spernere seipsum, spernere se sperni*, [to scorn the world, to scorn no man, to scorn oneself, to scorn being scorned], which has been attributed to St. Bernard, comes from Hildebert of Le Mans (*PL*, CLXXI, 1437).

16

dignity and who is adverse to anything loud and conspicuous right to the bottom of his heart. He too has performed his own divine follies as a pilgrim and as a fool who was soundly thrashed among the coarse Spanish soldiers in northern Italy and with the cudgels of the lovers of the nuns in a cloister at Barcelona whom he had tried to instruct in proper behavior. All this has been vanquished long ago. Yet we would misjudge the noble Roman culture of this man if we did not press on into the depths of this soul blessed with mystical graces. Indeed, Ignatius realized and grasped with all the acuteness of his "discernment of spirits" that one can also comprehend and honor the majesty of the Trinity (and perhaps more authentically) in an "ordinary" life, in a return to the commonplace, in "devotion to inconspicuous dress."[54] This is for the service of souls, for winning the world, that belongs to Christ, in the mysticism of joy in the things of God's world.[55]

Yet the "entirely other" remained alive in the depths of his soul, ready at any moment to break out like lava from the shell of the commonplace that he had fashioned about himself purely for the sake of helping souls. Here we grasp another "Philippian" tendency in Ignatius. In the first attempt at a biography of Ignatius, as early as 1547, the following testimony is given by one who knew him perfectly, Diego Laynez: "Ignatius is actually a despiser of the world. He told me that, if it depended on his own personal preference, he would be not in the least adverse to be considered insane as he would walk along with bare feet and with his deformed leg clearly in view or with horns on his head. But for the sake of souls he allowed none of this to become public knowledge."[56] Here Ignatius is like Philip. We have a similar account from Pedro de Ribadeneyra: "He said to me that, if the salvation of souls were at stake, he would be ready at any time to walk through the streets in bare feet or fitted with horns. He would not be ashamed to wear any sort of ridiculous or shabby clothes were it of use to men — and he proved this in deeds whenever an opportunity presented itself."[57]

---

54 *FN*, I, 609. Hugo Rahner, *Ignatius von Loyola und das geschichtliche Werden seiner Frömmigkeit* (Graz-Salzburg, 1949), pp. 60-62, 84. [English translation by Francis John Smith, *The Spirituality of St. Ignatius of Loyola: An Account of its Historical Development* (Westminster, Md., 1953), pp. 56-58, 84].
55 Karl Rahner, "Die Ignatianische Mystik der Weltfreudigkeit," ZAM, XII (1937), pp. 121-137; B. Schneider, "Der weltliche Heilige. Ignatius von Loyola und die Fürsten seiner zeit", *Geist und Leben*, XXVII (1954), pp. 35-58.
56 *FN*, I, 140.
57 Ribadeneyra, *Vita Ignatii*, V, ch. 2, no. 28, in *FN*, IV, 760.

In Rome Ignatius refused to succumb to this "temptation"; everything was concealed under the mask of the inconspicuous. Prudent discretion always kept him as if in suspension over the abyss into which the person with mystical graces would like to cast himself in order to annihilate himself in his own nothingness. When Simão Rodrigues, who was less experienced in this discernment, wrote to Ignatius from Portugal about the "holy follies" to which his subjects were enthusiastically devoting themselves and said that the true Jesuit must be "a man who has become a fool for the sake of Christ" (*loco por Cristo*),[58] Ignatius answered with much understanding for such *locuras santas*; but he added to this that everything must be "reduced to the moderation of discretion" (*reducir a la mediocridad de la discreción*).[59] This is the true Ignatius, and his prudent self-possession can only be understood in light of his secret love for the folly of the cross. This is the Ignatius who quietly and unobtrusively goes to a death "like all the world dies."[60] Yet Ribadeneyra testifies that it was Ignatius' desire to be buried secretly after his death somewhere on a dung-heap, for he said that he had never been anything else but refuse and dung.[61] In the records of Ignatius' canonization process there is this statement that is just as true of Philip, "*Cupiebat omnibus ludibrio esse*," he desired to be an object of derision to everyone.[62] No, the man from Loyola was never a charming humanist, and we would never grasp the depths and abysses in him if we wished to praise him merely as the man of prudent self-possession — just as Goethe once completely misunderstood Philip Neri when he called him the "humorous saint" and praised his maxim, *spernere se sperni*, as a principle "of the most exalted human spirits, of those inwardly most self-assured."

In both Philip and Ignatius the influx of mystical graces shattered the vessel of their natural emotional, and even physical, well-balance. In the case of Philip, one might say that this vessel remained smashed to bits to the end of his life and that the bent ribs next to his heart were the incarnate symbol of this.[63] Ignatius on the other hand, after years of mystical disintegration, formed himself into a man of calm, spiritualized self-possession that was even able to subordinate to reason and to the orders of his doctors the stream of tears caused by the delights of prayer. In the same year that Ignatius noted down

58 *MonBroet*, (Rodrigues), p. 548.
59 *EppIgn*, I, 507; *LettersIgn*, 128.
60 *FN*, I, 768.
61 *SdeSI*, II, 571, 851, 1009; Ribadeneyra, *Vita Ignatii*, V, ch. 3, no. 52, in *FN*, IV, 780.
62 *SdeSI*, II, 571.
63 Ponelle, 79-82, [127-130].

day by day in his spiritual diary the tears and ardors of his graces in prayer, 1544, Philip was seized by that "supernatural madness" that scorched his heart and of which he would never be healed. From that time on fearful awe of the divine, sobbing in the presence of God, sweet tears, and the "net of love that holds him prisoner"[54] have all become part of his daily life. After he had become a priest in 1551, Philip often became deathly pale while offering Mass; he bit hard on the rim of the chalice when the blood, the real, living blood of the Lord, made him drunk. Exhausted, he would collapse in the sacristy. Later on, he celebrated Mass alone in a private chamber — and it would take him hours for just one Mass. Thus it remained until his death; the broken fragments of his nature can no longer hold together.

During 1544 the same experiences happened to Ignatius, and here he was still completely Philippian. He was like Philip in being painfully alert and nervously sensitive to any noise or disturbance from outside while celebrating the Holy Mysteries. At one time he thought seriously of renting a room in another house "to escape the noise"[65] — just as Philip, in his old age, prepared a Mass-room, defended against everyone and everything, on the top floor of the house at Vallicella.[66] No words appear more frequently in Ignatius' diary than "sobbing" (*sollozo*) and "ardent fire" (*color intenso*), which spreads throughout his whole body (*ardor in todo el cuerpo*). His hair stands on end; his breast contracts; his heart leaps in agitation. Exhausted, he often breaks down and becomes unable to rise from his knees. He loses his power of speech because of the sobbing and interior sweetness (*duulçra interior*).[67]

However, just as he had applied the discretion of spirits and renounced folly without relinquishing the longing for it, so he acted in this case also. In the midst of the pages describing his mystical flights, this is found: "Because of the violent pain that I felt in one eye as a result of the tears, this thought came to me: if I continue saying Mass I could lose this eye, whereas it is better to keep it."[68] With this one word "better," discernment and the "reasonable" insert themselves with quiet authority into the mystical process, and there is scarcely anything more characteristic of Ignatius and his

64 Ibid., 79, [126].

65 *Cons*MHSJ, I, p. 124; *SpDiar*, [145].

66 Ponelle, 467-468, [516-517].

67 *Cons*MHSJ, I, pp. 88, 91, 93, 99-100; *SpDiar*, [11], [16], [24], [27], [28], [45], [47]. See also Victoriano Larranaga, *Obras completas de San Ignacio*. (Madrid, 1947), I, 687, no. 10; Hugo Rahner, "Die Vision von La Storta," *ZAM*, X (1935), 266.

68 *Cons*MHSJ, I, p. 114; *SpDiar*, [107].

development as a mystic. In this there comes into play that spiritualization [of the mystical phenomena] that distinguishes him from Philip and which, in the last years of his life, he once acknowledged to his trusted friend, Polanco: " Earlier I felt disconsolate if I could not weep three times during one Mass. But the doctor has forbidden me to weep, and I took that as a command of obedience. Since then, I experience much more consolation without tears."[69]

To be sure, to the end of his life there also remains in Ignatius a susceptibility to serious disturbances in his health during encounters with the divine mysteries. Nadal testifies: " He constantly had a great longing to say Mass; and he therein felt such great and such extraordinary consolation that, when this consolation overwhelmed him, he immediately began to suffer again from his stomach ailment. He was ill for two weeks when he had said three Masses at the request of the daughter of Don Juan de Vega."[70] But even here Ignatius submits to the powerful intervention of " reason "; he chooses rather to forego the celebration of Mass in order to escape the convulsions of soul and body (*vehemens commotio*).[71] That which is recorded in a memoir of Father Codretti is truly an " unphilippian " saying: " Later Ignatius celebrated only on Sundays and feast days because of his fear of visions (*ob metum visionum*)."[72] At the end of his life Ignatius is filled with a sweet spiritualization: All the earlier visions, tears, and ardors are things of the past; only the burning love and the contemplation of the Holy Spirit remain. " His spiritual life is on a purely intellectual plane " (*versatur in pure intellectualibus*) Nadal says about him.[73] Ribadeneyra gives this testimony about the Ignatius of the final years in Rome, who was transfigured by the presentiment that he would soon die: " He felt how he was always making progress and how the fire within him was becoming continually more ardent. And so, during the course of those last years in Rome, he did not hesitate to apply the name of elementary school and novitiate to the period at Manresa, which he had once called his ' primitive church ' because of the wonderful illumination."[74]

Nevertheless, this differentiation in the mystical development of Ignatius and of Philip is not the last point that we are capable of making in this regard. In the mystical depths of a soul that has once been touched by God and received an incurable wound, all disturbance

69 *FN*, I, 638-639.
70 *FN*, II, 158; *Letters to Women*, p. 456.
71 *FN*, II, 122.
72 *SdeSI*, I, 573; *FN*, III, 467.
73 *MonNad*, IV, 645.
74 *SdeSI*, I, 353-354.

is at an end — however much the body may or may not still be affected by this. At those depths the soul stands in a mysterious immediacy before God; it perceives Him acting directly upon it (Ignatius has spoken of this in those difficult-to-interpret Rules for Discernment of Spirits for the Second Week);[75] and it is therefore always alert and ready to break into prayer and to find God in all things. Cardinal Tarugi, one of the greatest of Philip's disciples, once said of his master: "*Haveva l'orazione pronta* — prayer had become so natural for him that the ardor which the Spirit enkindled in him was much stronger than if he had needed first to fan the flame of prayer by meditation."[76] In this lay one of the secrets of his pastoral success in the Oratory; everyone felt that speaking here was one who was filled with prayer and who made every word of God sound new.

The followers of Ignatius give us exactly the same testimony. When someone once told him that he regularly tried to make a connection between his morning prayer and what he had experienced the day before, Ignatius answered, "I, however, find devotion in everything and wherever I want."[77] He was often lifted up to God right in the middle of a conversation; and once he stammered like a drunkard, "Just now I was above the heavens for a moment," and then tried to cover this confession up with a shy reserve.[78] Nadal, who best knew the mystical secrets of the father, later wrote about him: "He always found a stimulus in any sort of object. Thus in the garden (I myself was there) he was aroused to profound contemplation and ecstasy over the Trinity at the sight of an orange leaf."[79] This mystical presence — what one might call an uninterrupted mastery of the divine — was common to both Philip and Ignatius. The founder of the Oratory, that wonderful school of prayer, could have made the same avowal that Ignatius once made about himself, "It seems to me that I could no longer live if I were not to perceive in my soul something that does not come from myself and which is not merely human, but comes from God alone."[30] If Philip saw the reflection of this relationship with God on the face of Ignatius (*la bellezza interna dell'anima sua*),[81] then he had a premonition of that which Ignatius' Jesuit brethren observed in him, with respectful love, during the last

75 *SpEx*, [330, 336], in *SpEx*MHSJ, 528, 534.
76 Ponelle, 43-44, [82]. See the judgment of Cardinal Tarugi on the sanctity of Ignatius (*SdeSI*, II, 487-488).
77 *FN*, II, 122-125.
78 *FN*, II, 125.
79 *FN*, II, 158.
80 *SdeSI*, I, 470, 349; *FN*, II, 338, no. 31.
81 *SdeSI*, II, 425-426, 491; *FN*, III, 447, 428.

few years of his life: " He received the grace to perceive the presence of God in all things, actions, and conversations, with a delicate sensitivity for the spiritual. Indeed, he gazed at this presence [of God] and so became a ' contemplative in action.' He was accustomed to express this in the phrase, ' We should find God in all things.' With profound admiration and sweet consolation of heart we saw how this grace, this light in his soul, made his countenance radiant and how it became manifest in the prudent and confident handling of all his affairs."[82]

The Religious Founder

Now these two men and mystics were also founders of religious orders, and both have left their institutes indelibly marked with their own personalities. Their human and mystical similarities and dissimilarities continue in the Society of Jesus and in the Oratory.

The history of the origin of both communities already reflects the inner history of Philip and Ignatius.

First of all there is the early history of the Society of Jesus. The companions whom Iñigo had won in Paris were united to him from the beginning with a completely personal devotion. In this they were like the companions that Philip later gathered about himself and whom he kept bound to him by his personal charm. The Parisian Masters wished simply to follow " Iñigo's way of life "[83] which he had placed before them in the Spiritual Exercises. Yet from the outset there was a force at work that clearly contrasted the origin of the Society of Jesus with that of the Oratory: Iñigo was not only the heart but also (in contrast to Philip) the will of the new community. Iñigo was the man who, as early as the writing of the *Spiritual Exercises*, always had before his eyes the concept of the " ordered life "— a man of proper order, of planning, of infallible instinct for hierarchy, subordination, and the power of authority.

This became apparent when the companions gathered at Rome in 1539 to discuss the problem, which would also be the subject of debate some decades later in the community of the Oratorians: Should we remain a voluntary association of secular priests, engaged in apostolic works, or unite into a religious order ? In many respects this *Deliberatio primorum Patrum* still bore Philippian tendencies. In the especially striking " differences of opinion " (*pluralitas sententiarum*),[84] with which the lively discussion began, there still pulsated what one

---

82 *MonNad*, IV, 651-652; H. Rahner, " Die Vision von La Storta," *ZAM*, X (1935), pp. 203-204.
83 *FN*, I, 183; II, 82.
84 *Cons*MHSJ, I,. p 2.

might call the "democratic" spirit of the unorganized community of friends which had existed at Paris and Vicenza. But as they all, under the powerful influence of the ideals of the Spiritual Exercises, were in agreement that they should give their lives as " total offerings " for Christ and for His Vicar on earth, there soon crystallizes out of this amorphous movement of spirits, under the direction of Iñigo, this resolution: to constitute themselves a religious family under obedience to an elected superior.[85] Among the arguments that seemed at first to be in opposition to this idea, we hear thoughts that reappear later in the deliberations at the Oratory in Vallicella: the slight mistrust abroad in the Church against the founding of new orders; and, above all, the greatest possible freedom for pastoral work, which for the sons of Ignatius consisted at that time almost exclusively of teaching catechism to children and serving in the hospitals — precisely that activity therefore that Philip always considered most essential. In Iñigo's circle the decision was in favor of obedience, and the most profound reason for this is actually Philippian —" One of us said in favor of obedience: ' Obedience gives birth to heroic deeds and to dispositions that last. For whoever sincerely lives under obedience is perfectly prepared to carry out anything he is commanded, even though it be something very difficult, something that stirs men of the world to ridicule, laughter, and wonder — for example, if I were to be ordered to walk through towns or along the roads naked or in garish clothing. Although such a command will certainly never be given, yet each would have to be ready to do so since he has mortified his own judgment and will. ''[86]

With this background we understand how Simão Rodrigues could many years later, as we have already mentioned, still characterize such ascetical follies as the " foundation of our order." At that time Ignatius called him back to the "norm of discretion." But there can be no doubt that in 1539 he was pleased by this concrete illustration, as expressed by one of his companions, of his basic idea of obedience as a way of ordering one's life when we recall what he confessed about himself and his desire to play the fool for God. So much the more astonishing, even when looked at from the standpoint of these first deliberations about the founding of the order, is the discretion with which he submitted to the cancellation of the " anti-ascetical " clauses in the final draft of the bull of September 27, 1540, which founded the order. For he had placed those clauses in the first draft of August,

85 *Cons*MHSJ, I, pp. 4-7; Schurhammer, *Franz Xaver*, I, 437-438; Schurhammer, trans. Costelloe, *Francis Xavier*, I, 455-456.
86 *Cons*MHSJ, I, pp. 6-7.

1539, so that the force of obedience might restrain the longing for that heroism of folly right from the beginning by means of the discretion of the " ordinary." From that time on his order has maintained its vitality by deriving an inner unity from the tension between the cross and everyday life, between folly and discretion, between the unconstrained law of love and the restraining force of obedience; and everything is controlled and harmonized by the ideal of obedience, viewed with stern and inexorable clarity, which guarantees the orientation toward their proper goals of all formation of souls and all pastoral work.

Is it not now completely understandable why the unrestrained Pippo buono, who had such an impetuous enthusiasm for all folly done for the love of God and who truly aroused " ridicule, laughter, and wonder in the men of the world," was not inclined to join this community of Master Ignatius ? The follies of these priests at Santa Maria della Strada, whom he also admired, were worthy of honor: they shared with him the mockery of the street boys, and people called them " twisted necks " and " rubbish and refuse of the city of Rome."[87] This also would have been a pleasure for Philip. But as long as he lived, he knew only one principle: " to live according to his own taste " (*vivere suo arbitrio*);[88] and he knew that this was God's style and his vocation within the broad expanse of the freedom of Christian men. Therefore, he had no taste for the Basque " order " of Master Ignatius. Even though he led others to Ignatius, he himself wanted to remain free and to gather around himself with a spontaneous, almost aimless improvisation those men whom he found strong enough to bear such freedom. In 1548 he and Persiano Rosa formed the first cell of the future Oratory. After that there gathered very slowly about him, with a blessed lack of any such intention, a small community — in meetings of spontaneous, fervent, but infinitely simple prayer; or in caring for pilgrims to Rome at the Ciambella near the Baths of Agrippa.[89] From the time that he became a priest in 1551, his narrow chamber at San Girolamo was the happy place where he exercised his freedom and his ardent pastoral labors. " Each one lived there as he liked, each in a small room, no community meals, no superior. For Philip's disposition and for his future work, these were the ideal conditions."[90] Let us turn our glance away from San Girolamo toward

---

87 *SdeSI*, II, 828; Benedetto Palmio, *Autobiographia*, ch. 13, no. 7, in *FN*, III, 160; also in Tacchi Venturi, *Storia*, Vol. I, Pt. 2, p. 247.

88 Ponelle, 95, [142]; 317-318, [367].

89 Ibid., 58-62, [106-109].

90 Ibid., 122, [169].

the Professed House next to the small church of Santa Maria della Strada — and in this glance we grasp how widely separated the paths of the two religious founders have now become.

Before the decisive year of 1551 there was already some ill feeling in Philip's circle with regard to the " Ignatians," precisely because at that time they were engaged in the same charitable and catechetical works as those for which Philip was expending his efforts. To be sure, the names of some of Philip's friends are also found on the list of patrons of the House of St. Martha that Ignatius had founded.[91] However, the slowly developing Oratory of Philip and Persiano Rosa certainly had little appreciation for the clear orientation and apparently excessive organization in the planning and execution of the work of reform that existed in the Company of Ignatius. Without a doubt they were of the same opinion as that expressed in 1546 to Pope Paul III by the Franciscan, Fray Barberán, in his complaint about the House of St. Martha, " These priests want to reform the whole world."[92] However, in 1548 (or somewhat later[93]) we read in the libelous complaint of the Dominican, Fra Teofilo da Tropea, " against the reformed priests that are also called *Illuminati* or Ignatians," about a certain priest, Francesco da Arezzo, who was living at San Girolamo, and who for some time had been in this Society of Ignatius and then had left in disappointment.[94] Now this is undoubtedly Francesco Marsuppini, who was a close friend of Philip and who later became his revered confessor.[95] Evidently he found the greater cordiality of the

91 Ibid., 54, n. 6, [102, n. 5]. The full text of the list is given by Tacchi Venturi, *Storia*, Vol. I, Pt. 2, pp. 296-307. The names of the three friends and members of the later Oratory who appear in the list of the members of the *Compagnia della Grazia*, which Ignatius founded to aid the work of the House of Martha, are Enrico Pietra (Tacchi Venturi, 305, n. 5), Teseo Raspa (305, n. 6), Prospero Crivelli (306, n. 1). On Philip's miraculous healing of Prospero Crivelli, see Ponelle, 110, [157].

92 *EppIgn*, I, 447; *Letters to Women*, p. 19.

93 Tacchi Venturi, *Storia*, Vol. I, Pt. 2, p. 278, dates the writ of complaint between 1547 and 1552.

94 Ibid., p. 281. It is not clear that we can place complete trust in this story, since the report of Fra Teofilo is demonstrably not entirely free of rumours and fake atrocity stories. Nevertheless, Fra Teofilo is likely to be better informed on this matter since he lived at Santa Maria sopra Minerva, where Philip so often went to pray with his friends. In point seven of his writ to the Inquisition, it is stated: " There is also a priest from Arezzo, who lives at San Girolamo, who is called Master Francesco d'Arezzo. He has been a member (of the Jesuits]. Thus he is acquainted with ' the cooked and the raw meat,' for they allowed him to make his profession: more accurately, the three vows. But afterwards, when he saw what he saw, he left them."

95 Ponelle, 57, n. 3, [104, no. 4]; 58, [105].

incipient Oratory more to his liking than the strict discipline under Master Ignatius at the Professed House. Here we learn once again and more clearly why Pippo almost instinctively, and presumably with his charming smile, declined to join Ignatius.

From 1551 on, the differences in the ideals of the two orders become even clearer. Philip's biographer correctly characterizes this year, in which Philip was ordained and began to live at San Girolamo, as a turning point in the development of the Jesuit order.[96] Ignatius had now completed the writing of his *Constitutions* and submitted it to the professed fathers assembled at Rome. The bulls of Julius III had completed his work by giving it canonical approval. Ignatius could now yield to a " Philippian " tendency deep in his heart; and, on January 30, 1551, he wrote his famous letter of resignation — which proved unavailing, of course.[97] The works of his order had grown worldwide. Even in Rome the works once practiced, labors of pastoral charity and the apostolate of teaching catechism to children, were receding into the background; and, in their place, the Roman College and the German College were in the process of formation. Education and the promotion of learning, theology at Trent, and missions as far away as Japan and Brazil had to be given direction and inspiration. The number of the members of the order and their training demanded the closest concentration. Ignatius would soon write the Letter on Obedience (1553); starting in 1551 the correspondence of the general of the order swelled beyond all limits. Out of the earlier small circle of friends there had grown, in ten years, a real monarchy, which had to be controlled firmly as well as prudently.

Men like Nicolás Bobadilla, despite all their enthusiasm for their former Master Iñigo, felt this change to be contrary to the happy, " democratic " beginnings of an earlier day. Bobadilla himself would write to Pope Paul IV, shortly after the death of Ignatius, " Ignatius was quite certainly father and absolute lord (*padrone assoluto*), and he did what he wanted."[98] Even the best of the sons of the first general, like Laynez and Polanco, sometimes found it difficult to discover the loving heart and radiant kindness of their father, concealed under the powers of the authority that gave them " hard bread and solid food "[99] to eat.

---

96 Ibid., 144-145, [192].
97 *EppIgn*, III, 303-304; *LettersIgn*, 230. See Leonard von Matt and Hugo Rahner, *St. Ignatius of Loyola: A Pictorial Biography* (Chicago: Regnery, 1956), p. 94. A reproduction of this last page of this letter is printed there as Plate 201.
98 *MonNad*, IV, 732-733; Tacchi Venturi, *Storia*, Vol. II, p. 543.
99 *SdeSI*, I, 424; *FN*, I, 588; 587; 673.

Though the personal ties to the spirit of Master Iñigo still remained as strong as ever, Father General Ignatius became ever more "unnecessary," one might say, precisely because of the strength of the *Constitutions* he had devised with such genius. He disappeared behind his work, and he vanished into the other world in full knowledge that he had left "no lacunae" behind. This was exactly the impression that his fellow Jesuits had and that they expressed in their letters of mourning after the thirty-first of July, 1556. Thus the loyal Polanco writes to Ignatius' favorite son, Ribadeneyra: "He did not summon us to come to him for his blessing; he did not designate a successor, not even a vicar; and he gave no sign like those the servants of God usually give at the time of their death. No, he wanted the Society of Jesus to build its hopes on no one else but God alone, precisely because he had such a contemptuous opinion of himself."[100]

Philip witnessed this development in the Society of Jesus during those especially happy years that, beginning in 1551, he experienced at San Girolamo della Carità. He honestly admired the Society; and, when they read Francis Xavier's letters from India, there came over Philip and his friends the longing to take part in this splendid work. But these longings were not in accord with his spirit (and therefore not in accord with his divine vocation). The mystical monk at Tre Fontane, to whom he went for advice, said to him, "Your India is in Rome."[101] Philip returned to his small room and lived as before, *suo arbitrio*. He would never have fitted into the Professed House at Santa Maria della Strada. In comparison with the reports about the exquisitely unrestrained life at San Girolamo, where one prayed and was charmed by the music of the Oratory, we must read the rules that General Ignatius, with his love for order, installed at the Professed House during the last years of his life — everything was regulated down to a common type of shoe.[102] Everything was designed for the strict formation of men who could be sent to Japan or to the Congo without blinking an eye. This also makes us understand why Ignatius refused so firmly the various offers to unite the Theatines or the Barnabites with his order.[103] These were the good Barnabites from Milan who later felt so at ease and so understood in Philip's Oratory at Vallicella.[104]

100 *SdeSI*, II, 21; *FN*, I, 768.
101 Ponelle, 164, [211].
102 *SdeSI*, I, 483-490; *FN*, III, 651-658.
103 *SdeSI*, I, 439-440; *FN*, II, 496-497. In regard to union with the Theatines: *EppIgn*, VI, 84; *PolChron*, III, 182; with the Barnabites: Letter of Ignatius to Archbishop Girolamo Sauli, *EppIgn*, IV, 495-496; Sauli's urgent request, ibid., 497-498.
104 Ponelle, 264-265, [313-314].

In comparison then with the origin and development of the Society of Jesus, the slow growth of the Oratory of St. Philip Neri, as we know it in its proper canonical form, is a final proof of the limitless range of Christian ideals within the one Church and toward the one common goal. Philip lived at San Girolamo for more than twenty years before he began, in 1575, the idea of founding an "organized" family of priests living in common. How different from the *Deliberatio primorum Patrum* of Ignatius' companions in 1539! In any case, there was one thing clear from the first to the brotherhood at Vallicella: there was no question of "founding a new order"; there was no question of taking religious vows. Indeed, Philip never developed a real, deliberate intention of founding an order.[105] Until his holy death he certainly remained the heart of his community, but the discussions seem to have passed right over his head. He seldom took part in the long sessions, for there grew up among his sons a second generation that sought consciously to form the new community into a "cloister in the world" and to make it the "golden mean" between order and freedom. Six years after the beginning of the deliberations, he was still living at San Girolamo, stubbornly and almost eccentrically. Only the command of the pope forced him to move to Vallicella. Pippo, always the same, knew how to fashion this change of dwelling into a delightful procession of a fool for the love of God.[106] The troublesome question as to whether the poverty of a common life might not require a vow he disposed of almost in anger.[107] The growth of the Oratory and the foundation of Oratories outside Rome, which he, as the revered and beloved father in the Spirit, should direct, were a worry for him. He seldom wrote letters and then with reluctance. In matters of obedience the most pleasing thing for him was to allow the spirit alone to rule; and he aspired to the sublime maxim (which one must compare with Ignatius' Letter on Obedience to savor properly): "If you want someone to obey you, then give no commands!"[108] Not until long after Philip's death (1612), did the Oratory find that permanent form in which the fragrance of the Philippian spirit could be preserved. Philip's biographer is correct in saying, "Without any exception, the Oratory is the exact opposite of the famous institute of the Society of Jesus."[109] For the Spirit of God breathes where He will.

105 Ibid., 268-269, [317-318].
106 Ibid., 353, [403].
107 Ibid., 327, [377].
108 Ibid., 317, [367].
109 Ibid., 58, [105]. The comparison between the Oratory's practice of prayer and the Spiritual Exercises (ibid., 237-238, [323-324]) is not entirely successful.

When we commemorate the death of Ignatius on July 31, 1956, we might gaze on the splendid altar-tomb in the Gesu at Rome and look at the gilded bronze images. In one of these Ignatius is portrayed greeting his Philip Neri with a most ardent love.[110] In the ante-chamber of the small room where Ignatius died, there is a painting that shows the two heroes of the Roman Reform fraternally united. They were canonized together, and they belong together forever in the kingdom of the Spirit. For with that penetrating vision which is characteristic of men of God, they recognized each other here on earth as men lost in the love of God. Our attempt to understand the depths of their souls has been awkward and incomplete. Let us comfort ourselves with the words that Olivier Mannaerts, whom Ignatius had accepted in his school, wrote after a meeting with Philip:

"The revered Father Philip Neri, the superior of the Oratory, told me that he had once seen the countenance of the holy Father Ignatius flooded with a supernatural brightness, and that it was therefore his opinion that no creation of the painter could represent him as he was in reality."[411]

110 A reproduction is found in Charles Clair, *La Vie de Saint Ignace de Loyola* (Paris, 1891), 310. On a tapestry in the Church of the Gesu which contains a similar representation of the two saintly friends, see P. Pecchiai, *Il Gesù di Roma* (Rome, 1952), p. 203.
111 *SdeSI*, I, 513; *FN*, III, 428.

IGNATIUS AS SEEN
BY HIS CONTEMPORARIES

Hubert Becher

EACH AGE has its own idea of sanctity, sometimes accentuating certain elements, sometimes others, as they seem to that age to give the clearest testimony of sanctity or to be important in a saint. The Middle Ages are said to have attached the greatest importance to extraordinary events and deeds. The Enlightenment wanted for its ideal a man who allowed himself to be guided by reason in everything. It considered St. Ignatius " like most true visionaries, ancient or more modern, a poor, crazed creature that went wherever his spirit drove him and otherwise let the world fare as well as it could and wanted to."[1]

In the most recent past the matter of chief importance became that of casting light on someone's inner psychological nature. Along with the outstanding features of his character, a writer sought to determine a man's limits, weaknesses, and sins and to explain his works, words, and thoughts on the basis of his natural predispositions toward them. This could lead to such a point that Heinrich Böhmer was able to write about Ignatius, " But the ultimate causes and strongest motives of his productivity were three qualities that are seldom found together in one individual: will power heightened by methodical schooling to an almost superhuman capability; an intellect directed entirely to the practical, yet capable of the sharpest concentration and penetration; and finally an ability, attained through iron self-discipline, to sacrifice one's own ego to the last breath for the sake

Study 3 was translated by Louis W. Roberts.

1 Anon., *Leben und Thaten des heiligen Ignatius von Loyola, Stifters und ersten Generals des Jesuiter-Ordens* (im Verlag der Republik der Gelehrten, 1788), p. 4.

of the ideal in which one believes."[2] Just which method of looking at him departs more from the truth, that of the Enlightenment or that of pure Psychologism, could be a point of dispute. Both have made of Ignatius an inhuman will-and-intellect-machine.

But even when a judgment according to purely naturalistic principles does not lead to such a one-sided view, it requires little reflection to see that whenever the supernatural guidance of God's grace is perceived and acknowledged, greater justice is done to a saint and we receive a more comprehensive view of the reality than when only the natural conditions and forces are examined. Even a lack of psychological analysis may be admissible as long as one sees and correctly portrays the workings of God in the saint.

Yet every age has the task of familiarizing itself afresh with the character and actions of a historical personality, that it may overcome as far as possible the one-sidedness of previous generations and may attenuate as much as it can the limitations of its own time and place by comparisons with earlier interpretations. Knowledge of what a man's contemporaries have thought about him and how they have judged him can contribute a great deal to this. Despite their being limited to the peculiarities of their own historical moment and perhaps despite their personal prejudices, one may yet presuppose that these contemporaries, through their direct contact with the man and their living experience of his personality, were still more qualified than anyone else to penetrate to the core of a man's nature and to cast light on his inner character.

These general considerations seem to have particular urgency in regard to research about Ignatius. The period of religious humanism and of the baroque readily glorified Ignatius. As was the case in the sculpture and painting of the period, the literary and oratorical portrayal of the saint stressed the heaven-storming and heroic aspects and overlooked or denied the frailty inherent in a son of this earth. The stormy youth of the page and officer that Ignatius of Loyola was up to his conversion in 1521 has scarcely any place in an exalted representation of this kind. At any rate, the temptation to deny it has to be reckoned with. It did happen in the biographies that Francisco García published in 1685 and Father Henao in 1689.[3] There is still need of research into the question as to whether the authors

2 Heinrich Böhmer, *Ignatius von Loyola*, ed. Hans Leube (Stuttgart, 1941), p. 50.
3 Antonio Astráin, *Historia de la Compañía de Jesús en la Asistencia de España* (Madrid, 1902), I, 11.

of the first lives of Ignatius, Ribadeneyra in particular, succumbed to this danger.[4]

Two further facts seem to suggest the possibility of falsification in the earliest portraits of Ignatius. Francis Borgia, the third general of the order, and Everard Mercurian, the fourth, had already ordered that everything that was in circulation about Ignatius was to be sent to Rome. This material was to be replaced by new biographies. Claudio Aquaviva, the fifth general, later denied the petition to allow the publication of the earlier writings about the saint. From all this one could conclude that it was of some importance to the superiors of the order that a particular image of the founder be traced out and that it should become the prevalent image — one perhaps not entirely in accord with the total reality of his life. In this article an attempt will be made to gain an impression from the early testimony about the saint as to whether and in what way such a development and transformation actually took place. For this purpose the judgments about Ignatius that were expressed by his enemies during the many times when he suffered persecution — in Alcalá, Salamanca, Paris, Venice, and Rome — may very properly be left out of consideration, since they always ended with a vindication of the saint.[5]

4 [At the time the article was written, the most recent edition of Ribadeneyra's *Vita Ignatii* was in the volume *Historias de la Contrarreforma*, ed. Eusebio Rey (Madrid: BAC, 1945), pp. 30-428. Since then a modern critical edition, in both Latin and Spanish, has been published by the *Institutum Historicum Societatis Jesu* as *FN*, IV (Rome, 1965). Therefore all references to the *Historias* refer to the introductory material by Rey. Ribadeneyra's *Vita Ignatii* itself will always be referred to, as was done in the previous articles, as it is found in *FN*, IV — this is the only edition likely to be widely available in English-speaking countries. A list of the earlier editions is given by Becher in no. 41, below. Also, an interesting account of the biographies of St. Ignatius, which naturally were much influenced by the circumstances and tastes of successive historical periods, is given by Ignacio Iparraguirre in *Obras completas de san Ignacio, Edición manual* (Madrid, 1963), pp. 2-35. This account is compressed in English in Mary Purcell, in *The First Jesuit* (Westminster, Md., 1957), pp. 369-376.]

5 For references to these persecutions, see for example: *FN*, I, 7, 8-10, 51-54, 94-99, 133, 174-177, 179-181, 201-203, 297, 308-310, 440-449, 452-463, 468-475; *Autobiog*, 57-61, 64-70, 78 and 81; *FN*, II, 69-72, 90-91, 546-552, 561-563, 575-576, 589-592; *SdeSI*, I, 598-623; Schurhammer, *Franz Xaver*, I, 127-132, 150, 230, 355-357, 403-406, 408-411, 564 — containing an abundance of references to the sources [pp. 137-142, 159-160, 242, 371-373, 421-425, 427-430, 587 are the corresponding pages of the English translation]. The English translation was first noted in fn. 74 of Study 1, above.

I

Even during the lifetime of St. Ignatius the wish was frequently expressed to learn about the course of his life and about his interior development. It was not simply the love and reverence of his spiritual sons for their father that gave rise to this wish. Much more important was the conviction that Ignatius personified the ideal of a Jesuit and therefore was a living model for his order. Nadal especially was of the opinion that the Society of Jesus had its basis in the life of its founder and that Ignatius would give it a firm foundation merely by relating his life.[6] He, therefore, did everything he could to move Ignatius to relate his way to God so that it might be left after him as a heritage for the order.

This opinion is of no little importance. It can also be said of earlier founders of religious orders, St. Benedict, Francis of Assisi, and Dominic, that their institutes reflect their personal way of life.[7] But the age of the Renaissance and of Humanism was marked in a very special manner by a newly experienced way of looking at man, particularly at the individual man. Even the societies that were then formed (academies, humanistic circles, and the like) were not so much realizations of a fixed sum of practical regulations, of goals, and of means ordered to those goals, as expressions of particular human models. Ignatius himself is a proof of this. In the *Exercises* he teaches one to search into the interior dispositions and the entire deportment of the God-Man in order to form oneself after Him as a model. As a preliminary to his *Constitutions*, he placed the *General Examen* as an exterior and interior test of the individual candidate.

---

6 *Autobiog, 4*,* in *FN*, I, 360; *FN*, II, 204.

7 This is especially true in the case of St. Francis. His first Rule, which he presented to Pope Innocent III (1209-1210) for confirmation and approval (and which has unfortunately been lost), consisted of only a few simple phrases. It could thus hardly be called a religious rule in the ordinary sense of the term. In place of such a rule, he emphasized all the more that he himself was the real norm, the epitome of the brothers' way of life, the living interpretation of the rules (see L. Casutt, O.F.M.Cap., *Das Erbe eines grossen Herzens. Studien zum franziskanischen Ideal* [Graz-Salzburg-Wien, 1949], p. 155.) Etienne Gilson, *Heloise and Abelard*, tr. L. K. Shook (Ann Arbor: University of Michigan Press, 1960), pp. 124-144, rightly emphasizes that the appreciation of the individual personality and setting up a particular person as a model to be followed were not unfamiliar concepts in the Middle Ages.— Ignatius himself never pointed to himself as the pattern for his order and the model for his sons. Yet it is a fact worthy of note that he called so many members of the order from all lands to Rome, more mature members as well as the young, so that he might personally direct their formation.

The Introduction to the *Constitutions*, which declares that the wisdom and goodness of God and the mutual love of the members of the order — the mutual encounter of individual persons — are the actual motive forces behind the foundation and the preservation of the order, is not to be taken as a mere pious formula. It is Ignatius' central concept, even though he proceeds to provide particular regulations with a thoroughness and a comprehensiveness never before met with in a religious institute, " since the vicar of Christ our Lord has ordered this, and since the examples given by the saints and reason itself teach us so." The detailed description of the personal characteristics of the general of the order given in Part IX of the *Constitutions* is also worthy of note. Ribadeneyra and others were of the opinion that, except for the quality of good health, Ignatius had here described himself. This concentration on individual personality, as a part of the intellectual current of the time, was as much a basic component of the thought of the Jesuits as it was of the thought of all their contemporaries; and they were conscious of it themselves. Therefore they took pains to commit to writing the personal characteristics of their spiritual father, and they must have expended considerable effort to learn as much as they could from him and about him and to make sure that that information was accurate.

On a given occasion Ignatius did not hesitate to speak about his sins and failings. Sometimes, under the strong impression made by an unusual event, he would also relate something about his spiritual experiences. Diego Laynez especially heard from him many details of his life history.[8] He was even allowed to inquire about them, though he did not always receive an answer.[9] In general, however, modesty and humility kept Ignatius from talking about himself. Still, the steady pressure by his associates and companions moved him to consider whether their reasons might not be worthy of consideration. He came to the conclusion that an account of his spiritual development would be an act of thanksgiving to God and a glorification of his Creator and Redeemer. So he chose to relate his life to the Portuguese Luís Gonçalves da Câmara. This man picturesquely relates how this happened, how Ignatius looked over the manuscript,[10] and how his fellow religious, especially Nadal, continually pressed for the completion of the report, which was delayed again and again by the frequent illness of the saint.[11] In these accounts, and on other occasions also,

---

8 *FN*, II, 321.
9 *FN*, II, 325-326.
10 *SdeSI*, I, 32-33; *FN*, I, 354-363.
11 *SdeSI*, I, 33; *FN*, I, 360.

Ignatius speaks about himself and his sublime graces and illuminations so modestly and openly that one senses how intensely he felt himself to be an unworthy recipient of the divine favor. Every sort of vanity lay far from him; he himself once asserted that he had experienced no temptations to vanity for some eighteen to twenty years.[12] Furthermore, many other sayings of the founder of their order and many details of his life were remembered by those who lived with him and had perhaps already been committed to writing.

If such a great longing for information about the saint's life already existed during his lifetime, the wish to collect everything known about him must have become stronger than ever after his death. The first to make an official report to the members of the order about the life and death of the founder was Laynez.[13] Similar reports were written by Gonçalves da Câmara, Ribadeneyra, Nadal, Polanco, and others. They passed their notes on or made copies for themselves.[14] Thus they tried to preserve as accurately as possible the image of their father. Accordingly we find protestations that the writer wishes to report only what actually took place or was actually said. The rigid objectivity of Polanco is beyond question.[15] The same thing can be said about the other fathers. Nonetheless it was unavoidable that the various presentations should differ in detail, and there were several who objected to this.[16] This also became perceptible when the first account of the saint's life, from the pen of Johann Albrecht Widmanstetter, appeared in print.[17] It contained several inaccuracies since it relied on the common oral tradition rather than on clearly reliable testimony. Because of this, Polanco expressed the opinion, in a letter to Father Vitoria in Vienna, that for the future it would be advisable to have everything that was to be printed about the Society first checked for accuracy in Rome.[18]

In the following years, the wish for an authentic life of Ignatius continued to grow. The rapid increase in the number of members and the continual interior development of the Society made reference to its source more urgent. Some of the fathers, among whom was Gonçalves, even thought that the Society had already departed from

---

12 *FN*, I, 163.
13 *FN*, I, 66.
14 See *MonNad*, III, 377; see also 534.
15 See Clara Englander, *Ignatius von Loyola und Johannes von Polanco* (Regensburg, 1955), p. 189.
16 *MonNad*, III, 540; see also *FN*, I, 346.
17 Otto Braunsberger, *B.P. Canisii epistulae*, II, 31-32, 912-913; *FN*, I, 780-805.
18 *FN*, I, 783.

the spirit of its founder. Therefore they wished to re-establish the earlier state of affairs, especially in the novitiate training.[19] The *Memoriale* of Gonçalves da Câmara owes its origin to these considerations. Thus the number of sources was growing constantly, but so was the number of variations in the tradition. Hence arose the first eff rts toward an official and complete biography of the saint, during the generalate of St. Francis Borgia. Pedro Ribadeneyra was given the task of composing it. In 1567, Borgia wrote to each province and called upon the provincials to send to Rome all writings about Ignatius since an accurate work was being prepared. If they contained anything good and true, it would be used in the production of a uniform and accurate image of their father.[20] Ribadeneyra, who himself testifies that he was the author of the measure that was proposed to the general's council of advisors and accepted by it, justifies the action, and gives as one of the reasons that Gonçalves' *Memoriale*, though it does give an excellent presentation of the major points, does not give sufficient coverage to less important ones; also, that Gonçalves was unreliable and inaccurate when giving dates because of failing memory caused by his age. Therefore, as well as all the other writings about Ignatius, it too was to be withdrawn from circulation and not allowed to be read or passed from hand to hand among those of the order or those outside it. This was of course to be accomplished with great care and prudence so that no disturbance might arise.[21]

We learn the response to this process of collection from a few letters. Canisius, at that time provincial of the southern German province, found nothing in Germany except one composition by Polanco "which I believe is not needed at Rome."[22] Salmerón wrote from Naples that he would see if he could find anything and then would send it to Rome.[23] Nadal, who received both the letters from the general and the explanation of the reasons for it from Ribadeneyra, did not find it easy to carry out their wishes. For the fathers to whom he turned did not wish to part with the documents until the promised book by Ribadeneyra had been published.[24] It was so important to them to have at hand something about the founder of the order.

19 *FN*, I, 523.
20 Braunsberger, *B.P. Canisii epistulae*, V, 510.
21 *MonNad*, III, 490, 540.
22 This probably refers to the letter printed in *SdeSI*, II, 18; Braunsberger, *B. P. Canisii epistulae*, VI, 85.
23 *MonSalm*, II, 137.
24 *MonNad*, III, 505, 518.

The purpose of the collection and recall of manuscripts was only to create as true a picture of the saint as possible. The desire was to avoid inconsistencies. The suspicion that they wanted the character of the founder to appear in some special light — according to some definite school of spirituality, for example — finds no support in the sources. If Francis Borgia, who for a time had a different idea about prayer than Ignatius had, especially valued those manuscripts of the saint that contain his spirituality and his spiritual experiences, the desire that motivated him too must have been to transmit the truth and not a concealed wish to have the founder appear as Francis would like him to appear. Otherwise Nadal's joy at the general's zeal could not be explained.[25]

In the year 1572 there appeared Ribadeneyra's Latin biography of St. Ignatius. How much care was taken not to publish such a book before it was faul less in every detail can be seen from the directive of the father general that the book was not yet to be shown to externs.[26] First it should be read by the members of the order and they should report what might be missing in certain cases and what was superfluous. It would be released to the public only after all possible corrections had been made.

Ribadeneyra's book was an excellent piece of workmanship. The writer of the history of recent historiography, Ernst Fueter, says of it, "Humanism produced no biography that is comparable to the work of Ribadeneyra." He passes this judgment not simply because of its fidelity to the facts but above all because it is the first biography to penetrate into the interior life of its hero and because its author advances "as a psychologist, far beyond his models."[27] The judgment of his contemporaries was similar.[28] According to Peter Canisius, the book cannot be recommended enough. There were nevertheless several objections to it. As Ribadeneyra was a disciple of the saint, he had woven personal recollections into it. This seemed to some to offend against modesty.[29] Peter Canisius was one of those who thought so and was furthermore of the opinion that the author had not preserved the proper mean between a description of the life of

---

25 *MonNad*, III, 365, 377, 534.

26 These directions were probably given by Francis Borgia, not, as the editors of the *Monumenta Historica Societatis Jesu* write, by Everard Mercurian; for the letter from Father Ramiro to Father Araoz was written May 5, 1572, and Francis Borgia did not die until September 30, 1572 (*SdeSI*, I, 712-713).

27 E. Fueter, *Geschichte der neueren Historiographie* (Munich, 1911), p. 283.

28 See Ribadeneyra, *Historias de la Contrarreforma*, pp. 14-15.

29 *SdeSI*, I, 720-725; *MonLain*, VIII, 874.

St. Ignatius and a history of the early Society of Jesus. He thought that he should have given more recognition to the activities of Bobadilla and that he should not have made such unqualified statements about supernatural illuminations.[30] The fathers who had assembled for the Third General Congregation (1573) expressed similar opinions and recommended that the new general, Mercurian, should see that a new, corrected edition should be brought out. He therefore once again endeavored to gather all the manuscripts about St. Ignatius that were in circulation, "which could serve the Society and be of use in her government."[31]

To be sure, a new current now became perceptible within the order, and this also had its effect on the writing of its history. At the just-mentioned Third General Congregation there had occurred those painful discussions aimed at lessening the Spanish influence.[32] While Ribadeneyra, who along with Nadal and Polanco had to leave Rome, was busy with the new edition of his Latin biography and the Spanish version of it,[33] Father Giampietro Maffei, an Italian, was also commissioned to write a life of the founder. He had already been chosen by Francis Borgia to write the history of the order.[34] Now all the writings about the order's founder were also put at his disposal. Ribadeneyra bore with patience this measure, which was actually directed against him and his fellow countrymen. Yet he did have this worry: "There are ... many items dealing with the faults of very venerable fathers such as Simão Rodrigues, Miró, De Torres, etc., and with admonitions addressed to them. It is not good that these things come into the hands of the younger men, or even of the older; for the remembrance of these events should not be perpetuated."[35] Maffei worked on his book for a number of years, and it appeared in 1585. Meanwhile, in 1581 Claudio Aquaviva had become general. He also devoted himself to the matter and sought to reassure Ribadeneyra. He said that Maffei's book would in no way prejudice Ribadeneyra's.[36] In his opinion it was worse than Ribadeneyra's, but it would "be of service to northerners, who enjoy a fine, rhetorical style and who,

30 *SdeSI*, I, 714, 715, 720; Braunsberger, *B.P. Canisii epistulae*, VII, 250-271; Astráin, *Historia*, I, xxxii and other places.
31 *MonRib*, I, 822.
32 Astráin, *Historia*, III, 4-21; Hubert Becher, *Die Jesuiten* (Munich, 1951), pp. 118-122.
33 *MonRib*, II, 475.
34 *MonBorg*, V, 484; *PolCompl*, I, xxiii.
35 Letter of October 8, 1572, in *MonRib*, I, 797.
36 *MonRib*, II, 280.

when they taste of it, also absorb the content enclosed within it."[37] When the book appeared, only a few copies were distributed at first, "lest anyone, especially the Spaniards, feel slighted."[38]

The new work was indeed far inferior to Ribadeneyra's. He could justifiably make many criticisms.[39] The difference in the success of the two books also showed their relative worth and Aquaviva's opinion that Maffei's classicizing style[40] would particularly please the northerners was not borne out.[41]

Until the day of his death Ribadeneyra was busy trying to perfect the style and accuracy of his book.[42] His greatest concern was to express the truth as accurately as possible. Because God is truth he wanted no fabricated stories or miracles. He made some additions. as he himself says, in the Spanish version. It was a question of things that he had not known at the time of the first edition or had not yet known with certainty.[43] When he was interrogated during his spiritual father's beatification process, he also swore that he had allowed himself to be guided only by the love for truth while writing his book.[44]

At the time of General Aquaviva, the attempt was made once more to collect the letters, sayings, and deeds of St. Ignatius that were not yet in the collection and to have the best of them published for edification and consolation. The General Congregation of 1584 suggested this. The congregation of the province of Castile, held in preparation for the general congregation, requested in particular the printing of the story of the saint's youth as composed by Luís Gonçalves. Aquaviva

---

37 " ... que esta del P. Maffei servirá a los tramontanos que gustan de aquella elocuencia y al sabor de ella se aprovechan tambien de la substancia que en ell se encierra " (Ribadeneyra, *Historias de la Contrarreforma*, p. 12).

38 *MonRib*, II, 282.

39 *SdeSI*, I, 749-756; *FN*, III, 217-236; *MonRib*, II, 282.

40 See also Fueter, *Geschichte der neueren Historiographie*, p. 284.

41 Ribadeneyra's *Vita Ignatii* was published in the Latin version at Naples in 1572; Madrid, 1586; Antwerp, 1587; Rome, 1589; Ingolstadt, 1590; Lyon, 1595; Madrid, 1595; Cologne, 1602; Augsburg, 1616; in Spanish — Madrid, 1583, 1584, 1586, 1594, 1595, 1596, 1605; the German translation — Ingolstadt, 1590 and 1640; the French — Paris, 1608; Tournai, 1614; the Italian — Venice, 1586, 1587, 1606; Naples, 1607. Maffei, *De vita et moribus Ignatii Loyolae* was published at Rome, 1585; Venice, 1580 [?]; Cologne, 1585; Douai, 1585; Milan, 1586; Cologne, 1587; Barcelona, 1589; Antwerp, 1605; Paris, 1612; Antwerp, 1638. See *SMV*, V, 296-297; 6, 1725-1731.

42 Ribadeneyra, *Historias de la Contrarreforma*, p. 15.

43 E. Portillo, " El original manuscrito de la primera edición castellana de la vida de N.P. San Ignacio por el P. Ribadeneyra," in *RazFe*, XLII (1915), 290-298.

44 *SdeSI*, I, 150-167.

referred both petitioners to Ribadeneyra's book as it contained everything from Gonçalves worth being made public. It was not advisable
to make the rest available to everyone.[45] Aquaviva himself remained
of this opinion; and yet he let Father Lancicius (Mikolaj Lenczycky)
use all the writings about Ignatius in his research just as Ribadeneyra
and Maffei had received them,[46] and also Bartoli later on. Not till
1731 was the *Memoriale* finally published by the Bollandists, "since
nothing seemed to stand in the way of publishing these documents."[47]

Astráin was of the opinion that Aquaviva had been so cautious
because of the founder's beatification, the object of his efforts at that
time. This cannot mean that anyone wished to conceal the facts contained in the documents. There exists explicit testimony that the
Memoriale of Gonçalves was submitted at the beatification process in
Madrid in 1606.[48] During that period a tendency to caution is noticeable in everything. So for example, Ribadeneyra was criticised because he spoke in his book about Laynez' ancestry. In order to avoid
scandal, one did not dare to touch upon many things. Furthermore,
witnesses and relatives of persons who had come into contact with
Ignatius were still living. The importance of these and other motives
cannot be ignored. In any case, there is no evidence that anything
was suppressed in order to produce a falsification of his life, a mytho-
logizing and heroizing of the saint.[49]

Insofar as the caution of Aquaviva in particular is concerned,
it is completely justifiable. Even today the use of the materials collected by Gonçalves, Ribadeneyra, and others demands a certain circumspection. As valuable as the individual contributions are, the
true content of each one is revealed only to one who is in a position
to place himself in the whole context and to penetrate to the heart
of the situation. Anyone who would wish to comprehend such
an item without exact knowledge of the whole situation could
receive a completely false picture of the saint, as is the case with Böhmer,
for example.[50] Even the picture of Ignatius' character constructed by
Anton Huonder, S.J., out of many building stones suffers from this.[51]

45 *FN*, I, 347, 511; Astráin, *Historia*, I, 17.
46 *FN*, I, 510, 513, 526.
47 *Acta sanctorum*, Julii, VII, 645-665.
48 *FN*, I, 518.
49 See *MonLain*, VIII, 855-875.
50 Böhmer, *Ignatius von Loyola*, pp. 214-215.
51 Huonder, *Ignatius von Loyola* (Cologne, 1932).

It lacks the inner unity of a comprehensive view. The way it stands, one can prove almost anything with it.[52]

In Aquaviva's time the effort to fashion a comprehensive picture of the character of the founder of the Society of Jesus was still motivated entirely by the desire to derive from the sources the basic elements of his nature and to make a clear presentation of them. In the seventeenth century this changed. Perhaps something of this can already be felt in Maffei.[53] In his case, to be sure, it is more a matter of the stylistic means of expression. Later, however, writers formed an image of the saint to fit in with the ideals of the period. They did not much carry on their investigation in the sources; and when anyone did use them, it was not so much a question of research into them as of developing from the commonly known facts of the saint's life a perfect and ideal figure, which one can characterize most vividly as *pietas victrix*, piety triumphant, the title of one of Avancini's (1611-1686) most famous plays. "The religious man goes through life as a victor and is more victorious than ever in death."[54] Here the seriousness of the struggle for eternal life is more and more forgotten, and in its place there enters the exultation and glory of extraordinary sanctity and greatness. The contemporaries of St. Ignatius had also looked upon him as a giant and called themselves mere boys and dwarves — as did Master Juan de Ávila.[55] But they did not forget the earthbound and commonplace details and his struggle to overcome them.

II

To some extent we can be said to be following a tendency of modern biographical method. But it also has a practical basis in the nature of our subject, if we first direct our attention to St. Ignatius' youth and to his failings. Ignatius himself had no problem about acknowledging them and, if there was a good reason for it, about speaking of them. Thus he relates in his memoirs how, after three days of preparation, he made his confession at Montserrat; and later at Manresa he continually recalled the sins of his youth. On the occasion of his election as general, and even later, he laid his past open before his

---

52 The book had not been completed at the time of its author's death, and it was published in this incomplete state by Balthasar Wilhelm, S.J. The author personally informed the writer of this article that he wished to give his work much greater condensation and unity.

53 See Fueter, *Geschichte der neueren Historiographie*, p. 284.

54 Hubert Becher, " Die Geistige Entwicklungsgeschichte der Jesuitendramas," in *Deutsche Vierteljahrsschrift für Literaturwissenschaft und Geistesgeschichte*, XIX (1935), 294.

55 *PolChron*, IV, 460.

confessor because he considered himself unworthy on account of it. Telling others of his own lapses was also of use to him in giving consolation and courage to tormented and confused souls.[56] When after prolonged prayer he decided to allow his memoirs to be written and informed Luís Gonçalves of this on August 4, 1553, he then also clearly and exactly related to him " his youthful adventures " (*las travesuras del mancebo*).[57] When he visited Loyola in 1535, he openly admitted a youthful theft.[58]

The saint's youth, then, was known to his companions. They often speak of it in their notes and reports. Thus Laynez reports that Ignatius made a vow of chastity on the road to Montserrat (probably at Aranzazu) because he was afraid that he might again be overcome by the vice of the flesh, which had often been a source of temptation for him and had led him into sin.[59] The same thing is reported by Polanco,[60] Nadal, and Ribadeneyra.[61] In addition to sins of the flesh, his desire for fame, his ambition, and his vanity are mentioned.[62] All these things led him to think of everything else but piety. Along with this they are glad to be able to record truthfully that Ignatius always displayed magnanimity and a noble cast of mind and never behaved ignobly.[63]

Later on this provides the opportunity to emphasize this last character trait alone. This is exemplified as early as 1556 in the first work published about Ignatius, by Johann Albrecht Widmanstetter.[64] In the translation by Stephan Agricola in 1660 it says: " [Ignatius] became an officer not long afterwards and performed his military duties with such prudence, courage, integrity, Christian spirit, and fidelity that he was a source of wonder to his own men and of terror to the enemy and was pleasing to God almighty, as his choice of a life of perfection later confirmed."[65]

The saint's failings were also known outside of the order, evidence of the existence of an oral tradition. The Carthusian monastery at Cologne knew that Ignatius had been excessively addicted to the

56 *FN*, I, 576; II, 314; *SdeSI*, I, 193; Ribadeneyra, *Vita Ignatii*, V, chaps. 2 and 10, in *FN*, IV, 769, 850-853.
57 *FN*, I, 330-331, 356, 358.
58 Ribadeneyra, *Vita Ignatii*, II, ch. 5, in *FN*, IV, 239.
59 *FN*, I, 74-76; II, 378.
60 *FN*, II, 513, 520; *PolChron*, I, 16.
61 *FN*, II, 149, 378.
62 *FN*, I, 155-156, 364; II, 5, 62-63, 149, 231, 307, 404, 513.
63 *FN*, I, 155-156; II, 5, 149; *SdeSI*, II, 879.
64 *FN*, I, 780-805.
65 *FN*, I, 789.

vanities of the world[66]; and a Portuguese theologian at the Council of Trent, Diogo Andrada de Payva, who had studied under the Jesuits at Coimbra, spoke in 1564 of the fact that Ignatius had been dazzled by the enticements of worldly honor and of the passions.[67] Yet we do not find much of this knowledge witnessed to in the beatification processes. The usual formula was simply: He was a soldier and then was converted.[68]

Even though his youthful lapses were thus known, other facts seem to argue that there were those who wished to suppress this knowledge. Just the fact that the report of a judicial process of 1515, dealing with the "nocturnal excesses, serious and grave offenses" that Ignatius had been guilty of as a companion to his brother, is preserved only in part could suggest the thought that they had been removed. The Jesuits or his Basque fellow countrymen, who were proud of their great saint, might here come in question. Such an undertaking, however, would certainly have destroyed everything. The records that are still preserved let it be clearly seen that Ignatius and his brother with the bad reputation were guilty of something, even if we do not know exactly what the crime in question was.[69]

Even if we go over each biography individually, we find that little or nothing is related about the youth of St. Ignatius. This is true, for example, of an anonymous author's biography that has been printed only recently.[70] Even Laynez mentions nothing about the early life of the saint in his recollections of Ignatius that he sent to Polanco on July 17, 1541. He begins with the events at Pamplona.[71] It is quite understandable that he followed the same procedure in a commemorative oration on the founder of the order that he delivered in 1559.[72] More important is the fact that Luis Gonçalves, to whom the saint related the story of his life, merely reports that he has heard the "*travesuras del manebo*"[73] but transmits no details of them. It will not be far wrong if this is explained by his reverence and his understandable conviction that these stories should be allowed to fall into

---

66 *FN*, II, 396.
67 *FN*, II, 287.
68 *SdeSI*, II, 868, and many other places.
69 *SdeSI*, I, 580-597; see Paul Dudon, trans. W. J. Young, *St. Ignatius of Loyola* (Milwaukee 1949), pp. 21-22; Pedro Leturia, trans. A. J. Owen, *Iñigo de Loyola* (Chicago: Loyola University Press, 1965), which gathers together in meticulous detail all the sources and portrays most completely the life of the young Ignatius, pp. 42-49, especially pp. 48-49.
70 *FN*, II, 422-447.
71 *SdeSI*, I, 98-152; *FN*, I, 70-145.
72 *FN*, II, 137: "Si levò dal mundo."
73 *FN*, I, 330-331.

oblivion. The same thing is true, and that is yet more important, of Pedro de Ribadeneyra in the first biography intended for the whole order and for the general public. After he has briefly discussed the family origins of his hero, he begins his story with the siege of the citadel of Pamplona.[74] But if he here omits the defects of his youth, he comes in the course of the narrative to speak about Ignatius' desire for fame, the thorns and thistles of his soul,[75] his vanity,[76] his coarse and unchaste desires,[77] his sins,[78] his fear of the weakness of his flesh,[79] and calls him a vain and shameless soldier.[80] This list should lead us to conclude that Ribadeneyra had no intention of falsifying the image of the saint's character. The saint's second biographer, Giampietro Maffei, speaks even more clearly when writing about his youth: " He wasted miserably the time given to him to work out his eternal salvation as most mortals do, partly in factional quarrels and affairs of honor, partly in love affairs and similar worldly vanities."[81] Only in the seventeenth and eighteenth centuries was the feeling for the actual facts lost, and there was fashioned a dream image of a soldier of serene sanctity.[82]

III

History has transmitted to us only a small group of unfavorable judgments about St. Ignatius. If we disregard the ecclesiastical protests raised in Alcalá, Salamanca, and Paris, which were settled in the hearings held in those places, the negative judgments stem principally from Nicolás Bobadilla and Simão Rodrigues, his first companions, and the Theatine Giampietro Carafa, later Pope Paul IV.

Since the criticisms show a basic agreement, they seem to have some sort of foundation in the saint's character. Without exception they come from men who had clashed with Ignatius and were spoken in the heat of passion. Bobadilla's excitable nature caused Ignatius a great deal of trouble. On the other hand he loved him and even knew how to joke about his thoughtlessness. Once, when the Jesuits had

74 Ribadeneyra, *Vita Ignatii*, I, ch. 1, in *FN*, IV, 78-81.
75 Ibid., ch. 2, in *FN*, IV, 87.
76 Ibid., in *FN*, IV, 91.
77 Ibid., in *FN*, IV, 93.
78 Ibid., chaps. 3, 4, 6; in *FN*, IV, 101, 107, 121.
79 Ibid., ch. 3, in *FN*, IV, 103.
80 " Soldado desgarrado y vano," ibid., II, ch. 18, in *FN*, IV, 315; see also V, chaps. 2, 10, in *FN*, IV, 769, 850-853.
81 Giampietro Maffei, *Historiarum indicarum libri* XVI. *Accessit Ignatii Loyolae vita* (Cologne, 1593), p. 457.
82 See Astráin, *Historia*, I, 10-12.

been called hypocrites, Ignatius said that after long consideration he had found no one who deserved this reproach unless perhaps Salmerón (who was of an almost childlike candor) and Bobadilla.[83] At times he had to admonish this man with love and firmness.[84] During the deliberations preparatory to the foundation of the order, since Bobadilla had his own personal opinions and would not let himself be convinced by anything, Ignatius suggested that a majority of votes be sufficient for the adoption of a specific regulation. With the exception of Bobadilla, all agreed.[85] The rest of the saint's companions did not find it so easy to put up with Bobadilla's manner and, because of this, even forgot his merits and services.[86] Bobadilla's abruptness sometimes showed itself in the statements about Ignatius, whom he once called " a rascally sophist and a Basque spoiled by flattery."[87]

Simão Rodrigues, whose contrariness developed to such a point that it caused Ignatius a great deal of worry so that he recalled him from Portugal, and whom he sought to guide back to the right spirit— in which, by the way, he also used help from Bobadilla — was in this situation naturally not full of love for the founder of the order whom, when in another mood, he expressed a great desire to see again.[88] He called Ignatius ambitious,[89] charged him with using the order for his own personal advantage and for that of his family,[90] and said that Ignatius had recalled him out of passion and hate and had taken no care for his good reputation.[91] Once he said to Luís Gonçalves, " You must understand that Father Ignatius is a good man and very virtuous; but he is a Basque, who, once he has undertaken something..." And it continues in this vein.[92]

We find Pope Paul IV making similar statements. The co-founder of the Theatine Order had already come into conflict with Ignatius in Venice because he felt insulted by a frank letter Ignatius had sent him.[93] There had followed two other disputes in Rome in which Cardinal Carafa had lost to Ignatius.[94] The news of the Cardinal's

---

83 *FN*, I, 541, 730.
84 *EppIgn*, I, 277-282; *LettersIgn*, pp. 72-77.
85 *Cons*MHSJ, I, 12-13.
86 See *MonNad*, II, 53; *SdeSI*, I, 715; *FN*, I, 75.
87 *MonNad*, II, 53.
88 *MonBroet*, p. 553.
89 *PolChron*, II, 711-712.
90 *EppMixt*, II, 808.
91 *EppMixt*, III, 180-191; IV, 186-187.
92 *EppMixt*, III, 34.
93 *EppIgn*, I, 114-118; *LettersIgn*, pp. 28-31.
94 *MonNad*, II, 14; Astráin, *Historia*, II, 30-32.

election as pope arrived while Ignatius was at recreation with his fellow religious. Immediately his facial expression altered perceptibly. He later reported that all the bones in his body had trembled. But after he had retired for a short period of prayer, he became calm and ever after spoke of the new pope only with praise.[95] He also warned the others — Ribadeneyra for example — to be circumspect because anything they said could come to the ears of His Holiness. Should anything happen that was hard to excuse, the behavior of Pope Marcellus II was to be praised and the good will of the Society affirmed — without speaking about Paul IV.[96] The pope, "often imprudent in his utterances and generally unnecessarily rude and caustic," knew no guile and no hypocrisy, but indulged "in the strongest, coarsest language, like a true Southern Italian."[97] However he always showed himself quite amiable toward Ignatius and never allowed him to stay kneeling or to stand with his head uncovered.[98] Yet after Ignatius' death he said that he had become general in a tyrannical election,[99] that he had ruled the Society tyranically,[100] and that the order had lost its idol with his passing.[101]

The core of these objections is the statement that Ignatius was dictatorial and stiff-necked. This is based mainly in popular stereotypes. Basques still have the same reputation among Spaniards even today. And the Portuguese accused Spaniards of a "national and almost inborn dislike for the Portuguese."[102] With these words Father Baltasar Tellez sought to defend the revered founder of the Portuguese province against the envoys sent by Ignatius, the Spanish Diego Miró and Miguel de Torres. The same attitude caused the Portuguese Leon Enriquez to revolt against the predominance of Spaniards after the death of St. Francis Borgia, and it thus caused the sad confusion at the Third General Congregation of 1573.[103] When Simão Rodrigues attributed selfish motives to the order's founder, this was due to a mistake. He was thinking primarily of the marriage of Ignatius' niece, Lorenza de Loyola, to St. Francis Borgia's son, Juan. Ignatius knew nothing about this; and, when he heard about it, he disapproved of it.

95 *FN*, I, 581-582.
96 *SdeSI*, I, 389; *FN*, II, 389.
97 Ludwig von Pastor, *History of the Popes* (40 vols., 1891-1953), XIV, 69-70.
98 *MonNad*, II, 14-15; *SdeSI*, II, 855; *Acta Sanctorum*, VII, Julii, 519E.
99 Astráin, *Historia*, II, 613.
100 *MonNad*, II, 50.
101 *MonNad*, II, 15.
102 *MonBroet*, p. 818.
103 Astráin, *Historia*, III, 4-21.

Anyway, this plan would have been more advantageous to Juan Borgia than to the bride.[104]

Bobadilla's opinion will be properly evaluated if we bear in mind that he wished all the first companions to have equal rights in a joint directorate over the Society.[105] This opinion was the source of the difficulties that arose in the order at the time Laynez was elected as general.[106]

It is certain that Bobadilla had worked to have Paul IV espouse this idea of his. He was quite close to the pope, and Paul seems to have made Bobadilla's opinion his own.[107] The saying about Ignatius' being the idol of the order should probably be interpreted as an expression, born in a moment of emotion, for the reverence that all paid to the order's founder. This reverence was indeed already so great that Araoz, a relative of the saint, wrote to Polanco on the occasion of a rather stiff admonition, " Even if he should beat me to death, I would still trust in him."[108]

Ignatius was indeed a Basque if this is meant to signify a man of an extremely determined and unbending will.[109] He could say of himself: " For thirty years I have never neglected to perform at the appointed time anything I have undertaken in the service of our Lord, neither because of water nor wind nor any other sort of bad weather."[110] Once he waited fourteen hours in the anteroom of a cardinal until the prelate finally received him.[111] It is obvious that such perseverance and inflexibility could be irksome and unpleasant. These qualities had their basis in his natural disposition, but they grew even stronger because of reverence for the Divine Majesty. This reverence was so great that he could say that to do something superficially for worldly purposes does no harm, but to do anything superficially for God is completely intolerable.[112]

Thus only those who failed in their duty experienced the unpleasant side of his strength of character in the founder's dealings with them. To the others he seemed to be kindness itself. As an example, here is a quotation from a letter of July 29, 1553, by the young Frans de Costere, who had been sent from Cologne to Rome: " The day

104 *PolChron*, II, 711-712; *EppMixt*, II, 808; III, 34, 180-191.
105 *MonNad*, II, 50-51.
106 Astráin, *Historia*, II, 15-21.
107 *MonNad*, II, 50-51.
108 *EppMixt*, IV, 80.
109 Ribadeneyra, *Vita Ignatii*, I, ch. 10, in *FN*, IV, 149.
110 *FN*, II, 414; *PolChron*, II, 427.
111 Ribadeneyra, *Vita Ignatii*, V, ch. 12, in *FN*, IV, 899.
112 *FN*, II, 480.

before yesterday I saw for the first time, with indescribable joy and eagerness, the Reverend Father Ignatius. I could not see enough of him. For his countenance is such that one cannot look upon it long enough. The old man was walking in the garden, leaning on a cane. His face shone with godliness. He is mild, friendly, and amiable so that he speaks with the learned and unlearned, with important people and little people, all in the same way: a man worthy of all praise and reverence. No one can deny that a great reward is prepared for him in heaven for everything."[113]

Ignatius appears to have made an exception to this amiable behavior in the case of his closest co-workers and intimates, Laynez, Nadal, Polanco, and also Luís Gonçalves.[114] Ribadeneyra says of Polanco that he had scarcely heard a good word through nine years as secretary.[115] Ignatius rebuked Nadal so much that he often could not keep from crying; and Laynez once complained to Ribadeneyra, " What have I done against the Society that this saint treats me this way ? "[116] Similar examples of the founder's severity are found in the letters.[117]

The reason for Ignatius' treatment of Laynez was probably the latter's inclination to the theoretical, which often led him to set his standards too high in the practical affairs of life. Ignatius accused him of acting " mathematically."[118] He could still lose his composure when he was general — Nadal relates a vivid example of this.[119] Laynez was his most intimate friend; and Ignatius, who probably saw in him his successor, evidently wanted to test him and lead him to perfection.[120] He succeeded in an extraordinary measure. Laynez displayed this during the difficult months of the First General Congregation, and it is significant that St. Francis Borgia asked God for the prudence and illumination of St. Ignatius and the gentleness of Laynez.[121]

With all their natural talents, Polanco and Nadal were also somewhat sober and men concerned for exact order. The basic motivation of Ignatius' treatment of them was probably the thought that it would be entirely for the glory of God if these men who were striving for

---

113 Joseph Jansen, *Rheinische Akten zur Geschichte des Jesuitenordens* 1542-1582, pp. 227-228.
114 *FN*, I, 587-588; *SdeSI*, I, 491.
115 Ribadeneyra, *De ratione gubernandi*, ch. 4, in *SdeSI*, I, 454; *FN*, III, 690.
116 Ibid.
117 For example, *EppIgn*, IV, 498-500; *LettersIgn*, pp. 269-271.
118 *MonLain*, I, 209; *PolChron*, II, 477.
119 *MonNad*, II, 45.
120 *FN*, II, 315.
121 *MonBorg*, V, 884.

perfection were exercised in self-denial. In their case he needed fear no lack of generosity. Moreover it is not too wide of the mark to suspect that these ever-present witnesses of his conduct before God might tread too close to that area of intimacy reserved to God alone.[122] Just how much he otherwise opened himself to them and entrusted himself into their hands is shown by the fact that he related his life story to Gonçalves and calmly abandoned himself to Polanco's discretion when the time came for the lonely death that had to take place before God alone.[123]

IV

In contrast to the few, insignificant objections against the character and behavior of the founder of the Jesuits there stands a boundless profusion of witnesses who saw in him a saint while he was still alive and who spoke of him in admiration after his death. Just the social position of the persons who sought him out, made him the advisor and director of their souls, and sought his friendship testifies to what a remarkable figure he was. Popes, cardinals and bishops, rulers, men and women of great name and influence were in communication with him. Even if the record says merely that they were friendly to the order as a whole, as in the case of Michelangelo Buonarroti — the great artist wanted to build the large Church of the Gesù for the Jesuits without remuneration[124] — it would probably not be too far wrong to attribute this attachment to reverence for the founder of the order.

Besides the opinion of important personages, that of the common people, who revered and loved the saint, must not be forgotten. He had drawn attention to himself quite early. That became evident shortly after his arrival in Manresa. It is related that his confessor, Juan de Chanones of Montserrat, used to say that his spiritual son, Ignatius, would be a great pillar of the Church.[125] An aged woman of Manresa, known in many parts of Spain as a servant of God and also much revered by Ignatius, said to him one day, "May it please our Lord Jesus Christ to appear to you one day."[126] In August, 1537, Ignatius met at Bassano a hermit known as a man of God, Francesco Antonio, who considered him at their first meeting to be a man lacking in perfection. But he was shown in prayer that Ignatius was a man

---

122 *FN*, I, 580.
123 *PolChron*, VI, 35-45.
124 *MonNad*, I, 284.
125 *SdeSI*, II, 446.
126 *FN*, I, 392, 412.

of apostolic zeal and courage.[127]   Despite his poor knowledge of Italian, graphically reported by Ribadeneyra,[128] Ignatius preached at Rome to large crowds, like one who had power.[129]   When he walked through the city, people gathered to see him.   They gazed after him even though he avoided anything striking or unusual, and they called him a man who always looks to heaven and speaks about God.[130]   Since he was involved in less external activity when he was general of the order, he was thought to be a man more inclined to the contemplative life, a spiritual man.   During the later beatification process, a witness told how his father had one day taken him to visit Ignatius.   Ignatius had [playfully] pulled at his ears, asked a few questions about Christian doctrine, and inquired about his last confession.   After confession he had caressed him affectionately as is usually done with children.   All good people had considered Ignatius a saint.   He had received many visits from cardinals, prelates, and nobles.   The lower class, however, had spoken of those "hypocrites," the Theatines.[131]   When Ignatius preached in the streets, children sometimes threw apples at him; but he did not turn around because of that.[132]

The Jesuits still had enemies that called them the "riffraff and scum of the city" as late as 1546, and scattered circles spoke ill of them.[133]   The testimony to the general reverence for the founder himself is thus all the more significant.[134]   The enormous crowds of the common people at his funeral and the numbers in which they visited his grave also indicated how much he was loved.[135]

The beatification processes held in Spain and Italy also testify to the high esteem in which he was generally held by the common people.   The individual statements in them are less noteworthy than the universal agreement.[136]   If it had been necessary, these would have more than made up for the false statements that had been made about Ignatius in the earlier processes at Alcalá, Salamanca, Paris, and Venice; and they confirmed the judgment of the process held at Rome

127 *FN*, I, 194.
128 *FN*, II, 349-350.
129 *FN*, I, 197.
130 *SdeSI*, II, 476.
131 *SdeSI*, II, 828; *FN*, III, 281.   At that time the people of Rome often mistook the Jesuits for Theatines.
132 *SdeSI*, II, 831.
133 Tacchi Venturi, *Storia*, I, 247-248; II, Pt. 2, 44.
134 *SdeSI*, II, 830, 914-920.
135 *SdeSI*, II, 839, 857-863, 878.
136 At Azpeitia, 20 witnesses; Barcelona, 91; Manresa, 57; Valencia, 41; Gandía, 30; etc.   For the records of these processes, see *SdeSI*, II, 112-126, 128-259, 262-401, 411-423, 461-468, 503-505, 521-927, 983-1015.

in 1538, at which by chance the three judges from Alcalá, Paris, and Venice were able to testify for Ignatius.[137]

The popes who ruled the Church during the lifetime of St. Ignatius esteemed him highly. Marcellus II especially displayed a " friendship of long standing."[138] While still a cardinal, he had a dispute with Father Olave and declared that it was a mistake for the Jesuits not to wish to accept ecclesiastical dignities. Olave, driven into a corner, appealed to the fact that this was the opinion of Ignatius. The Cardinal said: " Now I yield, Olave. Though I still think my reasons are better, the authority of Ignatius carries even more weight."[139]

Cardinals Scipio Rebiba, Julius Sanctorinus of Santa Severina, Guglielmo Sirleto, Stanislaus Hosius, Antonio Carafa, Fulvio della Corgna, Giambattista Cestagna, later Pope Urban VII, all considered him a saint.[140] Francesco Maria Tarugi, the holy and beloved disciple of St. Philip Neri, expressed the same opinion and kissed the hand of the dead Ignatius.[141] Cardinal Pietro Bertano of Fano, reporting on an audience with Charles V in a letter of February 3, 1552, said that the Emperor had spoken so well about the position of the pope and about ecclesiastical benefices that Ignatius could not have done better.[142] Cardinal Gabriele Palleoti called him a luminary of the Church.[143] St. Charles Borromeo celebrated his second Holy Mass in the room where Ignatius had died.[144] Cardinal Gaspar de Quiroga, Archbishop of Toledo, had known Ignatius in Rome and was a friend of his. This is his testimony: Ignatius never spoke one word or performed any action that was contrary to the dignity of a saint. He was humble, gentle, patient, loving, zealous for the honor of God and the salvation of the neighbor. He despised the world, was prudent and magnanimous, remained the same on good days and on bad days. He always possessed a restrained joyousness, with an expression of peace and equanimity such as I have never seen before. He needed no miracle to testify to his sanctity.[145]

137 *FN*, II, 591; Schurhammer, *Franz Xaver*, I, 417; Schurhammer, trans. Costelloe, *Francis Xavier*, I, 436.
138 *Acta Sanctorum*, VII, Julii, 519C.
139 *FN*, II, 352-353.
140 *SdeSI*, II, 919, 925-926.
141 *SdeSI*, II, 487-488, 877. On Cardinal Tarugi see Ludwig von Pastor, *History of the Popes*, XIX, 169; XXIV, 158, 161, 192.
142 *Acta Concilii Tridentini* (Freiburg im Breisgau: Societas Goerresiana, 1901-), XI, 814.
143 *SdeSI*, II, 855.
144 *PolCompl*, I, 423.
145 *SdeSI*, I, 726-727; II, 110-111, 403, 822.

The reverence that many cardinals paid him finds particular expression in the letters of condolence which they sent to his fellow religious following his death. Among them was Cardinal Alessandro Farnese, who wrote that he had lost a friend on whose counsel and prudence, devotion and friendliness he had relied; also Ippolito d'Este of Ferrara, Reginald Cardinal Pole, and Otto Cardinal von Truchsess, who had recourse to him in all his difficulties.[146] Considering this universal admiration it is no wonder that Ignatius received five votes at the conclave in which Julius III was elected pope.[147]

The cardinals were joined by many bishops like Johannes Antonius Viperanus, who stressed his balanced attitude,[148] Fabio Mirto, bishop of Caiazzo, Louis Prat of Clermont, and others.[149] Blessed Juan de Ribera, archbishop of Valencia, who presided over the beatification process held at Gandía, was deeply moved by the many physical and spiritual miracles that he discovered; and he delivered a panegyric on the saint.[150] The bishops of the ecclesiastical province of Tarragona expressed themselves in a like manner and " testified to what we have seen and have been able to grasp in our own hands.''[151]

We should not be surprised that the saints and the great apostolic laborers of the age felt a spiritual kinship with Ignatius, flowing from an inner sense of recognition, and esteemed him. Philip Neri, who, by his own testimony, learnt meditative prayer from him,[152] saw his countenance illuminated as a sign of the inner beauty of his soul and his union with God.[153] The apostle of Andalusia, Blessed Juan de Ávila, also revered him and thought of himself as a boy in comparison to that giant.[154] The venerable Luis de Granada admired him as a mirror of all virtues, especially of prudence.[155] In addition there are the Carthusians of Cologne, who expressed approval of the young order while he was still alive;[156] the Barnabites of Milan;[157] Father Luis de Estrada, O.Cist., who paid him homage with rhetorical pomp and compared him to a mustard seed;[158] Juan Gutierrez, O.P., who criticised

---

146 *SdeSI*, II, 33-40; *Cartas*, VI, 419-420.
147 *SdeSI*, I, 339-340; *FN*, II, 325-326.
148 *SdeSI*, 925-926.
149 *SdeSI*, II, 40, 926.
150 *SdeSI*, II, 932-935.
151 *SdeSI*, II, 501.
152 *Acta Sanctorum*, VII, Julii, 332A.
153 *SdeSI*, II, 425-426, 488, 499.
154 *SdeSI*, II, 823, 824, 836, 855.
155 *SdeSI*, II, 855.
156 *FN*, I, 753-761.
157 *Cartas*, VI, 413-414.
158 *FN*, II, 15-37; *SdeSI*, II, 42-71.

the members of his order for their reserve and antipathy [toward the Jesuits];[159] St. Mary Magdalen dei Pazzi, who saw him in heaven in one of her visions.[160]

Let us mention a few other witnesses: Luis Vives, whom Ignatius had met on one of his begging journeys in Flanders (1529 ?), considered him a holy man who might some day found a religious order.[161] Ignatius himself was not greatly impressed by the great scholar and forbade the reading of his books in the schools of the order. At the expostulation of the fathers working in the colleges, however, he lifted the ban and allowed the use of his writings.[162] The historian Esteban de Garibay, in his *Compendio Historial*, called him a noble and holy man, a man worthy of eternal memory, who had been of a gentle earnestness edifying to all in his relationships with others.[163] The homage of the German Johann Albert Widmanstetter for "the brave soldier of Jesus Christ" has already been mentioned.[164] The saint's doctor, Alexander Petronius, once saw him bathed in shining light.[165] The Viceroy of Sicily, Juan de Vega, whose wife had helped Ignatius in his works in the social apostolate and whose secretary, Pedro de Marquina, had also been very devoted to him, wrote a letter to Laynez after the saint's death in which he celebrated the holy captain in military images and thus, along with the bull of Paul III, *Regimini militantis Ecclesiae*, originated one particular view of the activity of the saint and of his order.[166] Finally let us mention King John III of Portugal, who had a great veneration for Ignatius. He wished to learn from Gonçalves everything Ignatius had said and done. In 1555 he was of the opinion that the cardinals would do well to elect him pope.[167]

All this can be fittingly summarized by stating that, with few exceptions, all his contemporaries recognized the greatness of the saint.

V

If the statements and testimony of non-Jesuits speak of the sanctity of the founder of the Society of Jesus in more general terms and, when

---

159 *SdeSI*, II, 824.
160 *SdeSI*, I, 534-535.
161 *FN*, II, 557.
162 *EppIgn*, III, 582, 688; IV, 106, 108, 484, 650; V, 421; VI, 267; *SdeSI*, II, 880; *PolChron*, III, 165.
163 *FN*, II, 451, 453, 454, 461.
164 *FN*, I, 788, 803.
165 *SdeSI*, II, 110-111.
166 *MonLain*, I, 653-655.
167 *SdeSI*, I, 530; *PolChron*, V, 603.

they do go into details, give special stress to his apostolic love, his equanimity, and his prudence, then we would expect his sons to give a more exact picture of their spiritual father. To them all he was a "father." Though one may think unsuitable the expression used by Pope Paul IV, the "idol" of his subjects, it still has a basis in reality. For Francis Xavier, who used to write to him on his knees, Ignatius was the "father of his soul," his "only father in the love of Christ."[168] It was noticed what reverence the Duke of Gandía, St. Francis Borgia, showed in his dealings with Ignatius.[169] Even Simão Rodrigues, in the self-possession of his old age, called him father.[170]

It is impossible to give even an approximate summation of the many observations and opinions of the saint's religious brethren. Even Anton Huonder could reproduce only a small selection from them.[171] First of all, Ignatius displayed in all his dealings with others the manners of a gentleman who strenuously avoids any sort of carelessness or coarseness in even the most unimportant details.[172] This was a natural result of his upbringing, but it became more and more the effect of an interior disposition that viewed men and all other creatures in the light of God. To refinement of manner he united a perpetual cheerfulness of spirit which entranced visitors and made them "always cheerful."[173] Of course he could also be severe when he perceived carelessness in the service of God or a spirit of insubordination. But this severity, which sometimes intensified into harshness, never repelled. The only way we can explain this is that everyone sensed that Ignatius' decisions and actions came from a man who viewed all things in a divine light. There was also no dissatisfaction caused by the fact that he usually had someone else administer his admonitions while he himself treated the one admonished very kindly. Later critics have interpreted this as insincerity. But it was simply the expression of the fact that he regarded the weaknesses of his followers as things of secondary importance and wished to preserve undisturbed the unity of what was essential in his relationship with them.

Alongside his unshakeable courage and his noble disposition, the natural gift everyone admired most in him was prudence. Deepened by a union with God that cast an other-worldly light on all earthly

168 *EppXav*, II, 5, 7; *CartasXav*, pp. 278, 280.
169 *SdeSI*, II, 825.
170 *MonBroet*, pp. 453, 655.
171 Huonder, *Ignatius*, pp. 132-136, and in many other places.
172 Tacchi Venturi, *Storia*, Vol. I, Pt. 2, 245, 249; Lancicius, *Dictamina S.P. Ignatii Generalia*, nos. 39-56, in *FN*, III, 653-656; and many other places.
173 *FN*, I, 121, 637.

things, free of all thoughtless haste,[174] his prudence awakened great admiration in everyone. He made use of different means to handle what seemed to be identical situations: in one case great severity and in other great gentleness. Even though one did not understand at first what he was doing, the results showed that he had been right.[175] Father Edmond Auger called him the great sculptor of men, who had made of Francis Xavier the immortal Apostle of India and thereby obtained no less fame than Alexander the Great, who had tamed the wild Bucephalus.[176] Before making decisions — in which process he was inclined to interpret the actions of others in the best light possible — he conferred with his fellow workers; but in this he showed himself "so superior to the others that, even if it was a Polanco, the other appeared to be a child compared with a wise man."[177] He was capable of this primarily because of a deep-rooted humility that let him forget himself.[178] He was completely in earnest when, in 1552, he presented his companions a written petition that they should elect another general. Of course no one complied with this wish with the exception of Andrés de Oviedo, known for his great simplicity of heart, who thought: When a saint says he is not fit for an office, one must believe him.[179]

His spirit of prayer and his piety towered above all these natural qualities, which were ordered and intensified by his sanctity. There was probably no one who did not know what intensity and heights his prayer life possessed. What is astonishing is that, despite the fulness of mystical graces, he continually examined himself, recollected himself, and prepared for prayer with incomparable fidelity.[180] In every sense of the word he lived with God. For this reason the most insignificant creature and the most unimportant action and the carelessly spoken word were for him all signs from God and part of His plan.

Here it must be observed that his companions had made their own the saint's basic principle that the extraordinary should not be considered of primary importance. They knew of course about the unusual gifts of grace which God had showered upon their founder, were

---

174 "Let us sleep on it" (*FN*, I, 629).

175 *SdeSI*, I, 195, 253, 397, 416-417; II, 900-901; *FN*, I, 136, 579, 646; *EppMixt*, II, 516; and in many other places.

176 Schurhammer, *Franz Xaver*, I, 162, fn. 2; Schurhammer, trans. Costelloe, *Francis Xavier*, I, 172.

177 *SdeSI*, I, 253, 397.

178 For example, in *FN*, II, 378.

179 *EppIgn*, III, 303-304; *LettersIgn*, p. 230; *FN*, II, 210.

180 *FN*, I, 140-141, 542, 644.

acquainted with the assaults of the devil that he had to endure,[181] and preserved as a precious souvenir the notations about his interior visions and his experiences in prayer;[182] but these were not the primary determinant of their judgment about him. For instance, when Nadal comes to speak about the beginning of Ignatius' recovery that took place on the night before June 29, 1521, he says: Although I am not one of those who easily assume that any event is a miracle, so long as there is a natural explanation possible, still such circumstances are worthy of note when there is question of individuals whom God has called to be founders of religious orders. Therefore I am glad to consider that God began to help and heal him on that very day, and so I truly revere this saint as a helper of the members of the Society.[183] Ribadeneyra holds a similar opinion in his biography of the saint. The sober St. Peter Canisius wrote after his death, "He lived in such a way that he could not die badly."[184] Thus they considered it quite right for Ignaitus to reprove and replace his own confessor, Diego de Eguía, who had often hinted at the extraordinary sanctity of the founder.[185] For all of them, the great miracle of God's grace that made him such a great saint was his daily life. " It is certain that some fathers of the Society who seemed to be great saints when considered as individuals, like Pierre Favre, Diego Laynez, Francis Xavier, Francis Borgia, and others, were like dwarves compared to a giant when they were compared to Ignatius. They recognized this themselves and so stood before him in reverent homage."[186]

Because the companions and disciples of the founder saw him primarily as a servant of God, his death was for them above all a journey home and only a momentary occasion for mourning. Reports from all the houses and all the members of the order, such as St. Francis Borgia, St. Peter Canisius, Nadal, Ribadeneyra, and others, were in agreement that they experienced a feeling of joy and a stimulus to their zeal in the knowledge that he was certainly in heaven.[187] All were convinced that piety and continuous, intimate association with

181 *FN*, I, 132-133.
182 *MonNad*, III, 377.
183 *FN*, II, 184.
184 Braunsberger, *B.P. Canisii epistulae*, II, 22-23.
185 *FN*, I, 628, and other places.
186 Ribadeneyra's testimony in the canonical process concerning the canonization of Ignatius held at Madrid in 1595, in *SdeSI*, II, 162.
187 *FN*, II, 125, 218; *SdeSI*, II, 18, 25, 27, 28; *PolChron*, VI, 35-45; *MonBorg*, III, 266; *MonNad*, I, 345; II, 48; *MonRib*, I, 63-64, 196-198; *EppMixt*, V, 458, 460, 487, 490, 511; *LittQuad*, IV, 548; V, 68, 78, 148-149; Braunsberger, *B.P. Canisii epistulae*, II, 22-23.

God were at the center of his being. He himself described his religious life as more passive toward God than active.[188] Although he was almost overwhelmed by consolations, he directed his attention less to the emotional than to that which was "more abstract and not perceptible to the senses" (*más abstractas, separadas*).[189] Thus he united the extraordinary life of grace given him by God with every detail of those preparations for prayer he advises for the exercitant in the *Spiritual Exercises*. It would almost appear as if, in a century that had given rise to a false definition of the relationship between God and man, in which man is saved exclusively by grace and can do nothing for his own salvation, the real situation had been given visible form in Ignatius: the cooperation of God and creature in which the grace of God helps man to remove the obstacles and to receive the supernatural life, for his own salvation and for his apostolate for others — according to the words of Christ, "I have come to cast fire upon the earth, and what will I but that it be kindled" (Luke 12:49).

188 *FN*, I, 138-139.
189 *FN*, I, 136.

PART II

ST. IGNATIUS' SPIRITUALITY

ELEMENTS OF CRUSADE SPIRITUALITY
IN ST. IGNATIUS

Hans Wolter

REGIMINI MILITANTIS ECCLESIAE are the opening words of the bull of Pope Paul III in which the Society of Jesus received its first official approval. It was issued September 27, 1540. The allusion to the *ecclesia militans* (Church militant) seems carefully chosen; the expression sounds like a program, like an indication of the mode of thought characteristic of the man whose work the bull approved.

The Augustinian concept of the *ecclesia militans* signifies that strife is a constituent form of the Church of Jesus Christ, together with suffering and triumph and as a stage between them. Ignatius took this form very seriously. He gave the idea new life, deepened it profoundly, and made it widely known. This ethos of strife was the motive force behind the historical accomplishments of the Society of Jesus as a missionary order, as forerunner and co-author of the Catholic Reformation of the sixteenth and seventeenth centuries. There appeared a crusade that gave battle in the remotest regions of the earth; and alongside it a stubborn struggle, full of inspired tactical measures and strategic plans, on the European front where those of the new faith and the old faith collided with each other. This battle used the weaponry of the spirit, humanism, a dynamic and burning love of Christ, a self-devouring will to serve one's brother through concern for the salvation of his soul. Contemporary observers were already impressed by this — if one may use the term — avant-garde zeal of the young order.[2] Scholars and historians

---

Study 4 was translated by Louis W. Roberts.

1 *Cons*MHSJ, I, 9-32.

2 See Ignacio Elizaldo, "San Ignacio de Loyola en la poesía española del siglo XVII," in *AHSJ*, XXV (1956), 201-240. In the poetic statements of the seventeenth century about Ignatius, there is considerable emphasis on the military and knightly aspect.

of St. Ignatius and the institute he founded have therefore been continually misled into considering the militant, indeed even the military, factor to be the central element of their make-up. The very language of the fundamental documents had to have a determining influence in the formation of this opinion. The diction has certainly been strongly influenced by the literary tradition of the " army of Christ."

Recently however doubts about this interpretation have been reported on both the Catholic and the Protestant side. In disagreeing with Karl Holl,[3] Karl Heussi pointed to the monastic, Platonic, and mystical traditions within the order.[4] Joseph de Guibert limits the concept of the "military" in St. Ignatius' spirituality to the *servitium per amorem*, the service of love, in opposition to all false images of narrow, sergeant-major type of discipline, of noisy flag-waving, of the spirit of the barracks, and of modern militarism.[5] He is certainly in the right. Yet the breath of knighthood rests on this "service of love," the breath of struggle, of daring, of readiness to act at any moment.

Students of the Society of Jesus usually try to understand its character and its labors, its influence and its dynamics, by analysing the planning, demanding, unique, creative, and — with all his limitations — magnificent personality of its founder. They then rightfully reverse the process and attempt to comprehend the human and religious character of its spiritual father by looking at the distinctive characteristics of the order and its history. If then, as we have said, strife on the European front and overseas was a characteristic feature of the young Society of Jesus, a natural

3 Karl Holl, " Die geistliche Übungen des Ignatius von Loyola," in *Gesammelt Aufsätze* (Tübingen, 1921-1928), III, 285-301.
4 Karl Heussi, *Kompendium der Kirchengeschichte*, tenth newly revised edition (Tübingen, 1949), p. 342.
5 *DeGuiJes*, 176-181.
6 M. de Iriarte, " Un doble encuentro decisivo para Ignacio," in *Manresa*, XXVIII (1956), 63: " al Instituto de la Compañia de Jesús creado a su imagen y semejanza." See J. Iturrioz, " Compañia de Jesús. Sentido histórico y ascético de este nombre," in *Manresa*, XXVII (1955), 43-53, especially p. 43: " Compañia de Jesús es en las apariencias un nombre militar, como en apariencas lo es también el espiritu de Ignacio. El fundo no es militar." This statement certainly carries the denial of the military element too far. Ignatius could no more completely divest himself of the military and knightly elements to be found in the milieu of his family, his people, and his epoch than Bernard of Clairvaux could at the time when he lived: " son atavisme militaire ne pouvait que se satisfaire de cet idéal et de ses lois " [of the Crusades, that is]; see A. Seguin, *Bernard de Clairvaux* (Paris: Commission d'Histoire de l'Ordre de Citeaux, 1953), p. 398.

conclusion from this is that the ethos of strife was a characteristic of St. Ignatius also. This was not merely because the circumstances of a troubled and unrestrained era necessarily involved this, but also — and especially — because it was demanded by the unique quality of his religious development, by his basic natural character, and by the interlacing of the history of his soul with the basic thought patterns of his epoch, his people, and his native land.

The history of Ignatius' conversion has been illuminated by scholarship in even its most insignificant and delicate details.[7] Light has been cast on the saint's consciousness of his status as a knight. Attempts have been made again and again to throw new light on his idea of obedience, which he pushed to extremes (Pope Paul IV believed he had ruled like a tyrant[8]), yet which allowed the individual a great deal of freedom.[9] His conduct of the official business of his office has been questioned repeatedly. It was marked by consistent though elastic methods, painful attention to detail and largeness of outlook, uniting the smallest details and the most far-reaching vision. Scholars have been able to discover the literary sources of his spirituality.[10] They have compared and contrasted the effects upon him of his life in his homeland, his life as a pilgrim, and his life as a student.[11] So it might seem a waste of time to want to treat the same subject once more. Everything has been explained. But is this really true of " everything " ? We believe that there is one area among the source materials that has not yet been examined and discussed, at least not thoroughly enough.[12] An examination of this group of sources complements our

7 See the most recent treatment: J. M. Granero, " Nuevos Derroteros. Estudio sobre la conversión de S. Ignacio," in *Manresa*, XXVIII (1956), 31-56. See also M. de Iriarte, " Un doble encuentro," in *Manresa*, XXVIII (1956), 57-70. This is a scholarly psychological treat-study that treats the period between that of the *caballero mundano* and that of the *caballero de Cristo*.

8 " Dixerat Patrem Ignatium tyrranice gubernasse societatem " (*MonNad*, II, 54).

9 See P. Blet, " Note sur les origines de l'obéissance ignatienne," in *Gregoria·num*, XXXV (1954), 99-111.

10 *DeGuiJes*, pp. 152-161; Hugo Rahner, *The Spirituality of St. Ignatius of Loyola: An Account of Its Historical Development*, trans. Francis J. Smith (Westminster: The Newman Press, 1953). Especially to be noted are the various works of Pedro Leturia.

11 See Böhmer, *Ignatius von Loyola*.

12 See P. Kellerwessel, " Geschichtliches zur Königsbetrachtung der Exerzitien," in *ZAM*, VII (1932), 70-79. Occasional references to this are made in the course of many scholarly works; for example, H. Monier-Vinard lays stress on the influence of crusade thought in *L'Appel du divin Roi. Les grandes directives des retraites fermées* (Paris, 1930), pp. 149-171.

knowledge of certain traits of St. Ignatius' spiritual character and labors, and lets us comprehend more clearly how they fit into the history of the period and the history of ideas.

This category of source materials is called "crusade spirituality." It would be a waste of effort to look through the manuals on the history of spirituality for a chapter that deals specifically with this area. It was a spirituality of the laity and thus did not produce written treatises. And since there is no body of literature, researchers make a careful detour around it.

Yet precisely because it is a lay spirituality, it must be examined by those who wish to have a complete understanding of the spiritual history of St. Ignatius. For Iñigo de Loyola was — as Jerônimo Nadal once expressed it[13] — before, during, and immediately after his conversion to a new mode of religious living (1521-1524) — a *Christianus popularis* (a folk Christian). Only later, at the age of thirty-three, did he begin to study at the universities of Spain and France. In his religion Iñigo was thus a man of the people, a simple soul without any particular intellectual pretensions, without involvement in the fine-spun web of European spirituality. He was just as far removed from the soft rhythms of humanism, later of conscious choice,[14] as he was from the world of scholastic and mystical conceptions of spiritual aspirations of sublime origins. We must therefore not start our investigation in the realms of humanism, scholastic theology, or monastic asceticism, but with the people of Spain, the people in the churches among the Basque mountains, his religiously naive companions in the circle about Juan Velázquez de Cuéllar, the people at the court of the Viceroy of Navarre, Duke Antonio Manrique de Nájera. Polanco says later, "God is accustomed to move each one according to his interior and exterior dispositions, his degree of understanding, and his inclinations."[15] Among these fundamental dispositions there belongs, as a psychological premise, "the national milieu; that is, the modes of thought, the ethos, and the life goals that were dominant among the Spaniards of his day."[16]

---

13 "Nihil spiritus, nihil egregiae pietatis attigit. Erat quidem catholice, sed populariter christianus " (*FN*, II, 231).

14 Pedro Leturia, " Genesis de los ejercicios de S. Ignacio y su influjo en la fundación de la Compañía de Jesús (1521-1540)" in *AHSJ*, X (1941), 16-36. The various stages in Ignatius' rejection of Erasmianism are sketched on page 36.

15 "Sumario de las cosas más notables que a la institución y progreso de la Compañía de Jesús togan," no. 13, in *FN*, I, 159.

16 M. de Iriarte, " Un doble encuentro," *Manresa*, XXVIII (1956), 59. Iriarte refers to Felix Olmedo, *Introducción a la vida de San Ignacio de Loyola* (Madrid, 1944). Unfortunately we were not able to obtain a copy of this book.

Now there we find that, together with a strong, clear, un-reflective belief, concentrated on the essentials, on God, Christ, and his Church,[17] it is *la actitud de Cruzada*[18] the crusading spirit, that gives its special cast to the spiritual countenance of the Spanish people. The heart of this is what we call crusade spirituality. Do not medieval vistas open up here that are alien to the modern image of St. Ignatius ? For an answer we refer to one acquainted with the problem:[19] "Ignatius himself ... remained a man of the Middle Ages. Assuredly he was very intelligently alert," very circumspect, very realistic. "But for his own interior life he borrowed nothing, or little more than nothing," from the spirit of his age; namely, the spirit of humanism.

This crusade spirituality will therefore be the first topic of discussion. We will speak of its origins in the concept of crusade and in the experiences of the crusaders, of its fortunes down to the time of Iñigo de Loyola. Certain essential elements of this spirituality will then be presented just as they can be gathered from the sources. Finally we will attempt to examine whether and to what extent they are found in the spirituality of St. Ignatius, whether, when they appear in his work, they at least hint at a derivation from the folk spirituality of the age, one still close to the crusades. Since it will often be a question of elements found in the main-stream of traditional Christian spirituality ever since its origins, it will not be easy to prove that they have their direct source in the special cast that was given them by the crusade mentality. The possibility always remains that they have come to Ignatius through other channels (monastic, Franciscan, or those of the *devotio moderna*).[20] So we shall not be able to say any more than that an influence from the crusade spirituality is ascertainable. This influence is indeed one less conscious, if not less powerful, than other influences. It is, so to speak, an influence from the climate of the times, an influence added to the direction of his soul which he consciously experienced at Montserrat and Manresa and in his freely chosen studies.

---

17 Granero, *Manresa*, XXVIII (1956), 32.

18 M. de Iriarte, ibid., 60. This concept is followed in the article by this other one that we will speak of later: "la actitud de Caballero Andante, nutrida en los libros que se ensalzan y el lee, los libros de Caballería."

19 *DeGuiJes*, p. 166.

20 See L. Zarncke, *Die Exercitia Spiritualia des Ignatius von Loyola in ihren geistesgeschichtlichen Zusammenhängen* ("Schriften des Vereins für Reforma-tionsgeschichte," no. 151. Leipzig, 1931); L. Casutt, *Die Erbe eines grossen Herzens*.

I

The Concept of Crusade and Crusade Spirituality

Georg Schreiber once remarked in his suggestive manner that the pilgrimage to Jerusalem (*peregrinatio Hierosolymitana*) — by which he means the crusades — has continued to have its effects down through the centuries. At the same time, he continues, it has profoundly influenced the history of spirituality, even the spirituality of the religious orders — something that has not been the object of much research.[21] Folk spirituality was apparently the first thing to be exposed to the overpowering experience of the events of the crusades.

The crusades developed their own ideology as well as their own unique spirituality. They must be carefully distinguished from each other. It is true that there is an evident interdependence between them. They encourage, define, and sometimes limit each other. Yet the appearance of the ideology does not necessarily indicate the presence of the spiritual attitude, especially when it appears in official form as in a crusade bull, in a manifesto, in preaching, as a political program, or in a panegyric. Yet the ideology in such statements can be a welcome means to bring into focus the spirituality of those who are the object of such calls, especially when we consider the large numbers of people to which they are appealing. Consequently the military, political, and social ramifications of the crusade concept are not here taken into consideration. On the other hand, its religious content is of great interpretative value to us.

It must furthermore be carefully noted that the concept of crusade, the origins of which Carl Erdmann[22] has described so masterfully, and the crusade spirituality that corresponded to that concept were exposed to continual modification from the eleventh

21 Georg Schreiber, "Prämonstratensische Frömmigkeit und die Anfänge des Herz-Jesu-Gedankens. Ein Beitrag zur Geschichte der Frömmigkeit, der Mystik und der monastischen Bewegung," in *Zeitschrift für katholische Theologie*, LXIV (1940), 189. More on the subject can be found in Georg Schreiber, *Gemeinschaften des Mittelalters. Recht und Verfassung, Kult una Frömmihkeit* (Münster, 1948): pp. 41 (the hospital), 88 (devotion to the Cross), 132 (judgment by ordeal, consecration of weapons, blessing of pilgrims), 167 (liturgy), 228 (pilgrimage), 264 (the emperor motif, Charlemagne), 275, (blessings and tribute), 402 (itinerant preachers), 410 (Cluniac dynamism), 416 (*Kultwanderungen* [religious journeys or processions ?]), 419 (the concept of Europe as a unity), and many others. Special emphasis is given to the lay spirituality of the period of the Crusades.
22 Carl Erdmann, *Die Entstehung des Kreuzzugsgedankens* ("Forschungen zur Kirchen-und Geistesgeschichte," Vol. VI. Stuttgart, 1935).

century to the seventeenth. Let us recall merely the popular and hierarchical form of crusade at the time of Gregory VII (pope 1073-1085), the classical crusade moving eastward in the years between Urban II (1088-1099) and Innocent IV (1243-1254), the Church's inner crusades against the Albigensians and Frederick II (emperor 1215-1250), the *Reconquista* on the Iberian Peninsula, the campaigns against the Moors in North Africa, the occupation of the whole African coastline by the Portuguese, the conquest of the New World that also claimed to be a crusade, and finally the European defensive against the Turks from the time of Nicholas V (1447-1455) to that of Innocent XI (1676-1689).

To these varied forms of the one central idea — simply compare the manifestos of Urban II with those of Innocent III (1198-1216) and Leo X (1513-1522)[23] — there corresponds a similar development in the history of crusade spirituality. It is rich in intensity and weaknesses, in depths of feeling and in superficiality, in a variety of religious gestures, in the power to organize forms of devotion — from the stay-at-home pilgrimage, in which a proxy was sent, to the Franciscan Way of the Cross, from the crusade indulgence to the blessing of those who fought the Turks. When the crusade has an offensive character, a militant spirituality is its ready companion; when the crusade shifts to the defensive, the spirituality is compelled to become more interior.

It is only after the victorious high point in 1683 that there begins a rapid decline in both ideology and spirituality; the Enlightenment then administers the death blow.

What is of crucial importance for our investigation is the fact that the crusade idea was very much alive during the youth and adulthood of St. Ignatius. We may therefore surmise that the corresponding spirituality was also active among the common people in Spain, France, and Italy. At the tenth International Historical Congress held in Rome in 1955, the medieval section dealt exhaustively

---

23 Ibid. On pp. 102-106, just before dealing with the manifestos mentioned in the text, Erdmann analyses the call to Crusade of Sergius IV (1009-1012). Several important elements are already contained in it. On Urban II's appeals at Piacenza and Clermont (1095) and his letters to the faithful of Flanders, see H. Hagenmeyer, *Die Kreuzzugsbriefe aus den Jahren* 1088-1100 (Innsbruck, 1901), p. 136; on the letter to Bologna, ibid., p. 137. See also Erdmann, *Kreuzzugsgedanke*, pp. 363-377, which contains precise documentation. For the call of Innocent III, see *PL*, CCXVI, 817: epistle XVI, 28. For Leo X (at the Fifth Lateran Council, 1513), see Harduin, *Acta Conciliorum*, IX (1714), 1742-1747. This last also contains several highly informative speeches concerning the Crusade, pp. 1700-1705, 1728-1732.

with the fate of the concept of crusade.[24] While Stephen Runciman pointed to the decline of the idea in the later Middle Ages — that is, of the classical crusade to the East[25] — Etienne Delaruelle could declare (also of the end of the Middle Ages): " Not that the idea of crusade had died out or that the Holy Land had lost its power of attraction; but it seems that at that time, doubtless under Franciscan influence, there came to pass something like an interiorizing of this spirituality of the Passion. Instead of taking the Cross, one made himself a crusader by becoming a member of the Order of the Holy Cross (*Ordo sanctae Crucis*) . . . instead of making a pilgrimage to Jerusalem (*iter Hierosolymitanum*) one makes the Way of the Cross, an exercise that developed at the end of the fourteenth century and became widespread during the fifteenth."[26]

We here perceive clearly how the fortunes of crusade spirituality are dependent on those of the ideology, and vice versa. But Stephen Runciman does not say everything. Carl Erdmann's researches have shown that the classic idea of the crusade was a late and ineffective arrival in the Iberian Peninsula, but that it then became useful during the wars against the Moors and thus became very powerful, continuing to have its effect during the Age of Discovery.[27] In Portugal the Order of Christ (from 1317) became the notional, martial, indeed the official state vehicle of the crusade idea.[28] Throughout the entire peninsula, especially in Spain, the public was kept familiar with the crusade idea by the *bulas de cruzada* (*bullae cruciatae*, papal " crusade " bulls) from the time of Callistus III (1455-1458) — a Borgia, and thus a Spaniard.

We call to mind, for example, the work of Christopher Columbus known as the *Libro de las profecias* (written 1501-1502 and published only in 1882 and 1894) and its informative heading: " The beginning of the book or compilation of authorities, sayings, opinions, and prophecies regarding the recnnquest of the Holy City and the

---

24 *Relazioni del X congresso internazionale di scienze storiche* (6 vols. Florence, 1955), Vol. III, *Storia del Medioevo*.

25 Ibid., Stephen Runciman, " The decline of the crusading idea," 637-652.

26 Ibid., E. Delaruelle, " La pietà popolare alla fine del Medioevo, 515-537, esp. p. 523.

27 Carl Erdmann, " Der Kreuzzugsgedanke in Portugal," *Historische Zeitschrift*, CXLI (1950), 23-53.

28 See *FN*, I, 795, where, in the apology of Johannes Albert Widmanstadius, " De Societatis Jesu initiis," 789-805, the author refers to the parallel with the Portuguese Order of Christ when defending the name " Society of Jesus ": " quemadmodum et Lusitanis equitibus, qui sub Jesu nomine et signis militant, gloriosi hujus tituli decus absque ulla cujusquam offensione relinquitur."

Mountain of God, Sion, as well as the discovery and conversion of the islands of India."[29] At that time (1502) he wrote to the pope that he had wished by his discoveries to create a means for the conquest of the Holy Land. *Conquista* [the conquest of the New World] and crusade belong together, outwardly as Columbus here sees it, and inwardly inasmuch as the *Conquista* is thought of and experienced as a crusade — consider merely the names given to the islands first discovered, San Salvador, Vera Cruz.

Joseph Höffner says about the Spanish crusader spirit of the *siglo de oro* (Golden Age): The Spanish felt that they had a vocation as crusaders in the West [in the battle against heresy] in addition to their task overseas. There the joy of discovery was intimately united with zeal for conversions in a people who had the crusader ideal in their blood."[30] Gerhard Jacob has recently expressed a similar opinion: "We see here — in the *Conquista* and in Columbus — how the spirit of the glory-seeking Renaissance, with its thirst for power and gold, worked hand-in-hand with the equally powerful zeal for the faith in which the idea of the crusades lived unmistakably on."[31]

Jan Huizinga informs us that even in Burgundy and France, where the autumn of the Middle Ages was allowing the old ideals to wither away: "There was a tremendous political drive that was inseparably joined to the ideals of knighthood: the crusade, Jerusalem! The primary and the most unavoidable concern of European politics ... was inseparable from the crusade idea. Europe could view the Turkish question only as one subordinate part of the great holy task at which her ancestors had failed, the liberation of Jerusalem."[32]

---

29 "Incipit liber sive manipulus de auctoritatibus, dictis ac sententiis et prophetiis circa materiam recuperandae sancte civitatis et montis Dei Syon, ac inventionis et conversionis insularum Indie," in Robert Streit, *Bibliotheca Missionum* (Münster), I (1916), 1.

30 Joseph Höffner, *Christentum und Menschenwürde. Das Anliegen der spanischen Kolonialethik im goldenen Zeitalter* (Trier, 1947), pp. 76, 112.

31 Gerhard Jacob, "Aus der ibero-amerikanischen Kulturwelt. Literaturbericht," in *Archivum für Kulturgeschichte*, XXXVII (1955), 381.

32 Jan Huizinga, *Herbst des Mittelalters. Studien über Lebens- und Geistesformen des 14. und 15. Jahrhunderts in Frankreich und in den Niederlanden* (3rd ed. Leipzig, 1930), pp. 132-133. Huizinga makes other notable observations: Wherever the purest form of the knightly ideal was promoted, asceticism was emphasized (p. 103); the noble warrior owned no property (p. 103); hero for love's sake (p. 104); Philippe de Mezières' Order "of the Passion" had four vows, the fourth being that of *summa perfectio* (p. 116); profession of vows at a festive meal, a secularizing counterpart to the profession of [religious] vows before Holy Communion — the eucharistic love feast! (pp. 127-128).

105

In this connection we should recall the African campaign of Emperor Charles V and his Viceroy in Sicily, Juan de Vega, to whom Ignatius presented his famous plan for the fleet.[33]

Huizinga continues: "The ideal of knighthood stood in the forefront of this thought [of freeing Jerusalem]; here it could, and necessarily did, have a particularly powerful effect. The religious content of the knightly ideal found here its object of greatest promise; and the freeing of Jerusalem could not be other than a holy, noble work for any knight. The small success of the struggle against the Turks can find some partial explanation precisely because the religio-chivalric ideal had such a strong influence on the evaluation of European policy in the East."[34]

Menendez Pelayo calls attention to the fact that the religious element is as clearly marked as the crusade element in the literature of knightly romance, in the style of Amadís de Gaula, Ignatius' favorite reading material during his worldly years.

We have already mentioned the "bulas de cruzada." As letters granting indulgences, they came directly into the hands of the faithful. Calixtus III, Julius II, Leo X, and Clement VII issued them especially in favor of the Spanish. Whoever wished to gain the indulgence was required to obtain and keep in his possession an authenticated copy of the bull (printed or hand-written) made out in his name. Anyone who, like Iñigo de Loyola, could read must certainly have made himself familiar with the content of the bull at some time or other. Ignatius mentions them once in the Rules for Correct Thinking in the Church Militant: " The sixth, to praise ... pilgrimages, indulgences, jubilees, *bullae cruciatae....*"[35]

Thus we may, in the first place, consider it as certain that at least the crusade idea was sufficiently alive in the West and South of Europe at the time of St. Ignatius[36] that we may rightly

---

33 " Ein Flottenplan des heiligen Ignatius von Loyola," in *Die katholischen Missionen*, XLIII (1914-1915), 49 53; Gisbert Beyerbaus, " Karl V und der Kreuzzugsplan des Ignatius von Loyola," in *Archivum für Kulturgeschichte*, XXXVI (1954), 9-17.

34 Huizinga, *Herbst*, p. 132.

35 *SpEx*, [353-370]: " Para el sentido verdadero que in la Iglesia militante debemos tener, se guarden las reglas siguientes "; rule 6 (no. 358), " alabar reliquios de sanctos ... alabando ... peregrinaciones, indulgencias, perdonanzas, cruzadas " (this last word signifies the bulls of crusade although the word itself can naturally also mean " crusades "). On the bulls of crusade, see Diendorfer in Kirchenlexikon, II (1883), 1469-1470; F. Heidingsfelder in Lexikon für Theologie und Kirche, VI (1934), 271-272.

36 See also Louis Brehier, " Croisades," in Dictionaire Apologétique, I (1925), 819-827. On page 825 he says: " A partir du XVIe siècle, le principe de la

expect that it influenced the intellectual attitude of the young knight. Furthermore, because of the intimate relationship between the crusade idea and crusade spirituality, we can assume that the essential elements of this spirituality were cultivated among the Spanish people — taking into account the modifications in them that we mentioned before. The élan that the discoverers and warriors of the age put into their undertakings cannot be explained by the drawing power of the ideology alone. Even more powerful influences were the above-mentioned vitality of the faith and the impulses of the intensive, if not very reflective, folk spirituality.[37]

Recall simply that, of the saint's brothers, one met his death in the *Conquista* and another on the crusade in Hungary — one more proof of the existence of the crusade spirit in the intimate family circle of Iñigo de Loyola.[38]

Before we turn to making an outline of the essential elements of crusade spirituality, reflections of which we hope to find in the spirituality of St. Ignatius, let us note once more that we are dealing with a merely supplemental approach to the understanding of the saint. We enter upon this path with great caution, recalling that the individual points call for substantial deepening and richer documentation. The tracing of Ignatian spiritual attitudes to elements in this group of sources will be tentative and not an assertion of fact. Finally, the full historical value of the many lines of influence successfully derived from the study of other groups of sources remains affirmed.

---

raison d'État, qui domine en Europe, rend tout projet de croisade chimérique . . . L'ardeur pour la croisade ne s'éteignit pas cependant: les "conquistadores," l'enfant don Enrique [Henry the Navigator], Cristoph Colomb, Albuquerque portaient la croix sur la poitrine et croyaient, en cherchant les nouvelles routes des Indes qui permettraient de prendre les Musulmans à revers, préparer la délivrance de la Terre Sainte." The house of Habsburg took care to keep the crusade spirit alive for the sake of defense against the Turks.

37 See also J. M. Granero in *Manresa*, XXVIII (1956), 32-33: "la fe era, por tanto, un clima colectivo más o menos confortable, que respiraba el pueblo en todas partes . . . una fe explosiva y hasta belicosa."

38 H. Böhmer, *Ignatius*, p. 16. On the death of Ignatius' brother in the war against the Turks (in Hungary), see *PolChron*, II, 267 — there is quoted a letter of Claude Jay from Vienna, dated April 21, 1551: "Cum de P. Ignatio loqueretur [Ferdinandus I], sibi notum esse ejus nobile et illustre genus significabat, et quidem dux Loyola, ejus frater, fere octo annos ante hoc tempus, cum contra turcas Regi inserviret, mortem obierat." Recently the opinion has been expressed that it could only have been a cousin, not the actual brother of the saint: I. de Olózaga, "Un hermano de S. Ignacio desconocida hasta ahora," in *RazFe*, CLIII (1956), 276.

II

Elements of Crusade Spirituality

Where will one have to look to come into contact with this form of Occidental spirituality ? Since the primary element from which it developed was the experience of the crusades themselves from the eleventh century on, the historians of the holy expeditions (*sanctissimae expeditiones*)[39] will be the first to have something to say about the religious attitude of the crusader as well as that of the crusader's homeland. Added to this is the preaching of the crusades by the Cistercians, Praemonstratensians, Dominicans, and Franciscans. This preaching could become effective only because it entered into the conceptual world of the common people. It also contributed to the development of the folk spirituality and to making it more conscious of itself. The papal bulls of crusade remained limited to the higher clerical circles; their testimony will therefore remain an indirect one insofar as they reveal the motivation of the Church authorities. Yet they had to become part of the common heritage of popular religious thought, especially since they offered lines of thought for the official crusade sermons. Furthermore, we will have to draw upon the poems and panegyrics praising successful crusaders. Finally, insights can be gained from the literary expression of the motivations for " vows and foundations, for penances and indulgences, at burials and the dedication of churches ";[40] for the pilgrimage to Jerusalem (*peregrinatio Hierosolymitana*) had its strongest influence in such matters.

Unfortunately nearly all of this is yet to be done. Even Wilhelm Maurer's indication of the influence of crusade spirituality on the spirituality of St. Elizabeth of Thuringia (or Hungary) can be considered primarily as merely a signpost showing us the road we should follow.[41]

Mention of St. Elizabeth leads us to an important distinction that we must make from the beginning. We make a distinction between

---

39 This expression is used frequently; for example, by Albertus Aquensis, in *PL*, CLXVI, 389. *Expeditio* became a technical term indicating the crusade. We will meet with it in St. Ignatius' Contemplation on the Kingdom of Christ.

40 Georg Schreiber, *Gemeinschaften*, p. 119; " Prämonstratensische Frömmigkeit," *Zeitschrift für katholische Theologie*, LXIV (1940), 189.

41 Wilhelm Maurer, " Zum Verständnis der heiligen Elisabeth von Thüringen," in *Zeitschrift für Kirchengeschichte*, LXV (1953-1954), 16-64; " Die heilige Elisabeth im Lichte der Frömmigkeit ihrer Zeit," in *Theologische Literaturzeitung*, LXXIX (1954), 401-410. See also Hans Wolter, " Die heilige Elisabeth von Thüringen — Quellen ihrer Frömmigkeit," in *Geist und Leben*, XXVIII (1955), 462-464.

the spirituality of the crusader himself and the spiritual attitude on the home front, which accompanied the crusade by prayer and penance. It is clear that we are here dealing with two very different things. We should not expect a complete and conclusive synthesis of these matters, especially since, as our goal is the understanding of the spirituality of St. Ignatius of Loyola, we will be inclined to pay most attention to those elements in the body of crusade thought that show a relationship in intent and intensity to the basic spiritual concepts of the founder of the Society of Jesus.

The Spirituality of the Crusader

Why did the medieval man, whether prince, knight or commoner, layman or cleric, decide to take up the crusade towards the south, north, or east ? Of course we are here passing over political, economic, and social motives as well as the mere desire for adventure. We are seeking to discover the religious motivations.

The crusader took the Cross and made his vow because he believed that God was calling him. He perceived the voice of God in the admonitions of the popes, the preachers, and of his bishop. The will of the divine Lord — and it was a question of recapturing His earthly home, of protecting His faithful, of extending His kingdom — was for the crusaders an inescapable duty. The call, " God wills it," was for centuries after the Council of Clermont (1095) the religious rallying cry of Christian military campaigns in all parts of the world (the *quattuor climata mundi*). In the fulfilment of the summoning will of God the crusader saw the justification for the immense sacrifice[42] he had to make to prepare for the journey and much more during the crusade itself.[43]

The crusade was for him a participation in the work of Christ. He thought of himself as drafted into the army of Christ,[44] placed under Christ's command.[45] The Kingdom of Christ was for him a

---

42 The long pilgrimage and the crusade cost money and more money (Schreiber, *Gemeinschaften*, p. 119). Duke Robert of Normandy mortgaged his whole duchy to his brother, King William the Red. " Only in the later Middle Ages does the familiar type of penniless pilgrim, who must beg or chooses to beg in voluntary poverty (like Queen Elisabeth Bona of Portugal, died 1336), appear to receive more emphasis" (ibid.).

43 It is always the " army of God " that goes on crusade; for example, in " epistola prima Stephani comitis Carnotensis ad Adelam uxorem suam," he says, "infinitum Dei exercitum ... repperimus" (Hagenmeyer, *Kreuzzugsbriefe*, p. 139).

44 " Cum omni electo Christi exercitu," in Stephen of Blois' second letter to Adele (Hagenmeyer, *Kreuzzugsbriefe*, p. 149).

45 " Christo praeeunte pugnavimus " (ibid., p. 150); Baudri of Bourgueil, *Historia Hierosolymitana*, in *PL*, CLXVI, 1068b: " Sub Jesu Christo duce nostro."

self-evident part of his faith.[46] The spirituality of the crusader was
in all its forms and at all times centered in Christ. His wish
was to fight for Christ, even to die for Christ. Christopher Columbus still begins his ship log "in the name of our Lord Jesus
Christ."[47]

At the end of the journey stood Christ and Holy Sion (*sancta
Sion*), the site of the life, death,[48] and glorification of Christ. The
road of the crusade was thus believed to be a road of the "following
of Christ." In Christ he saw the true leader (*Christo duce*) whom
one must follow. And in a yet deeper sense it was a following of
Christ, because the crusader considered the exertions, deprivations,
and sufferings of the journey into foreign lands — he wished to be
homeless with his homeless Lord[49] — and especially the constant
threat of death, to be a spiritual participation in the suffering and
death of Christ. Beyond that, victory — granted but seldom — was
experienced as a participation in the victory of Christ and the
glorification of Christ.

We find a witness to this attitude in a poem written on the
occasion of the occupation of Jerusalem by Emperor Frederick II (1229).
Even though it does not necessarily express the thought of the
emperor himself, it does reveal the crusader's attitude toward the
crusade.

> Rejoice, Jerusalem, to revere the name of the Lord...
> Since as noble king once Jesus, now Emperor Frederick,
> Both ready to suffer, are exalted in Thy splendor.
> Both brought offerings: the First Himself for the second,
> And for the First's honor, the second himself and his own...[50]

---

46 "Tali imperatori [i.e., Christo] militare debetis" (ibid., 1068c). In this we
hear the theme of the emperorship of Christ, which continues on down until
it enters into the *Vulgata Versio* of the *Spiritual Exercises*.

47 Höffner, *Christentum und Menschenwürde*, p. 117.

48 *Militia Christi*, the crusade, Baudri of Bourgueil, in *PL*, CLXVI, 1067d;
"Pulchrum sit vobis in illa civitate [Jerusalem] pro Christo mori," ibid., 1068b.

49 Albertus Aquensis, *Historia Hierosolymitana*, in *PL*, CLXVI, 389b: "et in
nomine Jesu exilia quaesierint"; ibid., 570d: "ad quid de terra et cogna-
tione vestra exiistis nisi ut animas vestras usque ad mortem pro nomine Jesu
daretis." All the chronicles of the crusades give evidence of this Christological
attitude in numberless texts.

50 "Jauchze, Jerusalem, den Namen des Herrn zu verehren...
Weil als hehrer König einst Jesus, jetzt Kaiser Friedrich,
Beiden zu dulden bereit, in Deinem Glanz erhöht sind.
Opfer brachten sie beide: der Erste sich selbst für den Zweiten
Und für des Ersten Ruhm der Zweite sich und das Seine..."
The author of the poem is Marquard von Ried; quoted from **Erast
Kantorowicz**, *Kaiser Friedrich der Zweite* (Berlin, 1936), p. 186.

Frederick himself spoke of his vow to go on crusade as a "holocaust."[51] Thus the crusade was seen as an oblation, and the "following of Christ" was taken seriously in all its consequences—one is tempted to say, even in its radical theological depths.

In reality this "holocaust" was accepted only too often and consummated in blood. In the consciousness of the crusader his anticipated death stood under the sign of "martyrdom."[52] This motif runs in undiminished force throughout the whole literature. One gave witness to Christ in the most absolute form that there was.[53] Even if there were no military or political success, the basic religious goal was achieved.

In the Christian consciousness, the Apostles always stand next to the martyrs: all, except John, had witnessed in their own blood to the truth of their teaching and to the divinity of their Master. It was not an unrelated phenomenon that, at the time of the most lively crusading activity, the spirituality of broad masses of the populace was supported by the thought of the "apostolic life" as it was proclaimed and lived by the wandering preachers and the reformers of religious orders in the twelfth century. Even in the religion of the crusaders there is an element of this "apostolic life,"[54] although they prepared themselves to preach not so much with the sword of the word as — in accordance with the spirit of the age — with the naked sword made of iron. The Augustinian "compel them to enter" (*compelle intrare*) was still not forgotten.

---

51 "Personam et posse nostrum non in sacrificium, sed in holocaustum humiliter obtulimus domino puro et sincero animo"; quoted from Kantorowicz, *Friedrich II*, p. 71. The complete text is printed in *Monumenta Germaniae Historica: Constitutiones*, II, 150.

52 See the letter of Archbishop Manasses of Theims to Bishop Lambert of Arras (1099) concerning the death of the papal legate while on crusade: "Orate pro Podiense episcopo ... qui tam glorioso martyrio coronati in pace defuncti sunt" (Hagenmeyer, *Kreuzzugsbriefe*, p. 176); *Chanson de Roland*, 11. 1126-1138 — Archbishop Turpin addresses the army: On to battle ... if you die, you will be holy martyrs and have your place in the highest part of Paradise (see Erdmann, *Kreuzzugsgedanke*, p. 264, n. 66; p. 265, n. 70). Other examples can be found in Hagenmeyer, *Kreuzzugsbriefe*, pp. 153, 297, 154; Lisiard of Tours, *Historia Hierosolymitana*, in *PL*, CLXXIV, 1953.

53 The crusader witnesses to the divinity of Christ simply by the fact that he is fighting. This idea is expressed by St. Bernard in letter no. 458, in *PL*, CLXXXII, 653; see "Bernard et la seconde Croisade," in *Bernard de Clairvaux* (Paris: Commission d'Histoire de l'Ordre de Cîteaux, 1953), pp. 379-409 — especially "La théorie de la croisade," pp. 395-400. Another highly informative book is: Joseph Calmette and Henri David, *Saint Bernard* (Paris, 1953), especially "Le lancement de la seconde croisade," pp. 227-258.

54 This is felt in one way because the crusaders leave home, family, and possessions; but also (see n. 52 above) because they bear witness to Christ.

This union of sword and gospel is best recognized in the Portuguese and Spanish *Conquista* during the lifetime of St. Ignatius himself. The heathen world was considered a battle front (*defensio fidei*) and a mission (*propagatio fidei*).

Christ therefore stood at the center of crusade spirituality. The military orders were wholly dedicated to the "service of Christ." It was for His sake that the brethren endured together their struggles and sufferings. These orders had their origin in the hospitals, the shelters for pilgrims and the sick, and for the crusaders themselves. The ideology of the hospital and of service in it also had a Christological stamp to it.[55]

The notion that Christ was the lord and leader of the crusaders had the result that the idea of the "Kingdom of Christ" also became widespread. For the Lord was King. The crusaders took the field for the defense of Christ's homeland (at the same time a symbol of the Kingdom of God). It was precisely because of this symbolism of the *terra sancta*, the Holy Land, as a type of the *universa terra*, the whole world, that the Reconquest of Spain for the Christian Faith (and for the Spanish authority, naturally) and the conquest of the New World for Christianity were seen as equivalent to the conquest of Palestine. The *terra sancta* and the whole earth belong together in the same way that mid-point and cincumference constitute one circle. In this connection it is interesting to observe that the Portuguese ventures in Africa during the fifteenth century were also motivated by the thought that in this way they could prepare and make possible the conquest of the Holy Land.[56] That the crusaders were following the path through Africa from the time of the Fifth Crusade on is witnessed to by Louis IX and, in the sixteenth century, by the African campaigns of Charles V, with which the above-mentioned "fleet plan" of St. Ignatius was connected.[57]

---

55 Schreiber, *Gemeinschaften*, pp. 28-35 (on the hospital as an appendage of the monastery). Motivation was primarily provided by the basic concept that service in the hospital is service of Christ (ibid., p. 29). Other concepts were that service to the sick is a kind of penance (p. 30), service of the sick is an act of love (p. 31), the sick are the masters (pp. 32-33). On the religious military orders as hospital orders, see p. 40: "Those who fought against Saladin and the front-lines of the Saracens wished at the same time to nurse those on their sickbed."

56 See Brehier, "Croisades," Dictionaire Apologétique, I (1925), 825.

57 Even though the political situation did not allow it to be carried out in 1552; see Huonder, *Ignatius von Loyola*, p. 367; and Beyerhaus, *Karl V*, pp. 16-17: "What is lacking to the plan in the Platonic sense is simply the *kairos*, the proper historical moment."

A fundamental principle of the kingdom of Christ is the law of dynamic expansion. Just as the medieval emperor felt that he was the bearer of a missionary vocation — quite clearly accented in the case of Frederick II, though in his case with a certain reserve toward the pope and so a little overdone[58] — in the same way the crusader saw himself obligated to the service of the spread of the faith (*propagatio fidei*). This was especially true of the knights of the Teutonic Order in the North-East, of the French form of crusade spirituality, and of the Iberian Peninsula. However, since the offensive in the Mediterranean area changed to a defense rather early, the impetus toward apostolic preaching — so passionately desired by Francis of Assisi — never became very strong there. In place of the *propagatio fidei*, the *defensio fidei* came to dominate the spiritual awareness of the crusader. Yet we must strongly emphasize that both are basic constituents of crusade spirituality.[59]

The crusader's ethos of struggle also belongs here. It showed itself to be completely religious in spirit and was encouraged by remembrance of the wars of the Old Testament. The ancient Christian concept of the *militia Christi* (army of Christ) took on an amazing reality. We cannot pursue its history here.[60] Let it simply be noted that the reform spirituality of the twelfth century, which stands in such conjunction with crusade spirituality, also put stronger emphasis on the Benedictine tradition of the *militia Christi* than had been done formerly. But for the crusader spiritual and secular warfare become one, as do interior and exterior achievements in the fight. Their mutual interdependence was recognized, the necessary relationship of one to the other. Inner spiritual motivation is indispensable. Only that man does full justice to the crusader's religious task who holds his own in the soul's struggle for purity of faith and freedom from moral fault. Recall the reception of the sacraments before battle,[61] before the decisive assault on the beleaguered city. Again and again it was stressed that God gives victory only to those who

---

58 This is the thesis of the book of Kantorowicz, *Friedrich II*.

59 The problems involved in the concept of religious war cannot be discussed here. See Erdmann, *Kreuzzugsgedanke*, pp. 1-29, 86-106, 212-249; Höffner, " Der Krieg gegen die Ungläubigen," in *Christentum und Menschenwürde*, pp. 52-59.

60 See M. Bernards, *Speculum Virginum. Geistigkeit und Seelenleben der Frau im Hochmittelalter* (Köln-Graz, 1955), pp. 102-106, along with the references there given; Erdmann, *Kreuzzugsgedanke*, in the index under *militia Christi*.

61 Recall the confession of St. Ignatius before the battle at Pamplona: "Ubi dies advenit qua pugna exspectabatur futura, uni nobilium, cum quo saepe armis contenderat, confessionem criminum fecit, ac ille vicissim ipsi " *Auto-biog*, 1).

are clean of heart. The explanation for lack of success was always the sinfulness of the whole army as well as that of the leaders. They said that God had abandoned them because their sins had demanded it (*exigentibus peccatis*).

Because of this, the crusade was thought of primarily as a *penance.* Even Johannes Haller admits, " The strongest motivation — we may assume this without hesitation — was the religious; and the pope offered the highest, most valued reward: the certain prospect of forgiveness of sin and of eternal life."[62] To be sure, Haller, a Protestant, here confuses the forgiveness of sin and the remission of punishment due to sin. The former was linked to the sacrament; the other (the promised indulgence), however, was basically merely an absolution of the canonical penalties incurred during the armed pilgrimage. Penance was to be performed for sins, only the form of the penance was changed. Now it was to be the preparations for war, the labors of the journey, the expectation of death.[63] The will to perform such penance was certainly nourished by a readiness to do penance in the gospel sense; but it was heightened by the consciousness that this private penance, because of the participation in the crusade, assumed a more sublime significance and also a public and vicarious character. Along with the satisfaction for personal guilt, the crusade resulted in bringing the concerns of Christendom more forcibly into the awareness of everyone. This was in accord with the common feeling of the Middle Ages. The candid reports of what went on during the crusades made men quite aware of what was in store for them, and so it was no blind enthusiasm that urged them into the holy war. For the rest, let us remember the close interrelationship between pilgrimage and penance.[64] The crusade was always considered to be also a pilgrimage in armor.

The idea just mentioned, that the crusader fought, suffered, and died vicariously, became a significant element of crusade spirituality.

---

62 Johannes Haller, *Das Papsttum, Idee und Wirklichkeit* (3 vols. Stuttgart, 1934-1945), II, Pt. 1, 439.

63 Lisiard of Tours, *Historia Hierosolymitana*, in *PL*, CLXXIV, 1600: " quot et quantas labores, timores, angores sustinuerint pro Christo . . . nam pro Christo laborare tanto gloriosius, quanto beatius." The language reminds one of the choice of words in the Contemplation on the Kingdom. Pain and labor have the same meaning when considered as forms of penance.

64 Yet pilgrimage and penance are not identical. While the idea of pilgrimage had its origin in " devotion," which urged one to seek physical proximity to the saint, thus not necessarily including the thought of penance, the idea of penance was usually in the foreground in the thought of those who went on the armed pilgrimage. It is one of the chief elements of crusader spirituality.

The obligation of the crusade was incumbent upon all Christians, but not everyone could personally fulfil it with sword in hand. Thus the crusader represented in the field those who had to stay at home or wanted to. The religious concept of the "communion of saints" here became a living reality.

Each man recognized his obligation to a holy service: of God, of Christ, of the Church, of his neighbor. This attitude also accorded with the requirements of the Gospel. Yet, in an age with a feudal social order, "service" took a distinct form. In addition to its basic religious meaning, it received a public, socially binding character. In the feudal relationship of vassalage,[65] which was based on the mutual fidelity of lord and vassal, a mutual service was included, the service of help that the lord had to give in case the vassal was threatened, the service of consultation, and then the actual service owed his lord by the vassal. The crusader viewed his relationship to Christ according to this pattern. He considered the crusade to be a feudally required service to which he was called by the vicar of Christ, his great feudal lord on earth, the pope. Here there comes once more into our field of view the service in the hospitals as a service of the knight of the Cross. It is always Christ whom one serves, Christ in the pope, Christ in the sick, Christ in the pilgrim, Christ in one's brother in arms.[66]

One element of the complex of motives we have just mentioned must still be given special emphasis. From the time of Gregory VII, and especially from the time of Urban II, the crusade was a concern of the papacy. From this time on the fate of the papacy was linked to that of the crusades. Their success accompanied it to its high point, and their ultimate failure introduced its decline.[67] The pope had taken the historical initiative; the crusade was considered to be "his war."[68] From this time on further planning was his responsibility. He assumed the organization, financing, propagandizing, and publicity. The lands and possessions of all crusaders were under his protection as long as they were on their pilgrimage. He had to see to it that those returning home could take possession of their

---

65 See I. Zeiger, "Gefolgschaft des Herrn. Ein rechtsgeschichtlicher Beitrag zu den Exerzitien des heiligen Ignatius," *ZAM*, XVII (1942), 1-16.
66 See n. 55 above.
67 Haller, *Papsttum*, II, Pt. 1, 426.
68 "Bellum, quod tuum proprium est," in a letter of September 11, 1098, rom Bohemund, Raymond, Godfrey, and Robert of Normandy to Urban II (Hagenmeyer, *Kreuzzugsbriefe*, p. 164); "tu inceptor sancti itineris" (ibid., p. 165). This conception remained always present, and consciously so.

rights without loss, that their property should suffer no damage during their absence.

The pope became, in consequence of this, a central figure in the consciousness of crusading Christendom. Criticism of Rome was thus unusually harsh right at the time of the crusades, and even more so after them. This attack issued from the camp of the saints[69] as well as from the camp of the papacy's political enemies. It was expressed with amazing freedom in letters and songs, in chronicles and sermons. Still this criticism could not kill the faith in the papal mission that manifested itself again and again in acceptance of participation in the crusade. In the fabric of crusade spirituality there must have been a thread of deeply felt devotion to Peter (similar to but also different from that found among the early Carolingians). It was directed beyond the imperfect successor of Peter who happened to be living at the time toward the saint himself, the first vassal of Christ to represent his Lord visibly on earth.

The pope had raised the banner of the Cross.[70] The princes, knights, and common people of the West took the field under this banner. Therefore devotion to the Cross, to the relics of the Cross, and to the tools of the Passion (lance, crown of thorns, nails) is a part of the sprituality whose outline we are trying to draw. Many individual passages of the literature show us that this devotion found the most tender and the most violent of forms. Let us merely recall the outbreak of enthusiasm that the discovery of the holy lance (obviously not genuine) gave rise to in beleagured Antioch. This devotion, which resulted in the intensification of the cult of relics, belongs to the religiously significant phenomena of the age of the crusades.

It should not be overlooked that poverty, as a symbol of the Cross, played a role in the crusader's spirituality. Entire duchies were mortgaged to allow their lords to go on crusade. A certain disregard for money belonged to the knightly ideal of the Middle

---

69 For example, from St. Bernard; see Calmette, *Saint Bernard*, pp. 100-110.

70 Thus Gianbattista Gargha of Siena, Knight of the Holy Sepulchre (*eques Hierosolymitanus*), in a speech at the Fifth Lateran Council, could still say to Leo X: " Huic Christi militiae a summo Deo invictus vexillifer praefectus fuisti " (Harduin, *Acta Conciliorum*, VIII, 1729); " tibi ... totius orbis Christiani principes parere affectant " (ibid., 1728). This reminds one of the Contemplation on the Kingdom: " un rey humano, eligido de mano de Dios ... a quien hazen reverencia y obedescen todos los principes ... christianos " (*SpEx*, [92]). The pope-emperor concept also finds expression: " Expergiscimini ... christiani principes et labenti Ecclesiae auxilium afferte et sub Leone felicissimo pastore invictoque duce de bello Turcis inferendo in medium consulite " (Harduin, VIII, 1731).

Ages right up to its final gasp during the time of St. Ignatius. Of course this can also be explained on the basis of other factors. But the poverty proper to the crusader was readily linked with the poverty of Christ. It allowed him to endure the renunciation of the security of his home. If one wanted to ignore this aspect of the matter completely, it would mean a devaluation of the statements of the sources into pious monastic or clerical reflections. To assume the poverty of the Cross and to give a religious assent to it is intrinsic to the very idea of the crusade. The concepts of the " following of Christ " and of penance also enter in here.

Let us close this section by mentioning a final, all-inclusive trait of crusade spirituality. In accordance with the knightly character of the armed pilgrimage, the motive of honor, of the " glory of God," had to have a powerful influence. The " glory of God," affronted by the incursion of the heathen into the holy places, must be redressed. This was the time of the First Crusade, echoing throughout all the accounts and deeply imprinted in the thought of the crusaders. Contained in this is one of the basic themes of Christian spiritual tradition. Yet here it has been transferred from the realm of the spiritual and interior into that of the militant and the externally visible — we might say into that of the concerns and tasks of the laity.[71] Out of the self-contained world of clerical and monastic endeavors there is formed the broad expanse of lay spirituality, in the middle of which stand the claims of the " glory of Christ " to be defended and extended.[72] One should read Friedrich Heer's discussion of the " honor of God," which was a great and powerful idea to the men of the twelfth century: the " honor of God " as the " king's honor," as the " honor of his name."[73] Here

71 " Plus quam D nostrorum peditum ad laudem Dei perdidimus," letter of Stephen of Blois to his wife Adele (Hagenmeyer, *Kreuzzugsbriefe*, p. 151).
72 Lisiard of Tours, *PL*, CLXXIV, 1610 and 1612: " Glorificatus ita Christus in Antiochenis, quam mirabiliter et in Hierosolvmitis glorificari dignatus sit."
73 Friedrich Heer, *Aufgang Europas. Eine Studie zu den Zusammenhängen zwischen politischer Religiosität, Frömmigkeitsstil und dem Werden Europas im 12. Jahrhundert* (Wien-Zürich, 1949), pp. 143-150 (under *honor Dei*). Heer then adds in his volume of commentary, referring to page 143, a comment worthy of some thought in regard to the introduction of the feast of the " name of Jesus " by Innocent XIII at the request of the Emperor Charles VI (1721): the name of Jesus was seen as a symbol of power, an expression of the *honor Dei*. Then he says: " The Baroque sought a magnificent restitution of the religio-political " God-World unity " of the early Middle Ages." Heer then says on page 163 that the concept of crusade, as expressed in the great public declarations, unites the religio-political concept of war with the secular concept; Christ the King is considered now to be the leader of both the religious and the secular army.

117

it becomes quite clear on what a broad basis crusade spirituality developed. We may stress this motif all the more forcefully since we will meet it again in Ignatius in such a well-defined form.

The Spirituality of the Home Front

It would be completely one-sided, and one would suppress something quite essential, if he wished to seek and find crusade spirituality only among the crusaders themselves. For it was the possession of whole generations and of whole epochs. The crusaders began their march from the midst of a world that had its own distinctive religious character; and on their return they shared their experiences and the beliefs that had guided their journey with their community, clan, or family, with their friends and vassals. Departure and homecoming were surrounded by customs and liturgy.[74]

It is therefore understandable that those remaining at home felt that they too were interiorly taking part in the " holy expedition." Their financial support was expected; but with the same frankness they were asked for their prayers of intercession, the support of their fasting, their spiritual participation in the hardships of the journey by their freely undertaken works of penance at home. The behavior of St. Elizabeth before and during her husband's crusade journey is also a model case from which we can gather the crusade spirituality of the home front.[75]

The spiritual character of taking part in the crusade is something that is presupposed and appealed to in the letters of popes, prelates, and crusaders to the people of Christendom. An example is an epistle sent from Antioch by Bohemund, Raymond of St. Gilles, Godfrey, and Hugo the Great (1098): " Therefore we beg you all earnestly that you fast, give alms, and piously and zealously attend holy Mass, ... that you devoutly support us with many prayers and alms."[76] In an appeal addressed to all the faithful by the clergy and people of Lucca: " You also (who remain at home) should

---

74 Schreiber, *Gemeinschaften*, pp. 132, 340-341; " Prämonstratensische Frömmigkeit," *Zeitschrift für katholische Theologie*, LXIV (1940), 190: " Thus the energies of the crusade idea long left their shining mark on pious statements of this sort. During the Baroque it actually sprang into new life." Ibid., 195: " One comes away from the newly revived research into pilgrimages and the places of pilgrimage with the strong awareness that the crusade fronts in Palestine and in Spain and Portugal were an important influence on the fact that new worlds of emotion sprang up in which the *amor spiritualis*, the life of religious love, developed and became more profound."
75 See fn. 41 above.
76 Hagenmeyer, *Kreuzzugsbriefe*, p. 155.

piously and diligently take part in the singing of psalms, the celebration of the vigils, and the prayers in order that those whose road leads them through barbarian lands may be protected by the merits of those interceding for them as well as by the weapons of war and so may live in tranquillity and security."[77]

Prayer and good works were thus considered to be spiritual weapons which should be put to the service of the same goal for which the crusader himself was striving. The "merits" of those at home were united to the labors of those fighting abroad in order to secure their success. Unfortunately we have too little literary testimony as to what echo this call to spiritual participation in the crusade found in the souls of those praying at home.[78]

Only one group at home constitutes an exception to this remark about the literature, the monks. The monks' crusade is the spiritualized counterpart of the pilgrimage in arms but should be viewed and evaluated as in complete spiritual unity with it.

The investigation of the influence of crusade spirituality on the development of monastic spirituality would be an intriguing field for research. In the last part of our discussion we will attempt to do this at least for St. Ignatius. At present it will suffice to call attention to the figure of St. Bernard and his function as a preacher of the crusade. Within the walls of his abbey he kept urging his monks to greater intensity, and especially to interest in the crusade. The duty of monks leads them to the heavenly Jerusalem, not to the Jerusalem on earth; they journey there not with their feet but with their hearts.[79] We should also mention the mendicant orders of the thirteenth century, especially the Order of Preachers, which had its origin in the climate of the crusade against the Albigensians, and the Order of Friars Minor, which the figure and spirituality of St. Francis familiarized with the crusade experience. Although the literary remains may not always provide us much on the point, we may still be certain that the crusade idea and the crusade reality had decisive influence on the lay spirituality of the later Middle Ages and that this spirituality, in turn, through its own vigor

77 Ibid., p. 167. The appeal to those at home to provide financial support for those returning from the crusade also belongs here (p. 174). Financial help and new contingents are awaited from the homeland (p. 175).
78 Schreiber, "Prämonstratensische Frömmigkeit," *Zeitschrift für katholische Theologie*, LXIV (1940), p. 188.
79 Epistle 299. See also letter 459, to G. de Stopho, *PL*, CLXXXII, 654; letter 64, to Alexander, bishop of Lincoln, ibid., 169; letter 57, to Wileneus, bishop of Langres, ibid., 166.

reawakened, time and again, the enthusiasm for a crusade either offensive or defensive in character.

III

Ignatian Spirituality and Crusade Spirituality

In our brief outline we could not mention all the themes present in western crusade spirituality. Much less could we give a thorough analysis of all of them or set forth their historical development. We have had to satisfy ourselves with certain basic characteristics, and we can expect that other variations and developments in them existed at various times and places.

We now approach the question whether Ignatius of Loyola was affected by this crusade spirituality during his youth and early manhood, at the time of his conversion, during his years as pilgrim and student, and after he had settled down in his final dwelling place at Rome. We must ask whether he was indebted to it in his prayer, his penance, his apostolic zeal, and whether it can throw light on some of the peculiarities in his way of life and in the product of his labors, the new order.

One possible way to answer all these questions — not the only way — is by an analysis of those texts that stem from Ignatius himself. We mean the *Acta Patris Ignatii*, the *Spiritual Exercises*, the *Formula Instituti* — in its double form as it was presented to Pope Paul III (1540) and Pope Julius III (1550) — the *Constitutions*, and his letters. To fill out the picture, we must also consider the statements and writings of his first companions.[80] Again, we can only give a preliminary outline of matters that deserve a more exact, detailed, and complete examination.

What we must do now is to endeavor to discover whether the verbal expression, or at least the ideas, of the themes we determined

---

80 Yet one must be very cautious in his interpretation. For example, when Jerónimo Nadal expresses the opinion that the ideas, *militare sub crucis vexillo*, came to Ignatius through the meditations on the heavenly King (*FN*, I, 313), one must say that he introduced it into those meditations. Mention is made of what Ignatius read at Loyola (the Cistercian Vagad's introduction to the *Flos Sanctorum*) by Leturia in " Génesis de los Ejercicios de San Ignacio y su influjo en la fundación de la Compañía de Jesús," *AHSJ*, X (1941), 20. We must go yet farther and say that this idea was current in popular crusade spirituality and there was no need of any literary illumination, much less one streaming from above, for a man of the time to be familiar with it. Nadal's pious interpretations are analysed by José Calveras, " La ilustración del Cardoner y el Instituto de la Compañía de Jesús según el P. Nadal," *AHSJ*, XXV (1956), 27-54, especially p. 43.

(in the second part of this artical) to be essential to crusade spirituality are also found in the works of St. Ignatius which we have just mentioned. We must exercise great caution in this. For most of the thoughts expressed in these documents are part of the common treasure of Christian thought, ideas that have always been current in the spiritual tradition of the Church in the West. Only the frequent recurrence of specific patterns of thought and their emphatic central position in the whole of Ignatian spirituality could make it clear that the influence of specifically crusade spirituality was at work.

These things do not lie on the surface. First of all, it is quite inadequate to try to understand Ignatius according to the model of the knight-errant found in the romances about Amadís de Gaula. One must be acquainted not merely with the ideals of the troubadours; but he must also look at that image of the Christian knight who, in the Spain and Portugal of the fourteenth and fifteenth centuries, still directed his efforts to undertakings higher than those of his own individual interests. Here in the southwest corner of Europe the common Christian spirit was still alive, social ties were still strong, the traditions of the people and of individual families were still vigorous.[81] Here the courtly *amor*, the "service of love," long hardened into an empty formula elsewhere, was still practised as an honestly lived-out reality. In this society lay the origins of the basic attitude of Ignatian spirituality that Joseph de Guibert called a *servitium per amorem*, a service through love.[82]

Above crusade and crusade spirituality there stand, controlling everything, the "will of God." From this, according to the common view, there came the call to the armed pilgrimage to Jerusalem. The dispositions of the Divine Majesty were seen and recognized in all phases of the campaign, in success and in failure.

In like manner, this reverence toward the Divine Majesty penetrates the spirituality of Ignatius. His will is law and His call is decisive: "if Your most holy Majesty should wish to choose and accept me for such a state of life."[83] In the *Formula Instituti* he says: *Deo volente, domino inspirante, a Deo propositum finem, spiritu sancto afflati* (as God wills, inspired by the Lord, the end proposed by God, inspired by the Holy Spirit). In such phrases there is

---

81 This is forcefully worked out by J. Granero, "la Conversion," in *Manresa*, XXVIII (1956), 31-56.
82 *DeGuiJes*, pp. 176-181.
83 Contemplation on the Kingdom (*SpEx*, [98]): "queriéndome vuestra sanctissima majestad elegir y recibir en tal vida y estado."

121

revealed a consciousness of the initiative of God, of the binding call that, once accepted, awakens an enthusiasm to fulfil it.

In all the prudent formulations of later years, in a readiness to serve that seems almost over-restricted by limiting conditions, the fact still shines through that the call of God is the one thing that counts. It is not of primary importance who makes this call heard, whether it be the pope, the bishop, the superior, or whether it is heard in the petitions of temporal rulers, this call demands a response and readiness to answer it: "... in order that his divine Majesty may dispose of the person and of all he possesses according to his most holy will."[84] This recalls the crusader who was ready to offer himself and, in many (probably most) cases, all he owned in order to be equal to the conviction that " God wills it."[85]

The Christocentricity of Ignatian spirituality is unquestioned. That Christ is King and Lord is the revelation that determines Iñigo's conversion.[86] This clearly reflects the fundamental spiritual attitude of the crusader. Ignatius' work is participation in the work of Christ (*mecum laborare, particeps mecum fiat victoriae, debet mecum laborare*[87]). The glory of the crusader was to be part of the army of Jesus Christ; Ignatius views things the same way. For example, he has the exercitant ask "to be accepted under His [Christ's] banner "; or again, he has the exercitant " consider the speech that Christ our Lord addresses to all His servants and friends whom He sends on such an expedition."[88]

Christ is the leader of the crusade (*Christo duce*). Ignatius calls Him the supreme and true leader (*summus et verus dux*).[89] The Vulgate version of the *Exercises* here[90] uses the expression *imperator Christus* — a theme that was certainly much used during the Middle Ages but is not primary in connection with crusade

---

84 Annotation 5 (*SpEx*, [5]): " para que su divina majestad así de su persona como de todo lo que tiene [as was the case with the crusader] se sirva conforme a su sanctissima voluntad."

85 See J. Ayerra, " San Ignacio y la voluntad de Dios," *Manresa*, XXVIII (1956), 71-90.

86 See J. Rimbaldi, " Temas cristologicas en el pensamiento ignaciano," *Manresa*, XXVIII (1956), 105-120, especially p. 105.

87 Contemplation on the Kingdom (*SpEx*, [93]): " trabajar ... vigilar ... después tenga parte conmigo en la victoria "; compare the " laborare pro Christo, vigilare, angores sustinere " of Lisiard of Tours, *PL*, CLXXIV, 1600.

88 The Two Standards (*SpEx*, [147]): " para que yo sea recibido debaxo de su bandera; " and (*SpEx*, [146]): " que a tal jornada embia."

89 Ibid., [143]: " el summo y verdadero capitan." The Versio Prima has for this: " summus et verus dux."

90 Ibid.

spirituality. For it the pope comes next after Christ. When Frederick II stressed the emperor's obligation to the crusade, he did it in conscious opposition to the primary right of the popes of Rome.

The following of Christ was therefore the theme of the pious crusader, not only literally on the road to Jerusalem, but also — as we saw — spiritually on the road of inner imitation. Now we know from the *Exercises* that the idea of the "following of Christ" dominates the spiritual life of Ignatius: "I desire ... to imitate You in bearing all injustice and scorn and poverty."[91] Here he makes mention of the typical difficulties and experiences of the crusade; for the crusaders had to, and wanted to, accept injustice (*injuria*) and scorn (*vituperia*) from the unbelievers in remembrance of the similar sufferings of the Lord. This "injustice" and "scorn" are often mentioned in the chronicles of the crusades. Ignatius expresses this in such phrases as: "which help us more closely to follow our Lord and to imitate him,"[92] "to beg for the grace of imitating him,"[93] "in order thereby to imitate him,"[94] "to become actually more like him."[95]

"Imitation" is at the same time participation. This realization of crusade spirituality has been deepened by Ignatius and elevated to be the theological nucleus of his asceticism.

It may be a merely superficial parallel; but we can, in this connection, compare the statement in the crusade vow of Frederick II, where he calls it a "holocaust," with the same expression that is found again in the vow formula of the scholastics: "that You deign to accept this holocaust in an odor of sweetness."[96]

The crusade was considered and conducted as an oblation. Something very similar is in the life of Ignatius and his companions. Just as crusade spirituality valued the ultimate sacrifice, death on the crusade, as a martyrdom; so the young Society of Jesus and

---

91 Kingdom (*SpEx*, [98]): "desidero ... imitari te in ferendis omnibus injuriis et in omni vituperio et omni paupertate."

92 *SpEx*, [109]): "quae juvent ad magis sequendum et imitandum Dominum nostrum."

93 Two Standards (*SpEx*, [139]): "rogare ... gratiam ad illum imitandum."

94 Ibid., [147]): "ad magis in illis eum imitandum."

95 The Three Degrees of Humility (*SpEx*, [165]): "utque ei magis actu similis fiam;" see n. 65 above and the text with which it goes.— The concept of the "imitation of Christ" was naturally not drawn first from the *Gersoncito* he read at Manresa. The wish to follow in the footsteps of the saints had already awakened in Iñigo de Loyola when at home, and it was alive in the people through crusade spirituality.

96 *Thesaurus Spiritualis Societatis Jesu* (Rome: Typis Polyglottis Vaticanis, 1948), k. 485.

its founder accepted death as the natural consequences of their dedication . . . indeed they greeted it.[97]

We saw above that from its beginnings, but especially after the influx of Franciscan thought, the element of preaching the Gospel — as it developed out of the religious movement of the twelfth century, the summons to the "apostolic life" — was fitted into crusade spirituality not as an external accretion, but as an organic part. We have here another obvious link with Ignatius. The concern for his own personal salvation soon broadened out into a concern for others, a concern that was to become the true end of his order. Indeed it "was founded especially that it might bend its efforts to the help of souls . . . and the spreading of the faith."[98] Is it not significant that Ignatius began his apostolate in Jerusalem ?

An instruction of Ignatius to Peter Canisius of August 13, 1554,[99] proves that this concern for the salvation of the faithful was in no way limited to those spiritual means listed in the *Formula Instituti* but that he also, in the spirit of the medieval crusader, wishes the resources of external power to be applied. In it Ignatius enumerates the points that Canisius, according to the measure of his own prudence, might lay before Ferdinand I: "Without doubt it would be the most obvious and best human remedy if His Royal Majesty would not only confess himself a Catholic, as he does continuously, but proclaim himself a resolute enemy of heresies and declare war on all heretical errors, not only in private but also publicly." Since later in the letter the death penalty is recommended for heretics (to give an example), this "war" cannot be understood as a merely intellectual conflict.

Crusades and wars against the Turks were judged to be just wars. That is the attitude of the whole of the Christian Middle Ages. A similar judgment was made regarding wars against heretics. Ignatius was in this point a completely medieval man.[100]

---

97 Leturia, "Genesis," *AHSJ*, X (1941), p. 38.

98 The Formula of the Institute, *Regimini militantis Ecclesiae* (1540), [3], in ConsMHSJ, I, 26. See R. de Ravinel, "L'appel du Christ," *RAM*, XXIX (1953), 327-336: De Ravinel sees an *appel a la vie apostolique* as early as the Contemplation on the Kingdom (p. 327), not merely the *agere contra* as an expression of the efforts made toward one's personal perfection. The Preludes, he says, set the tone with their *rôle evocateur* — against Monier-Vinard and Valensin (p. 329, n. 8).

99 Braunsberger, *B.P. Canisii epistulae*, I, 448-449.

100 The episode with the Saracen who said that he could not believe in the Mother of God's virginity *a partu* and Ignatius' wish: "darle de puñaladas por lo que habia dicho," show clearly how closely the spread of the faith and physical force still belonged together in the mind of Ignatius (*Autobiog*, 15).

If it is just, then even war works toward the glory of God.[101]

Along with the affirmation of the Lord as leader of the march, the belief in His kingship and thus in His kingdom is an essential part of the Christ-concept of crusade spirituality. Here we encounter themes that are too well known from the *Exercises*, the *Constitutions*, and the saint's life to need to be presented once more in detail. It need only be mentioned how the concepts of the kingdom and of the " propagation of the faith " complement each other. Research attributes the first appearance of the tendency toward the apostolic life to the Contemplation on the Call of the King rather than to the later Meditation on the Two Standards.[102] In the saint's spirituality kingdom and propagation of the faith belong together.[103]

The militant ardor of this " propagation " was expressed in the terminology of the " army of Christ." It is also found in the meditations on the Call of Christ and on the Two Standards. Ignatius had these two concepts in mind " ever since his first arrival at Montserrat; "[104] that is, while he still stood completely under the spell of the popular crusade piety of his homeland and of his youth. It is therefore not impossible that we have here a visible point of interconnection between the spirituality of St. Ignatius and the crusade spirituality of his times.

Therefore the following affirmation of Leturia is insufficient: " Apart from this influence of an external kind [naturally together with that from the New Testament and his Book of Hours as well as the other books he read during his illness], all the basic influences came from unusual inner phenomena — from the illuminating light."[105] This fails to give due consideration to the traditions of popular piety. Yet we must note that this popular tradition was also present

---

101 See Ignatius' letter to the army of the Viceroy Juan de Vega (on the expedition to Africa), *EppIgn*, III, 112-113. Here we meet a perfect example of crusade terminology: " Vobis, qui in bello pro Christi gloria ac fidei sancta exaltatione gerendo cum infidelibus distinemini, apererit ejus Sanctitas [Julius III] hilari animo, de benignitate apostolica omnibus vobis (qui tamen contriti et confessi essetis) eam gratiam concessit, ut tanto alacrius, animosius, et fortius cum inimicis sanctae crucis dimicetis, quanto effusiorem Dei altissimi et sponsae ejus Ecclesiae liberalitatem et foeliciorem belli eventum (sive viventibus victoria sive alicui morienti beatitudo obtingat, impetrata omnium peccatorum remissione) cernetis." See *PolChron*, II, 47-52. Military chaplaincy was one of the works often exercised by Ignatius' first companions.
102 See De Ravinel, *RAM*, XXIX (1953), 329, n. 8.
103 See n. 98 above.
104 Leturia, " Genesis," *AHSJ*, X (1941), 22.
105 Ibid., 25.

in the books read during his sickness; in the prologue to the *Flos Sanctorum* by the Cistercian, Gauberto Maria Vagad, and in the courtly style of the Franciscan Fray Ambrosio de Montesinos with which he introduces the *Life of Christ* by the Carthusian Ludolph of Saxony.[106] In this last, sanctity is proclaimed a " deed of heroic following of the eternal Prince, Jesus Christ, the King and Lord of virtues; " and the saints are seen as knightly followers (*caballeros imitadores*).

That Ignatius viewed the " army of Christ " ever more as an interior battle is understandable (though we saw that crusade spirituality did not exclude but rather included this element). But the Ignatian " army of Christ " immediately advanced beyond the realm of purely interior struggle as the apostolate, the world mission, the defensive battle against the advancing reformation entered into the sphere of his active spirituality. Yet this " army of Christ " occasionally assumed again a quite worldly character (we cited the letter to Canisius).[107]

Among the essential concepts of popular crusade spirituality there also belonged the affirmation and performance of penance. The crusade was a penitential journey. This theme is also found in the early meditations of the *Exercises* when he speaks of following Christ in pain.[108] Of course penance is found in the purgative way of the First Week; but there the connection with the crusade is not very evident, and he goes back to the common Christian understanding of sin, conversion, and penance. In the Call of the King poverty and humility stand in the foreground as virtues, as positive acts, not as works of penance or " negative " achievements. This should be noted. Ignatius puts little emphasis on the vicarious nature of penance.[109]

---

106 Recently J. Tarre, in " El *Retablo de la vida de Cristo*," *AHSJ*, XXV (1956), 243-253, has expressed the doubt that the *Vita Christi* mentioned in Ignatius' *Autobiography* (no. 5) refers to the Spanish translation of Ludolph of Saxony. Tarre believes rather that the *Retablo de la vida de Cristo*, by the Carthusian Juan de Padilla [Serille], is the work in question. This is a work in popular style, at that time widely disseminated in Spain.

107 See n. 99 above; remember also the plan for the fleet (n. 33) and the letter to the army of Juan de Vega (n. 101).

108 Kingdom (*SpEx*, [95]); see also the section on the crusade in the letter of the clergy of Lucca (Hagenmeyer, *Kreuzzugsbriefe*, pp. 165-166): " ubi laboris comes et periculi, triumphat particeps et gaudii, pugnavit cum pugnantibus, esuriit cum esurientibus, vicit quoque cum vincentibus; " also the letter of Anselm of Ribodimont to Archbishop Manasses of Rheims (ibid., p. 157): " ut pariter nobiscum patiamini et in prosperis nobiscum gaudeatis."

109 The Formula of the Institute, *Regimini*, [4], in *Cons*MHSJ, I, 27-28.

Yet one element of this community consciousness of crusade spirituality has been absorbed into Ignatian spirituality: the idea of existing for others. This becomes a necessity on the field of battle where the first commandment of self-preservation is to hold together and to support one another. Thus from the basic notion of the " army of Christ " there was born the idea of founding an order[110] and also the desire for an apostolate of service.

The comprehensive notion of penance which was so strong in all forms of crusade spirituality, is such an obvious and emphatic element in Ignatian spirituality that Joseph de Guibert has declared that this is its basic formula. We have presented this in our introduction. " To serve Christ " is a fundamental chord ringing through the most important meditations of the *Exercises*: " those who wish to distinguish themselves in the undivided service of their King,"[111] " the greater service,"[112] " the address of Christ to all His servants,"[113] " what the individual thinks will be of greater service," " the exclusive service of God our Lord,"[114] " in order to serve better,"[115] in the *Formula Instituti*: " they have dedicated their lives forever to the service of our Lord Jesus Christ ... and the popes of Rome; " " to serve the Lord alone and ... the Roman pontiff, His vicar on earth."[116]

We have seen that devotion to Peter was not wanting in the sphere of crusade spirituality, in accordance wtih the central position of the popes in the crusades. From this point of view, we think, light can be thrown on the oft-studied question of why Ignatius devoted himself to Rome and the popes, completely subordinated himself to them, and declared them to be in a certain sense the " origin and head " of his work.

Before placing themselves under a superior of their own, the first companions and Ignatius himself had, as Burkhard Schneider recently emphasized,[117] already promised entire obedience (*omnem*

---

110 This is also the opinion of recent scholars on the relationship between the illumination at the Cardoner at Manresa and the basic character of the two meditations on the heavenly King (Kingdom and Two Standards); see Leturia, " Genesis " and Iriarte, " Un doble encuentro," etc.
111 Kingdom (*SpEx*, [97]).
112 Ibid., [98]). " que sea vuestro mayor servicio."
113 Two Standards (*SpEx*, [146]).
114 The Three Classes of Men (*SpEx*, [155]).
115 Three Degrees of Humility (*SpEx*, [168]).
116 The Formula of the Institute, *Regimini*, [3], in *Cons*MHSJ, I, 26.
117 Burkhard Schneider, " Nuestro Principio y principal Fundamento. Zum historischen Verständnis des Papstgehorsamsgelübdes," *AHSJ*, XXV (1956), 488-513.

obedientiam) to the papacy. That is an important observation. Schneider indeed alludes to the parallel of this promise and the *suscipe* of the *Exercises* to, respectively, the visible head of the Church and Christ.[118] With this, however, not everything is said. Obedience to the pope belongs to the original proposals (*prima desideria*) of Ignatius and of the community around him.[119] In the well-known deliberations as to whether it was necessary to organize the community at Rome into something like a religious order, the service of God is identified for the first time with the service of the visible Church.[120] Here *militare Deo* (to war for God) means *servire Ecclesiae* (to serve the Church).

The thought of placing themselves under the direct command of the pope first found expression (still hypothetically) on Montmartre (1534). Leturia recalls the young Ignatius' devotion to St. Peter.[121] Heinrich Böhmer refers to the "reaction produced in the small group around Ignatius when they encountered the Protestant movement in Paris."[122] Burkhard Schneider alludes to the personal experiences of Ignatius during the first stages of his journey to self-sanctification (difficulties with bishops that led him to turn his eyes toward the highest ecclesiastical authority). Schneider also believes that while in Paris Ignatius took notice of the great practical value of the exemptions of the old mendicant orders.[123]

One must certainly add to this the fact that the Spaniards of the turn of the century possessed an unshakeable loyalty to the papacy (Cardinal Ximénez, Adrian of Utrecht, the part papal recognition played in the *Conquista*).

On the other hand, it should be mentioned how shaky the reputation of the Holy See was, what effects the Italianization of the renaissance papacy had had, how strong the tendencies toward Gallicanism were in Paris.

---

118 Ibid., p. 492.
119 Ignatius was well acquainted with the Rome of his day. In the *Autobiography* (no. 36) the "pilgrim" reports that he wanted to go to Rome and that people asked him with astonishment: You want to go to Rome? Don't you know how those come back who have gone there?
120 Schneider, "Nuestro Principio," p. 493.
121 Leturia, "Genesis," p. 40.
122 Böhmer, *Ignatius*, p. 115. Yet Böhmer rejects the idea that this thought was considered as a reaction against the Protestants. Neither Loyola nor any of his companions ever had the thought (in 1534) of founding an order to fight the Protestants. "The seven had no thought at all of fighting against anything. They desired to accomplish something positive" (ibid., p. 114).
123 Schneider, "Nuestro Principio," pp. 499-500.

Nevertheless Ignatius opted for Rome.[124] Here we must recall that, besides the above-mentioned reasons, besides the saint's mystical graces, this devotion to Peter had its roots in crusade spirituality, that the climate of thought about the crusade (*actitud de cruzada*) in which Iñigo de Loyola grew up always thought of the crusade and the papacy together — as they always had been united in historical fact. The popes had been patrons of both the *Conquista* and the campaign against the Turks. Their authority had seen to it that the conquistadors were accompanied by missionaries. They also kept even the defensive against the danger from the East always joined to a concern for the spreading of the faith.

The promise to obey the pope also stated explicitly that it would be an obedience in regard to the missions (*circa missiones*). The group inserted itself into the holy enterprise (*santa impresa*); into the most holy expeditions (*sacratissimae expeditiones*); into the mission promoted by Urban II, Innocent III, Pius II, and Leo X; into the *missiones* of the popes against the East, the Turks, and overseas. Thus the *romanità* of Ignatius can be understood as an inheritance from crusade thought. The crusade movement brought together the peoples of Europe, who had not known each other very well. Out of many peoples, the chroniclers say, there was formed the one "flock of the Lord."[125] During the common expedition, in their common success, they came to experience and recognize the unity of Western Christianity.[126] That all marched together was a characteristic of the crusade and also had its effect on crusade spirituality. Men fought for each other and prayed for each other. The "merits" of those at home helped those at the front, whether they came from England or Flanders, France or Germany, Burgundy or Italy. Everyone felt that the center of their Christian faith was in the radiant circle about "Holy Sion." They all saw in it the common goal of their religious strivings and felt themselves motivated from there to pious activity.

124 See Leturia, " Alle fonti della romanità della Compagnia di Gesù," *La Civiltà Cattolica*, LXXXV (1941); a translation into French can be found in *Christus*, V (1955), 81-100, under the title, "Aux sources de la ' Romanité' de la Compagnie de Jésus."

125 Ordericus Vitalis, *Historia Ecclesiastica*, Bk. 9, in *PL*, CLXXXVIII, 647.

126 See Hans Wolter, *Ordericus Vitalis. Ein Beitrag zur kluniazensischen Geschichtsschreibung* (Wiesbaden, 1955), pp. 150-151; Calmette, *Saint Bernard*, p. 258: " Et Bernard de Clairvaux, en ces maîtresses années 1146-1147 [the time of preparation for the Second Crusade] aura été, par excellence, la voix européenne du XIIe siècle."

We must notice this element of the universal if the spirituality of St. Ignatius is to be understood from the point of view of crusade spirituality. How strongly the saint affirmed this pull toward the universal and let it develop ! The language of the early meditations of the *Exercises* already betrays this: " See how the king addresses all his followers . . . to subdue (*conquistar*) all the land of the unbelievers . . . before him the whole world; He has His call go out to all of them and to each in particular. . . It is my will to conquer the whole world and to overcome all enemies."[127] " He wills to gather all under His banner . . . throughout the whole world . . . they should desire to help all."[128]

This universality of purpose (to win the world for Christ), of laborers (from the lands of all princes), and of means (all created things) is an essential aspect of the Ignatian apostolate and is supported by his all-inclusive spirituality, which here seems to indicate how it has been influenced by the popular form of crusade thought. This is all the more true because it was precisely at the time of Ignatius that the Mediterranean horizon of the Iberian Peninsula was broadening into one that embraced continents, since the crusade as a Western enterprise was being transformed into the world enterprise of the *Conquista*. And just as this was accompanied by the spirituality of its land of origin, Portugal and Spain,[129] so we sense in back of the missionary planning of St. Ignatius a universal spirituality which is related to that of his native land.

We have observed how the crusade and its spirituality deepened the religious concept of the hospital which stood on the pilgrimage route and developed out of the needs of the crusade. It is not without significance that the origins of the orders of knights lay in service in the hospitals. Hospital and crusade belong together.[130] That practical asceticism that was involved in the service in the hospitals is incomprehensible without the power of the faith that lay behind it. Caring for the poor pilgrims, for the sick crusaders, was a service to Christ. This was as true at home as in foreign lands (simply recall the hospital service of St. Elizabeth of Thuringia which was carried out under the influence of her crusade spirituality).

This may perhaps explain the conspicuous role that the hospital played in the life and asceticism of St. Ignatius. The pilgrim — quite symbolically, Ignatius always called himself this — believed

127 Kingdom (*SpEx*, [93, 95]).
128 Two Standards (*SpEx*, [137-147]).
129 Iriarte, " Un doble encuentro," *Manresa*, XXVIII (1956), 60.
130 Schreiber, *Gemeinschaften*, pp. 10. 13, 40.

that he was best cared for in a hospital, whether as a guest or as
a nurse.[131] He needed it if he wanted to live according to his
original plans. In conformity with the ideology of the crusade hospital,
he here actualized his ideal of the "following of Christ;" he could
proclaim and carry out his "service of love." In the hospital experiment of the novitiate we have one last effect of this attitude.[132]

Would it be wrong to discover traces of crusade spirituality
in the hospital asceticism (we can hardly say "hospital mysticism")
of St. Ignatius? Hospital and poverty, each implies the other.
As a matter of fact, crusade spirituality had to consider the question
of apostolic poverty. Certainly there were those who went on crusade
to become rich[133] — in particular the Normans of southern Italy.
Yet the fundamental desire was not to earn but to give (offerings
for the Holy City, one's own labors in battle, if necessary, one's
life). Despite all the questionable aspects of the crusades (did not
even St. Bernard recommend participation in them because something
could thereby be won for the spice trade?),[134] let it not be forgotten
that for the crusader honor was more important than money. The
chivalric element, basic to crusade spirituality, disdained money.
Recall the voluntary poverty of St. Elizabeth, the enormous financial
sacrifices that the crusaders had to make. They wanted to be poor
along with the poor Christ who was their leader and for whom they
fought. This did not have a great deal to do with the notion of
monastic poverty.

St. Ignatius' desire for poverty grew out of his intention to
emulate the saints. In poverty he saw something difficult and
burdensome (*cosa dificultosa y grave*).[135]

A very informative parallel is found in a speech given at the
Fifth Council of the Lateran on December 18, 1513, by the Knight

---

131 *Autobiog*, 24.

132 Schreiber, *Gemeinschaften*, p. 32, refers to this relationship. He mentions a
reason given for doing this that is found in the Prague edition of the Institute
(*Institutum Societatis Jesu*, auctoritate Congregationis Generalis XVIII melio-
rem in ordinem digestum auctum et recusum [Prague, 1757]), I, 347: " ut
omnino (in the hospital) suo Creatori et Domino pro ipsorum salute crucifixo
serviant." That service in the hospitals was promoted by Ignatius for other
reasons also, we know, for example, from the instructions that he gave Laynez
for the way he was to act at Trent (*PolChron*, I, 179).

133 " Facultates etiam inimicorum vestrae erunt: quoniam et illorum thesauros ex-
spoliabitis," Baudri of Bourgueil, *Historia Hierosolymitana*, in *PL*, CLXVI, 1068.

134 St. Bernard, letter 363, to the clergy and people of Germany, in *PL*, CLXXXII,
567: " Si prudens mercator es, si conquisitor hujus saeculi, magnas quasdam
nundinas indico: vide ne pereant." This was intended to have a completely
concrete sense and to be in no way symbolical.

135 *Autobiog*, 7.

of Jerusalem, Giovanni Battista Gargha from Siena. He says: "Whoever becomes a member of this army of Christ may build no house nor acquire any goods. He partakes of the King's table and receives his pay from the Emperor (Christ)."[136] These are familiar themes of crusade spirituality.

In the *Formula Instituti* of 1540 we read: "... and since we know that our Lord Jesus Christ will grant His servants who seek only the kingdom of God that which is necessary for food and clothing, so all without exception should vow eternal poverty."[137] The similarity of images is amazing: the Lord of the pilgrimage will provide.

We should make mention of a point that has seldom been treated. Among the goals set for the Society there stand not only that her members defend and spread the faith, help souls by teaching and instruction, conduct retreats and administer the sacraments, but also that they should show themselves useful in works of love of neighbor — among these latter, besides serving in the hospitals and visiting prisons, there is specified the reconciliation of enemies (*ad dissidentium reconciliationem*).[138] This concern for peace is an elementary Christian attitude. But in the present context it is important that the effort for peace is among the most important elements of the crusade ideology. The popes, as originators and organizers of the crusades, always called for the preservation or re-establishment of peace. This was a precondition to any possibility whatever of an expedition and meant security for the home front.

In the course of the centuries, this concern for peace always took first place in the publicity for the crusades, in sermons, in speeches at councils, in diplomatic negotiations, and in preparatory conferences — from the time of Urban II to that of Gregory XIII and Innocent XI.[139] So it is understandable that the concept of

---

136 Harduin, *Acta Conciliorum*, IX, 1729.

137 The Formula of the Institute, *Regimini*, [6] and *Exposcit debitum*, [5], in ConsMHSJ, I, 29, 379.

138 The Formula of the Institute, *Exposcit*, [4], in ConsMHSJ, I, 378. This is among the additions to the Formula found in *Exposcit*, an Apostolic Letter of Julius III, July 21, 1550.

139 St. Bernard, letter 363, in *PL*, CLXXXII, 566: "Cesset pristina illa non militia, sed plane malitia, qua soletis invicem sternere, invicem perdere, ut ab invicem consumamini ... habes nunc, fortis miles, habes, vir bellicose, ubi dimices absque periculo." See the speeches on the crusade given at the Fifth Lateran Council, which also demand first of all peace among the countries of Europe as a precondition for an expedition against the Turks; for example that of Simon Begnius, bishop of Modrusi (Harduin, *Acta Conciliorum*, IX, 1684); Leo X himself: "eaque [pace] composita sancta et necessaria contra infidelium rabiem Christianorum sanguinem sitientium expeditio fieri valeat" (ibid., 1698).

peacemaking was already familiar to the saint from the sphere of popular crusade spirituality. Later, in the exercise of his pastoral ministry, he was usually able to achieve success in actually bringing about reconciliations. Yet it must be noted that this *reconciliatio dissidentium* is first mentioned in the second *Formula Instituti* of 1550. Thus it should probably be understood as the result of those ten years of experience.

In conclusion let us compare the theme of the " glory of God," so familiar to crusade spirituality, with the dominant idea of Ignatian spirituality. This theme has found its classic expression in the motto of the Society of Jesus, for the greater glory of God. Fame and honor were the highest goods in the knightly ethos of the crusader — one's own glory, of course, but embedded in the glory of God and elevated by the glory of " Holy Sion " which was to be freed from all heathen darkness. The crusader wished to prove that God, as the God of the Christians, is conqueror, lord, " conquestador." The glory and honor of the Divine Name was to be defended and magnified in the crusade. It was also expected, with reason, that a luminous glow would stream back from the glory of Christ, thus preserved, upon the " soldiers of Christ " since every increase in the authority and power of the lord ennobles the vassal to a corresponding degree.

This eagerness to serve the glory of God knew no bounds, not even that of death, since one passed over it into the " eternal glory " of final union with Christ, the commander of the expedition.

The *Plus ultra* (farther still) on the commemorative coin of Charles V (1548) is not meant in merely a geographical sense, though this seems to be indicated by the double-headed imperial eagle over the waves between the Pillars of Hercules. Rather it manifests inner rhythm of the vital force behind the *Conquista* and the crusades.[140]

The *Plus ultra* of the Hapsburg and the *magis* (more) of the saint of Loyola are in harmony with each other. Both were born from the convictions of the age that urged men out into distant lands and to the heroic and the conquering. In the case of Ignatius of Loyola this knightly ideal, derived from the world of the crusades, undergoes a transformation into the ideal of absolute service of God.[141] The glory of God now becomes the only norm

140 M. Bernhart, *Die Bildnismedaillen Karls V* (Munich, 1919), pp. 103-104; quoted from Karl Brandi, *Kaiser Karl V* (2 vols. Munich, 1937), II, 423.
141 See also J. F. Wickham, " The worldly Ideal of Iñigo de Loyola," *Thought*, XXIX (1954), 209-236.

for all self-dedication.[142] The descent of Ignatian spirituality from crusade spirituality is here unmistakeable.

We summarize: For an understanding of the genesis and nature of Ignatian spirituality a study of crusade spirituality as it existed in the West, especially on the Iberian Peninsula, from early days right up to the days of Ignatius, is indispensable. Such a study, the outline and direction of which we have indicated, shows how a heritage has been handed down to the saint, through his ties with the spirituality of his homeland and his people, and that this heritage then becomes visible in a new and purified form in the maturity and perfection of Ignatius after his conversion. Many other forces have also been at work in the development of this new form — that must not be forgotten.

Difficulties in finding documentary proof should not hinder us from carefully pursuing every trace that leads from the specifically lay spirituality of his age to the great themes of the Ignatian spiritual life.

We do in actual fact discover important elements of crusade spirituality mirrored in the spirituality of St. Ignatius. Let us once more call to mind the Christocentricity, the desire to follow the suffering and crowned Lord, the penitential pilgrimage and the readiness for poverty, service of the sick in the hospitals and subordination to the leadership of the pope of Rome, the interrelationship between defense and spread of the faith.

It is not the fact that one or the other of these elements can be perceived in Ignatius that leads us to surmise that the saint stood in the midstream of crusade tradition and that he preserved and absorbed these elements of the treasure of its piety. It is rather the special interrelationship of all these themes, both in the personal life of the founder and in the program of his foundation, the Society of Jesus, that leads us to judge that in the spirituality of St. Ignatius, the spiritual knight of Loyola, essential elements of Western crusade spirituality have been molded into a new synthesis.

The spirituality of St. Ignatius is at the same time a mirror of the past and a formative force for the future.

---

142 Letter of July 9, 1550, to Juan de Vega, in *EppIgn*, III, 111: "esa santa empresa [the expedition against the infidels in Africa] . . . por occupación de tan justa guerra . . . el servicio de Vuestra Señoría a gloria de Dios Nuestro Señor."

IGNATIAN PRAYER:
SEEKING GOD IN ALL THINGS

Josef Stierli

THE FOUNDING of the Society of Jesus appeared to the sixteenth century as a revolutionary break with the one-thousand-year tradition of Western monasticism. For, in spite of changing forms, in all monastic orders from Benedict to Dominic, contemplation had been the center of monastic life. Even the order of St. Dominic is considered by its own members a contemplative order in spite of its apostolic orientation. The expression and guarantee of this contemplation was the enclosure of the monastery and also choir, which was the center of the monastic day. In the Benedictine formula, " pray and work " (*ora et labora*), the accent is on "pray." Monastic occupations like farming, handicraft, and study are only meaningful interruptions of liturgical prayer. Even in the Dominican formula, " to give to others what one has contemplated " (*contemplata aliis tradere* [*Summa theologiae*, II-II, Q. 188, a. 6]), apostolic work is considered the organic expression of contemplation and study.

Ignatius made the first daring break with these forms and formulas. This innovation of Ignatius accounts for the difficulties and resistance he had to overcome before receiving the approbation of the Church. This innovation accounts too for the repeated attempts of the popes who came from the old orders to fit the Constitutions of the Society of Jesus into the tradition of monasticism, especially by the introduction of choir.

The innovation of St. Ignatius was not so much to be found in the carefully thought-out apostolic nature of his order. The Praemonstratensians and the mendicant orders of the high Middle

Study 5 was translated by Morton J. Hill, S.J., in *Woodstock Letters*, XC (1961), 135-166.

Ages were pioneers in apostolic spirituality and his predecessors in it. It was not in the universality of his apostolate and in his apostolic method that Ignatius surpassed the earlier orders. It was the radically different adaptation of the entire order to the labor of the apostolic ministry that appeared as a revolution to the representatives of a firmly established monastic tradition. Yet it was only by this adaptation that Ignatius created an apostolic order in all its purity.

In the realization of his ideas, Ignatius abandoned many of the exercises of the monastic life that had been considered essential up to that time. First among these was the Office in choir. On the other hand, he created new ways of community life. In place of choir as the essential expression of contemplation, he presented a new religious ideal, "Seeking God in all things." This he made the central principle of religious life. With this highly dynamic formula, Ignatius not only gave his own order a unique spirituality, he also gave the layman an anxiously awaited method of unifying his faith and his everyday living. If by his Constitutions Ignatius paved the way for many modern religious communities, he also developed a religious ideal by the formula of seeking God in all things. This ideal — along with the Spiritual Exercises — is effective outside the Society of Jesus. Therefore, an examination of this basic principle is a matter not merely of historical and ascetical interest to the Jesuit, but may also become fruitful for modern apostolic religious and for the layman.

We shall treat our theme in four steps. First, the source and content of the formula, "Seeking God in all things," must be sought for in the life of St. Ignatius himself, because this formula grows from the depths of his own God-given mystical prayer. Second, it is worth noting that Ignatius makes this ideal an essential principle in the ascetical and religious training of his followers, and in it he finds the specific holiness of a Jesuit. Third, because of the central position he gives to the seek-God-in-all-things formula, it will be necessary to ascertain its true meaning. Fourth and last, we will ask by what means this disposition can be acquired and fostered in the spirit of St. Ignatius.

I. The Example of The Master
At the end of the *Autobiography*, the original form of an Ignatian biography, dictated to Da Câmara in the years 1553-1555 after repeated pressure from Ignatius' disciples, the saint admitted that "since he began to serve God, he advanced constantly in devotion; that is, in facility to find God, now more than ever in his

life."[1] This is a remarkable statement because Ignatius here equates devotion with the formula of "Seeking God in all things" and so characterizes his own spirituality. What he intends to say can be understood only in connection with his deep mystical prayer, whose nature we can now trace to some degree from the writings of the saint himself and from the testimony of contemporaries. Especially valuable are *The Spiritual Diary* of the years 1544-1545, his *Autobiography*, and the *Spiritual Exercises*. The mystical prayer of St. Ignatius is essentially trinitarian. Since the triune God has revealed himself in Christ crucified, his prayer is also Christ-centered and cross-centered. His prayer is Church-centered too, since we meet Christ in the Church, and centered on the Holy Eucharist and the priesthood, especially after his ordination in Venice in 1537.

In his *Autobiography*, when describing the third Manresan period, the great mystic invasion of God into his life, Ignatius gives a systematic summary of the graces of this time that influenced his entire spiritual life. "First, he practiced great devotion to the Holy Trinity, addressing himself daily to each Person of the Trinity."[2] On the steps of the Dominican church, he received a vision of the Holy Trinity that was both a grace and a mission. "This impression was so tremendous that it remained with him all his life and he always felt great consolation when praying to the Holy Trinity."[3] Laynez, to whom the master confided much of his interior life, has more to tell of those hours of grace. "During the year he spent at Manresa, he had so much light from our Lord that his mind was deeply consoled. Almost all the mysteries of the faith were shown to him. It was especially the mystery of the Holy Trinity which refreshed his mind so that he thought of writing a book about the Holy Trinity, even though he was a very simple man who knew only how to read and write in Spanish."[4]

Jerónimo Nadal, Ignatius' right hand in the introduction of the Constitutions and the inner formation of the order, testifies from his own experience and from the confidences entrusted to him by Ignatius, that "Ignatius is uniquely united to God. Father Ignatius told me personally that he is in constant relation with the Divine Persons and that he receives graces proper to each Person from the individual Persons."[5] On another occasion he writes, "I do not wish

1 *Autobiog*, 99, in *FN*, I, 504.
2 *Autobiog*, 28.
3 Ibid.
4 *FN*, I, 82.
5 *MonNad*, IV, 645.

to omit that our Father Ignatius has received the unique grace to be able to pray and to rest freely in the vision of the Holy Trinity. He had these visions also earlier in life, but I am inclined to say he experienced them most frequently in the last years of his stay on earth."[6] The last years in Rome were a time of deep mystical union with God, a constant union with the Trinity. Nadal testifies: "Ignatius is united to God in a special way. His soul has experienced every type of vision, not merely visions of a sensible nature as, for instance, the vision of Christ or of the Blessed Virgin, but also visions that were directed to his purely intellectual powers. He constantly lives the life of the spirit in a high state of union with God."[7] Ribadeneyra (author of the first Ignatian biography) testifies to the maturity of Ignatius' mystical life of prayer in the years of his greatest labor and torturing illness: "Ignatius felt that he was always advancing and that the fire in his soul ever burned with a warmer glow. Hence, Ignatius did not hesitate, during his last years at Rome, to call the time spent at Manresa his 'kindergarten' days, although earlier during his studies, by reason of the wonderful graces received then, he had called it his 'primitive church'."[8]

But we shall have a few passages from his own *Spiritual Diary* as our confirming witness. On February 16, 1544, he wrote:

I wanted to get ready for Mass, but doubted to whom and how to commend myself first. In this doubt, I knelt down, and wondering how I should begin, I thought that the Father would reveal Himself more to me and draw me to His mercies, feeling that He was more favorable and readier to grant what I desired (not being able to apply myself to my mediators). This feeling kept growing, with a flood of tears on my cheeks, and the greatest confidence in the Father, as though He were recalling me from my former exile. Later, while on my way to Mass, preparing the altar and vesting, and beginning Mass, everywhere with intense tears which drew me to the Father, to whom I directed everything concerning the Son, while I experienced many remarkable intellectual lights, which were delightful and very spiritual.[9]

---

6 Ibid., 651.

7 Ibid., 645.

8 *FN*, II, 344.

9 *SpDiar*, [33], in *Obras completas de san Ignacio* (1963), p. 327. Henceforth references are to this edition. The English translation is from W. J. Young, S.J., *The Spiritual Journal of St. Ignatius Loyola* (Woodstock College Press, 1958; reprint by Program to Adapt the Spiritual Exercises, Jersey City, 1971).

February 19, 1544:

On awakening in the morning and beginning my examination of conscience and prayer, with a great and abundant flood of tears, I felt much devotion with many intellectual lights and spiritual remembrances of the Most Holy Trinity, which quieted me and delighted me immensely, even to producing a pressure in my chest, because of the intense love I felt for the Most Holy Trinity[10]... On the way to Mass and just before it, I was not without tears; an abundance of them during it, but very peacefully, with very many lights and spiritual memories concerning the Most Holy Trinity which served as a great illumination to my mind, so much so that I thought I could never learn so much by hard study; and later, as I examined the matter more closely, I felt and understood, I thought, more than if I had studied all my life.[11]

February 21, 1544:

In this Mass I recognized, felt, or saw, the Lord knows, that in speaking to the Father, in seeing that He was a Person of the Most Holy Trinity, I was moved to love the Trinity all the more that the other Persons were present in it essentially. I felt the same in the prayer to the Son, and the same in the prayer to the Holy Spirit, rejoicing in any One of Them and feeling consolations, attributing it to and rejoicing in belonging to all Three.[12]

February 27, 1544:

I felt or rather saw beyond my natural strength the Most Holy Trinity and Jesus, presenting me, or placing me, or simply being the means of union in the midst of the Most Holy Trinity in order that this intellectual vision be communicated to me. With this knowledge and sight, I was deluged with tears and love, directing to Jesus and to the Most Holy Trinity a respectful worship which was more on the side of a reverential love than anything else. Later, I thought of Jesus doing the same duty in thinking of praying to the Father, thinking and feeling interiorly that He was doing everything with the Father and the Most Holy Trinity.[13]

March 4, 1544:

I entered the chapel with fresh devotion and tears, always ending in the Most Holy Trinity; and also at the altar, after having vested,

10 Ibid., [51].
11 Ibid., [52].
12 Ibid., [63].
13 Ibid., [83-84].

I was overcome with a much greater flood of tears, sobs, and most intense love for the Most Holy Trinity.[14]

Trinitarian mystical prayer has many forms. It is again Nadal who points out to us the characteristics of Ignatius' prayer that centered on the Trinity. "We know that Father Ignatius received from God the singular grace of occupying himself freely in the contemplation of the Trinity and of reposing in it... Father Ignatius received this manner of praying by reason of a great privilege and in a most singular manner; and also this, that in all things, actions, and conversations he perceived and contemplated the presence of God and had an affection for spiritual things, being contemplative even while in action (a matter which he customarily explained by saying: 'God must be found in all things.')"[15] An exact analysis of text and context shows that Nadal does not intend to speak of two different graces, but of one unique vital grace of the master that is at the same time directed fruitfully toward the Trinity and the created universe. The inner, indissoluble connection in the case of Ignatius between Trinitarian mystical prayer and the formula of "finding God in all things" is based on his unique mystical picture of God. The triune God whom he met in grace and prayer, and consequently in all his work, is the creator of the world and the lord of history. We should never forget that creator and lord, in the mind of Ignatius, are not philosophic, but extremely rich theological ideas. For Ignatius, God is always the triune cause and origin of all natural and supernatural reality. For him history is the fullness of all communicated divine love. Therefore, history is above all the history of grace and salvation. Logically, the Ignatian picture of Christ bears the same traits that are seen in the picture of God. For the intoxicated mystic of Manresa and for the wise organizer of the Society of Jesus, Christ is above all the king, not the king of glory of the Benedictine liturgy, but the ambassador of the Father, come to conquer a kingdom for him. He is head of the Church Militant, which is here and now continuing the work of salvation, the battle of the cross against Satan.

We must explain the series of the systematic reflections of Ignatius concerning the Manresa graces, not merely as an historical sequence, but as organically interlocked and connected graces that were constantly evolving. In his *Autobiography*, we are told of a second Trinitarian mystical grace. "Another time he was shown the manner in which God created the world. In this he experienced

14 Ibid., [106].
15 *MonNad*, IV, 651.

140

great spiritual joy. It seemed that he saw something white, producing certain rays out of which God created light."[16] Then the progression goes on, from creation-centered prayer to Christ-centered prayer (already a Eucharistic note!), then Church-centered prayer, as Nadal expressly states. That we may not consider these mystical graces his own self-willed invention, but gifts, that "fifth" in his review, that final and complete grace of Manresa shows: "One day, to satisfy his thirst for devotion, he went to a church, one mile from Manresa. I believe it is St. Paul's Church. He walked along the river that leads to the church, deep in his pious thoughts. After a while, he sat down. He turned his face toward the river, which flowed deep below him. The eyes of his mind began to open. He did not have a vision, but he grasped and understood many questions concerning the spiritual life, and matters of faith and learning, and this was with such clarity, that all seemed to be new.

"It is impossible to indicate everything he understood at this time, however much it was. But it is certain that his soul was filled with such brightness that he thought if he could unite all the graces he had received in his life up to the age of sixty-two and all the knowledge he possessed, he did not receive as much as on this one occasion.

"As a result of these experiences, his mind was so illuminated that he thought he was a different man and had another mind. As this illumination lasted quite a while, he went to a cross that stood nearby, and knelt down to give thanks to God."[17] This great illumination that gave him "the new understanding," also presented him with an insight into the architectonic fabric of all reality in the world and of every mystery of faith. In the great clearness of his spirit, he could examine and evaluate all things proceeding from the triune God and coming to himself. Thus at Manresa was established that formula of "Finding God in all things," during an hour of grace of inconceivable fruitfulness.

That which first appears at this time like a rare ray of divine grace became increasingly the perpetual state of his spiritual life during his time at Rome. His soul was indeed endowed with this "new understanding," the clarity of which never left him. The very intimate pages of his *Spiritual Diary*, that were never meant to be for any foreign eyes, prove nearly day by day that Ignatius lived at that time in an habitual mystical union with the Trinity. Furthermore, the concept, "Finding God in all things," during this

16 *Autobiog*, 29, in *FN*, I, 402.
17 *Autobiog*, 30, in *FN*, I, 404.

time had a predominantly mystical character, and for this very reason proved fruitful in all his actions, as Nadal again testifies. For in immediate connection with the testimony just mentioned of the " contemplative in action " he continues: " But we saw with deep amazement and sweet consolation how this grace, which was a light in his soul, manifested itself in the wisdom and sureness of all his actions. It was as if a light shone over his countenance. Indeed, we felt that this grace was communicated to us in a mysterious way."[18] Another testimony sums it up more briefly: " Nearly always he was directed to God, even if at times he seemed to do something else."[19]

Since Manresa, Ignatius was ever more intoxicated with the light of God and consequently could see everything else only in this light. The triune God had become a powerful magnet in his life. Under the force of this central experience, all truths are now seen in relation to divine truth, and all activities are directed towards this divine goal. Trinitarian holiness and " Finding God in all things " have become one formula for Ignatius. Finding God in all things is the special characteristic of his trinitarian prayer. The contemplation of this trinitarian mysticism becomes the " action " of " Seeking God in all things."

II. The Lesson for His Followers

After Manresa, where Ignatius began to " help some souls who had come seeking him there to advance spiritually," the mysticism of Ignatius was translated into an ascetical doctrine for his band of followers. We learn about Ignatian spirituality first of all in the booklet of the *Spiritual Exercises*, and then in the *Constitutions*, which are more of a spiritual manual than a code of laws. We also learn about Ignatian spirituality in his rich correspondence, where practical decisions and questions of organization are harmoniously united with fatherly advice, and finally, in the personal method of instruction employed by the saint which we learn from the manifold testimony of his pupils and associates.[20] Moreover, the first generation of Jesuits was convinced that the tremendous graces of their father were not only his personal privilege, but also a promise to his sons. Nadal testifies to this among other things concerning the vision of La Storta. In this vision Ignatius was placed by the

---

18 *MonNad*, IV, 651-652.
19 *Responsio Manarei*, no. 37, in *FN*, III, 438.
20 Joseph de Guibert, " St. Ignatius' Spiritual Training of His Followers," chap. 2 in *DeGuiJes*, pp. 74-108.

heavenly Father next to Christ bearing his Cross. This marked the fulfillment of the triple colloquy of the Two Standards. To find God in all things is a grace promised to the sons of Ignatius. Nadal says: "We believe that what we have recognized here as a privilege given to Father Ignatius has also been granted to the whole Society; and we are confident that the grace of that prayer has been prepared in the Society for all of us, and is indeed something connected with our vocation."[21] As Manresa was for Ignatius the "primitive church" of his mysticism, so for his successors the concept, "Finding God in all things," is established in the "Manresa of the Exercises." These culminate in the Contemplation for Obtaining Divine Love. In retrospect, this Contemplation summarizes the entire Exercises in focal point. It shows the First Principle and Foundation in the light of the four weeks of the Exercises. Looking forward, it projects the radiation and translation of retreat ideals into the everyday routine of Christian life which is to be resumed. The second prelude describes the purpose of this meditation: "Ask for an interior knowledge of the great favors received, so that, in grateful recognition of them, I may love and serve His Divine Majesty."[22]

The common theme of the four points is God's picture of our life's history. Again and again we must renew for ourselves the rich contents of this concept of "Finding God in all things" as grasped by Ignatius. "All things" must be experienced as gifts of God and as an expression of his love in the first point. The beneficent God is viewed in the second point as present in his gifts, because the presence of the giver gives the deepest possible meaning to all gifts. In the third point, which treats about the presence of an ever-active God, he is also discovered as continually working in all things. In the fourth point the mystery of divine descent into all earthly reality is brought to our attention. All things are seen in their continual issuance from God as Ignatius at Manresa had the grace to experience. All things must be returned to God by a person "who has gone out of himself," through a pure love that serves. This is the meaning of the answer, the fourfold *Suscipe*. Thus the retreatant should be transformed by the Spiritual Exercises into a man who seeks in all things the presence of our Lord,[23] who finds God in all things,[24] who lives with God ever before his eyes,[25]

21 *MonNad*, IV, 652.
22 *SpEx*, [233].
23 *EppIgn*, III, 510; *LettersIgn*, p. 240.
24 *EppIgn*, III, 502, 510, and many other places; *LettersIgn*, pp. 236, 240.
25 *Autobiog*, 44, in *FN*, I, 422, 432.

and who is always directed towards God,[26] to use the different formulas of the saint.

We meet the same ideal again in the Constitutions of the order. In Part Three, Ignatius demands as the basic principle for the religious training of his followers: " All should make diligent efforts to keep their intention right, not only in regard to their state of life but also in all particular details. In these they should always aim at serving and pleasing the Divine Goodness for its own sake and because of the incomparable love and benefits with which God has anticipated us... Further, they should often be exhorted to seek God our Lord in all things, stripping off from themselves the love of creatures to the extent that this is possible, in order to turn their love upon the Creator of them, by loving Him in all creatures and all of them in Him, in conformity with His holy and divine will."[27]

Employing other words, but to the same effect, he gives the scholastics (students of the order) this golden rule: " In order to make great progress in these branches, the scholastics should strive first of all to keep their souls pure and their intention in studying right, by seeking in their studies nothing except the glory of God and the good of souls."[28] In the spirit of Saint Ignatius, Nadal, during his first Spanish visitation to introduce the Constitutions, sketched this ideal for the scholastics: " Everyone, who advances in the world of prayer and of the spiritual life, should strive in Our Lord to find God in all their exercises and employments, that they may walk exclusively in the way of the spirit, and form the habit of being recollected and devout in all things. They should profit from the fruits of contemplation and prayer in all their occupations insofar as the weakness of our nature permits."[29] This thought recurs in the rules framed by Nadal for the students of the order, called " Rules for Scholastics " which are wholly fashioned in the spirit of the Constitutions.[30]

What has its foundation in the Exercises and Constitutions should become fruitful in everyday living. To this end, an abundance of directions was issued from the chamber of Ignatius at Rome to the entire world. Most of the letters treating the theme " Seeking God in all things " are in the same context. They are either a part of

26 *Responsio Manarei*, no. 37, in *FN*, III, 438.
27 *Cons*, [288].
28 *Cons*, [360].
29 Nadal, *Orationis Ordo*, no. 14, in *Cons*MHSJ, IV, 490.
30 *Cons*MHSJ, IV, 481, 486.

that difficult struggle against extension of the time for prayer which Ignatius had to wage in the last ten years of his life — such tendencies were noticeable especially in Spain and Portugal — or they contained decisions and advice for scholastics "for whom study did not leave much time for prayer" (a repeated thought of St. Ignatius which is also treated in the Fourth Part of the *Constitutions*). Sometimes his letters are for very busy fathers who groan under the burden of their occupations and carry in their hearts a longing for quiet prayer. So we read near the end of the famous letter to the students at Coimbra, dated May 7th, 1547: "Your study does not allow you much time to engage in long prayer. However, such time can be made up for by the desires of the person who turns all his actions into a continual prayer, by undertaking them solely for the service of God."[31]

Four years later, a letter from Ignatius' secretary, Polanco, to the rector of the same college repeats these wise principles, under the inspiration of the saint. "Regarding prayer and meditation, if there are not special necessities in consequence of temptations, I notice that he [Ignatius] has greater approval for one's effort to find God in all things a man does, rather than for his giving a long time to prayer. The spirit he wishes to see in the members of the Society is that, as far as possible, they should not find less devotion in any work of charity and obedience than in prayer or meditation; for they ought not to do anything except for the love and service of God. Therefore, each one should find greater satisfaction in what he is ordered to do; for then he can have no doubt that he is conforming himself to the will of God our Lord."[32]

Under the same date of June 1, 1551, Antonio Brandão, a scholastic priest from Coimbra, received this directive along with other valuable advice concerning the spiritual life: "In view of the purpose of our studies, the scholastics cannot devote themselves to long meditations. Over and above the exercises which they have for the acquisition of virtue, namely daily Mass, one hour for prayer and the examen of conscience, and confession and communion every eighth day, they can exercise themselves in seeking the presence of our Lord in all things — for example, in conversing with someone, in walking, looking, tasting, hearing, thinking, and in everything that they do, since it is true that his Divine Majesty is in all things by his presence, power, and essence. This manner of meditating,

---

31 *EppIgn*, I, 509; *LettersIgn*, p. 129.
32 *EppIgn*, III, 502; *LettersIgn*, pp. 235-236.

by which one finds God our Lord in all things, is easier than trying to elevate ourselves to spiritual things which are more abstract and which require more effort to make them present to ourselves. Furthermore, this splendid exercise will dispose us for great visitations from the Lord, even during a short prayer. Moreover, the scholastics can train themselves to offer frequently to God our Lord their studies and the difficulties they bring, by remembering that they have undertaken them out of love for God, and by putting aside their personal inclinations, in order to serve his Divine Majesty, and to help those for whose life he himself suffered death."[33]

On this theme about time for prayer in the midst of studies, Da Câmara reports in his *Memoriale* an interesting discussion between Ignatius and Nadal. "When on last November 22 [of 1554] Father Nadal was speaking to our Father about the hour and a half of prayer he had permitted in Spain [as a compromise between the two hours the Spaniards demanded and the one hour Ignatius had appointed], the Father said that his opinion, from which no one would ever move him, was that for the scholastics one hour of prayer is sufficient, it being supposed that they are practicing mortification and self-denial; and that such a one would easily accomplish more prayer in a quarter of an hour than another, who is not mortified, would do in two hours. However, that does not prevent one who is under great trial and in greater need from being allowed more time for prayer.

"When the Father was speaking to me on another day about the same subject, he told me that he thought there was no greater mistake in spiritual things than to desire to lead others as oneself. He was speaking about the long prayers he had made. He then added 'hat out of a hundred men who give themselves to long prayers and severe penances, the majority expose themselves to great harm. The Father was referring especially to stubbornness of judgment; and thus he placed the whole foundation in mortification and abnegation of will. When he told Nadal that an hour of prayer was enough for those in the colleges, he was placing the chief stress upon this presupposition of mortification and abnegation. Thus it is clear that the great foundation of all the things of the Society, for example, of the indifference which is presupposed, consists for our Father in the examination after the probationary experiences and in the testimony which remains from them, and not in prayer — except for that which arises from these. Thereupon

---

33 *EppIgn*, III, 510; *LettersIgn*, pp. 240-241.

the Father praised prayer highly, especially that which is made by keeping God always before one's eyes."[34]

In the same manner Ignatius drew the ideal of holiness for fathers in the active ministry. To them he gives as the sole rule for prayer and mortification — "discreet charity": "In view of the time and approval of their life through which those wait before being admitted among the professed and even among the formed coadjutors, it is presupposed that they will be men who are spiritual and sufficiently advanced to run in the path of Christ our Lord to the extent that their bodily strength and the exterior occupations undertaken through charity and obedience allow. Therefore, in what pertains to prayer, meditation, and study and also in regard to the bodily practices of fasts, vigils, and other austerities or penances, it does not seem expedient to give them any other rule than that which discreet charity dictates to them, provided that the confessor should always be informed and also, when a doubt about expediency arises, the superior."[35]

Ignatius finds it quite all right that the apostolic worker does not have much time for formal prayer. He must rather make a prayer out of every task: "He did not wish that the members of the Society seek God only in prayer, but in all their actions, and that these be a prayer. He approved this method more than long-drawn-out contemplation."[36]

Close to eternity, Ignatius wrote half a year before his death: "One should reflect that man does not serve God only when he prays. Otherwise all prayer would be too short that does not last twenty-four hours daily (if that were possible), since everyone indeed should give himself to God as completely as possible. But in reality, God is served better at certain times through other means than prayer, so that God is well pleased if for them one omits prayer or, *a fortiori*, if he shortens it. Thus, one should pray constantly and not lose heart, but he should understand that correctly after the manner of the saints and of the doctors of the Church."[37]

And Nadal repeats this idea in one of his instructions: "It is helpful to seek God our Lord continually in all things, by laying aside as far as possible the love of all creatures, in order to place it

---

34 *FN*, I, 676-677.
35 *Cons*, [582].
36 *FN*, II, 419.
37 *EppIgn*, XII, 652.

in their Creator, by loving him in them all and all of them in him, in conformity with his holy and divine will."[38]

Instead of prolonged time for prayer, one's work should become prayer, precisely by finding God in all things. Thus Ignatius, through Polanco, instructed Andrés de Oviedo, one of the most obstinate champions of extended prayer: "Besides the obligatory breviary, he should not employ more time in prayer, meditation, and examination of conscience than one hour [therefore, the same length of time as prescribed for scholastics], so that he might have more time remaining for other things in the service of God. In the midst of duties, he can keep himself in the presence of God, and thus pray continuously, while directing everything to the greater service and the greater glory of God."[39]

Furthermore, Ignatius personally wrote to Francis Borgia, who, under the influence of Oviedo and others, always remained somewhat inclined to the "longing for the desert" of extended prayer (so that the question may be asked whether Ignatius entirely succeeded in "converting" him): "As far as I can judge about you in our Lord, you would do better to give half the time [you have hitherto devoted to prayer] to study (for knowledge, not only infused but also acquired, will be very useful to you in the future), to the government of your estate, and to spiritual conversations. Seek always to preserve your soul in interior peace and calm, disposed for the moment when our Lord may desire to work in it; for without doubt there is more virtue and grace in the ability to enjoy God in various employments and places than in only one. We ought, in the Divine Goodness, to try to arrive at this state."[40]

Father Gaspar Berze, an outstanding Netherlander, the best co-worker of Francis Xavier in India, received a letter from Ignatius, probably occasioned by further Portuguese attempts for longer periods of prayer: "If the climate there is even less suited for meditations than it is here, there is so much the less reason for extending the time for prayer than here. In the midst of actions and studies, the mind can be lifted to God; and by means of this directing everything to the divine service, everything is prayer. Hence, all the members of the Society should be convinced that when exercises of charity very often take away from them the time of prayer, they are not for that reason any the less acceptable to God than during prayer."[41]

38 *MonNad*, IV, 677.
39 *EppIgn*, III, 309.
40 *EppIgn*, II, 234; *LettersIgn*, p. 180.
41 *EppIgn*, VI, 91.

The same thought recurs in a consoling letter from Ignatius to Father Godinho who had complained about the prayer-disturbing burden of administrative occupations: " Although the care of temporal affairs may seem to be and is somewhat distracting, I do not doubt that your good and holy intention and the direction of all you do makes your work into something spiritual and highly pleasing to the Divine Goodness. For the distractions, undertaken for God's greater service and in conformity with his divine will, as interpreted through obedience, can be not only equivalent to the union and recollection of assiduous contemplation, but even more acceptable to God, proceeding as they do from an even more ardent charity. May God, our Creator and Lord, deign to preserve and increase this charity in your soul and in the souls of all."[42]

And again to another superior who was saddened under the yoke of his office: " One need not be surprised if on account of the burden of government he sometimes experiences a lack of devotion and is full of distractions. But if one only bears this lack of devotion and these distractions with patience — with the thought of the holy obligation which is imposed through obedience and brotherly love, and adding the intention of serving God better thereby — then he will not be without high reward before God — nay, an even greater reward will be his."[43]

What the previous texts have already indicated is expressly emphasized by Ignatius and his faithful interpreter, Nadal. The Jesuit has to direct all prayer to the apostolate and by the apostolate his prayer is fructified. Ignatius formulated this briefly in one instance as follows: " A distraction borne according to the will of God in the service of one's neighbor cannot do any harm."[44] And again, in his very beautiful instruction concerning prayer in the Society of Jesus, Nadal does not leave room for any doubt that for the Jesuit the value of his prayer must be judged by its apostolic fruitfulness: "... prayer should be the guide, and it increases, directs, and enhances all the activities with spiritual relish, by imparting to them its greater breadth and strength; and the activities in turn increase and enhance the prayer with strength and joy. In this way, Martha and Mary are united; and through their giving mutual aid to each other, not one part alone of the Christian life (even though it be the better one, contemplation) is embraced;

42 Ibid., IV, 127; *LettersIgn*, pp. 254-255. [Cf. Summa theologiae, Q. 182, a. 3, and *ConsSJComm*, fn. 4 on p. 183.]
43 *EppIgn*, IX, 125.
44 *Responsio Manarei*, no. 17, in *FN*, III, 431.

rather, with the anxiety and trouble over many things now banished, Mary helps Martha and is united with her in our Lord."[45] Prayer and meditation as they are practiced in the Society of Jesus must as a consequence give each one of us the strength and courage to apply himself entirely to the works which the Society undertakes and which are all of the same type: "preaching, explaining Scripture, teaching Christian Doctrine, giving the Exercises, hearing confessions, dispensing the Blessed Sacrament, and practicing other good works. In these labors we must find God in peace and calm, in an inner surrender of the whole man, in light and inner serenity, with a contented heart, that glows with the love of God. And all this we should seek in all other works, even if these are exterior."[46]

How well Nadal here expresses the mind of St. Ignatius is shown by this testimony of a companion: " Ignatius wished that the same spirit he himself possessed in a high degree should be found also in the sons of the Society: namely that in each and every work of love they should have no less devotion than in prayer and meditation since it is fitting that we do everything only out of love and for the service of God and to his honor and glory."[47]

Thus according to the mind and spirit of the Father of the order, the daily life of its sons is realized in work, study for the scholastics, the apostolate for the fathers. The consequent impossibility for extended prayer is fully compensated by " Seeking God in all things." Then the whole day is a prayer as well for the Jesuit as for the monks, only in a different way.

III. What Does Ignatius Mean by " Seeking God in All Things "?

To prevent any false interpretation of this central religious ideal, after a proof of the facts has been furnished, we must here seek a deeper comprehension of the meaning and essence of this principle — " Seeking God in all things." In doing this we shall always look to its connection with Ignatian spirituality as a whole.

Regarding Creation from the Viewpoint of Faith

That which became Ignatius' possession in that hour of grace on the river Cardoner was never to be lost but ever grew in

---

45 *MonNad*, IV, 674.
46 Ibid., 681.
47 *Responsio Manarei*, no. 27, in *FN*, III, 435.

meaning. Each of his disciples should grow in understanding this grace of their founder. " All things," that is, the whole created world, natural and supernatural, the history of individuals, of nations and of the Church, all should be seen in their relation to God — the deepest of all relations. They must be seen in the light of God, and, therefore, in their basic truth. In this regard "they can exercise themselves in seeking the presence of our Lord in all things, for example, in conversing with someone, in walking, looking, tasting, hearing, thinking, and in everything that they do, since it is true that the Divine Majesty is in all things by his presence, power, and essence."[48] Or as Nadal once said, " in these creatures we should consider with sweetness the power of God, and thus the truth of that power in God."[49]

Francis Borgia, when still a duke, received some valuable advice from Ignatius on this matter: " When men go outside themselves, and enter wholly into their Creator and Lord, they have a continual awareness, attention, and consolation; and they perceive with relish how our eternal and highest Good dwells in all created things, giving existence and conservation to all of them by his own infinite being and presence. I readily believe that these and many other considerations will give you abundant consolation. For all things help those who love the Lord entirely, and aid them toward greater merit, joy, and union through intense charity with their Creator and Lord."[50]

In a more particular way, Ignatius teaches his followers to find God in their fellow man. Thus, for example, he instructs the novices in the *Constitutions*: " In everything they should try and desire to give the advantage to the others, esteeming them all in their hearts as better than themselves and showing exteriorly, in an unassuming and simple religious manner, the respect and reverence befitting each one's state, in such a manner that by observing one another they grow in devotion and praise God our Lord, whom each one should endeavor to recognize in his neighbor as in his image."[51]

Wholly in the spirit of St. Ignatius, Nadal has said on this point: " Let us place the perfection of our prayer in the contemplation of the Most Holy Trinity, which extends itself to our neighbor in the employments of our calling."[52]

48 *EppIgn*, III, 510; *LettersIgn*, p. 240.
49 *MonNad*, IV, 678.
50 *EppIgn*, I, 339-342; *LettersIgn*, pp. 82-86.
51 *Cons*, [250].
52 From *Annotationes in Examen*; quoted by Miguel Nicolau, *Jerónimo Nadal* (Madrid, 1949), p. 256.

According to Ignatius, in the *Constitutions* and in his classic Letter on Obedience, a genuine religious foundation in obedience demands that all see in a superior the supreme authority of God and hear in his command the word of God. " In our superiors who have charge of us, we should always behold the person of Christ, whom they represent."[53]

Since the Divine Trinity has appeared to us in Jesus Christ and all history is centered in him, the religious view of the world is Christological: " The condition of prayer is one condition of the spiritual life in Jesus Christ. Therefore, just as he is the eternal light and infinite goodness, so he should be known and loved above everything, and everything else should be known and loved in him; ... we should see and recognize the Divine Virtue and Goodness in all things."[54]

Of course that deep mystic insight into the unity of all things in God is not given to the disciple as it was to the holy founder of the order. But in a living faith, through contemplation and study, he should seek in his own way to attain an ever more unified view of all things in God. A view of all creation in the spirit of the Contemplation for Obtaining Love will be for him on that account a constant desire and a growing joyous discovery.

The Continual Search for the Divine Will

Ignatius never considered this viewing of creation through the eyes of faith, as the first meaning of " Finding God in all things," to be a goal and end in itself. We find in him nothing of that Neo-Platonic intellectualism that is found in other forms of Christo-centric mysticism, even in the theory of the great masters. In his view of God, central to which are God's holy will and omnipotent activity, he does not consider mere knowledge as the most exalted thing. It is deeds that matter: surrender to the will of God and loving service. Therefore, for St. Ignatius, " Seeking God in all things " meant search for the will of God through humble prayer and personal effort in all decisions occurring in human life.

After his conversion at Loyola, Ignatius was constantly searching for this divine will, first for his personal life, then increasingly more, especially after 1539, for the group of followers entrusted to him.

---

53 Letter to the scholastics at Alcalá, no. 8, in *EppIgn*, XII, 675: *LettersIgn*, p. 441.

54 From Nadal's treatise, *On Prayer, Especially for Those of the Society*, in *Mon-Nad*, IV, 676. [A translation of this important document is to be found in *Woodstock Letters*, LXXXIX (1960), 285-294.]

It is deeply stirring how systematically he labored between the years 1521 and 1539 to find the will of God, step by step, for his life and his work. " During this time, Ignatius did not know what our Lord intended him to do. But God knew and so directed everything in order to make him founder of the Society," as Ribadeneyra once testified.[55] Walter Nigg in his book, *Warriors of God*, has masterfully described this passionate searching for the will of God: " To find the will of God was the central problem of his life... His concern was always to discover the will of God. Around this goal and around nothing else he revolved incessantly as around a fireplace. It is the source of the compelling charm of his career. Unless one considers this constant effort, Ignatius' later life remains an incomprehensible puzzle. Above all we must center our attention on how Ignatius never wanted to act according to his own will, therefore never to do what appealed to him just at that moment. He continually strives to discover what God wants him to do in this particular situation... Ignatius knew that this search for the divine will is not easy, but he never surrendered. Throughout his whole life we find this often painful effort at continually renewed enquiries after the divine will. His constant prayer for the manifestation of God's will is exceedingly touching to observe, and one becomes absorbed with him in his search. One cannot imagine a more exciting struggle. If you want to become familiar with his heart, you have to view this man as restlessly seeking after the will of God."[56]

The search for the will of God is also the central theme and the burning concern of the Exercises, as Ignatius expresses it in the very introduction —"... by the term ' spiritual exercises ' is meant every method ... of preparing and disposing the soul ... to seek and find the will of God in the disposition of one's life."[57] Each individual exercise contributes to this effort to know the will of God, first and foremost, however, in the choice of a vocation and way of life. Once again, the final meditation seeks to expand this humble and noble-minded readiness for the will of God into an all-embracing plan of life. Thus " Finding God in all things " means precisely to seek, find, and perform the divine will at every hour and in every action. Unreserved readiness for the service of God and complete submission to God's will, in all matters, whether great or small, is the meaning of the *Suscipe*.

55 *MonRib*, II, 903.
56 Walter Nigg, *Vom Geheimnis der Mönche* (Zürich-Stuttgart, 1953), p. 378.
57 *SpEx*, [1].

Another gripping testimony to this is the *Spiritual Diary* of the saint. His main concern for forty days focused on the poverty of the order's churches. More basically, however, he asked what was the holy will of God in this regard. Therefore we are not surprised to meet this passionate concern about the recognition of God's will in the closing formula of innumerable letters written by the saint.

"I beseech God our Lord, who one day will judge us, to bestow upon us in His infinite goodness the grace that we may perceive His most holy will and fulfill it entirely," we read in a letter from Paris to his brother Martín García, the Lord of Loyola.[58] And in a letter to Sister Teresa Rejadella from Venice, half a year before the arrival of his companions from Paris, he wrote: "I conclude by begging the Most Holy Trinity in its infinite goodness to give us abundant grace to perceive God's most holy will and to accomplish it entirely."[59] And to Polanco, shortly before he took up his post as secretary to Ignatius: "May God in His infinite goodness bestow upon us the fullness of His grace so that we may always perceive his most holy will and accomplish it entirely."[60]

He wrote to the prior of the Teutonic Order in Venice: "In recommending ourselves to the prayers of Your Grace, we beg the infinite goodness of our Lord that he will give us all abundant grace always to know his most holy will and fulfill it completely."[61]

He wrote to Father Godinho at Coimbra: "May Christ our Lord help us all with his abundant grace that we may know his holy will and fulfill it entirely."[62] He wrote to the Carthusian Prior Kalckbrenner in Cologne: "May God in his immeasurable charity grant to all of us his grace and holy spirit, that we may be able always to know and fulfill his divine will."[63]

We should not say that these are mere formulas. Ignatius was never a man of empty formulas, least of all in religious matters. Rather these closures of his letters are an everyday testimony of his passionate concern for the will of God in his life and in his order.

How this deep concern for the recognition of the divine will has passed over to his followers as an enkindling spark of burning zeal appears in the letters of St. Francis Xavier. No one would

---

58 *EppIgn*, I, 83; *LettersIgn*, p. 8.
59 *EppIgn*, I, 107; *LettersIgn*, p. 18.
60 *EppIgn*, I, 459; *LettersIgn*, p. 115.
61 *EppIgn*, II, 446.
62 Ibid., IV, 127; *LettersIgn*, p. 255.
63 *EppIgn*, VIII, 585; *LettersIgn*, p. 378.

suspect Xavier of a merely exterior imitation of Ignatius' style, though he loved him so intensely.

Xavier wrote Ignatius, on January 12, 1549: " So I conclude, begging your holy and fatherly love (and I write this on my knees as if I had you before me, beloved Father of my soul) to recommend me to God, our Lord, in your Holy Sacrifices and in your prayers so that he may let me understand his most holy will in this life and grant me his grace to fulfill it entirely. Amen. In the same spirit I recommend myself to all the members of our Society."[64] He wrote to King John III of Portugal: " May our Lord permit Your Majesty to realize his most holy will in your innermost soul and grant you the grace that you may be able to perform it in such a manner as one day at the hour of death you shall rejoice to have acted..."[65] And once more Xavier addressed the same person: " May God, our Lord, in his love and inexhaustible mercy illumine Your Majesty in your innermost soul and make you understand his will so that you may be enabled to perform it in such a manner as one day at the hour of death before the divine judgment seat may redound to your joy."[66] Finally Xavier on another occasion wrote to Ignatius: " For the love of God and His service, I beg your holy paternal love and the entire Society continually to remember me in your prayers; and it is my deepest desire that your holy paternal love itself may recommend me to all of Ours and especially to the professed. May our Lord, in response to this widespread intercession, give me the grace to recognize correctly his most holy will in this life and accomplish it to perfection."[67]

We stand here face to face with the true meaning of " Seeking God in all things," much more than when we focus on the faith view of the world, which is, to be sure, a presupposition for Ignatius' phrase. The genuine Ignatian interpretation means: At every hour of the day and before making any decision, one must inquire after the will of God and then allow God to dispose of oneself entirely. Or, after the example of Christ, " to be free to devote oneself exclusively to the service of the eternal Father."[68] Thus the formula " To seek God in all things " has a far deeper significance than merely serving God in all things. We can see why

---

64 *EppXav*, II, 16; *CartasXav*, p. 286; Coleridge, *Xavier*, II, 75.
65 *EppXav*, II, 63; *CartasXav*, p. 305; Coleridge, *Xavier*, II, 83.
66 *EppXav*, II, 119; *CartasXav*, p. 338; Coleridge, *Xavier*. II, 153.
67 *EppXav*, II, 293; *CartasXav*, p. 425; Coleridge, *Xavier*, II, 374-375.
68 *SpEx*, [135].

the mysticism of Ignatius is aptly termed by De Guibert a mysticism of service.[69] Ignatius, therefore, understands prayer as being conformity to the will of God.[70] He does not consider service as a mere consequence of mystical favors but rather as their substance and goal.

In this respect "Seeking God in all things" is also closely united to the ideal of perfect obedience. It is from this same source that the Ignatian concept of an instrument receives its special meaning.

Pure Intention

"Seeking God in all things" signifies for Ignatius not only an external conformity to the will of God but an interior surrender of the heart to Divine Providence. Therefore, universal purity of intention, in the interpretation of the saint himself, is the primary concern of the "election meditations" of the Exercises.

In a previously quoted text of the *Constitutions* the concepts of "finding God," "pure intention," and "wholehearted love" are considered by St. Ignatius as essentially interjoined: "All should make diligent efforts to keep their intention right, not only in regard to their state of life but also in all particular details. In these they should always aim at serving and pleasing the Divine Goodness for its own sake..."[71]

In many other places too, the author of the *Constitutions* has occasion to speak about a pure intention in every act, especially in the Fourth Part, which treats of the scholastics. Then again, in the Seventh Part, which treats of the choice of apostolic labors, and in the Tenth Part. There, purity of intention is reckoned as part of that supernatural foundation which contributes more than any other means to the preservation of the proper spirit in the Society.

While the scholastics "are applying themselves to their studies, just as care must be taken that through fervor in study they do not grow cool in their love of true virtues and of religious life, so also during that time there will not be much place for mortifications and long prayers and meditations. For their devoting themselves to learning, which they acquire with a pure intention of serving God and which in a certain way requires the whole man, will be not less but rather more pleasing to God our Lord during this time of

---

69 *RAM*, XIX (1938), 16.
70 *EppIgn*, III, 502; *LettersIgn*, p. 236.
71 *Cons*, [288].

study."[72] " Furthermore, they should keep their resolution firm to be genuine and earnest students, by persuading themselves that while they are in the colleges they cannot do anything more pleasing to God our Lord than to study with the intention mentioned above."[73]

When Father Miró as confessor at the Court of Lisbon proposed his difficulties, Ignatius wrote him a letter which treats with the greatest freedom of the true apostolic sentiment towards high and low stations. In the middle of this reply we read the sentence: " If we proceed with a right intention, not seeking our own advantage, but rather solely the interests of Jesus Christ, he in his infinite goodness will certainly protect us."[74] The same advice he transmits through Polanco in an instruction to the fathers at the college in Prague: " The better we ourselves are, the more fit instruments we are for the spiritual welfare of our neighbor. Therefore everyone should strive . . . to seek solely the things of Jesus Christ and should awaken in himself lively desires of being a truer and more loyal servant of God and of procuring the success of his cause in everything. Therefore everyone should genuinely deny his own will and judgment according to the divine direction which obedience gives him, whether he be employed in great matters or small."[75]

Just as Ignatius considers conformity to the will of God as prayer, so also he considers a pure intention, directing all to God, as prayer.[76] Or: the members of the Society " should not find less devotion in any work of charity and obedience than in prayer or meditation; for they ought not to do anything except for the love and service of God."[77]

In connection with " Seeking God in all things," the saint repeatedly refers to the necessity of a pure intention. " He desired very much that all members of the Society should have an intention completely right, pure, and unmixed, without any mingling of vanity or stain of self-will and self-interest. He desired that they seek the glory of God in their souls, bodies, and works, and the good of souls in all things, each according to the talent that God has given him."[78]

Purity of intention in every act is nothing else than genuine conformity to the will of God. It is interior surrender to our Lord. It is the constant raising of the heart to God. It is continual

72 *Cons*, [340].
73 *Cons*, [361].
74 *EppIgn*, IV, 627; *LettersIgn*, p. 284
75 *EppIgn*, X, 693-694.
76 Ibid., VI, 91.
77 Ibid., III, 502; *LettersIgn*, p. 236.
78 *FN*, III, 613.

prayer. The ideal of maintaining a pure intention and the necessity of seeking God in all things are essentially identical in the mind of Ignatius.

Pure Love That Serves

Again and again in these texts, the final and deepest motive of every act has been that which the full meaning of " Seeking God in all things " implies, namely pure, selfless, wholehearted love. Conformity to the will of God is brought to perfection by a pure intention which, in the spirituality of Ignatius, is achieved chiefly by love. Therefore, once again we meet the theme of the Contemplation for Obtaining Love. Because God meets us with his love in all things, we should answer him with a like love in all things. This love corresponds with our total dependence upon God, a dependence that is not lessened even through love. We should answer God with a love that serves; that is, a love that fulfills the will and desire of the beloved in everything without any admixture of self-love.

" We should employ continual care to keep our heart with great purity in the love of God, so that we do not love anything created except in him; and also to desire to converse with God alone, and with our neighbor for the love of God, and not for our own pleasure and pastime."[79] Such is the first of those twelve golden rules of the holy Founder to the scholastics of Alcalá. And midway through the religious instruction for the young members of the order, Ignatius completes the idea of the necessity of seeking God in all things and of a pure intention by referring to love. " . . . they should often be exhorted to seek God our Lord in all things, stripping off from themselves the love of creatures to the extent that this is possible, in order to turn their love upon the Creator of them, by loving him in all creatures and all of them in him, in conformity with his holy and divine will."[80]

We meet the same motive in a letter of the saint to Francis Borgia in 1545, at that time still the Duke of Gandía: " All things help those who love the Lord entirely, and aid them toward greater merit, joy, and union through intense charity with their Creator and Lord."[81]

Nadal says in his great instruction on prayer: " . . . there is in our hearts the charity that God, our Lord, inspired there. In

79 *EppIgn*, XII, 674; *LettersIgn*, p. 440.
80 *Cons*, [288].
81 *EppIgn*, I, 342.

this source must be found our fervor and the manifestation of it to all men. This source will be a wonderful help in all the activities of the Society within and without."[82]

Thus the essential similarity of the different formulas has been proven: holiness is equivalent to meeting God in all things in a spirit of faith. This is equivalent to seeking and fulfilling his most holy will in every situation of life. This is equivalent to a pure intention in every act. This is equivalent to a love which serves in the entire breadth and depth of human existence. Ignatius considered contemplation not only as familiarity with God in prayer but in every activity of life.[83] The unity of the love of God and neighbor is also implied here as the sole precept and the epitome of holiness.

IV. *The Way to This Religious Ideal*

The formula "Finding God in all things" came from God, according to Ignatius, in two ways. The idea was granted to him personally as a great and pure grace of his mystical life. Secondly, the Trinity, from whom Ignatius descended to creatures, helped him to execute the ideal. His follower too, who treads the same path of seeking God in all things, must notice this twofold primacy of God. That is, he must pray often and confidently for the grace to be able to find God in all things, to serve and love him. He must first of all come to God with a heart genuinely converted so as never again to lose him even in a busy apostolic ministry.

To cooperate with divine grace and to help in constantly turning the heart to God that one may find God in all things, Ignatius points to three indispensable presuppositions.

1. The first demands, again in the spirit of the Exercises, continual mortification and self-denial. During his battle against protracted prayers, Ignatius had continually returned to this presupposition, without which neither conformity to the will of God nor purity of intention nor constant recollection are possible.

Let us recall once again that conversation between Ignatius and Nadal on November 22, 1554, which Da Câmara relates in his *Memoriale*: "The Father said that his opinion, from which no one would ever move him, was that for the scholastics one hour of prayer is sufficient, it being supposed that they are practicing mortification and self-denial."[84] And Da Câmara sums up his conversation

82 Nadal, *On Prayer*, in *MonNad*, IV, 681.
83 *Cons*, [723].
84 Da Câmara, *Memoriale*, no. 256, in *FN*, I, 676-677.

of the next day with Ignatius as follows: " Thus our Father placed the whole foundation " of the spiritual life " in mortification and abnegation of will."[85]

Again and again in his battle against many exterior works of penance and lengthy time for prayer, Ignatius emphasizes the connection between finding God in all things and mortification and self-denial. Thus, for instance, in the already mentioned letter to the scholastics of Coimbra on May 7, 1547, and again in a letter of June 1, 1551, to the rector of Coimbra concerning the direction of the scholastics we find: " The truly mortified man who has conquered his passions finds in his prayer what he desires much more readily than a person who is unmortified and imperfect. This is the reason why our blessed Father held mortification in such high esteem. He preferred it to the prayer which does not have mortification as its end, and then, through this means, union of oneself with God."[86]

In the discussions concerning the settlement of the time for prayer which several provincial congregations engaged in after the death of Francis Borgia, general of the order, the Portuguese Province proposed an exceptionally wise solution. It rested upon the supposition that the life of prayer in the Society had suffered considerable damage. To be sure, the time devoted to prayer had not been curtailed, but it was bearing much less fruit as was evidenced in the decline of apostolic zeal. First on the list among the remedies and the most necessary was a constant mortification. Then the rich graces of prayer of the former period could be expected. The other recommendations of the assembled fathers were as follows: cultivation of the life of prayer in the true spirit and according to the genuine methods of the Exercises instead of adopting ways of prayer foreign and strange to the order which only furthered the interests of self-will; elimination of all secular employments; moderation in bodily recreation and in the thirst for knowledge; and finally, the practice of the presence of God which belongs to the spiritual essence of the order.[87] All in all, this is a document dictated in the genuine spirit of Ignatius. It was not in vain that Da Câmara was one of the leading men of this provincial congregation.

According to Ignatius only the individual who has leapt out of all disordered attachment to the world and his own ego is capable

85 Ibid.
86 *FN*, III, 636.
87 *AHSJ*, III (1934), 97.

of truly finding God in all things. In the opinion of Nadal, few reach the very height of this ideal of holiness precisely because many lack that complete indifference of the will and true freedom of heart requisite for it.

2. The second presupposition is a constant source of help in finding God in all things. It is true prayer, which is absolutely necessary and implies for Ignatius not only perseverance but skill. Without formal prayer at determined times, the ideal of finding God in all things remains a dangerous illusion. On the other hand, methodical prayer must be surpassed and developed into a habitual attitude of prayer that is no longer bound by time or by method.

" Recollection and solitude in the beginning " are good.[88] There is need for a " definite rule and method," " a period of training."[89] This training in prayer from which Ignatius expects much fruit of personal prayer is given especially in the Exercises. But above and beyond this training, there is demanded a continual cultivation of an attitude of prayer through a regular program of interior prayer and meditation. " Once a person has made the Exercises," says Nadal, " the life of prayer must be guided, preserved, and increased through perseverance in prayer and in the ministries of our vocation."[90] But this practice in prayer should further develop organically, as he adds in the very next paragraph: " Finally, we must find God, our Lord, in all things and in our own individual method of prayer."[91]

3. The third presupposition is the explicit practice of seeking God in all things which is bound up with constant renewal of recollection. Only by the constant repetition of this will a habit gradually be acquired. Even Ignatius himself, one of the greatest mystics, once wrote to Simão Rodrigues: " I have been thinking in our Lord of telling you how much I desire to recollect myself every hour and often to remember, how the good angels, in matters which are delicate and important, are wont to keep themselves continually alert to strengthen and build up, ..."[92]

As regards this exercise, Father Mannaerts relates a striking example: " When a certain father once complained to Ignatius that he was called often to the door by strangers and that this was seriously distracting him from interior union with God, the saint replied: ' You should always receive with great charity those who

88 Nadal, *On Prayer*, in *MonNad*, IV, 673.
89 *MonNad*, IV, 645, 691.
90 Ibid., 675.
91 Ibid.
92 *EppIgn*, XII, 630; *LettersIgn*, p. 130.

come to you to obtain spiritual help and consolation. But after you have been called, or while you are on the way, make use beforehand of some ejaculatory prayer. Beg God that he may deign to help that person through you. Then you should direct all your thoughts and conversations toward helping your visitor to make spiritual progress. In this way you will not be experiencing distractions to no avail, but you will be making progress. And if in these circumstances you do not feel yourself to be as united with God as you were while undisturbed, you should not be worried. For a distraction which has been undertaken for the glory of God will not be detrimental to you.' "[93]

We come upon the same advice in another saying of the founder: " We should do nothing of any importance without first asking, however briefly, counsel from God as from a very good and wise Father."[94] The examination of conscience, to be made twice a day, on which Ignatius laid more stress and considered of greater importance than meditation, also has as its object daily recollection in God's presence.

How " Finding God in all things " is at the same time a grace from God and an exercise for us, Nadal has explained in his instruction on prayer. He wrote: " It is good to know that there are two ways to enter into prayer. The one way is through simple and humble meditation on creatures, whether natural or supernatural, such as the Incarnation ... the sacraments, all infused graces; and in these creatures we should consider with sweetness the power of God, and thus the truth of that power in God. The other way occurs when grace anticipates one with a higher illumination, so that he comes to consider and contemplate God in every lower being."[95] The trinitarian mysticism of St. Ignatius is a good example of this second method in its purest form. It does not lie in the power of man to procure or even to merit such moments of grace. But he can prepare himself for them with humility and holy desire by raising his mind to God in a spirit of faith in all the activities of daily life, a practice constantly accessible to him.

Concluding Reflection

In an essentially monastic spirituality, apostolic labors are considered if not a disturbance of contemplative recollection, at least as

---

93 *Responsio Manarei*, no. 17, in *FN*, III, 430-431; quoted in Huonder, *Ignatius*, p. 179.

94 *Responsio Manarei*, no. 16, in *FN*, III, 430.

95 *MonNad*, IV, 678-679.

its interruption. Through " Seeking God in all things," Ignatius has indicated to his order, which is entirely directed to the apostolate, the way to an interior union of prayer and work. Prayer urges to work, work enriches prayer, so that they become increasingly one. The follower of Ignatius is a contemplative in action.

Nadal in his treatise " On Prayer, Especially for Those of the Society " has a paragraph which is worth noting. And we should not forget that Polanco in his *Chronicon* says that Nadal had a deeper understanding of Ignatius and a better knowledge of his spirit than any other.[96] Nadal writes: " Consider that the active life and the contemplative life should make their way side by side. The time of probation, so exacting, brings it about that the active life reaches a certain perfection, and also that the contemplative life already dominates, governs, and guides the active life with peace and light in the Lord. And in this way one arrives at a superior active life, one which supposes both the active life and the contemplative life and has the power to impress them both deeply in all souls, in accordance with what is more conducive to greater service of God. Briefly, the action of charity, when united to God, is perfect action."[97]

96 *PolChron*, III, 427.
97 *MonNad*, IV, 679.

THE MYSTICISM OF ST. IGNATIUS
ACCORDING TO HIS *SPIRITUAL DIARY*

Adolf Haas

IGNATIUS OF LOYOLA was "a man of the most penetrating intellect, immense strength of will and untiring energy, averse to all fanaticism and fantasy, filled with the purest love of God and neighbor.[1] Who could even suspect that this same saint "was an incomparable mystic"[2] to the very depths of his being ? And yet, one would fail to recognize the deepest source from which the Ignatian energy took its origin, if one were to overlook the life of faith of this great religious founder, a life aflame with mystic ardor.

We must treasure the historically faithful, voluminous, and illuminating accomplishments of hagiographers, whose work is directed to collecting all available historical facts, as an indispensable foundation. Nevertheless, it cannot be too strongly emphasized that the self-portrait sketched by Ignatius in his *Autobiography* and in his *Spiritual Diary*, with its fresh and colorful expressiveness, far surpasses all other sources, even the letters which are so important for forming a picture of the saint's character. Alfred Feder, S.J., has said of the *Autobiography*, which Ignatius dictated a few years before his death at the request of his fellow religious: "There are, to be sure, only a few streams of light that make their way through to us from within his mystical interior life; but they suffice to give us a vague idea of what splendid beams of shining grace blazed in his soul."[3] This is even more evident in his *Spiritual Diary*, of which the few pages preserved for us "belong together with the most

Study 6 was translated by G. Richard Dimler, S.J.

1 Alfred Feder, *Aus dem Geistlichen Tagebuch des heiligen Ignatius* (Regensburg, 1922), p. vi.
2 "un contemplativo y mistico incomparable," Larrañaga, *Obras Completas*, I, 629.
3 Feder, *Tagebuch*, p. 29.

beautiful and most noble pages that Christian mystics have set down on paper."[4] Here the saint is alone with God and himself. The tender, manly shyness so characteristic of him does not disturb him for a moment as he records and reveals the most intimate secrets existing between himself and God. This shyness left in meaningful obscurity what is most profound in the reminiscences that were meant for others, and thereby endowed his story of the " pilgrim " with an inimitable literary charm.

In the *Diary*, however, Ignatius lays completely bare the mystery of his intimacy with God. Consequently, no other document offers us a more penetrating insight into the magnificent world of faith that was the inner life of Ignatius. Only with discretion and reverence will the reader or interpreter of these records enter the most intimate area of the saint's soul. Therefore, in our investigation, we are not interested in describing the subjective properties of Ignatian mysticism as the *Diary* reveals them to us (for example, the gift of tears, different forms of mystical exaltation, all that belongs to a " psychology " of this type of mysticism). Ignatius' mysticism comprehended the whole history of salvation in a manner unusually extensive; and our primary purpose is to expose this horizon, the marvelous guidance of God, and the gradual development by which the mysteries of faith were the influence molding the saint's spirituality.

The *Spiritual Diary* of St. Ignatius and the mysticism manifesting itself therein do not have the poetic flights of the artistic style of John of the Cross nor the profound philosophico-theological speculation and linguistic splendor of Augustine's *Confessions*. Neither do we find, among its characteristics, the clear and at the same time interiorly glowing pedagogy of the autobiography of St. Theresa, nor the heavenly sweetness of the writings of Suso. The uniqueness of this mysticism lies purely and simply in an overpowering fullness of the lived and experienced deposit of faith and also in a knowledge which stems from this inner richness of spiritual vision, a knowledge regarded by Nadal as an orderly arrangement in the spiritual life (*ordo vitae spiritualis*).

The Writing of the Diary and the Interior Life of Ignatius

The fact that Ignatius, who had so little literary talent, kept a diary from the days of his conversion is amazing, but it is also significant. Two reasons make this fact somewhat understandable: gratitude to God and vigilance of conscience.

4 Ibid., p. 1.

Ignatius thought of the recording of the graces he received
above all as an act of personal thanksgiving.[5] He wishes to recall
again and again the divine favor, particularly since he confesses on
more than one occasion to a " weakness of memory " in regard to
these graces. This can be understood as a sign of the genuinity of
his mysticism.[6] We know that, at the time of his first spiritual
conversion at the castle of Loyola, " when he had already begun to
move a little about the house,"[7] he not only compiled those
passages and mysteries from the lives of Jesus and of the saints
whom he thought most important to himself, but also planned a
diary in which he carefully recorded the " movements " of his soul.
This diary he took with him on his journey to Manresa. " Here
he decided to spend a few days in the hospital and to make a few
notes in his book which he carried very carefully with him and
which brought him many consolations."[8] Even during his journey to
Jerusalem the " pilgrim " kept a diary.[9] In particular, however, he
made daily entries during the composition of the *Constitutions*.[10] We
may therefore presume that throughout his whole life he wrote down
in diary fashion the most important occurrences in the history of his
soul. We also know that he read through these entries again and
again, corrected them, supplemented them.[11] In so doing he frequently reawakened within his heart the mystical ardor of past
experiences.[12] Indeed, at the very moment of writing, the fullness

---

5 Arturo Codina is therefore correct when he writes in his introduction to the
critical edition of the *Spiritual Diary* (*Cons*MHSJ, I, ciii): " This diary is a
catalogue of the benefits received from God, which our father, Ignatius,
drew up because of his great gratitude to God and man. Ignatius did this
not only to stamp them more firmly in his memory, but also to inflame
his heart with an ever-increasing love for such benefactors by a frequent
re-reading of them." Pierre Favre also begins his diary with the psalm
verse: " Bless the Lord, O my soul, and forget not all his benefits "
(Ps 102: 2).
6 *Autobiog*, 29, in *FN*, I, 402; see also the *Spiritual Diary* for April 2, 1544,
and Hugo Rahner, *ZAM*, X (1935), beginning at page 270.
7 *Autobiog*, 11, in *FN*, I, 376.
8 *Autobiog*, 18, in *FN*, I, 388.
9 His first biographer still had access to this; see Ribadeneyra, *Vita Ignatii*,
I, ch. 11, no. 54, in *FN*, IV, 156.
10 *Autobiog*, 100, in *FN*, I, 504-507.
11 Feder, *Tagebuch*, p. 20.
12 *SpDiar*, [9, 125]. The numbers in square brackets, which facilitate otherwise
cumbersome references to the text of the *Spiritual Diary*, are those found
in the edition of Ignacio Iparraguirre in *Obras completas de san Ignacio de
Loyola*, Biblioteca de autores cristianos, no. 86 (Madrid, 1963), pp. 318-386.

of what he had seen often overwhelmed him anew. Thus, he relates on February 27, 1544: " Even while writing this, I feel my understanding drawn to behold the Most Holy Trinity, and behold I see, although not as distinctly as formerly, Three Persons . . .''

Closely linked with his gratitude to God, there is in his daily entries a genuinely Ignatian solicitude for the calm and clear spiritual awareness of the Spirit in the interior life. This clarity and alertness is such a conspicuous part of the spiritual character of the saint that it left behind a deep impression on those around him and became characteristic of the spirituality of the entire order. " The spirit of the Society,'' writes one of his most intimate companions, " is a certain clarity which fills and guides [the soul]; one had the impression that Father Ignatius was so guided.''[13] In this respect it is interesting that even in the *Spiritual Exercises* the recording of meditations and illuminations plays a definite role, one that today is perhaps taken too little into account.[14] Ignatius feared nothing in the religious life so much as an unenlightened soul which, not having learned discernment, allowed itself to be governed by every pious emotion. Moreover, no one surpassed him in his masterful knowledge of the many self-deceptions and the many deceits of the evil spirit that disguise themselves under the appearance of the good. In this practical knowledge we have the other source of the entries in the saint's *Diary*. Thus Laynez was able to say of him: " He exercises such constant guard over his conscience that each day he spends time comparing month with month, week with week, and day with day, always intent on making progress. . .''[15] As the context shows, this scrupulous carefulness is directed not so much to efforts at conquering faults as to the ever more delicate knowledge of the soul-guiding movements of grace

---

13 *MonNad*, IV, 690.
14 The Ignatian *Directories* to the *Spiritual Exercises* (in *SpEx*MHSJ, pp. 778-794; and in *DirSpEx*) often encourage this. For example, " For one who has the time, it is better not to bring the points already written out, but, after having explained the matter, to dictate them so that the exercitant may write them in his own hand '' (*SpEx*MHSJ, p. 780; *DirSpEx*, p. 74). Or: " One could encourage him to write down his insights and [inner] movements '' (*SpEx*, p. 784; *DirSpEx*, p. 84). In regard to methods of meditation using writing, see R. Graber, *Aus der Kraft des Glaubens* (Würzburg, 1950), pp. 139ff.; E. Roellenbleck, " Über des Schreiben von ' Betrachtungen,' '' *Der Psychologe. Psychologische Monatsschrift*, V (1953), 9ff.; G. Trapp, " Betrachten und Schreiben. Zur Frage einer schriftlichen Betrachtungsmethode,'' *GeistLeb*, XXVI (1953), 437ff.; A. Rodewyk, " Wir schreiben Gott einen Brief,'' *GeistLeb*, XXVII (1954), 153ff.
15 *SdeSI*, I, 127; *FN*, I, 140.

which God imparted to him from the time of Manresa and to the ever more exact correspondence with them.

Unfortunately, only a small portion of the " History of a Soul," as Ignatius wrote it down, has been preserved. The saint himself destroyed most of it toward the end of his life. A small remnant was found in his desk after he died. There are two notebooks. The first contains the period from February 2 to March 12, 1544. On many of the days there are very detailed entries on the astonishingly rich, mystic interior life of the saint. During these forty days the question of poverty in the Society preoccupied him above all others. In regard to this matter he wanted to make a decision completely under the influence of the divine light.[16] The second small notebook, with its first entry on March 13, 1544, immediately follows the first and ends on February 27, 1545. It contains only very short notations and symbols for the individual days.

The following facts prove that Ignatius must have been greatly preoccupied with his entries in the diary. Some of the entries were subsequently framed with lines in order to designate them expressly as being of particular importance.[17] In addition, the saint made transcriptions of these places which were so full of meaning for him. Luckily, we possess still another page on which just such " italicized " passages from the first part of the *Diary* are transcribed.[18] One may reasonably assume[19] that still other pages with similar excerpts in Ignatius' own hand must have existed. In all likelihood they played a role in the process of the election on the question of poverty along with the pages on which the reasons for and against the choice to be made were placed side by side. According to the testimony of his mass server, Paul Borell,[20] Ignatius frequently placed these pages on the altar in order to ask for new illumination while celebrating the holy mysteries.

16 Further historical details concerning the origin and significance of the *Spiritual Diary* are to be found in the excellent introduction to Feder's German translation mentioned in footnote 1 above; see also *Cons*MHSJ, I, ccv.
17 With regard to the places that Ignatius placed in parentheses with his own hand, there is no question of any deletions or erasures as Feder thinks (*Tagebuch*, p. vi); but, on the contrary, these are places that he wishes to emphasize; see *Cons*MHSJ, I, xcvi.
18 *Cons*MHSJ, I, xcvi-xcvii.
19 See Codina in *Cons*MHSJ; also in Feder.
20 Feder, *Tagebuch*, p. 12.

The Structure and Lines of Development in the Spiritual Diary

The saint's *Diary* points to such a central position for the mystery of the Trinity in his life that an expert on mysticism like De Guibert could say, " I believe it will be difficult to find a mystical development of this mystery of spirituality which is more perfect than that which is revealed in the *Spiritual Diary* we are studying here."[21]

We will now attempt to show first of all how this trinitarian spirituality not only dominated the entire course of Ignatius' life after Manresa, but also how from the very beginning in the fourfold prayer of Manresa, this mystery considered in itself was comprehended in its most fundamental reality; that is, from the aspect of the powerful trinitarian tension existing between the personal fullness of the three Divine Persons and their eternal unity in the divine Essence. Here we have probably encountered the deepest theological nucleus of the Ignatian concept of God, the ever greater God (*Deus semper major*), whose simplicity, which comprehends everything in its eternal and essential unity, is eternally being " surpassed " by the equally eternal fruitfulness and plenitude of the Divine Persons. Their personal plenitude, however, is just as necessarily and eternally being gathered into the all-unifying depths of the divine Essence.

Furthermore, the Ignatian *Diary* gives us testimony as to how the saint was led by God step by step through the abysses and heights of this trinitarian tension. A more penetrating, comparative examination of this gradual process shows us, however, that the unfolding of this trinitarian mystery takes place in two directions. The one is the intra-trinitarian aspect with its powerful tension between the trinity of Persons and the unity of the divine Being. The other aspect is the extra-trinitarian in which, through the mystery of the Incarnation, the trinitarian fullness communicates itself to the created and sin-decayed world and thus through Christ draws it back into the threefold life of God. In the *Diary* the intra-trinitarian cycle of development is linked and intertwined so organically with the salvational that the salvational aspect itself appears as nothing but the development of the trinitarian aspect out into the cosmos, which so needs redemption.

At the same time the salvational cycle of thought, at certain stages of Ignatius' interior development, is so clearly contrasted

---

21 Jeseph de Guibert, *St. Ignace mystique d'après son Journal Spirituel* (Toulouse, 1938), p. 35.

with the trinitarian cycle, that the person and work of Christ can completely " replace " the trinitarian, or at least stand as a substitute for it. We see in this the justification for giving particular emphasis to this salvational aspect in the mysticism of the *Diary* and for setting it over against the trinitarian cycle. However, in order to be able to point this out, we must first trace the important stages of development within the *Diary*. Only then will we be able to present the depths of the trinitarian and christological mysticism of Ignatius and the rich interplay between the two aspects. In the *Diary* the mystical journey takes place in four stages.

First Stage: *From the Divine Persons to the Unity of Their Mutual Indwelling* (*Perichoresis*)

Ignatius begins with the blissful experience[22] of how the intercessors (Mary, the divine Son) place petitions before the Father, and how the three Divine Persons communicate themselves in their personal individuality and according to the character of their divine missions to the suppliant who presents the offering of complete poverty (*Spiritual Diary*, [16, 46, 54]). He understands his own mission entirely from the aspect of the missions of the individual Persons of the Trinity (*SpDiar*, [15]). The divine guidance reaches its luminous climax on February 21 in the bounteous and exceptionally powerful vision of the circumincession (*perichoresis*), the mutual indwelling of the three Persons in the same divine Being ([15]). Now Ignatius sees, in this powerful vision of unity, how he " belongs to all three [Persons]" in the mystery of the circumincession ([63]); how the intense trinitarian tension is thereby resolved (this tension had actually become for him a " knot and a difficulty "); and how his own mission is contained within the trinitarian unity.

Second Stage: *From Jesus as Man to Jesus as God*

The following days[23] are in very clear contrast to the first trinitarian stage. Jesus now stands at the center of the inner experiences. On February 23 and 24, Ignatius wrote in the margin, in large letters, the leading idea of these and the following days: " Confirmation of Jesus " (*confirmación de Jesús*) [of the election on poverty]. Although the picture of Jesus during these days shows Christ in the humble form of a man, it is nonetheless completely

---

22 *SpDiar*, [1-64], Feb. 2-22, 1544.
23 *SpDiar*, [65-88], Feb. 23-28, 1544.

illuminated by the light of the Trinity. "It seemed to me that this self-manifestation or self-communication of Jesus was somehow the work of the Most Holy Trinity..." wrote Ignatius on February 23, and he is reminded of the hour of grace at La Storta. At the same time this remark is an indication of the inner connection between the Jesus-mysticism of the *Diary* and the priest-mysticism of La Storta, which in turn points back to the Christ-mysticism of Ignatius' "primitive church" at Manresa. On February 24, Ignatius emphasized, by drawing lines around it, a passage in his *Diary* which shows with what intimacy he is united in love with the "Head of the Society" during these days. "At these times, when I perceived or saw Jesus, I felt so great a love within me that I thought that nothing could happen in the future that would separate me from him, or cause me to doubt about the graces or confirmation I had received" ([75]). Jesus stands so completely in the focus of these days that Ignatius, who desired a renewed confirmation by the Trinity of his choice of poverty, received it only through Jesus. Yet the image of Jesus during these days is totally transparent to the Holy Trinity. Jesus is wholly Son of the eternal Father, so that over and over the exclamation, "What a Father and what a Son!" ([72]), escapes from Ignatius' soul. In a vision which is incapable of being described in words, Ignatius sees how the prayers at Mass are directed to the Father by Jesus. On the two final days of this stage of development (February 27-28) the vision of the unity of Jesus and the Most Holy Trinity reaches its climax. Both are revealed simultaneously. Jesus "at the feet of the Most Holy Trinity" ([88]) appears to him no longer as before, in his most holy humanity alone ("in a white light; that is, his humanity"), but as "completely God." Thus this stage of development consists in the inner ascent from Jesus-Man to Jesus-God.

Third Stage: From the Perichoretic Unity of Persons to the Divine Essence

The following days[24] lead Ignatius further on into the trinitarian mystery and thus they are in clear contrast with the days of the visions of Jesus. The first stage had led Ignatius right up to the blissful unity of the perichoresis of the Divine Persons. Now the divine leadership resumes, first allowing him to experience once more the mutual indwelling of the Divine Persons ([89-95]). Then, however, something new breaks in with overwhelming force, the glorious vision

24 *SpDiar*, [89-125], Feb. 29-March 6, 1544.

of the one divine essence ([99-125]). This divine essence had already appeared in the perichoresis as the all-unifying background. Now, however, Ignatius is led to this all-embracing and all-unifying divine essence itself. St. Ignatius' own words indicate that the visions are so illuminating that he believes " this intense consolation and love to be more significant and excellent than all the former consolations " ([105]). At this point we have reached, without the slightest doubt, the most profound section of the mystical way in the *Diary*, the basic foundation of the Trinity and of all things. On the last two days of this stage the vision of the Divine Persons is again developed out of this divine foundation. At first, he sees the Father as " the source and origin of the divinity " (*fons et origo divinitatis*), and then the other Persons. This " essential " experience remains so memorable in the life of St. Ignatius that he now comprehends all the trinitarian and salvational events from the viewpoint of this divine foundation.

Fourth Stage : A Mysticism of Reverential Love
(amor reverencial)

After these days[25] of most profound trinitarian experiences, a sharp break takes place in the further development of the *Diary*. In the following weeks there is not very much in the way of content. The depths of the mystery of the Trinity were traversed in an incomparable mystical journey (first and third stages) ; and in the ascent from Christ as Man to Christ as God (second stage) the salvational line of development was attributed to the trinitarian. In addition, the election of poverty had found a double confirmation : through the Trinity and through Jesus. The new aspect which now presses into the foreground in this stage of the *Diary* is a spiritual attitude, reverential love. Ignatius embraces this notion, at this time repeatedly suggested to him by God, with such interior ardor that, along with De Guibert (p. 58), we can name the mysticism of this final period of the *Diary* as the mysticism of reverential love (*amor reverencial*), or also, of the service of God (*mystique du service de Dieu*). Undoubtedly, here we have once again encountered an essential element of Ignatian spirituality as it was first conceived at Manresa, a basic attitude pervading the whole of the *Exercises*. Now, however, in the mysticism of the mature Ignatius, it has plainly become the all-pervading milieu of his profound mystical experiences.

25 *SpDiar*, [126-490], March 7, 1544-Feb. 27, 1545.

After the overwhelming trinitarian experiences of the third stage of the *Spiritual Diary*, the redemptive and intercessory aspects are again, and more intensely, dominant in this final period. This is not to be understood as if the mystery of salvation would be the only content of these days. For during these days all the former trinitarian and salvational visions recur in succession. But all these mystical experiences now stand almost exclusively and indeed emphatically within an atmosphere of creaturely reverence and humble, willing love. It is the "mood" of the proximity to earth of the salvation mystery. The new situation is clearly expressed in the interior direction that Ignatius is now following. Up to this point (first through third stages) his whole view was directed away from earth and out toward the great mysteries "up there high above the heavens." On March 6, after the vision of the divine essence and of the Father, which surpassed all previous ones, Ignatius says: "Thus I had the feeling of great security without being able to doubt the correctness of what had been revealed to me. Rather, as I examined and considered it again, I felt new interior movements, bearing me wholly to the love of what I had seen, to the point that I thought I saw more clearly illumined beyond the heavens what I sought to consider here with the understanding, as I have said" ([122]). One can perceive the decisive, interior "change of situation," the new direction in which Ignatius is moved when one reads immediately afterwards the first sentence of the following day (March 7): "When I entered into the customary prayer I had great devotion in the beginning, but I did not succeed in growing in devotion although I desired it and cast my glance upwards" ([126]).

As always, whenever a new interior path is opened up to him, Ignatius at this moment assumes an attitude of complete spiritual indifference ([127]): "Later, while vesting, new emotions forced me to tears and to conformity with the Divine Will, towards which the Lord was leading me, guiding me, etc. 'I am now indeed just a child' (Jer. 1: 6)" ([127]). Thus Ignatius, no longer looking heavenward, "but midway" ([127-128]), is once again given a share in the interior visitation (*la visita interior*). This is accompanied by a growing sense of reverence and reverential awe (*acatamiento y reverencia*). The visitations are related both to the trinitarian and the redemptive spheres. In a mighty descending movement, Ignatius sees the depths of the Trinity, then the Father and the Son, and finally our Blessed Lady and the saints ([129]). It sounds like his own "descent into hell" when Ignatius on that very same day meditates on hell in order to confirm himself in the paths of indifference and reverence. " The thought occurred to me: if God were to send me to hell! Two things appeared before my imagination. The first, the pain I should suffer there; the second, how His name would be blasphemed. As to the first, I was not able to feel or see the punishment, and so it seemed to me that it would be more frightful to hear His holy name blasphemed " ([132]).

The following days serve to confirm the humble path of creaturely reverence more and more. " There was a deep contentment in the preparatory prayer and in the chapel. While vesting, I had fresh inspirations, lasting to the end, becoming greater, and with many tears. I felt such a great humility that it kept me from even looking up to the heavens. The less I wished to look above, and the more I desired to humble and lower myself, the more I felt the relish of spiritual consolation " ([135]). Ignatius now sees an angel as the great example of continual standing in the presence of God and of constant sensitivity and readiness for the duties of his mission ([141]). He begins at this time to turn away decisively from the consolation of the gift of tears which had always accompanied his visitations up to this time. " Without tears or any sign of them before Mass or during it. But I found in the customary prayer very special grace and in the Mass, during the greater part of it, much sweet consolation. I thought that it was a greater perfection to find interior devotion and love without tears, as the angels do. Part of the time there was no diminution but rather an increase in consolation in comparison with the previous day " ([176]). Thus this last stage of the *Diary* is the beginning of the spiritualization characteristic of the mature mystic. We shall call this stage, as did Hugo Rahner, his spiritual period (*Geistperiode*).

During these days he makes his final decision in the matter of poverty. After many tormenting doubts and " temptations " (particularly on March 12), Ignatius recognizes in the light of his deepened indifference that further waiting for confirmatory consolations serves more his " own satisfaction " than the pleasure of God, our Lord ([146]). Thus the way is now open for the new path upon which the Lord wills to lead him to the ultimate responsiveness of reverential love. " During all this time before, during, and after Mass, I was penetrated with the thought of the deep reverence and respect with which I ought to pronounce the name of God, our Lord, etc., while on the way to say Mass; and how I ought to look not for tears but for this respect and reverence. And this to such an extent, that, exercising myself often in this reverence, in my room, before Mass and in the chapel, if tears came during Mass

174

I at once repressed them, turning my mind to this reverence... As a result, I gained the conviction that this was the path our Lord wished to show me, since during the past two days I kept thinking that he wanted to show me something. While I said Mass, I was persuaded that this grace and knowledge meant more for my own spiritual advantage than all those that went before" (no. 157). Yet it is precisely into this accented attitude of humility that the former trinitarian grace now descends "in an abundance of knowledge, consolation, and spiritual relish" ([164]).

On May 11, Ignatius notices for the first time that the gift of tears is again given to him in an entirely novel, interiorized manner. "The tears of today seemed to be much different from those of former days since they came more slowly, interiorly, and gently, without noise or notable movements; and it seemed to me that they came from within, without my knowing how to explain them" ([222]). Moreover, during these days he shared in the mystical gift of "interior speech" (*loquela*), which caused him to perceive interiorly such rapturous harmony and music that he was unable to express it. "Everything moved me to divine love and to the gift of the divinely bestowed locution, with so much interior harmony in the spiritual locution that I cannot explain it" ([222]).

All these experiences, however, are the result of his reverential love which is filled with a completely mystical ardor. "In this interval of time, I thought that humility, reverence, and respect should not be fearful but loving; and this was so firmly imprinted in my mind that I said with confidence, 'Give me a loving humility and also reverence and respect!'; and I received fresh consolation at these words" ([178]). In the love of the Trinity pouring itself out into the world in the mystery of creation and redemption, Ignatius feels himself also sent out into the world since he realizes that he "should not stop there," at the memories of all he had experienced, but that he "should have the same attitude towards creatures; that is, humility filled with love" ([179]).

This then is the culmination of Ignatian mysticism as found in the *Spiritual Diary*: a humble love of reverence and service oriented toward this world. At the end of the process there is no smothering of creation in the presence of the all-overwhelming Trinitarian God; but, just as in the Contemplation to Attain Love at the end of the *Exercises*, there is an awakening of creation's most profound and inner harmony since the Triune God bends down in eternal love toward the universe and pours himself out into the world through his gifts.

I

The Mysticism of the Trinity in the Spiritual Diary

After having indicated the gradual development of the trinitarian and christological mysteries in the *Diary*, it is necessary to introduce once more the focal point, hitherto little stressed, of the development of the trinitarian mystery as contained in the *Diary*: the grace-laden experience of the overpowering tension between the threeness of the Divine Persons and their absolute unity within the divine essence; in other words, of the tension between being threefold and being three-in-one. From a dogmatic point of view, Ignatius has been introduced to the most essential and profound content of the greatest mystery of the faith. Scheeben says in contemplating the oneness in threeness: " This is the greatest marvel, the supernatural mystery which faith presents to our contemplation, the mystery which our minds cannot approach without faith, which they cannot see as it is even with faith, not to mention being able to exhaust and fathom it in its depths. Yet our minds can contemplate it as reflected in the mirror of belief and can recognize and confess it to be an immeasurable sea of light, an infinitely rich system of the most glorious and exalted truths. It is a mystery which, precisely because it is so superior to them, must draw our minds, and which, through the least glimpse that it may allow them to take into its depths, must fill them with indescribable rapture."[26]

The Development of the Trinitarian Tension from the Time of Manresa

The *Autobiography* of the saint gives us clear evidence that, even at the beginning of his mystical journey at Manresa, the God three and one (*Deus trinus et unus*) entered into the soul of Ignatius with superabundant power so that it might from then on become the ever more fundamental chord that harmonized everything in his life. In his old age he still remembered those days at Manresa when " he had a great devotion to the Most Holy Trinity, and thus daily prayed to the Three Persons individually. But since he was praying to the Holy Trinity as such, the thought occurred to him that he could say four prayers to the Trinity."[27] At that time the trinitarian tension was apparently not yet of particular significance to him. For he adds, " But this thought gave him little or no trouble, since it seemed something of only slight

---

26 Matthias Joseph Scheeben, *The Mysteries of Christianity*, trans. Cyril Vollert (St. Louis: Herder, 1947), pp. 116-117.
27 *Autobiog*, 28, in *FN*, I, 402.

importance." In any case the trinitarian tension (as it appears in the fourfold prayer and in the visions of this time)[28] is present at Manresa, though not felt to be a problem and unsolved.

Even the first entries in the *Diary* show this juxtaposition of the three individual Divine Persons and of the "Trinity as such"; that is, of the three-in-one. But now this unsolved trinitarian tension is for Ignatius no longer "a thing of only slight significance." On the contrary! Ignatius is carried almost to the limit of the creature's power of comprehension under the influence of the almost daily inpouring of this trinitarian light, which reveals its deepest mysteries. The trinitarian tension actually becomes for him an interior "difficulty," a "knot," as he expresses it.

On February 18 the *Diary* still clearly reports the same fourfold prayer to the Divine Persons and the Trinity as a whole, just like the one Ignatius was already in the habit of using at Manresa. "Later, while preparing the altar and vesting, I had a strong impulse to say: 'Eternal Father, strengthen me in my choice; Eternal Son, strengthen me; Eternal Spirit, strengthen me; Holy Trinity, strengthen me; You, my only true God (*un solo Dio mio*), strengthen me'" ([48]). This parallel vision of the three Divine Persons together with the divine unity is still frequently mentioned on the following days. Nadal, one of the most intimate companions of the saint, was well aware of this characteristic prayer of Ignatius, now directed to the one God, now to the three Divine Persons individually. He writes: "Our Father Ignatius received from God the singular grace of occupying himself freely in the contemplation of the Most Holy Trinity and of reposing in it. Sometimes he was led on by the grace of contemplating the whole Trinity (*totius Trinitatis*), was carried into it, and was united with it ... ; at sometimes he contemplated the Father, at another time the Son, and at still other times the Holy Spirit."[29]

The Solution of the Trinitarian Tension in the Circumincession

On February 21 Ignatius experienced something totally new. The illuminations during the Mass were so overpowering on this particular day that he was overwhelmed by an uncontrollable abundance of tears and lost his voice. "It seemed that I understood so much that there was scarcely anything more to learn about the Most Holy Trinity" ([62]). In the midst of such an overflow of heavenly light and divine love, he reports that "this knot and

28 Ibid.: as three organ keys; "many similes of many different kinds."
29 *MonNad*, IV, 651.

difficulty" was solved. The manner of expression reveals that we are touching upon something here which was very important to him and which he had been considering within himself for quite some time. Accordingly, the joy and reverence were also extremely intense. " This conviction was so strong that I could not stop saying to myself: ' Who are you ?   Where do you come from ? ...   How did you deserve this ? ' or ' Where did these consolations come from ? ' " ([63]).

It is quite evident from the context which " knot " and which " difficulty " concern him. Ignatius describes the contents of his illuminations to the last detail. Whereas he complained frequently at other times that he could not express himself or even goes so far as to remark that the visions had been merely thought-provoking and not clear,[30] here the manner of expression is unequivocal and theologically precise.   In addition, the decisive text in the manuscript is placed in parentheses and is underlined.   It is as follows: " But in this Mass I recognized, felt, or saw, the Lord knows, that in speaking to the Father, and in seeing that He was a Person of the Most Holy Trinity, I was moved to love the Trinity all the more since the other Persons were present in it essentially (*essencialmente*). I felt the same in the prayer to the Son, and the same in the prayer to the Holy Spirit, rejoicing in each one of them and feeling consolation. And attributing this to all Three, I was filled with joy because I belonged to all Three and thus the " knot " was solved.   The conviction was so strong that I could not stop saying to myself: ' Who are you ?   Where do you come from ? ...   How did you deserve this ? ' or ' Where did those consolations come from ? ' and so on."[31]

Ignatius sees on this day the mystery of the circumincession (perichoresis); that is, of the mutual interpenetration and existing-in-each-other of the Persons of the Trinity in virtue of the same essence as well as the processions and relations within the one God. The vision of this central point in the Trinity brings him suddenly

---

30 For example: "... in the inner speech I received so much inner harmony that I cannot express it " (*SpDiar*, [222]); " I felt much devotion and certain illuminations with some clarity of view " (ibid., [15]); " the devotion and tears were directed now to one Person, now to another, without clear or distinct visions " (ibid., [159]).

31 The critical edition of the *Diary* appeared in 1934 (*Cons*MHSJ, I, 86-158). Therefore Feder's translation into German, which appeared before that, contains many places that do not agree with the original text ... especially on this page (*SpDiar*, 60-63). Thus, using La Torre's edition of the *Constitutiones* (Madrid, 1892), he translated as *auf besondere Weise*, " especially," the word he found printed, *especialmente*. According to the critical edition (*Cons*MHSJ, I, 103, n. 33), the correct word is *essencialmente*, " essentially."

into a relationship with the Three Persons which surpasses all former relationships in intimacy and ardor. He no longer meets them as if from outside but from within, from the center of their essence. He sees and understands them in their vital, eternal relationship to one another, in their begetting and processions, their unity in individuality and their individuality in their unity. He feels himself encompassed by them and drawn into their unity. This experience must have filled him with an unutterable joy and reverence; joy because of the close intimacy with the Divine Persons and the knowledge that he belonged to all Three in the same manner and at the same time just as they belong to one another; reverence because of the infinite distance between the Creator and his creature. It is somehow an anticipation of the Beatific Vision. At least Ignatius experienced it as such, for he compares his experience with the ecstasy of St. Paul in which the latter was lifted up into the " third heaven." He interrupts himself at the very beginning of this decisive entry and places the Latin interjection — *Deus scit,* " God knows " (2 Cor. 12: 2) — in the middle of the Spanish text. The Apostle of the Gentiles begins the description of his visions with this expression. It is an experience that touches the entire human soul. For this reason, we find a multiplicity of expressions for the type and manner of experience: *conoçia, sentia o veia* — I understood, I felt, or I saw.

In the combined vision of the divine being and the individuality of the Persons, the " difficulty " of the fourfold prayer, which he directed to God from the time of Manresa on, is solved for Ignatius. It is entirely possible that, when he was examined in Salamanca before the court of Inquisition with regard to the mystery of the Trinity, it was this fourfold prayer that had been the occasion for the inquiry. At the Fourth Lateran Council (1215), had not the question of quaternity in God already been the subject of a condemnation ? At that time Joachim de Fiore had erroneously understood the unity of the Divine Persons, not as a real unity of essence, but as a collective unity of those with the same specific nature.[32] From that time on Ignatius may have experienced a

---

32 " Unde asserit, quod ille non tam trinitatem, quam quaternitatem astruebat in Deo, videlicet tres personas et illam communem essentiam quasi quartam " (Denzinger-Schönmetzer, 830). The Council, on the contrary, maintains as a truth of faith: "... that there is one certain supreme reality, which is incomprehensible and beyond description, which truly is Father and Son and Holy Spirit: three Persons as one, and each of them an individual Person; and therefore in God there is only a Trinity and not a Quaternity. For each of the three Persons is that reality; that is, the divine substance, essence, or nature " (ibid., 831).

certain uneasiness in regard to this question which was probably not completely overcome even by his theological studies. The frequent visions of this great mystery, which did not bring him final clarity regarding the relationship between divine essence and personal individuality, were too overpowering to accomplish this. In any case the *Diary* permits no doubt to arise about the importance which we must assign to this innermost nucleus of the trinitarian mystery in the mystical experience of Ignatius.

We also find an echo of the "mystical difficulties" of the saintly founder in Nadal, who had penetrated the depths of the Ignatian prayer life as had no other. Nadal notes among his illuminations in prayer, which in so many places are the echo of conversations with Ignatius: "A certain man contemplated on the feast of the Trinity the divine processions from the divine infinity, in which everything appeared comprehensible and easy to believe. At the same time thoughts arose concerning the eternal goodness of God. This man went into this contemplation with ease and in it he found sweet repose. On the other hand, in contemplating the divine essence he had difficulties and felt uneasy, as if he were being repelled by something harsh, and as if he understood better the meaning of 'Whoever searches the majesty of God is overcome by splendor'" (Prov. 25:27).[33]

From the Circumincession to the Basic Principle of the Divine Being

The first stage of the trinitarian development in the *Diary* concludes with the grace-laden vision of the circumincession. Under the wondrous guidance of grace Ignatius is led to the God-Man. These are the days of the Jesus-mysticism (second stage). But this soteriological path leads back to the trinitarian, which returns on February 29 and is developed further.

From the time that Ignatius had been absorbed into the centermost principle of the Triune God, the "mystical way" to the essence of God had become easier for him than it had previously been. On February 29, "Before Mass I saw the heavenly fatherland or its Lord, recognizing the Three Persons, and the Second and Third Persons in the Father... After Mass I saw again in like manner the fatherland, or its Lord; this time, however, not so as to distinguish one Person from another (*in modo indistincto*), yet in a clear manner such as frequently happens at

33 *MonNad*, IV, 716.

other times " ([90]). This passage is also the last in the *Diary* that Ignatius set off by special markings. From now on a grace-impelled contemplation of the Trinity's essence moves into the center of Ignatius' visions. On March 2, " conceiving a certain confidence and love for the Most Holy Trinity, I wished to commend myself to it as to distinct Persons (*distintas*); but, not finding what I sought, I felt something (*alguna cosa*) in the Father, as though the other Persons were in him (*seyendo*) " ([95]). On the following day March 3 Ignatius is exalted to a grace-laden vision (*siempre assistente la gracia*) of the essence of the Trinity " without seeing the Persons distinctly, as on the previous days, but perceiving in one luminous clarity a single essence, I was drawn entirely to love of it. . ." ([99]). On March 4 Ignatius, in his prayers before Mass, turned to Jesus; but he was able to see him only indistinctly and in an obscure manner. On the other hand, the absolutely clear and luminous vision of the Most Holy Trinity itself filled him with such strong love that he believed that it surpassed all former measure and that this extraordinarily intense visitation (*intensa visitación*) was of greater significance than any previous one.[34] In conclusion, Ignatius once again clearly emphasizes that all the visions " terminated in the name and essence of the Most Holy Trinity, without however perceiving or seeing each Divine Person clearly and distinctly in itself " ([110]).

Final Development: The Trinitarian " Turn " from Essence to Persons

Ignatius has now arrived, one might say, at the most profound place in his first path, from the threeness of Persons to Their three-in-oneness of essence. The divine love now draws him along the second path,[35] guiding him in an awe-inspiring manner from the

---

34 On this day Ignatius uses all the terms in the most superlative form possible: " en mucha mayor abundancia de lágrimas," " amor intensissimo," " con mucho grandes tocamientos y intensissima devoción," " un mucho excesivo amor," " tanto amor y tanta suavidad espiritual " (*SpDiar*, [106-109]).

35 We know that, in the historical development of the theology of the mystery of the Trinity, this second path, from unity of essence to trinity of persons, was adopted by Augustine in his great work, *De Trinitate*. St. Thomas then brought to perfection Augustine's teaching on the psychological manner of procession (procession of the Son from the Father as an act of knowledge, procession of the Holy Spirit from Father and Son as an act of mutual love) through his brilliant incorporation of Aristotelian psychology into this schema. Thus this second path is the road that the whole theology of the West has followed. The great problem as to how unity of nature and

unfathomable depths of the divine essence to its unfolding in the three Divine Persons. Of course, this proceeds in such a way that the Persons always appear in their unity within the same common essence. This " change in direction " begins on March 5. Ignatius wants to begin his prayers with Jesus. But the clear revelation of the Most Holy Trinity again comes over him as on previous days. Now, however, the " new direction," namely from the triune essence to the Person of the Father, presents itself. This new element is inserted so powerfully into the previous vision that Ignatius takes refuge in Jesus in a spirit full of loving fear, asking that he be his guide along this new path to the Trinity. " . . . as the devotion began to tend towards the Most Holy Trinity, it drew me at the same time in a different direction, namely to the Father, with the result that I felt in myself that God wanted to communicate with me in a different way. That feeling was so strong that, as I was preparing the altar, I said interiorly and also aloud the words, ' Where do you wish to take me, Lord ? ' . . . Since under the circumstances it was beyond my understanding where he wished to take me, and since, after vesting, I did not know just where to begin, I took Jesus for my guide . . . and said to him, ' Lord, where am I going, or where are you leading me ? Following you, my Lord, I shall never be lost ' " ([113]).

During this time of the " trinitarian turn " there is also another " turn," the significant change in Ignatius' attitude toward tears and all consolations not yet purely spiritual. With God's guidance he begins slowly to detach himself from these. It is almost as if the vision of the spiritual substance of the Trinity (March 4), which had surpassed all former ones, had caused him, with the help of grace, to strip away the final, most sublime activity of the senses.

---

threeness of Persons can be brought into harmony with this approach has been solved in Western theology by the concept of real relations. The relations themselves are then founded upon the primary acts of generation and spiration. Thus the " relations " and the " processions " become essentially identical. In our creaturely mode of thinking — even mystical knowledge remains essentially such a creaturely, partial perception of the content of faith — we distinguish between them in this manner, that we perceive " the processions as expressing the *fieri* (*via ad personas*) [the eternal process by which the Son and Holy Spirit " become " persons], and the relations as denoting the complete state (*in facto esse, forma permanens*) "; as it is expressed in Pohle-Press, *The Divine Trinity* (St. Louis: B. Herder Book Company, 1919), pp. 233-234. The first path, from the Persons to the unity of nature, is the way that has been followed by Greek trinitarian theology.

Accordingly, there begins Ignatius' turn toward the final period of his mysticism, which Hugo Rahner has aptly termed his "spiritual period."[36]

On the day just mentioned (March 5), Ignatius does not yet find the way to the Person of the Father. This new way is just now being hinted at. Only on the following day, March 6, is the mystical path (if we may so describe it) from the three-in-oneness of essence to the threefoldness of the Divine Persons open to him. Ignatius sees the divine essence in the form of a sphere (*en figura esferica*) like the sun. This image is presented in such a way that first the divine essence shows itself to him and then the Father is seen as the unoriginated possessor of this substance. In like manner, on March 10 and 11, as well as on April 2, the divine essence again manifests itself to him first; and then the Father is revealed.

The First Person of the Trinity holds a predominant role in the visions of St. Ignatius. He is comprehended entirely from the aspect of the depths of the divine essence. This Person, the Father, is the being whom the Council of Toledo proclaimed in words of incomparable depth: "He is, therefore, the source and origin of the whole divinity; he is also the Father of his own essence who from his indescribable essence begot the Son in an indescribable manner. Nevertheless, he did not beget a being different from what he himself is. God begot God, light begot light. From him, therefore, is all fatherhood in heaven and on earth."[37] In this basic source and origin of the entire divinity, Ignatius sees the original principle, the source and root of the other Persons. The Father is in the Trinity somewhat like the central point of relationship, from which everything proceeds and to which everything is directed. That is the reason why Ignatius sees the other Persons again and again as they dwell within the Father. On February 23, Ignatius recalls the hour of grace at La Storta where the Father gave him to the Son as a companion. To the Father Ignatius directs the petition, "that He might give me His Spirit, that I may be able to examine and

36 Hugo Rahner, "Die Psychologie der Vision von La Storta im Lichte der Mystik des heiligen Ignatius," *ZAM*, X (1935), beginning on page 266.
From one point of view, the *Spiritual Diary*, which was written about twelve years before the saint's death, belongs to the mysticism of his old age, a time of autumnal glory and of a maturity ready for the harvest. Therefore De Guibert, *Saint Ignace mystique*, p. 16, characterizes the mystical graces of the *Diary* as *graces de la maturité*. From another point of view, we encounter in it only the period of transition into the final stage of Ignatian mysticism, the "Spirit-stage."
37 Denzinger-Schönmetzer, 525.

distinguish " ([15]). The offering of total poverty is presented to the Father ([16]). For Ignatius, Christ is completely transparent to the Father so that he frequently cries out in the Spirit, " What a Father and what a Son ! " ([72]). Jesus brings these prayers before the face of the Father and the vision of this " presentation " is so marvelous that it is impossible for Ignatius to find fitting words for it ([77]). Thus the Father is the origin and the point of return which dominates Ignatius' whole spirituality.

On March 6, then, the day on which our investigation paused above, Ignatius sees the Father alone, in his complete personal individuality ([121]). But on the same day the trinitarian vision is also brought to completion; for Ignatius, after Holy Mass, sees the divine essence again and in it now not the Father alone but all three Persons. " After unvesting, during the thanksgiving, the divine essence and the spherical vision presented themselves to my sight again; in some way or other I saw the three Divine Persons in the same manner as I saw the First Person; that is, how the Father on one side, the Son on another, and the Holy Spirit on yet another, came forward from the divine essence but without leaving the outlines of the sphere " ([123]). Here the marvelous trinitarian " cycle," in which all three Persons are seen simultaneously as the unfolding and the unity of the divine essence, has come full circle.

It was our intention to give a clear exposition of this basic core of the trinitarian mysticism of Ignatius. Previously it has been almost completely overlooked. It embraced the entire mystery of the Trinity at the point of its most vital tension. Ignatius begins his *Diary* with the vision of the Divine Persons as individuals. Then he is gradually led through the mystery of the mutual indwelling of the Three Divine Persons to the unity of the Divine Being. Then, under the wonderful guidance of grace, the Most Holy Trinity again unfolds, progressing from the divine essence to the personal fullness of the Three Divine Persons. What was present as in a bud in the fourfold prayer of Manresa has now developed into full bloom, an unforgettable part of the mystical experience of Ignatius. Now he understands how unity of being and Trinity of Persons stand in living harmony. " Everything here is unity, communion, harmony in the highest and most beautiful sense of the word. The threefoldness of the Trinity not only does not destroy the unity and simplicity of God; rather, this unity and simplicity reveals itself in its full power and magnitude precisely through the three-in-oneness, through the absolute concord and harmony with which it penetrates and governs the threefoldness in

God. Here it appears as a completely rich and vital unity; just as rich in repose and communicativeness as in self-sufficiency, in diversity as in simplicity, in dependence as in independence."[38]

II
The Portrait of Christ in Ignatian Mysticism as Seen in the Spiritual Diary

A glance at the structure and the lines of development in the *Diary* is sufficient to show that the trinitarian point of view was not always predominant in the mysticism of St. Ignatius. There are stages in this mystical development in which the figure and the work of Jesus fill the interior experience and, we might say, act as a substitute for the entire trinitarian cycle. Since Christ as Eternal Son of the Father belongs to the trinitarian cycle, but as a man capable of suffering is the center and embodiment of the redemptive cycle, the result is that the portrait of Christ in the *Diary* is determined by both elements. From a trinitarian standpoint he is the Only Begotten of the Father; from the soteriological he is the Firstborn among many brothers. The entire theology of St. Paul revolves around this twofold concept: Only Begotten and yet Firstborn. This was also a favorite notion among the Greek Fathers of the fourth century (for example, Cyril of Alexandria). Expressed in different terminology, this twofold Christological concept now returns in Ignatius. As a Person of the Trinity, Christ is almost always called " Son " in the *Diary*, while, as the God-Man Redeemer, he is designated by the name " Jesus." Both concepts, however, because of the intensity of Ignatius' mystical experiences and visions, have a very specific and profound meaning which thus often oversteps the theological limitations and precision of customary terminology.

Probably in no other document has the Ignatian portrait of Christ with its twofold designation of him as " Son " and " Jesus " found shorter, clearer, more precise expression than in the short explanation of the Sign of the Cross that was given by Ignatius towards the end of his life. He says: " When we make the holy Sign of the Cross, we place our fingers first on the head; and this is to signify God the Father, who proceeds from no one. When we touch our breast, this signifies the Son, our Lord, who proceeds from the Father and who descended into the womb of the Blessed Virgin Mary. When we place our fingers on both shoulders,

---

38 Scheeben, *Mysteries of Christianity*, p. 116.

this signifies the Holy Spirit, who proceeds from the Father and the Son. And when we fold our hands together again, this symbolizes that the Three Persons are one single substance. And finally, when we seal our lips with the Sign of the Cross, this means that in Jesus, our Saviour and Redeemer, dwells the Father, the Son, and Holy Spirit, one single God, our Creator and Lord — and that the divinity was never separated from the body of Jesus, not even at His Death."[39]

In this passage Christ is mentioned twice. In the large Sign of the Cross, which symbolizes the trinitarian sphere, Ignatius calls Him " the Son, our Lord, who is begotten of the Father and who descended into the body of the Blessed Virgin Mary." In the small Sign of the Cross, which symbolizes the redemptive sphere, he calls Him " Jesus, our Saviour and Redeemer, in whom dwells the Father, the Son, and the Holy Spirit, one single God, our Creator and Lord." This formula of the Sign of the Cross shall now be for us the leading theological theme for the evaluation of the portrait of Christ as we find it in Ignatius' *Spiritual Diary*.

The Portrait of the Son in the Spiritual Diary of Ignatius

From the very outset a twofold sonship characterizes the Ignatian picture of Christ. We see the eternal sonship with respect to the eternal begetting from the Father, and the sonship undertaken in time with respect to the birth through the Virgin Mother, Mary. It is of extraordinary significance for the theological depths and individuality of the Ignatian contemplation that the temporal sonship from Mary is completely subsumed within the trinitarian relations. Thus the temporal birth from Mary is nothing else than the continuation of the eternal birth from the Father in the temporal universe. In the first stage of development in the *Diary* (which is characterized completely by the Trinity of Persons and Their perichoretic unity in the Father), Ignatius employs exclusively the concept " Son " in reference to Christ — the name Jesus does not appear at all in this period. Not only this, but he also frequently speaks of the Son almost in the same breath with His human mother, " our dear Lady." " I saw Mother and Son disposed to intercede with the Father " ([4]). Ignatius is also raised up interiorly to the Father through the intercession of Mother and Son ([8]). On many days Mother and Son are called upon or seen as inter-cessors with the Eternal Father and the Most Holy Trinity ([15, 23,

39 *EppIgn*, XII, 667; *Geistliche Briefe*, p. 340.

31, 46]). During thanksgiving, which plays a significant role in Ignatian mysticism, Ignatius offers thanks, "first to the Divine Persons, then to our Lady and her Son, then to the angels, the holy Fathers, the Apostles and disciples, and to all the saints for the help they had given me in this matter" ([47]). The inner relationship between Mother and Son and the intercessory office of the Mother is manifested to Ignatius in a highly unusual manner at the celebration of the eucharistic mysteries. "After the end of Mass, and for long periods during Mass, in preparing and afterwards, much perception and vision of our Lady, very propitious before the Father; to such an extent that in the prayers to the Father, to the Son, and even at the consecration, I could not help feeling and seeing her, as if she were the channel or the gateway of all the grace I felt in my soul. At the consecration she showed me how her flesh was in that of her Son and this with such enlightenment that I cannot write about it" ([31]).[40]

It becomes sufficiently clear from these few texts how the concept "Son" indicates for Ignatius a twofold tendency: the inner-trinitarian, eternal sonship through the generation from the Father and the continuation of this eternal sonship in time through the Incarnation from Mary, the Virgin. Thus Christ is, even as Ignatius experienced him in the center of the trinitarian relationships, not only the enthroned Son of God, ruling with his Father in divine transcendence above all creation, but always and at the same time the Servant of God and the Son of the Virgin who entered our world in obedience to his Eternal Father. The powerful soteriological dynamism, which characterizes the Ignatian picture of Christ, is thus already present in the depths of the trinitarian cycle.

The Portrait of Jesus in the Diary

As we already pointed out in the presentation of the stages of development in the *Diary*, the first trinitarian period, in which Ignatius makes exclusive use of the concept "Son," is set off clearly from the second stage which is completely dominated by the vision of Jesus. What are the essential features that characterize the Ignatian picture of Jesus? The formula of the Sign of the Cross provides us once again with the leading idea. "In Jesus, our Saviour and Redeemer, dwell the Father, the Son, and the Holy Spirit, one only God, our Creator and Lord, and the divinity

---

40 For a more detailed interpretation of this passage, see Pinard de la Boullaye, *Saint Ignace de Loyola, directeur d'âmes* (Paris, 1947), p. 96.

was never separated from the body of Christ, not even in death."
Each and every word of this sentence, profound in its theological
significance, must be given careful consideration in order that we
may comprehend the fullness of the Ignatian portrait of Jesus:
the fullness of everything human, and, above all, the fullness of
everything divine. While the Ignatian portrait of the Son proceeds
from the inner trinitarian relationships and emphasizes the descent
of the eternal Logos in the Incarnation, the portrait of Jesus
embraces the dynamism of the ascent from Jesus as Man (Saviour
and Redeemer) to Jesus as God (Trinity, Creator, Lord). However,
by no means is this to be understood as if we could leave at any
time the "sphere" of this picture of Jesus to be with the Triune
God. This God-Man, Jesus, is and remains the place in which the
totality of the Divinity dwells; and, indeed, His divinized humanity
is just the place where we encounter the fullness of God.

1. The Meaning of the Humanity in the Portrait of Jesus in the Diary

De Guibert[41] also maintains, " When Ignatius speaks of Jesus
in the entries in his *Diary*, the context clearly shows that he is
then referring to the humanity of Christ." It is interesting that
Ignatius describes the human appearance of Jesus in the *Diary*
almost in the same way as he does his vision of Jesus at Manresa;[42]
that is, " in a white light "[43] or as " a white body, without
distinguishing the individual members." This proves to us once again
that even on this point there exists an extensive temporal continuity
in the visions of Ignatius.

That Ignatius grasped the complete integrity of the human
nature of Christ, and that he always speaks of the total breadth of
its historical reality, need no special proof. The *Exercises*, the fruit
of the Jesus-mysticism at Manresa, have already clearly testified
to the prominent significance that the totality of the mysteries of
Jesus' earthly life has for the closest imitation of the humble Lord
(*imitatio Christi*). One must continually keep in mind how, in the
second through the fourth weeks of the *Exercises*, e.g. in the
meditations on the Birth and Incarnation of Jesus (which he looks
upon as models for all the other contemplations), Ignatius desires to
make the total concrete historical context of the event present
to the soul of the exercitant. Ignatius has him see " with the inner

41 De Guibert, *Saint Ignace mystique*, p. 37.
42 *Autobiog*, 29, in *FN*, I, 402.
43 *SpDiar*, [87].

eyes of the soul the road from Nazareth to Bethlehem, measuring its length and breadth, and whether the road is flat or leads through valleys or over hills; and in like manner, contemplating the place or cave of birth, how roomy, narrow, low, or high it is, and how it is furnished." Then he should look upon the persons as he serves them, a "small, poor, worthless servant, with the greatest possible reverence and respect, just as if he were present there with them"; then he should consider what the persons are saying and doing. Thus the mysteries of the earthly life of Jesus in their concrete existential form should become the history of his own soul. This is still more evident in the method of the "application of the five senses" in which the world of his sense experience should be "assimilated" in faith to the life of Jesus as he tries to see the holy persons and to listen to them, to smell and to taste "... the infinite sweetness of the Divinity, of the soul and its virtues, and so of all else...."

Thus the whole life of the God-Man should be experienced in contemplative prayer as if within the realm of one's own personal experience. By means of interior imitation there is elevated into a living, conscious reality that which is an existential reality: I live no longer, Christ lives in me. In the degree to which the one who is praying has assimilated and absorbed the mysteries of Jesus into the total context of his existence, to that extent is he able, in all that he encounters, "to seek and find the presence of our Lord."[44] The medium or milieu of this imitation, which is conceived by Ignatius in such extraordinarily literal and concrete terms, is the human nature of Christ: to the extent that it is permeated and thoroughly irradiated by the Second Person of the Trinity and by the divine nature that it has in common with the Father and the Holy Spirit, filled "with the infinite fragrance and sweetness of the Divinity." Also due to the concreteness of this very direct imitation of Jesus is the fact that Ignatius first desires to realize his ideal in the Holy Land, by actually following in the footsteps of the historical Jesus. When God later points out another path to him, he binds himself and his companions in an irrevocable vow of obedience to the pope, the vicar of Christ. His Jesus-mysticism thus flows directly into a dynamic apostolic activity in the here and now of the Church as it actually is.

The portrayal of Jesus found in the *Exercises* is also found in the *Spiritual Diary*, viewed in the same comprehensive manner.

44 " la presencia de nuestro Señor en todas las cosas " (*Cons*MHSJ, I, 510).

This is particularly explicit in the second and fourth stages. It is precisely during these days that Ignatius sees Jesus as the Head of his Society, which is just taking its place in history. The vision of this Jesus is for him a confirmation of his election that transcends all others. This vision complements and almost acts as a substitute for the confirmation by the Trinity. For this reason he writes in large letters in the margin of the *Diary: Confirmación de Jesús*. And in these days yet another word stands in the text near confirmation (*confirmación*), reconciliation (*reconciliación*). This concept always appears in connection with Jesus. It also allows Him to appear along with the Trinity in the most sublime experiences of Ignatius' mature mysticism as Savior, Redeemer, Intercessor and Guide. In an overpowering vision Ignatius sees how Jesus brings his prayers into the presence of the Father. " During the orations addressed to the Father, it seemed to me that Jesus presented them, or that He was accompanying before the Father those that I was saying. I felt or saw this in a way that I cannot explain " ([77]). How important Ignatius thought this intercessory function of Jesus to be for our petitions and offerings is shown by the fact that he framed these sentences with heavy lines in his *Diary*. The next underlined passage in the *Diary* again relates " a vision of the most Holy Trinity and of Jesus beyond the powers of nature " ([83]). Again Ignatius perceives how Jesus " presents everything to the Father and to the most Holy Trinity " ([84]).

On the same day of the second period (February 27) there is heard for the first time a fundamental Ignatian idea which later on becomes the dominant theme of the fourth period of the *Diary*; that is, the mysticism of the reverent love of service (*amor reverencial*). The mystical vision of St. Ignatius here makes us understand clearly that there is more to this reverence inspired by love and this humble service than a virtuous readiness to serve. The reverential love (*amor reverencial*) is rather a climate, given to redeemed man once and for all through the God-Man, Jesus, of openness to the Father and to the most Holy Trinity. In Jesus, the humble servant, this climate has for Ignatius received an unmistakable impress as a service of humility and reverence inspired by love. Ignatius comes to share, through this path of humility in the service of the servant of God, Jesus, in all the exalted trinitarian visitations; and he himself, the more he appears in the raiment of his humble Lord, completes the final spiritualization of his attitude. This probably also presents us with one of the most decisive reasons for the striking fact that there is no trace of bride-mysticism in the strict sense in Ignatian spirituality although it is highly mystical and full of inner ardor. De Guibert[45] rightly sees in this one of the most distinctive characteristics of Ignatian mysticism in contrast to the "nuptial aspect of the mystical union" found in John of the Cross and other masters of the interior life.

2. *The Meaning of the Divinity in the Portrait of Jesus in the* Diary

Even though the humanity of Jesus is of such vital significance for Ignatius, he never delays on a meditation that considers this humanity in isolation. The line of development in the second stage of the *Diary* leads him on to Jesus "as He is totally God" ([87]), the dwelling-place of the most Holy Trinity, our Creator and Lord (formula of the Sign of the Cross). For Ignatius the humanity of Jesus is always, even in the smallest and apparently least significant fact of its historical existence, totally divinized; and it pours out, as it were, "the unending fragrance of the Divinity" (*Exercises*) and becomes for this reason eternally significant. For even though the divine and human natures exist together unmixed in the mysterious unity of the hypostatic union with the eternal Logos, still both penetrate each other in the most intimate and indivisible fashion. Ignatius experiences both polarities of the mystery of Christ in the mystical visions in the *Diary*. First he sees the humanity of Jesus, and then he sees how it is completely permeated by the Logos. "It seemed to me in the Spirit that I saw Jesus first, as I have said before, in a white light; that is, the humanity. The second time I perceived Him in my soul in a different way; not as before, the humanity alone, but as completely and totally God" ([87]).

Just as in the development of the trinitarian mystery the trinitarian circumincession was both the high point and the solution of the tension between threefoldness and three-in-oneness, so likewise in the portrait of Christ the central core of this mystery is met in the Christological circumincession. In a different way, however, from the trinitarian circumincession, the unifying and penetrating power of the Christological perichoresis emanates entirely from the person of the eternal Logos, "who, in spite of his own impenetrability, penetrates the human nature in an ineffable and mysterious manner and inhabits it as his possession."[46] The eternal Logos, however, dwells at the same time, together with the Holy Spirit, in the

---

45 *DeGuiJes*, pp. 55-56.
46 Pohle-Preuss, *Christology* (St. Louis: B. Herder Book Company, 1919), p. 181.

eternal Father; and the Divine Persons mutually penetrate one another in the most vital manner (trinitarian circumincession) — as Ignatius was permitted to experience, in the first period of the *Diary*, under the influence of grace. This trinitarian circumincession now throws its determining light also on the figure of Jesus. If the divine Logos completely permeates the human nature of Jesus and if he, on the other hand, dwells together with the Holy Spirit in the Father by reason of the same divine essence, then it is necessary that this Jesus be in a very special manner the dwelling of the most Holy Trinity-in-Unity and, as it were, its presence among us.[47]

In Jesus the complete fullness of God dwells bodily (Col. 2: 9). Therefore, Ignatius can also call Him Creator with complete accuracy. All the trinitarian and soteriological experiences of the last period of the *Diary* have, as it were, " a new place " in the " corporeality " of the figure of Jesus. Ignatius consequently no longer needs to look " heavenwards " ([122]) in separation from the world in order to seek and to find the trinitarian mysteries as he had done up to the last decisive turning-point (between the third and fourth stages). The way to the divine fullness lies in the attitude of love-inspired humility and reverence, turned toward the world which is in such great need of redemption — therefore, " in the garment of the Lord." This final perfection of mystical understanding is now turned also toward creatures so that Ignatius can " find God in all things " through Jesus. " Later in the day, I had much joy in remembering this, and I thought that I should not stop there, but that from now on I should have the same attitude towards creatures; that is, loving humility, etc." ([179]). Thus the fundamental Ignatian principle " to find our Lord in all things " is the result, the crown, and the final wisdom of his Jesus-mysticism.

The Soteriological Dynamism of the Ignatian Mysticism of the Diary

Just as the picture of the most Holy Trinity was grasped in its most intense profundity, just as Ignatius' picture of Christ binds the most extreme polarities into one, so too the work of redemption, as represented in the *Diary*, is filled with lively tensions. It is a rolling tide of ascent and descent between heaven and earth. It is the fulfillment of the words which our Lord spoke to Nathaniel

---

47 Concerning the question as to how the Incarnation of the eternal Logos does not signify an incarnation of the whole Trinity, see Pohle-Preuss, *Christology*, pp. 132-137.

and his first disciples at the beginning of His earthly mission, " Truly I say to you, you will see heaven open and the angels of God ascending and descending upon the Son of Man " (John 1: 51). In Christ this return of the world to the triune God has become possible. In Jesus " soteriological unrest " has entered sinful creation. In Him all creation is directed along the path of salvation and is brought into the rising and descending movement of salvation. The task of each man is none other than, in imitation of Christ, to perceive through faith this movement of salvation and humbly to follow it out. The *Diary*, which shows us this movement of salvation in the saint's prayer, is completely filled with this soteriological dynamism of ascent and descent: ascent through " the intercessors " to the Father and to the whole of the Trinity, and descent again through " the intercessors " to the world. One does not need to cite texts to prove this since almost every page of the *Diary* provides evidence for this extraordinarily characteristic movement in the spirituality of the saint.[48]

We must emphasize, however, one point in this soteriological process: for Ignatius the normal way to salvation is only through the mediators through whom God himself has come to us. Ignatian spirituality, as it is revealed with particular clarity in the *Diary*, could therefore be designated as a " mysticism of mediation." In the first place, there stands the universal mediator between God and man, Jesus Christ, whom Ignatius perceived in his Jesus-mysticism as the basic mediator because of the hypostatic union. After the universal Mediator comes the Mother of the Divine Son, who is called the " gate of great graces." Then follow " the angels, the holy Fathers, Apostles, disciples, and all the saints, etc." ([47]), and all those creatures that God has established as mediators along the path of salvation. Normally Ignatius does not recognize an ascent to God without intercessors even in prayer and contemplation. Of course, God himself has the liberty of touching the soul in prayer and of raising it up to himself without mediators. The *Diary* offers abundant evidence for this. However, Ignatius does not look on this as the normal situation. On the contrary, the first thing he asks himself at the beginning of his prayers is always with which intercessors he should pray and meditate, presupposing that God has not granted him an illumination or a vision at the very outset.

This prayer through the intercessors is also found again and again in the observations on prayer of Nadal, who had more intimate

---

48 A typical example is in *SpDiar*, [46-47].

knowledge of Ignatius' spiritual life than any of his contemporaries. This attitude dominates the whole spirituality of Pierre Favre, another companion of the saint, though with a characteristic " one-sidedness " so that in many ways the entire curve of the ascent and descent of this soteriological process, which culminates in Christ, the Father and the Blessed Trinity, is no longer fully visible nor does it become conscious in his prayer. Because of this the theological content of this type of prayer appears much less profound than in the magnificent universality of the Ignatian world of faith. Regarding the configuration of each individual's interior life, Ignatius always judged freedom of spirit, especially the freedom of the Holy Spirit, to be the supreme law. Regarding the necessity of intercession itself, however, he certainly left not the least doubt. For it is nothing else than the fulfillment or manifestation of the soteriological structure of our approach to the Father and to the Trinity as it was existentially established, once and for all, in the Incarnation of the eternal Son: *Per Jesum Christum Dominum nostrum*, and through the entirety of creation, called in Christ to its intercessory function.

Furthermore, in Ignatian thought there exists a well-ordered and well-thought-out hierarchy of intercessors. In his prayer they stand in the places assigned them by theology. Jesus is " at the feet of the Blessed Trinity." Mary is the gateway to her Son and, with the Son, is intercessor with the Father. Then comes the circle of the angels, Apostles, and disciples of our Lord; further on the circle of the saints, from among whom frequently a particular one is chosen as patron; and then finally the circle of all those persons who were helpful in the particular case.[49] Usually he calls upon only a few of these levels of intercessors and generally the essential ones, as in the " colloquies " of the *Exercises*: Mary - Son - Father. But never in the *Diary* does a significant rearrangement of this order of intercession take place. We are dealing here with one of those points of Nadal's " order in the spiritual life " (*ordo vitae spiritualis*), often forgotten today, which was of inestimable significance for Ignatius and his first companions. Ignatius consciously rejected a forced systematization of the spiritual life, but he did have a knowledge, ripened by extensive experience, of the necessity of an orderly arrangement in the interior life. Here in this *ordo vitae spiritualis*, he is concerned with nothing else than an insight into all the interrelationships of faith; and this insight is one manifesting and developing iteslf in an interior life which springs

49 Ibid.

from a faith truly lived. There is question, then, of everything with which Ignatius was gifted in unforgettable manner beside the Cardoner — of that experience which Leturia called the "synthetic vision." That same experience is what Nadal, whose terminology is so remarkably accurate, has described most precisely as "the spirit of an architectonic wisdom."[50]

Supplementary Remarks on the Ignatian Mysticism

1. *Eucharistic Mysticism and Gratitude*

Some — for example, De Guibert — have characterized the mysticism of the *Diary* as "eucharistic." This, of course, cannot be understood in the same sense as when one speaks of the trinitarian mysticism of the *Diary*. For there are relatively few references to the mystery of the Eucharist to be found in the *Diary*. But from another point of view one must indeed speak of a eucharistic mysticism in Ignatius, for the celebration of the eucharistic mysteries is the almost exclusive milieu in which his mystical life develops. Even a fleeting glance at his entries reveals how the work of his entire day was focused on the celebration of the most Holy Eucharist as the central event. The great trinitarian visions occur within the framework of the preparation, the celebration itself, and the act of thanksgiving that filled the rest of his day. This is also the milieu in which many unrelated "worldly" decisions are made. We may therefore well believe that one of the most prominent virtues of the saint, his extraordinary gratitude,[51] which has even found its legal repercussions within the *Constitutions* of the Society of Jesus,[52] does not have its ultimate roots in his human greatness of soul alone, but arises ultimately from his trinitarian and eucharistic mysticism; for the Eucharist *is* the mystery of thanksgiving. This view can be substantiated from the *Diary* itself; thanksgiving plays such a significant role in it. Thus it should cause no amazement if thanksgiving was considered by the first fathers of the Society of Jesus (according to Nadal's testimony in his *Orationis observationes*) to be among the most important foundations of the spiritual life and of interior progress.

---

50 "Ignace avait alors tout reçu du Seigneur dans une sorte d'esprit de sagesse architectonique"; quoted from *Christus* (Paris, 1953), no. 1, p. 28. The earliest source of this saying of Nadal is F. Sacchini in his introduction to Nicolas Orlandini, *Historia Societatis Jesu* (Cologne, 1721), p. 2.
51 Huonder, *Ignatius*, p. 276.
52 *Cons*, [309-319].

2. " *Finding God in All Things* " — *Understood Christologically*

What has concerned us in our remarks up to this point has been simply to outline the general structure of the theological content of Ignatian mysticism. To substantiate our view of this structure and to give it life with concrete examples from the other sources of Ignatian thought was not the goal of our present work. We would like to call attention, though, to one particular point since important practical consequences result from it. Throughout almost all the directives of St. Ignatius on the spiritual life, the ever repeated formula, " to seek and find God in all things," appears as the principal theme. However, it has been too little noticed and considered that in many places where he gives expression to this fundamental point, and where the context permits us a more exact identification, by " God " is simply meant Jesus Christ. It is true that in those cases Ignatius always places before our eyes the universal picture of Christ found in his mystical understanding of the faith, as we have attempted to point out in the course of the above treatment: Jesus Christ, Son of the Eternal Father, Mediator, Abode of the Trinity.

A first indication of the correctness of our interpretation we find in the fact that not only in the letters of the saint but also in the *Exercises* and in the *Constitutions* expressions like " Creator," " Eternal Lord of all things," and the like are very frequently understood of Christ.[53] Even the term " Divine Majesty " or " Your most holy Majesty " is applied to Christ.[54] The formula of the last vows in the Society of Jesus speaks significantly of " Almighty God and His Virgin Mother."[55] For those who wish to be accepted into the order, the *Examen generale* prescribes a service to the sick; and the ultimate motivation indicated for this is Christ as " Creator and Lord crucified for our salvation."[56] In the Tenth Part of the *Constitutions*, which treats of the preservation and growth of the Society, Ignatius says at the very beginning that it can only be preserved and increased " through the grace of Almighty God and our Lord, Jesus Christ."[57] By means of such texts, to which many

---

53 For example: "... ut major gloria et laus Christi Creatoris ac Domini nostri consequatur " (*Cons*, [602]); " O aeterne Domine rerum omnium " (*SpEx*, [98]).

54 *SpEx*, [98].

55 " Ego NN ... professionem facio et promitto omnipotenti Deo, coram ejus virgine Matre..." (*Cons*, [527, 532]).

56 "... ut omnino suo Creatori et Domino pro ipsorum salute crucifixo serviant " (*GenExam*, [66]).

57 *Cons*, [812].

others could be added, a christological interpretation of the basic formula of Ignatian spirituality and prayer, "to seek and to find God in all things," is made quite obvious.

Our hypothesis becomes a certainty, however, if we investigate the letters of St. Ignatius in which he has expressed himself at greater length on this basic formula and its meaning. As a typical text let us cite the answer which the saint once gave to a question about the problem of the spiritual life of those in the order who are in studies. "In view of the purpose of our studies, the scholastics cannot devote themselves to long meditations. Over and above the exercises which they have for the acquisition of virtue, namely daily Mass, one hour for prayer and the examen of conscience, and confession and communion every eighth day, they can exercise themselves in seeking the presence of our Lord in all things (*la presencia de nuestro Señor en todas las cosas*) — for example, in conversing with someone, in walking, looking, tasting, hearing, thinking, and in everything that they do, since it is true that his Divine Majesty is in all things by his presence, power, and essence. This manner of meditating, by which one finds God our Lord (*nuestro Señor Dios*) in all things, is easier than trying to elevate ourselves to spiritual things which are more abstract and which require more effort to make them present to ourselves. Furthermore, this splendid exercise will dispose us for great visitations from the Lord, even during a short prayer. Moreover, the scholastics can train themselves to offer frequently to God our Lord their studies and the difficulties they bring, by remembering that they have undertaken them out of love for God, and by putting aside their personal inclinations, in order to serve his Divine Majesty, and to help those for whose life he suffered death."[58]

We surely do not err if we have already seen in the words "to seek the presence of our Lord in all things, in their

---

58 *EppIgn*, III, 510. The original text does not say "to seek the presence of *God* in all things, but "the presence of *our Lord*" (*la presencia de nuestro Señor*) — a meaningful nuance! For "our Lord" means for Ignatius only Jesus Christ, who does appear in this passage as Creator — that is true. Most translators (for example: *Geistliche Briefe*, p. 206; *LettersIgn*, p. 240) are too free with the text since they simply say "God" in a passage where a more specific expression is found in the original. Further along in the passage Ignatius does not speak of the "visitations by God," but of "visitationes del Señor." [*LettersIgn* is accurate here.] At the end of the passage is a significant reference to "His Majesty" (again Christ is meant), whom we are to serve "so that we may be of help to those for whom He died."

conversations, their walks, in all they see, taste, hear, understand. . ." an indication and an echo of the application of the senses in the contemplation of the mysteries of our Lord in the *Exercises*. It is really nothing else than a transfer or application of the same exercise, in accordance with its basic meaning, to all things since, as Ignatius himself says, " His Divine Majesty is already in all things by His presence, power, and essence." This " Divine Majesty " is, significantly, understood of Christ at the end of the above text (" for whose life he suffered death "). Obviously, there are two possibilities for finding God in all things in the Ignatian text cited above. A more abstract method (" *cosas divinas más abstractas* ") recognizes or infers God from the created universe by the light of an untroubled reason. Another more concrete and therefore easier method, which also prepares us rapidly for great visitations from the Lord, seems to consist for Ignatius in seeking and finding our Lord, who has created us and redeemed us and who through His Incarnation has entered into the closest possible relationship to us and to all created things, as the One who is present in them all.[59] According to the mind of Ignatius, the soul that has contemplated the mysteries of Jesus in the *Exercises* and that has sensed some of the " infinite fragrance and sweetness of the Divinity, of the soul, of its virtues, and so of all things "[60] should not find it at all difficult to find everywhere this " Eternal Lord of all things "[61] who has come so close to us.

Nevertheless the value of a more abstract form of " seeking and finding God in all things " should by no means be denied. The only point we wished to emphasize clearly was that the more concrete, salvific, christological interpretation and practice of this important basic formula is simply a consequence of the universal portrait of Christ as it shows up in Ignatian spirituality and mysticism.

Perhaps a passage from the marvelous letter to the scholastics at Coimbra may serve to allow the total universality of the Ignatian understanding of Christ to shine forth one last time. " Yet there is one thing I wish you to excel in above all others; and that is that you be outstanding in the pure love for Jesus Christ, in zeal for his glory and the salvation of the souls whom he has redeemed.

---

59 The teaching on the omnipresence of Christ has nothing to do with Luther's teaching on ubiquity, his teaching on the omnipresence of the body of Christ; see Pohle-Preuss, *Christology*, pp. 194-195.
60 *SpEx*, [124].
61 *SpEx*, [98].

For you are his soldiers, with a special wage and title. Special, I say, for there are certainly many other general reasons that bind you to his honor and service. Wages from him is all that you are and possess in the natural order; for he it is who gives us being and life, and all the powers and perfections of the soul and body together with all external goods. His wages too are the gifts of grace with which he has endowed us so liberally and so lovingly and which he still continues to give to you even when you oppose him and rebel against him. His wages are the inestimable riches of his glory which, without any advantage to himself, he has prepared and promised to you, sharing with you all the riches of his happiness, so as to make you, by a remarkable participation in his divine perfection, what he is by his very essence and nature. Lastly, the whole universe is his wages and all the fullness thereof, whether of the material or spiritual order. Not only has he placed everything under heaven at our service, but the whole of his sublime heavenly court, not excepting even one of the celestial hierarchies. For they are all ministering spirits, sent to minister unto those who are to receive the inheritance of salvation (Heb. 1:14). And as if all this were not enough, he has given us his own self as wage, becoming our brother in the flesh, the price of our salvation on the cross, the support and companion of our pilgrimage in the most Holy Sacrament."[62]

62 *EppIgn*, I, 501; *LettersIgn*, pp. 124-125.

PART III

ST. IGNATIUS' SPIRITUAL EXERCISES

EARLY MONASTIC ELEMENTS
IN IGNATIAN SPIRITUALITY:
TOWARD CLARIFYING
SOME FUNDAMENTAL CONCEPTS
OF THE EXERCISES

Heinrich Bacht

THE YEAR 1548 yielded for Ignatius of Loyola and his young order a great success. On July 31 of this year Paul III pronounced in the bull *Pastoralis Officii* a solemn approbation of the *Spiritual Exercises*, the text of which had been presented to him in a double form, in the *Versio Prima* and in the more elegant Latin version of Father André des Freux.[1] But that same year saw also the rise of one of the harshest and most stubborn opponents of the new institute in the person of the Dominican theologian Melchor Cano, the author of the classic *Loci Theologici*.[2] Highly gifted and of overpowering oratorial ability, this man devoted a large part of his talent and energy to fighting the danger of the Alumbrados[3] which

---

Study 7 was translated by Louis W. Roberts.

1 See Dudon, *St. Ignatius*, pp. 213-214; also Albert Feder's introduction to this German translation of the *Spiritual Exercises*: Ignatius von Loyola, *Geistliche Übungen* (Freiburg, 1939), pp. 11-12.

2 Ignacio Iparraguirre, *Historia de la Práctica de los Ejercicios Espirituales de san Ignacio de Loyola* (2 vols. Rome and Bilbao, 1946, 1955), I, 94-98; a more detailed report on Melchor Cano's attacks is found in Astráin, *Historia*, I, 321-340, 368-370, 377-379; a short summary of the controversy in Ludwig Koch, *Jesuitenlexicon* (Paderborn, 1934), pp. 297-298, and in A. Lang's article on Cano in *Lexicon für Theologie und Kirche* (1930-1938), II, 731-732; the reference articles by Pierre Mandonnet in *Dictionnaire de Théologie Catholique*, II, 1537-1540, and by Francis Courtney in *NCathEnc*, III, 28-29, are unsatisfactory on this point.

3 On the *Alumbrados* or Illuminati see Koch, *Jesuitenlexicon*, pp. 51-53; *NCathEnc*, I, 356.

was at that time threatening Spain. He involved in this fight the spirituality of the *Exercises* and of their author. He accused Ignatius of nothing less than being an innovator, and a revolutionary, one who was destroying the well-ordered and well-tried structures of tradition. He said that it was madness " to leave the even and secure ways which the Church had traveled for 1,500 years."[4] In truth, that which was unusual and original about Ignatius and his Institute was so strongly felt at the time that for many spirits this accusation appeared anything but insignificant. It is well known that Cano did not stand alone. The friends of the new order, on the other hand, greeted in Ignatius the " modern " man who dared to take the concerns of the new age seriously and to form out of its spirit the program of his order and the frame for his spirituality.

Everyone •admits today that Ignatius and his goals and his spirituality did not fall like a meteor from heaven. The sources from which he more or less consciously drew are known. But when it comes to citing these sources, one does not usually get much beyond the New Devotion (*Devotio Moderna*) and medieval mysticism.[5] Thereby the fact is overlooked that there is a profound law for the renovation of all spiritual institutions, according to which they are always regenerated only by a return to the source from which they have drawn their first beginnings.

Now it is without doubt true that, seen in the light of this fundamental principle, Holy Scripture stands as the basis and origin of Ignatian piety.[6] So the first defender of the Jesuits in their struggle with Cano, Bartolomé de Torres, was right when he said of the *Exercises* that they contained nothing other than that which is presented in Holy Scripture as the norm and law of Christian

---

4 Melchor Cano wrote in a letter of March 28, 1556: " Es gran locura en cosas nuevas y dudosas arrojasas los hombres a aprovecharlas y sanctificarlas dejando los caminos llanos y seguros que mil quinientos años ha la Iglesia tenido. Lo que yo puedo pedir a cualquier cristiano es que esté a la mira y abra los ojos sin cautivarse de nadie, sino con libertad, siguiendo la vida y doctrina de los santos, la cual siguiendo no puede errar "; see Iparraguirre, *Historia*, I, 96.

5 A typical example is Pastor, *History of the Popes*, XII, 15-16; even De Guibert, in his chapter on the sources of Ignatian spirituality (*DeGuiJes*, pp. 152-181), does not provide much more. An exception is Hugo Rahner in " Ignatius von Loyola und die aszetische Tradition der Kirchenväter," *ZAM*, XVII (1942), pp. 61-77; and in *Ignatius the Theologian* (New York, 1967), pp. 32-52.

6 See J. Daniélou, " La vision ignatienne du monde et de l'homme," *RAM*, XXVI (1950), 5-17; J. Levie, " La méditation fondamentale à la lumière de Saint Paul," *Nouvelle revue théologique*, LXXV (1953), 815-827.

life.[7] In addition to this accepted fact, however, another source of Ignatian spirituality, of course completely subordinate to biblical piety,[8] may not be overlooked. This is the spirituality of early monasticism, as we have come to view it ever more clearly on the basis of the numerous editions and publications in which the last eighty years have been especially rich.[9] However true it is that Ignatius has traveled new ways, it still may not be forgotten that he received powerful and even determining impulses and directions from the documents of the early history of monasticism, even though for the most part only indirectly.[10] This is so true that his really history-making deed was the revival of the ideals of the early monastic fathers — a revival which is anything but a sterile repetition, one rather in which essential elements of the new approach to life and the spirit of the times can be felt.

It would be false and a methodological error if one wanted to see a dependence on the spirituality of the early Church only where a literary relationship to early monastic teaching can be shown in the form of citations or allusions in the writings of Ignatius. Certainly these are to be found also, especially from the time when Ignatius applied himself to theological studies onward.[11] Already during the first period of his spiritual life he had come to know the monastic world, especially through his careful reading of the

---

7 See Astráin, *Historia*, I, 380-381.

8 Ancient monasticism took this subordination to the direction of the Bible very seriously; typical of this is what Basil writes at the beginning of his short treatise on the Rule: " An liceat, aut expediat alicui, ut sibi ipsi permittat facere dicereve quae bona existimat, citra testimonium divinarum Scripturarum ? " (PG 31, 1079); see Heussi, *Ursprung*, pp. 276-280; Heinrich Bacht, *Antonius und Pachomius. Von der Anachorese zum Cönobitentum.*

9 The most important literature on the subject (up to 1938) is found in M. Viller and K. Rahner, *Aszese und Mystik in der Väterzeit* (Freiburg, 1938), pp. 81-83, 84-85, 90-91, 96-99, 110-113, 115-116.

10 That the spirituality of St. Ignatius is oriented according to that of the early monks has been stressed by Louis Bouyer in his book, *Du Protestantisme à l'Église* (Paris, 1954), p. 122. This is especially obvious in his understanding of obedience as presented in the famous letter on obedience; on this see H. Rahner, " Ignatius und die aszetische Tradition," *ZAM,* XVII (1942), 66-72.

11 See H. Rahner, ibid., 66. Rahner refers to the fact that the saint's secretary, Juan de Polanco, helped him, from 1547 on, by gathering " patristic " material for use in the composition of the *Constitutions* and in his correspondence.

Flos Sanctorum by Jacobus de Voragine,[12] in which are sketched a large number of the old monastic figures, partly through literal excerpts from the early sources.[13] It is known that, alongside St. Francis and St. Dominic, the venerable anchorite of the Egyptian desert, St. Onuphrius, made a particularly deep impression on Ignatius.[14]

But even more important is the fact that the entire spirituality of the age in which Ignatius lived was filled with and formed by themes, ideas, and values taken over from the writings of the great monastic Fathers of the East and the West. Let only the *Following of Christ* by Thomas à Kempis be mentioned. After Manresa the reading of this book became dearer to St. Ignatius than any other. In it there is great insistence on the " models of the holy Fathers."[15] Whoever is acquainted with early ascetical literature will perceive with surprise how even the terminology of the spiritual tradition of the Church has for the most part already found its final form in the first centuries.[16] It must not be overlooked — to mention but a few of the most important examples — that everything essential and important that Christian asceticism and mysticism has to say is already found in the *Vita Antonii* of Athanasius, in the writings of Evagrius Ponticus and of Diadochus of Photice, in the *Apophthegmata Patrum*, in John Climacus and John Moschus, in Cassian, Jerome, and Benedict. The succeeding centuries have drawn again and again from these rich sources, as is proved by the numberless manuscripts still extant today. If many ascetical writers of the modern period often appear to us to be superficial and poor in ideas, then one of the reasons for this must certainly be the fact that they have lost a living contact with the ancient sources, since the study of them has been left to the historians and philologists. This complaint

---

12 German translation: R. Benz, *Die Legenda Aurea des Jacobus de Voragine* (Heidelberg); English translation: *The Golden Legend of Jacobus de Voragine* (New York, 1941).

13 For example: Paul the Hermit, Macarius, Anthony, Basil, Benedict.

14 See Pedro de Leturia, " El influjo de San Onofre in San Ignacio a base de un texto inedito de Nadal," *Manresa*, II (1926), 224-238.

15 Thomas à Kempis, *The Imitation of Christ*, Bk. I, ch. 18, " Of the examples of the Holy Fathers "; the chapter is actually a compendium of what Cassian and other early monastic fathers had said.

16 It is gratifying to see that the philology of this question has recently been the object of research, especially under the direction of Professor C. Mohrmann of Nijmegen; see, for example, a work that has come from this school: L. T. A. Lorié, *Spiritual Terminology in the Latin Translation of the Vita Antonii* (Nijmegen, 1955).

could not yet be made at the time when Ignatius lived.[17] What wonder then if we find the echo of early monastic piety in him. One need only make it perceptible.

We need not fear that in doing this we are simply satisfying the curiosity of the historian. Rather we believe that in this we are serving the living assimilation of the Ignatian spiritual heritage, a task given to us and to every generation. Perhaps it is no exaggeration if we say that it is precisely due to a lack of familiarity with the early monastic roots of Ignatian spirituality that we no longer know how to value completely and make use of many important elements in the *Exercises* as well as in the *Constitutions* of the saint. To mention but a few examples, what do the " spiritual motions " (*Motiones spirituales, mociones*) about which we hear so much mean for many interpreters of the book of the *Exercises* ? What role is played in practice, not theory, by the rules for the discernment of the various spirits, so thoroughly developed by Ignatius ? What has become of the duties of the one who gives the *Exercises*, duties which are so clearly outlined in the text itself ? Is it not true that only too often the interplay demanded by Ignatius between ascetical and mystical, active and contemplative elements is misunderstood ? And is not the case the same with the *Constitutions*, which Ignatius drew up in the spirit of the *Exercises* ? Is it not hard at times for us to understand the original meaning of the " account of conscience " ? Are not many of the controversies regarding the role of " Jesuit obedience " and the role of the superior to be understood as arising because of the fact that we have lost sufficient understanding of the historical background ? These few examples should be enough to lead us to suspect what light would fall on central elements of Ignatian spirituality if we were to trace them to their really fundamental sources. Our concern is to give these elements a fruitful vitality, not to make a purely academic study — even and precisely when we make history the critical touchstone.

What we offer in the following is only a preliminary approach, what is called in French " une étude approximative." In order to show the total breadth and depth of the dependence of Ignatian spirituality on early monastic spirituality, we would also have to consider, in addition to the *Exercises*, the other writings of the saint, especially the *Constitutions* and the twelve volumes of the

---

17 Let us mention merely the many citations from ancient monastic spirituality contained in the classic work of the Jesuit Alfonso Rodríguez, *Practice of Perfection and Christian Virtues.*

letters. Here we must abandon such a broad goal and limit ourselves to the *Exercises*. The material to be mastered still remains sufficiently extensive since it is not enough simply to discover literary dependencies and show how they were handed down to posterity.[18] This could be done in a relatively short time. We are concerned with topics or groups of thematic material in the *Spiritual Exercises*, the source of which can be shown to lie in the spirituality of ancient monasticism. We are also interested in evidence as to whether and to what extent these earlier elements can enrich our understanding of the *Exercises*. This question appears up to now to have been little studied.

Let one more remark be allowed by way of preface. It is well known that the question regarding the "originality" of the *Exercises* and the spirituality manifested in them have been discussed for a long time.[19] There have been two contrary opinions. Some went too far in that they disposed too quickly of all questions regarding possible sources from which Ignatius might have drawn.[20] They would have the *Exercises* existing already in Manresa at a time when Ignatius had not as yet studied theology, when he was, so to speak, spiritually "self-taught" (or more exactly "taught by God").[21] Others did not go far enough inasmuch as they made of Ignatius at best a clever compiler, trying to make out of every similarity of thought, if they could find any hint of a proof, an immediate dependency. Arturo Codina[22] has rightly stressed, answering the latter, that Ignatius would have had to be a widely read man of letters — which he really was not — if the dependencies affirmed by some scholars were all to prove true.

In this case also, the truth lies in the middle. On the one hand, we know from the research of Henri Bernard, Pedro de

---

18 Herein lies the difference between what we are attempting in this article and what Hugo Rahner has done in his valuable study, "Ignatius und die aszetische Tradition," *ZAM*, XVII (1942), 66-72. His chief interest lies in determining what authors Ignatius consulted and what expressions in his writings are drawn from those sources. Our principal concern is the "motifs" that reached Ignatius directly or indirectly from monastic spirituality. One must know their original meaning if he is to understand their function in the whole complex of Ignatian spirituality.

19 See *DeGuiJes*, p. 152.

20 See Arturo Codina, *Los orígenes de los Ejercicios espirituales de san Ignacio de Loyola, Estudio histórico* (Barcelona, 1925), pp. 127-215.

21 This conception left a rather strange relic in the legend that the *Exercises* had been "dictated" to the saint at Manresa by the Blessed Virgin; see on this the sober remarks in Dudon, *St. Ignatius*, p. 203.

22 Codina, *Los Orígenes*, p. 215; H. Rahner, *ZAM*, XVII (1942), p. 72.

Leturia, Ignacio Iparraguirre, and especially Henri Pinard de la Boullaye[23] that the *Exercises* had not achieved their definitive form at Manresa,[24] but were filled in little by little. On the other hand, it is undisputed that the *Exercises*, in their basic conception as well as in their realization, bear the unmistakable stamp of their author; even more, that in them expression is given to the personal grace-given experiences of a life abundantly rich in mystical phenomena. But this fact alone is not enough to explain the place which the book of the *Exercises* has taken in the history of spirituality during the last four centuries. If only the experiences and visions of Manresa stood behind the *Exercises*, this little book would still be an important document about an individual who was supremely gifted with grace; and one that has produced wonderful effects in other men, giving them the foundation for sanctity. But they would lack an authorization of their value for the whole Church. Only because the rich treasures of the ascetical-mystical tradition that has been in the Church from its very beginnings are alive in them, could the Church officially accept them and take them into the inalienable treasure of Church tradition that is given anew to each generation. Hugo Rahner has rightly called attention to this essential relationship to the tradition of Christian life and piety, a relationship that marks a spirituality as genuine and authentic.[25] Viewed from this aspect the following is a renewed justification of the " basic Christian " character of the spirituality of the *Exercises*, in both senses of the term " character."

Exercitia " spiritualia "

Perhaps we may begin with a comparison. Everyone knows of Dante's *Divina Commedia*, at least by its title. But does everyone know precisely what this title means? Is not the case the same with the " Spiritual Exercises " of St. Ignatius? Do not many people perceive in the word only that it is a matter of " spiritual " (and thus not corporal) exercises, or more precisely, of " religious " exercises in general? The reason for this is that we have lost the

---

23 Henri Bernard, *Essai historique sur les Exercices spirituels de S. Ignace, depuis la conversion d'Ignace* (1521) *jusqu'à la publication du Directoire* (1599) (Louvain, 1926); Leturia, " Genesis," *AHSJ*, X (1941), 16-59; Iparraguirre, *Historia*, I, 34-40; Henri Pinard de la Boullaye, *Les étapes de rédaction des Exercices de S. Ignace* (Paris, 1950).

24 Laynez wrote in 1547 to Polanco, the saint's secretary from 1547 until his death in 1556, that the Exercises had existed in Manresa *quanto a la substancia* (*FN*, I, 82).

25 H. Rahner, *Spirituality of St. Ignatius*, pp. 16-45.

content, the meaning of the word *spiritualis* — and we are not the first to lose it. For how else could the word have come to be used, already in the Middle Ages, to stand for the " clergy " as differentiated from the " laity " (*spirituales vs. temporales*) ?[26] It is well known that Ignatius did not invent the term *exercitia spiritualia*. It had long been a technical term in ascetical literature.[27] But something further and undeniable arose as a result of the extensive use of the term " spiritual exercises " in a technical sense in ascetical literature. Much of the rich fullness of Christian meaning which originally inhered in the root *spiritualis* was no longer suggested to those who used the word. Even where Ignatius himself gives a sort of commentary on his title (*Spiritual Exercises*, [1]), we see little of original meaning. What Irénée Hausherr writes in his recently published book about the direction of souls in the ancient Orient is just as valid for the word " *spiritualis* ": "... in the course of centuries these words have lost almost all their meaning, as the sacred vessels gradually lose their gilding through being handled by priests and polished by sacristans."[28] In the same work, the learned orientalist has indicated the path by which we can come to an understanding of the original meaning of the term.[29] In the course of our study we will see just how much this original understanding of the term determines the total conception of the *Spiritual Exercises* of St. Ignatius.

Hausherr rightly points out that this understanding becomes easier if we put the earlier Greek word *pneumatikos* in place of the

---

26 See C. du Cange, *Glossarium ad Scriptores mediae et infimae latinitatis*, under the entry *spiritualis*.

27 Thus, for example, the Carthusian prior, Guigo the Younger, in his much-read book, *Scala claustralium* (written about 1145), uses the term *exercitium spirituale* to denote the four stages of contemplative prayer: *lectio, meditatio, oratio, contemplatio* (PL 184, 475). The book of the Benedictine abbot, García de Cisneros, which Ignatius had on hand at Montserrat, is called *Ejercitatorio de la vida espiritual*; see Codina, *Los orígenes*, pp. 169-170; also ibid., pp. 166-177, where the whole question concerning the dependence of the *Exercises* on the Benedictine's work is discussed. [Also, on the terminology of "spiritual exercises," see L. Hertling, "De usu nominis Exercitiorum Spiritualium ante S. P. Ignatium,' *AHSJ*, II (1923), 316-318. Ed.]

28 "... en traversant les siècles ces vocables ont perdu a peu près toute leur valeur comme des vases sacrés perdent peu a peu leur dorure à force d'être maniés par des mains de prêtres et frottés par des mains de sacristains ": Irénée Hausherr, "Direction spirituelle en Orient autre fois," *Orientalia Christiana Analecta*, 144 (1955), 19.

29 Ibid., 39-55.

polished Latin or German term. This immediately places us right in the middle of the world of biblical language. *Paul* it is who, especially in the First Epistle to the Corinthians, introduced the term into the language of the Church and gave it the fullness of its Christian meaning.[30] In contrast to its meaning in Hellenistic philosophy, which is unnecessarily dragged in here by Richard Reitzenstein, Hans Leisegang, and others,[31] *pneumatikos* calls attention to the order of super-nature, of the Spirit of God, who is given to those who are reborn in Christ. For Paul, " spiritual men " are those who are filled with the Holy Spirit and who are led and driven by him.[32] Accordingly, " spiritual " works are those that spring from the Spirit of God and are united to God, those that bear His seal. Paul likewise makes clear[33] the intimate union of " spiritual " and " charisma ": the spiritual man shares in those marvelous effects of the Spirit described by Paul in the famous chapter on the charismata (I Cor. 12).[34]

The rationalism of the Gnostics endangered the understanding of the " pneumatic," the basis of which had been laid down by Paul. The similarity of the terminology should not delude one into disregarding the radical difference in the theology behind that terminology.[35] While the Gnostics made the " pneumatic " a constitutive part of nature — one is by his very nature either " hylic " (material) or " pneumatic " — the concern of the Christian theologians from the time of Irenaeus on has been to safeguard the supernatural character of the " spiritual " as arising from the free grace of God.[36] From Irenaeus also comes the classic formula to describe the " spiritual man ": " The union of soul and body, when it receives

---

30 See F. Büchsel, *Der Geist Gottes im Neuen Testament* (Gütersloh, 1926).

31 Hausherr, " Direction spirituelle, " pp. 29-40; a detailed argument against the authors mentioned in the text is found in K. Prümm, *Der christliche Glaube und die altheidnische Welt* (2 vols. Leipzig, 1935), I, 269-281; II, 111-162.

32 See Rom. 8:14; 12:11.

33 Rom. 1:11; 1 Cor. 14:1.

34 See J. Brosch, *Charismen und Ämter der Urkirche* (Bonn, 1951); Paul Gächter, " Zum Pneumabegriff des heiligen Paulus," *Zeitschrift für katholische Theologie*, LIII (1929), 345-408.

35 See K. Prümm, *Religionsgeschichtliches Handbuch für den Raum der altchristlichen Umwelt* (Rome, 1954), pp. 588-589.

36 The following section is taken from Hausherr, " Direction spirituelle," pp. 39-55.

the Spirit of God, constitutes the . . . spiritual man."[37] Man becomes
"spiritual" by means of the Holy Spirit who is given to him and
whose effects are witnessed to by the martyrs in their superhuman
fortitude in the face of suffering.[38] Furthermore the Holy Spirit
announces his presence in the spiritual man through the charismata,
particularly that of prophecy, which was still alive in the days of
Irenaeus.[39] But another thought is also proclaimed by Irenaeus.
No one grows to "spiritual manhood" who does not walk in the
way of stern asceticism: "They therefore who possess the pledge
of the Spirit, who do not serve the lusts of the flesh but submit
themselves to the Spirit and live according to reason in all things,
these the Apostle rightly calls spiritual men since the Spirit of God
dwells within them."[40]

Although even in Irenaeus the "spiritual life" appears in close
union with the charismata, or else with their visible manifestations,
still it was recognized from the start that these outward manifestations in no way constituted the essence of the "spiritual."[41] On the
contrary, since the crisis of Montanism, the men of the time were
very suspicious of everything unusual and ecstatic.[42]

For the further development within the Church of the understanding of the "spiritual," Origen must be considered.[43] For
Origen, only that man is a true *pneumatikos* in whom are united
praxis and *theoria*, *gnosis* and the active pursuit of virtue, care for
his own progress and the service of his brother.[44] Of the charismata
granted to the *pneumatikos*, he stressed especially *diakrisis*, the gift
of differentiating the various kinds of spirits. It has been rightly
said: "If the details that are spread out through two or three
chapters of his book *De Principiis* were collected, then it would be

37 St. Irenaeus, *Adversus haereses*, Bk. V, ch. 8, no. 2 — in the edition of
W. W. Harvey (2 vols. Cambridge, 1857), II, 340: ". . . animae et carnis
adunatio assumens Spiritum Dei, spiritalem hominem perficit."
38 *Adversus haereses*, V, 9, 2: Harvey, II, 343.
39 *Adversus haereses*, V, 6, 1: Harvey, II, 334.
40 *Adversus haereses*, V, 8, 2: Harvey, II, 339-340.
41 Hausherr, "Direction spirituelle," p. 43, rightly stresses that the distinction
between *gratia gratis data* and *gratia gratum faciens* stems from the early
Church, even though the terminology was developed later.
42 See P. de Labriolle, *La crise montaniste* (Paris, 1913), p. 555. Yet even
before this it was well known how to distinguish between true inspiration
and that which came from demonic sources; see Heinrich Bacht, "Wahres
und falsches Prophetentum," *Biblica*, XXXII (1951), 237-262.
43 See W. Völker, *Das Vollkommenheitsideal des Origenes* (Tübingen, 1931),
pp. 145-196; Jean Daniélou, *Origène* (Paris, 1948).
44 Völker, *Vollkommenheitsideal*, p. 145.

easy to compile an essay on the 'discernment of spirits' that would be a concise summary of the entire teaching of Holy Scripture on this subject,"[45] and which, we may add, anticipates the whole future development of the teaching up to the time of Ignatius of Loyola.

Just as Irenaeus, and even more than he does, Origen stresses the union of the pneumatic with the Holy Spirit. In his trinitarian view of reality, the Father works in all creatures, endowing them with their being; the Son, on the other hand, works in all intelligent beings, procuring them knowledge. " But participation in the Holy Spirit is found only in the saints."[46] Through this participation one becomes " spiritual."

Now it is of basic importance to know that Origen, unlike his predecessor in the direction of the Alexandrian catechetical school, had a decisive influence on the spirituality of *ancient monasticism*.[47] Not only did he become through his own ascetical development[48] a " pioneer of monasticism " (Heussi), but he also gave it its theological foundation. It is certainly true that there is a great difference between the simple, not to say homely, piety of the Coptic fathers of monasticism and the subtle spiritual culture of Alexandrians like Evagrius and others.[49] But it is still true that essential elements of the spirituality of Origen spread in a short period of time through the whole of Eastern monasticism — even among those who belonged to the party of the anti-Origenists in the dogmatic feuds of the time. One need only compare the ten points with which Karl Heussi, following Walther Völker, summarizes the spiritual teaching of Origen with the model sketched by early monastic literature of the monk as *pneumatophoros* (spirit-bearer) in order to recognize the similarity.[50] Still if there is a difference, then it lies in this, that in the early monastic documents, everything appears to be more full of life and more real and concrete. But one should not overlook the fact that here too clichés rapidly take over, and idealizations replace genuine experience. Joined with them are pained

---

45 Viller-Rahner, *Aszese*, p. 75; see Hans Urs von Balthasar, *Origenes — Geist und Feuer* (Salzburg-Leipzig), pp. 330-341.

46 Origen, *De principiis*, Bk. I, ch. 3, no. 7.

47 Daniélou, *Origène*, p. 294; see also Heussi, *Ursprung*, pp. 44-49 — he there refers to Völker's *Vollkommenheitsideal*.

48 Eusebius of Caesarea, *Historia Ecclesiastica*, Bk. VI, ch. 2.

49 It is unfortunate that no scholar has worked out in sufficient detail the specific nature of the pre-Alexandrine period of Egyptian monasticism.

50 Heussi, *Ursprung*, pp. 45-47, 164-186.

complaints about the changed times and the decadence of the disciples of the earlier Fathers of the desert.[51]

To be sure the *Vita Antonii* of St. Athanasius, which has been called not without reason the Magna Charta of Christian monasticism,[52] is a disappointment. Anthony is certainly pictured in it as a perfect spirit-bearer, but the word *pneumatikos* is not used for this. The only time the word appears in the work it has quite a different meaning.[53]

The use of the term "spiritual" is however all the more frequent and instructive in the writings of the great theoretician of Eastern monasticism, Evagrius Ponticus.[54] No wonder, since he stands in close dependence on Origen, together with whom he was later condemned by the Church.[55] Nevertheless he was zealously read far and wide, although — *ad cautelam* — many of his writings were circulated under fictitious names. Evagrius speaks in his *Capita practica ad Anatolium*[56] of the "consolation" (*pneumatike hedone*) which angels awaken in the soul,[57] and of the "spiritual vision" (*pneumatike theoria*) with which is united such consolation as surpasses all earthly rapture,[58] and of the "spiritual love" (*pneumatike agape*) which alone can overcome the passions in the soul of man.[59] Elsewhere Evagrius speaks of the "spiritual refreshment" (*pneumatike anapausis*) for the sake of which the monk must be willing to sacrifice all bodily refreshment.[60] Those who live according to this law are "brothers in the spirit, holy fathers."[61] From all these citations we see that in Evagrius the term "spiritual" still appears in no way leveled off or placed on the same plane with "ascetical," as we find it in later writers. Still, he too stresses the indissoluble

---

51 Thus the complaints voiced in *The Imitation of Christ*, Bk. I, ch. 18, are in no way original; see Hausherr, "Direction spirituelle," pp. 178-179.
52 See Louis Bouyer, *La vie de Saint Antoine. Essai sur la spiritualité du monachisme primitif* (Saint Wandrille, 1950), pp. 1-5.
53 St. Athanasius, *Vita Antonii*, ch. 45, in PG 26, 909: *pneumatikè trophè*.
54 On Evagrius, see Viller-Rahner, *Aszese*, pp. 97-109; references to the sources and to other works are given, ibid., pp. 97-99.
55 See F. Diekamp, *Die origenistischen Streitigkeiten im sechsten Jahrhundert und das fünfte Allgemeine Konzil* (Münster, 1899).
56 PG 40, 1220-1236, 1244-1252, 1272-1276; see J. Muyldermans, "La teneur du Practicos d'Evagre le Pontique," *Le Muséon*, XLII (1929), 74-89; Viller-Rahner, *Aszese*, p. 97.
57 *Capita Practica*, ch. 15, in PG 40, 1225; see also ch. 48, in PG 40, 1233.
58 Ibid., ch. 21, in PG 40, 1228.
59 Ibid., ch. 24, in PG 40, 1228.
60 Evagrius, *Rerum monachalium rationes*, ch. 5, in PG 40, 1256.
61 Ibid., ch. 7, in PG 40, 1260.

union between "mysticism" and "asceticism," between "spiritual perfection" and one's "practical" (that is, ascetical) efforts. In this sense no. 50 in the *Capita practica* is to be understood: "The active [ascetical] life is that spiritual path on which is cleansed the part of the soul entangled in passions."[62]

We have to forego the temptation to cite examples from the rest of Eastern monasticism, however enticing it might be to pursue the living stream of this thought; for instance, in the works of Evagrius' greatest "pupil," Diadochus of Photice.[63] We go straight to Cassian who, as the bridge between East and West, naturally deserves special attention. "As the most read among the old spiritual authors, he nourished innumerable generations of monks with his teaching. Everywhere one can encounter his influence on the entire tradition; for example, even as late as in the authors of the 'Devotio moderna' ... or in that classical book, *On Christian Perfection*, by the Jesuit Alphonsus Rodriquez."[64] Unfortunately there is as yet no one who has summarized the vocabulary of the "great organizer of Western cenobitism before Benedict"[65] in a lexicon, as Guido Müller, S.J., has done for the works of St. Athanasius. Even so, it can be quickly discovered that *spiritalis* (*spiritualis*) is a word used by him very often. To be sure, we have to ignore all those places where the term is to be understood metaphysically or anthropologically;[66] also those where the word is used in connection with Holy Scripture, the meaning of which is to be understood "spiritually."[67] Yet even here the thought shines through that, if one is to interpret the Scriptures properly, one must be a "spiritual" man; or rather, one must possess a special "charisma of the Spirit."[68] We are interested only in those texts in which *spiritalis* refers to the ascetical-mystical realm. Here

---

62 Evagrius, *Capita Practica*, ch. 50, in PG 40, 1253: "Practica [vita] est spiritualis methodus quae animae partem circa affectus versantem expurgat."
63 Viller-Rahner, *Aszese*, pp. 216-226.
64 Ibid., p. 186.
65 Ibid., p. 185.
66 For example, Cassian, *Collatio* VII, ch. 13, no. 2: *spirituales atque intellectuales ... substantiae* (that is, angels).
67 Cassian, *Collatio* XIV, 13, 2: *spiritalibus studiis*; by this he means efforts towards gaining *spiritalis doctrina* as the spiritual understanding of Scripture, the *scientia spiritualis* mentioned in the same *Collatio*, 14, 2.
68 This idea is found right at the beginnings of Christian theology; see D. van den Eynde, *Les normes de l'enseignement chrétien dans la littérature patristique des trois premiers siècles* (Gembloux-Paris, 1933), pp. 77-85; Heinrich Bacht, "Die Lehre des heiligen Justinus Martyr von der prophetischen Inspiration," *Scholastik*, XXVII (1952), 23-24.

we observe something interesting. If for a long time the word "spiritalis" had expressed that which was worked by the Spirit, the "charismatic" moment in the "spiritual life," Cassian uses it primarily as an expression for man's efforts in the moral sphere, thus signifying the ascetical side of his labors in this life. For instance, when he speaks of monastic life as a *militia spiritalis*,[69] or as the sum of the *spiritalia studia* (spiritual efforts),[70] and when he calls the "interior" asceticism (in contrast to the corporal) a *spiritalis animae cura* (spiritual care of the soul).[71] Whoever will devote himself conscientiously to this struggle (*spiritalis quaestus*[72]) becomes himself *spiritalis*.[73] As a *spiritalis vir* (spiritual man) he can speak from experience and effectively hand on to others the *spiritalium rerum . . . doctrina* (teaching on spiritual matters).[74]

The term *spiritalis* passes from Cassian into Western terminology with this limitation to ascetical effort, to the *exercitia virtutum* (exercise of virtues).[75] As far as I can see, the expression *exercitia spiritualia* was not yet used by Cassian — although both components are found in him. Yet he shows us the direction in which we will have to look for the more precise sense of the term since his influence has been so significant in the development of Western ascetical-mystical theology. This theology puts the primary emphasis on the ascetical aspect, as well in the noun *exercitia* as in the modifier *spiritualia*. Yet this ascetical effort is aimed at and open to the mystical-charismatic side of the "spiritual life" — just as its earthly perfection consists for Cassian in the "contemplation" which only God can give.[76]

If we summarize the result of this first section, we have to state that the title *Exercitia spiritualia* must be interpreted, not directly from the biblical meaning of "spiritual," but from the historical development which the term *spiritualis* has undergone, especially since the time of Cassian. Without doubt the stress lies

---

69 Cassian, *Collatio* I, ch. 1; see Lorié, *Spiritual Terminology*, pp. 102-105.
70 Cassian, *Instituta*, VI, ch. 2; Lorié translates the phrase as "practice of the ascetic life" (*Spiritual Terminology*, p. 99). Would it not also be possible to understand *spiritalia studia* in this text as "efforts to understand Holy Scripture"?
71 Cassian, *Collatio* V, 4, 3.
72 Cassian, *Instituta*, X, 2, 1.
73 Ibid.
74 Cassian, *Collatio* XIV, 18; see also XIV, 14, 1.
75 *Collatio* XIII, 18, 4; XXI, 15, 1.
76 See L. Cristiani, *Jean Cassien — La spiritualité du désert* (2 vols. Saint Wandrille, 1946), pp. 194-222.

for Ignatius also on the ascetic-active component. The first Annotation (*Spiritual Exercises*, [1]) shows this clearly. In it "spiritual exercises" are defined in the following manner, in analogy with bodily exercises: " All methods of preparing the soul . . . to free itself from all inordinate affections and, after it has freed itself from them, to seek and find the will of God concerning the ordering (*disposición*) of one's life for the salvation of his soul are called spiritual exercises." But to give an interpretation exclusively ascetical to what Ignatius sets forth and means in this connection, as has happened only too often, would be to err completely. The *Exercises* are no school of the will, however original. The ascetic-active element is only one component. Its function is subsidiary to the other, passive element that is produced by the Spirit. It is precisely here that we see how much the spirituality of the book of the *Exercises* owes to the early monastic spirituality. On the other hand, it will be clear from this just how much the knowledge of this early monastic spirituality will contribute to our understanding of the spirituality of the *Exercises*. This will become even clearer when we try to interpret the many passages in the book of the *Exercises* where we read about the " motiones spirituales " or " cogitationes."

" *Spirituales motiones* "

Ignatius has left us an important observation regarding the history of the origin of the *Exercises* in his *Autobiography*.[77] He says that those sections of the book which refer to " the methods of election " go back to the experience of " the diversity of spirits and thoughts " to which he had been subjected at Loyola. What is particularly worth noting in these words is the close association of " spirits " and of " thoughts." Usually we do not notice this because we have become used to this manner of speaking without questioning ourselves very much about its validity. The *Exercises* themselves gives us an authentic commentary on this autobiographical text. We need only make the effort to check through the references to *cogitationes* and related concepts. We read as early as the sixth Annotation (*SpEx*, [6]) — in apparent analogy to the above-mentioned passage in the *Autobiography*: " When he who gives the Exercises finds that no " spiritual motions,"[78] such as consolation or desolation, are experienced in the soul of the exercitant, and that he is " not

---

77 *Autobiog*, 99, in *FN*, I, 504.
78 *Nullas incidere spirituales motiones* (Roothaan's version); *spirituales animi commotiones* (Versio Vulgata).

agitated by various spirits,"[79] then he is to inquire closely whether
the exercitant is making really earnest effort. So we have here
once again the close association of the two above-mentioned factors,
only this time in place of *cogitationes* we read *motiones*. We can
perceive from this that *cogitationes* need not be at all the same
thing as " thoughts " or something of this kind. Beyond that, the
sixth Annotation is important because it shows us what value
Ignatius places on the observation of these motions; for him their
presence is evidently a criterion as to whether one has honestly
allowed himself to become more intimate with God. Finally it
must not be overlooked that here, again in analogy with the text
from the *Autobiography*, it is a matter of " different " or " varied "
spirits, the effect of which the exercitant is to experience within
himself. Evidently the alternation between the contrary motions is
just what produces the possibility of making a discriminating
judgment.

In the following Annotations ([7-10]), we read about these same
" movements " and their possible " spiritual " causation, without the
term itself being repeated. The important point in this is the fact
that the necessity of using the " Rules for the Discernment of
Spirits," given at the end of the book (*SpEx*, [313-336]), is expressly
pointed out. From this it becomes clear just how little one does
justice to the purpose of the book of the *Exercises*, if one (as Feder
does in translating Annotation 6) lets the impression arise, by the
use of the German word *geistig* [which can mean either " spiritual "
or " intellectual "], that these *spirituales motiones* are simply " psychological " happenings. On the other hand, the fullness of detail
with which Ignatius discusses this point, in the otherwise quite
laconic text of the *Exercises*, lets one recognize how essential, in the
mind of Ignatius, is the part of the Exercises being touched on
here. From this alone it can be seen that the traditional manner of
giving the Exercises, without serious attention to these spiritual
movements in the soul and to the discernment of spirits, does not
give sufficient recognition to the full content of that which Ignatius
intended.

Our previous observations are confirmed by the opening remarks
to the General Examination of Conscience ([32]). There we read:
" I presuppose that there are in me three kinds of thoughts,[80]

---

79 *agitari variis spiritibus* (Roothaan); *diversorum spirituum agitationibus*
(Vulgata).
80 *tres cogitationes* (Roothaan); *triplex...cogitationum genus* (Vulgata).

my own, which spring simply from my own liberty and free will,[81] and two others which come from without, one from the good and one from the evil spirit." It here becomes clear that for Ignatius the "thoughts" in a man are ambiguous and therefore subject to the discernment (*discretio*); yet at this place and in the following considerations on the different types of sins of thought ([33-37; 74]), nothing more is said about this.

These things are handled all the more completely in connection with the Rules for the Discernment of Spirits. The very title to the rules that are intended for the situation of the First Week of the *Exercises* speaks about the "different motions . . . in the soul."[82] Here the "purely natural" happenings in the soul are not meant, but rather movements of the soul (imaginative images, moods, movements of synderesis,[83] thoughts, inspirations, and similar phenomena) that spring from the good or the evil spirit. Ignatius summarizes all this and what follows under two catchwords, "consolation" and "desolation" ([316-324]). Both times it is a question of a *motio* [movement] by which the soul is "excited." No matter to what extent superhuman spiritual powers are at work in these "movements," they still do not imply any lessening of human freedom. Just the opposite. Ignatius warns about this and says that it is precisely at such times that a man should be most watchful and in certain cases should bring himself to do just the opposite of that toward which he feels himself moved ([318-321]). At the same time he should keep alive in himself the conviction that it is God who in his wise providence delivers him over to the "various influences and temptations of the enemy."[84] The ninth rule of this group ([322]) shows how clearly conscious Ignatius was of the mysterious collaboration of natural and supernatural causality. This rule alone is enough to refute the often raised objection that

---

81 The translation in the Versio Vulgata, *ex proprio surgens motu ipsius hominis*, destroys the nuances; for "freedom" and "will" are in no way necessarily synonyms. There are "thoughts" that are "natural" without having their origin in a free human act.

82 *SpEx*, [313]: *varias motiones . . . in anima* (Roothaan); *motus animae* (Vulgata).

83 This term comes from Jerome, long before scholasticism; see H. Rahner, "Ignatius und die aszetische Tradition," *ZAM*, XVII (1942), 62.

84 *SpEx*, [320]: *variis agitationibus et tentationibus inimici* (Roothaan); *insultibus . . . inimici nostri* (Vulgata). The Vulgata, by omitting the ideas expressed by *variis* and *agitationibus*, has weakened the force of the statement.

the primacy of grace and the unconditional sovereignty of God do not receive their due in the *Exercises*.[85]

The Rules of Discernment for the Second Week treat even more subtly of these motiones, which according to Ignatius are aroused in the soul by transcendent powers ([328-336]). In the second of these rules, *facere motionem*, " to cause movements," is named as one of the various effects in the soul which can have God alone as their cause.[86] Yet even the devil may awaken good and holy thoughts in the soul[87] — to be sure only under the presupposition that the person is suitably disposed for this — but only in order to deceive him.

The weight of these citations can only be properly felt if one considers the extent to which the observation and testing of the *motiones* is woven into the real heart of the *Exercises*, the election. Here we need not prove once more that the election is the culmination to which the rest of the *Exercises* is ordered. Let it merely be noted that the very first Annotation (no. 1), which summarizes the entire *Exercises*, provides evidence for this. We are only interested here in showing that Ignatius is convinced that the call of God, the will of God for a man in a concrete situation, will be revealed in a genuine election.[88] All the human activity that precedes the election has only the role of " disposing," of " making oneself available." The election itself is a gift of God — despite all the exert'ons of the natural powers — and (in a sense which is not easy to determine) a revelation of God; and yet it is still a completely individual decision. This is especially noticeable where Ignatius speaks of the " three times in each of which one can make a sound and good election " ([175]). We are particularly concerned with the " second time," which is expressly distinguished from the " third time ... of tranquillity " ([176-177]). In this second time " sufficient clarity and insight is received " to recognize the will of God, and that comes " by the experience of consolation and desolation and by the experience of the discernment

85 See A. Steger, " Der Primat der göttlichen Gnadenführung im geistlichen Leben nach dem heiligen Ignatius von Loyola," *Geist und Leben*, XXIV (1948), 94-108.

86 The Versio Vulgata leaves this out.

87 *SpEx*, [332] *cogitatus* (Roothaan); *cogitationes* (Vulgata); see also [333-334].

88 See *SpEx*, [172], where the " choice " (of man) and the " call " (of God) are set in relationship with each other.

of the various spirits.''[89] On the other hand, the third time '' of tranquillity '' is so described that in it '' the soul is not moved back and forth by various spirits, and makes use of its natural powers in peace and freedom.''[90]

If one reviews the statements given here, it is impossible to deny that the experiences described by Ignatius with the terms *motiones, cogitationes,* and *agitationes* have a truly central position in the structure of his book. Perhaps it is not an exaggeration to say that the teaching on the *spirituales motiones* and practice in the discernment of them so belong to the substance of what Ignatius thought the *Exercises* to be that all forms of spiritual exercises which do not allow these elements to come into play may only be styled Ignatian Exercises in a reductive or adapted sense.[91] This observation is confirmed by the fact that even historically the experience and spiritual discernment of '' various spirits '' stand at the beginning of the *Exercises* and almost seem to be their root foundation. This is evidenced not only by the passage from the *Autobiography* cited at the beginning of this section but also by the latest studies on the gradual development of the book of the *Exercises*. At any rate, after a careful study of the various testimonies to the history of the origins of the book of the *Exercises*, Henri Pinard de la Boullaye comes to the conclusion that in the year 1523, when Ignatius set out for Jerusalem, the preliminary outlines of at least the Rules for the Discernment of Spirits and the Methods of Election were already in existence.[92]

Decisive for the analysis of the nature of these phenomena is the fact that for Ignatius they belong to the realm of the '' supernatural.'' In them the operation of transcendent powers within

---

89 *SpEx*, [176]: *et per experientiam discretionis diversorum spirituum* (Roothaan); *vel diversorum spirituum praevio experimento* (Vulgata). Note the difference in meaning!

90 *SpEx*, [177]; see Henri Bremond, '' Notes sur les Exercices de S. Ignace,'' *Vie spirituelle, Supplement* (June, 1929), pp. 147-190. Bremond attempts (pp. 185-186) to reduce the third '' time '' to the second. But he is mistaken when he deduces from [180] that the one in the process of making the Election should, even in the third time, pray to God to lead him out of that state and to bestow upon him the signs which are spoken of in the second time.

91 Everything being said here refers to the '' long retreat,'' the full course of the Exercises, which goes beyond the limits of the first week and leads to the Election. We will not treat here of the many varied ways in which the Exercises can be adapted to practical pastoral situations and necessities.

92 Pinard de la Boullaye, *Les étapes,* pp. 8-9.

the soul makes its presence known. Without this " spiritual realism " everything that is so completely and forcibly developed by Ignatius simply cannot be understood — even the *Exercises* taken as a whole cannot be understood. Every attempt to make them into merely a " logic " or a " psychology " is misguided. Of course this is not to say that logic and psychology do not have their place in them. It is indeed of decisive importance to know that these spiritual effects insert themselves so noiselessly among the purely natural phenomena that there is need of a special spiritual gift of discernment in order not to be deceived.

Now if one wants to understand these descriptions and instructions in the *Exercises* historically, it is not enough to point to the experiences and mystic graces that Ignatius received at Loyola and Manresa. Rather, in addition to these, the testimony of tradition must be included. Naturally one can say that the writings of all ascetical authors of the time were full of this discernment of spirits. We will mention only that famous chapter 54 of the Third Book of the *Following of Christ*, in which a large number of norms for the discernment of the " different motions of nature and grace " is presented. But as we have known for a long time, the entire ascetical literature of that time was only an echo and outgrowth of the uncommonly diverse spirituality of the early monastic period, in particular that of the East, which also became familiar in the West through Cassian, Rufinus, and Jerome (to mention only the most important middle-men). Therefore for an understanding of these things we must examine those sources also.

As evidence for this statement we need not explore the entire body of early monastic literature. We select one author who, because he was astonishingly well read and was a prolific writer, deserves special attention. He is Evagrius Ponticus, whom we have mentioned earlier. The true importance of this unusual man has only recently been revealed by the studies of Wilhelm Frankenberg, Jean Muyldermans, and Irénée Hausherr. As a pupil of Macarius, Basil, and Gregory of Nazianzen, and as a zealous reader of the works of the great Alexandrians, Clement and Origen, he assimilated and handed on what was most valuable in the spiritual experience and tradition of that age. Hausherr especially has shown what a fundamental role, unsurpassed up to now, Evagrius plays.[93] His

---

93 A list of Irénée Hausherr's various articles is in Viller-Rahner, *Aszese*, pp. 98-99.

thought, which was carried over into Latin by Rufinus and Gennadius, was able to influence Western spirituality directly.

Among the works of Evagrius which were once spread under the name of Nilus and were also published as such by Migne, is found the treatise *De diversis malignis cogitationibus*.[94] Here Evagrius develops, with astonishing sensitivity and with the vivid language of a man speaking from experience, a strategy for fighting various temptations and passions which could be dangerous to the monk or, more exactly, to the anchorite. Here we already find in essence all the elements that we emphasized and abstracted from the *Exercises* earlier.[95]

We learn from Evagrius what Ignatius means by the *cogitationes* which are to be discerned "in the Spirit." They are the *logismoi* of which Evagrius speaks repeatedly. In contrast to the secular Greek as well as to the language of the Old and New Testaments,[96] the word does not signify the "highest activity, constituting man as man,"[97] his reason, but chiefly the imaginations and impulses aroused in the soul by the good and even more by the evil spirits.[98] These *logismoi* are already distinguished terminologically from the purely natural *noemata*.[99] The former are caused "supernaturally,"[100] particularly by the demons. So they are called *daimoniodeis logismoi*.[101] The relation between the demons that cause them and the "thoughts" they arouse is so very close that they seem to be identical: the "thought" is the "spirit" — though we ought not to think because of this that he has returned to merely psychological terminology. Therefore, we find here exactly the same ambivalence that we perceive in the book of the *Exercises*, where the "various spirits" which agitate the soul are to be understood

---

94 The first part of this work is found in PG 79, 1200-1233; the rest is in J. Muyldermans, *A travers la tradition manuscrite d'Evagre le Pontique* (Louvain, 1932), pp. 47-55; see on this the important comment in Viller-Rahner, *Aszese*, p. 97.

95 Naturally we are not stating that Ignatius is directly dependent upon Evagrius.

96 Rom. 2:15; 2 Cor. 10:4.

97 See Heidland in Gerhard Kittel, *Theologisches Wörterbuch zum Neuen Testament*, IV, 289.

98 It is stated thus already in Athanasius, *Vita Antonii*; examples in G. Müller, *Lexicon Athanasianum*, p. 828.

99 Evagrius (Pseudo-Nilus), *De diversis malignis cogitationibus*, ch. 2, in PG 79, 1201 and throughout.

100 Ibid.: *para physin*.

101 Ibid.

at one time as affections of the soul and at another time as personified causes of these agitations.[102]

Furthermore we find already in Evagrius the threefold division of "thoughts" which Ignatius too discusses (*SpEx*, [32]). He too contrasts the suggestions of the demons with the occurrences in the soul that spring from ourselves, as well as those that are awakened in us by the "holy powers."[103] We also find the use of the terms *motio* and *movere* (*kinema*, *kinesis*, *kinein*) that we are already accustomed to from the book of the *Exercises*. This word group is characteristic of him when there is question of describing psychic occurrences.[104] That in this he has created no new terminology but adheres to the terminology of Stoic psychology[105] is not of great importance for us. We are interested only in determining to what extent the language of the book of the *Exercises* is dependent on the terminology of early monastic spirituality.

Finally we must note the intense "spiritual realism" which — just as in the *Exercises* — also marks Evagrius' description of psychic occurrences. For, just as in the case of Ignatius, the descriptions and analyses in Evagrius are not at the service of an abstract psychology but are elements of a "discernment of spirits" which can only be understood on the basis of this "realism."

It would now be very easy to show how the same images and the same terminology are encountered in monastic documents after Evagrius. For the sake of brevity let it suffice to note the role of "thoughts" within the *Apophthegmata Patrum*, that anonymous collection of maxims and examples of the virtues from the lives of famous monks that was produced toward the end of the fifth century and became one of the favorite books of the Christian

---

102 See J. Clémence, "Le discernement des esprits dans les *Exercices spirituels* de S. Ignace de Loyola," *RAM*, XXVII (1951), 347-375, especially 348; XXVIII (1952), 64-81.

103 Evagrius, *De cogitationibus*, ch. 4, in PG 79, 1204; ch. 7, in PG 79, 1209: "Cum multa observatione cognovimus, quod inter cogitationes angelicas et humanas, ac eas quae a demonibus proveniunt, haec sit differentia." The same threefold division is found already in Origen, *De principiis*, III, ch. 2, no. 4; see Clémence, *RAM*, XXVII (1951), 349, n. 4.

104 Evagrius, *De cogitationibus*, chs. 2 and 4, in PG 79, 1201, 1204, 1205.

105 See E. Andres' article on *Daimon* in Pauly-Wissowa, *Real-Encyclopedie der Classischen Altertumswissenschaft*, Supplement III, 297-311; Heinrich Bacht, "Religionsgeschichtliches zum Inspirationsproblem. Die Pythischen Dialoge Plutarchs von Chäronea," *Scholastik*, XVII (1942), 50-69, especially 64-65.

Middle Ages.[106] Heussi has already pointed out that here "the tempting thought, the *logismos,* is almost conceived as an autonomous power within the soul of the monk; this is in accordance with the conception that the demons infuse evil thoughts. The *logismos* speaks to the monk. The expression also signifies brooding, 'cultivation' of thoughts. The *logismos* comes, disturbs the monk, leaves him no rest; and yet it is unable to perform the action, but is only a hindrance to virtue."[107] Thus we also have here, as was to be expected, the same "spiritual realism" supporting and controlling everything. The same realization would force itself upon us if we were to analyze the teaching of Cassian on the "*cogitationes ... et internos motus.*"[108] But we must hurry onward.

The Early Monastic Background of the Rules for the Discernment of Spirits

Although in the previous sections we have repeatedly spoken of the place of the discernment of spirits within the *Exercises,* still we shall now discuss it in particular because the dependence of the spirituality of the *Exercises* upon early monastic spirituality shows itself most clearly in this area.

Without doubt it was a misunderstanding of far-reaching significance when, through a failure to recognize the "spiritual" design and intent of the *Exercises,* they were understood purely "ascetically" as an excellent school of the will. This misunderstanding was of course quite natural since the ascetical and pedagogical elements of the *Exercises* are so obvious to everyone. But what is to become of the Rules for the Discernment of Spirits when such a limited view takes the place of the original design of the Exercises? No wonder that they were considered a foreign body and a remnant from a vanished world, something that had to be preserved out of respect. Moreover, effective inclusion of these Rules within the course of the *Exercises* became more or less impossible because, in contrast to the original practice, the entire Exercises (therefore not merely the first week) were no longer given only to individuals, but to entire groups.[109] It was no longer possible to determine the

---

106 See Berthold Altaner, *Patrology,* trans. Hilda C. Graef (Freiburg and Edinburgh-London: Herder and Nelson, 1960), p. 256; Viller-Rahner, *Aszese,* pp. 115-121; Heussi, *Ursprung,* pp. 132-280.
107 Heussi, *Ursprung,* p. 258.
108 Cassian, *Collatio* VII, ch. 13, no. 12.
109 On Exercises given to individual exercitants as the original practice, see *DeGuiJes,* pp. 131-132; and especially, Iparraguirre, *Historia,* I.

course of the Exercises according to the present spiritual state of the exercitant, but they had to be adapted to an average "spiritual climate." These Rules, which in the intention of St. Ignatius belong primarily in the hand of the one who gives the Exercises and should only be used to deal with the case of an exercitant who is troubled by various spirits, and then only in accordance with the stage of his spiritual progress, now became a harmless text that everyone was allowed to read.

The urgent warning in the ninth Annotation of the *Exercises* was thus completely overlooked. There one is warned against giving the Rules for Discernment of the second week to a man who "has had no experience in spiritual matters and is tempted grossly and openly as, for example, if he exhibits impediments to making further progress in the service of God our Lord." Ignatius adds this explanation: "Because, to the degree that those of the first week will benefit him, those of the second week will do him harm because they contain matter too subtle and too exalted for him to understand." This prescription is immediately intelligible to one who knows the many warnings of ascetical and mystical literature about giving higher forms of spiritual knowledge to the inexperienced.[110] But how was one to appreciate such a prescription when one no longer possessed or cultivated a living continuity with spiritual tradition?

A genuine understanding of what Ignatius says regarding the necessity and the difficulty of the discernment of spirits presupposes above all an uninterrupted contact with the spiritual realism which was a truism for all Christians prior to the time of the Enlightenment. No matter how eloquently one speaks about the theology and mysticism of the *Exercises*, where this continuity is lacking such eloquence remains at bottom merely literature. But if one wants to convince himself of this realism, then one can find no better way than to study the testimony of early monasticism, where the rules for the discernment of spirits were developed in detail long before Ignatius. And if it also remains uncontested that behind what Ignatius writes stands his own personal experience, still it cannot be doubted that he was directly and indirectly in contact with that which is to be found in such detail and with such pertinence in ancient monastic literature about the various spirits and the discernment of them.[111]

---

110 Cassian, *Collatio* XIV, ch. 17.
111 Ignatius had already found many references to his theme in the lives of the early monastic fathers in the *Flos Sanctorum* (or the *Golden Legend*) of Jacobus de Voragine.

If we want to demonstrate this again in detail, we stand once more before an embarrassment of riches. Whether we take up the *Life of St. Anthony* by St. Athanasius[112] or the writings of Evagrius Ponticus or the works of Cassian or of any other of the many authors of that period, we meet everywhere these questions in a more or less systematic presentation.[113] We will have to satisfy ourselves with letting only a few of the more important voices speak.

Earlier we have pointed out the inestimable importance of Origen in the development of early monastic spirituality. Perhaps this is most evident in the elaboration of the rules for the discernment of spirits. Hans Urs von Balthasar has brought together in his anthology of Origen, under the title " Essence and Division of Spirits," forty-three such rules " which anticipate in an astonishing manner the Ignatian Rules of Discernment."[114]

We set down here some of the more interesting texts: " Our soul is illuminated either by the true light which never goes out, which is Christ, or if she does not have this eternal light in herself, she is ... irradiated by a temporal and transitory light from him who ' transforms himself into an angel of light '[115] and who illuminates the soul of the sinner with a false light in order that that which is of the present and passes away may appear to him to be good and valuable."[116] " If we see that a soul is troubled by sins, by faults, by sadness, by anger, by desires, by covetousness, then we know that she it is whom the devil ' leads away to Babylon.' If, on the other hand, quiet, joy, and peace produce their fruit in the depths of the heart, we know that ' Jerusalem ' dwells in her; that is, the

---

112 See the excellent commentary on this of Louis Bouyer, *Vie de Saint Antoine*, pp. 67-98, 142-144; see also the valuable discussion of " Cosmologie et démonologie dans le Christianisme antique," ibid., pp. 181-219.

113 The history of the theme of discernment of spirits reaches back to before the beginnings of Christianity. Whoever would set himself to write its (long overdue) history would have to begin with the *Manual of Discipline* found among the Dead Sea Scrolls; see H. Holstein, " Les ' deux esprits ' dans la règle de la communauté essénienne du Désert de Juda," *RAM*, XXXI (1955), 297-303. The historian would then have to take into account the *Testament of the Twelve Patriarchs*, the *Pastor Hermae*, Origen's *De principiis*, and especially the rich abundance of references to be found in the literature of ancient monasticism. A comprehensive sketch of this is given by A. Chollet in *Dictionnaire de Théologie Catholique*, IV, 1375-1415.

114 Urs von Balthasar, *Origenes*, pp. 330-341; the quotation given in the text is on p. 330.

115 This text from 2 Cor. 11:14 is also mentioned by Ignatius, *SpEx*, [332].

116 Urs von Balthasar, *Origenes*, p. 331; see *SpEx*, [314, 332].

' vision of peace' is within her."[117] " By many signs, therefore, it can become manifest that the human soul ... can be subject to manifold influences of various good and evil spirits... One is subject to the influence of the good spirit ... when he is moved and called to what is good and is full of enthusiasm for the heavenly and the divine ... of course, always in such a way that it is left to the freedom and judgment of the person whether he will follow or not. So it is possible through this obvious ' discernment' to recognize in what way the soul is moved by the presence of the good spirit: namely, if she suffers not the least darkening of the spirit through the present inspiration."[118]

Evagrius Ponticus reveals himself here also to be a pupil of Origen. The treatise we mentioned earlier, *De diversis malignis cogitationibus*, is already shown by its title to be an instruction on the discernment of spirits.[119] The first part of this tract could rightly be called a commentary on the Meditation on the Two Standards of the book of the *Exercises*. For here also, just as in Ignatius, the insidious strategy of the tempter is laid bare. Satan proceeds according to a clever plan of attack: first there come by turns the demons (temptations) of the desires of the palate, of avarice, and of vain ambition; only when these have conquered do the demons of unchastity and anger follow; and the demon of pride — just as in *Exercises*, ([142]) — cannot enter victoriously until the three first-mentioned tempters have made themselves at home in the soul.[120] In contrast to the order given by Ignatius (riches, honor, pride: see ([142]), which is evidently based on a definite type of man,[121] Evagrius adds to his " scheme " a biblical foundation; namely a reference to the three temptations of Jesus in the desert.[122]

---

117 Urs von Balthasar, *Origenes*, p. 332; note the echoes found in the Exercises: the Two Standards, Babylon — Jerusalem.

118 Ibid.

119 Evagrius, *De cogitationibus*, in PG 79, 1199.

120 Ibid., 1200.

121 One will not go wrong who, when he reads the concrete details in the section on the Election in the *Spiritual Exercises*, thinks especially of academicians and clerics who, though they basically desire to serve God (thus fitting within the " realm " of the second week), are held back from following Christ more closely in the religious state through " riches " (benefices) and " honors " (ecclesiastical offices and dignities); see Pinard de Boullaye, *Les étapes*, p. 27: " Les dignitaires et les bénéficiaires ecclésiastiques sont constamment évoqués." From this fact he deduces correctly that the present form of the section on the Election could not have already existed when Ignatius was at Manresa.

122 Evagrius, *De cogitationibus*, in PG 79, 1201.

Just as Ignatius does, Evagrius advises careful observation of what goes on within the soul.[123] He recommends in particular a continual testing of ultimate motives, since the good which one does can only too easily spring from concealed hypocrisy.[124] As one having deep knowledge of the heart he knows about the deceptions of the devil.[125] One must have gathered a rich fund of experience in the interior life[126] in order not to let oneself be deceived. In this connection he lets fall the warning: "Therefore the anchorite must carefully observe where that demon begins and where he ends."[127] This recalls the similar instruction in the *Exercises*, where Ignatius also advises "to pay attention to the process of the thoughts," and to test well "the beginning, middle, and end" in order not to succumb inadvertently to the infiltrations of the Evil One ([333]).

The first time Ignatius came to notice the movements of the various spirits, he devoted a great deal of time to recalling afterwards what had happened within him; the Rules for the Discernment of Spirits are the far-reaching fruit of these considerations. Similarly Evagrius advises that, after the period of temptation, one should reconstruct what happened, how things began, where they have led, and how everything has taken place, and that one should imprint this on the memory in order to be able in the future better to ward off the attack of the temptation.[128] Likewise he advises that one who has been wounded by the tempter should study the *logismos* carefully, of what sort it was, of what elements it consisted, and what it was that most disturbed the soul.[129]

Still another idea that reminds us of Ignatius must be mentioned: In chapter twenty-seven Evagrius teaches that the demons cannot look directly into our hearts, for only God can see into hearts. Rather the demons can know something about our interior only from our statements[130] and from the "movements" of the body. When the book of the *Exercises* declares ([330]) in a similar context that it is a property of God alone to go in and out of the soul, the same thought and the same experience stand behind this statement.

---

123 Ibid.
124 Ibid., 1204.
125 Ibid., 1205: *kakotechnia.*
126 Ibid., 1209: *mystikōs gymnazomenos, mystice exercitatus.*
127 Ibid.
128 Ibid., 1212.
129 Ibid., 1221.
130 That is, through the *prophorikos logos*, ibid., 1232.

Diadochus, bishop of Photice in Epirus (fifth century), has written about the discernment of spirits in even more detail,[131] though in clear dependence on Evagrius. In his chief work, *De perfectione spirituali capita centum*, which was one of the most widely read spiritual books of the Eastern Church,[132] Diadochus treats of the discernment of spirits in two places, in chapters 26-40 and 75-89.[133] One need only skim over the basic thought of these sections to perceive the striking relationship with what Ignatius writes in his *Spiritual Exercises*. Diadochus warns the one who desires perfection to test his " thoughts " continually in order to preserve the good ones which come from God and to reject the evil ones which stem from the devil (ch. 26). Just as Ignatius does, Diadochus speaks of two sorts of interior consolation, divine and demonic (chs. 30-33). He also knows that, to the extent that a soul makes progress, she has to prepare herself for a more dangerous struggle with the cunning devil. He recalls the warning of the Apostle (2 Cor. 11:14) — cited by Ignatius also — that Satan can change himself into an angel of light (ch. 40). It belongs to the nature of the diabolic to change form continually (ch. 37). Diadochus loves, as Ignatius does, to illuminate the workings of the various spiritual powers in the soul by the use of imagery. Thus he once compares the contrasting operations of God and the devil within the soul to the north wind and the south wind, to clear weather and fog (ch. 75). He speaks at length — again in this anticipating Ignatius — about the " disconsolation " and examines the forms under which it appears and its causes (chs. 86ff). All this is described with an alert sensitivity for what really occurs within the soul. No wonder that precisely these sections were often copied separately from the " Hundred Chapters " and thus handed on.

To the testimony of the Eastern Church let us add that of a Latin author, who admittedly owes his entire spiritual wisdom to the

---

131 On Diadochus see Viller-Rahner, *Aszese*, pp. 216-228 — a bibliography is given on pp. 216-218; Altaner, *Patrology*, p. 319.

132 Critical edition by J. E. Weis-Liebersdorf (Leipzig, 1911); Latin translation by Francisco Torres, S.J., in PL 65, 1167-1212; French translation, with introduction, Edouard des Places, *Diadoque de Photicé, Cent Chapitres sur la perfection spirituelle* (" Sources Chrétiennes." Paris, 1943).

133 The Latin translation of Francisco Torres appeared in 1570, thus long after the death of St. Ignatius. Des Places, *Diadoque*, p. 67, notes however that Diadochus was one of a list of early monastic authors who were recommended reading for the members of the early Society of Jesus.

East, Cassian. Berthold Altaner[134] rightly calls him "one of the great educators of the West."[135] It cannot be said that Cassian was particularly original. But he had the precious gift of cleverly arranging and handing on in still more eloquent language what he had heard and read elsewhere. Here it should not be overlooked that he, the imitator, obviously intellectualizes and even rationalizes the things of the spiritual life. At times one cannot avoid the impression that often it is no longer the charismatic experience that stands behind his statements and that in his case the matters discussed are beginning to become "literature." He does still use the terminology that was current among the ancient monastic fathers, but under his pen they take on another ring. In an earlier article we have tried to show the truth of this for the term *meditatio*.[136] It seems to us that something similar is valid for *discretio spirituum*. If one should read the chapter on this subject in Christiani's[137] study just once, that would be enough to convince him to what an extent Cassian has turned the charisma of the discernment of spirits into the gift of prudence and tact. Yet in other places, in the Collation of the Abbot Moses,[138] for example, it becomes quite clear, through his reference to the famous text in the chapter on charismata of the First Epistle to the Corinthians (1 Cor. 12:10), that Cassian consciously maintained a continuity with the ancient tradition. In this and similar places we recognize that the "gift of discernment" is more than just prudence and reserve. It is the ability to discern within one's own or another's heart the source and meaning of the various agitations and spiritual influences. How much Cassian, and with him the entire monastic tradition, valued this gift is shown by the words of the above-mentioned Abbot Moses: "You see therefore that the gift of discernment is not something earthly or unimportant, but the highest gift of divine grace. When the monk does not bend all his efforts to obtaining this and thereby become capable of discerning with confidence the spirits that press upon him, it cannot but soon come to pass that, like one who wanders about

---

134 Altaner, *Patrology*, p. 538.
135 For an overall picture of Cassian, see Cristiani, *Jean Cassien*; the article "Cassien" in *Dictionnaire de spiritualité*, II, 214-276. Furthermore, Cassian drew a great deal from Evagrius Ponticus; see Cristiani, *Jean Cassien*, I, 261-262.
136 Heinrich Bacht, "*Meditatio* in den ältesten Mönchsquellen," *Geist und Leben*, XXVIII (1955), 370-371, where the chief point is that Cassian altered the meaning of the terminology that he took from earlier tradition.
137 Cristiani, *Jean Cassien*, II, 27-40.
138 Cassian, *Collatio* II, ch. 1, no. 3.

in black night and awful darkness, he falls into dangerous pits and holes and even stumbles on flat and level terrain."[139]

In the course of the conversation Abbot Moses also gives us to understand why the monks value this ability above all else. It is this alone that "can keep the monk untouched by the snares and tricks of the devil and lead him on the right way with sure steps to the crown of perfection."[140] Without this gift of discernment, the monk cannot remain on the "royal road."[141] What is at first a surprisingly high evaluation of discernment as the "greatest gift of divine grace" thus becomes understandable.[142] According to Cassian it is the "mother, protector, and guide of all virtues."[143] Consequently, if Ignatius puts such emphasis in the *Exercises* on the use of this gift of discernment, then it only shows how dependent he was on the early monastic tradition.

At the start of his instructions on the discernment of spirits, Cassian places, as does his favorite teacher Evagrius,[144] the axiom concerning the three sources of our "thoughts" (*cogitationes*): God, the devil, ourselves.[145] It is characteristic of God to visit us with the illumination of the Holy Spirit, to awaken in us the desire for progress, and to goad on our indolence for our own good. It is characteristic of the devil, on the other hand, to entice us openly through the desire for evil or secretly through his art of deceiving, "with subtle cunning deceitfully showing evil things as good" (*subtillissima calliditate mala pro bonis fraudulenter ostentans*).[146] In this connection the expression used by Ignatius occurs again, that the devil clothes himself in the robe of an angel of light. And quite in the sense of the *Exercises* is Cassian's warning that the monk should "study with prudent discretion every motion that stirs in his heart, inasmuch as we notice the beginning, the cause, and the originator of the thoughts."[147] For the rest, the images and comparisons which Cassian uses are certainly of a different nature

---

139 Ibid.
140 Ibid., ch. 2, no. 1.
141 Ibid., no. 4.
142 Ibid., ch. 2, no. 4: *divinae gratiae maximum praemium*. The word *praemium* probably intimates that this gift is not given to beginners, but to those who have labored long to advance in the spiritual life.
143 Ibid., ch. 4, no. 4: *omnium ... virtutum generatrix, custos, moderatrixque*.
144 See S. Marsili, *Giovanni ed Evagrio Pontico. Dottrina sulla carità e contemplazione* (Rome, 1936).
145 Cassian, *Collatio* I, ch. 19.
146 Ibid., no. 3.
147 Ibid., ch. 20, no. 1.

than those employed by Ignatius. But common to both is the emphasis with which they insist on the continual exercise of this discernment.[148]

The Role of the One Who Gives the Exercises

In connection with the necessity of striving for the gift of discernment of spirits, Cassian mentions (here also speaking for the entirety of early monastic tradition) a fourth aspect that can contribute to understanding the *Exercises* of St. Ignatius and reveals how deep are their roots in the spirituality of early monasticism. In the conversation with Abbot Moses one of the conversationalists asks how one achieves this exalted gift of discernment.[149] The answer runs: God grants it only to him who exercises himself in humility. But the first requisite for this humility is that one open himself to his spiritual director.[150] This theme is then developed at length, a sign of how essential the attachment to a spiritual father was considered by ancient monasticism.[151] The reasons for this necessity are many and varied. At one time it is pointed out that our secret passions deceive our judgment only too easily. So behind this there stands an awareness of the dangers of the spiritual way, where the evil enemy lies in ambush with all his malice and deceit. Finally there is also the consideration that, just as in the sphere of natural life, so also in the spiritual life there must be fatherhood and sonship.[152]

In this demand for close attachment to a spiritual guide, to whom the disciple must reveal all the thoughts that arise in his heart, Cassian stands, as we said, in the broad stream of the traditions of incipient monasticism. The *Life of St. Anthony* speaks of this.[153] Certainly Holy Scripture is in itself sufficient for our instruction. Still it is useful to encourage one another in the faith. " Therefore like children you must bring everything before your father and tell him everything that you know."

On the other hand, those who have been proved by temptations have the duty of acting for others as guides along the right way.[154]

---

148 For an overall picture, see Cristiani, *Jean Cassien*, II, 37-40.
149 Cassian, *Collatio* II, ch. 9.
150 Ibid., ch. 10, no. 1.
151 For what follows, see Hausherr, " Direction spirituelle," pp. 178-186.
152 See P. Resch, *La doctrine ascétique des premiers maîtres égyptiens du quatrième siècle* (Paris, 1931), pp. 194-203.
153 Athanasius, *Vita Antonii*, ch. 16, in PG 26, 868.
154 PG 26, 876.

It was for the Fathers of early monasticism an impracticable idea that one could become a " self-taught " monk. Therefore Heussi is quite correct in stating about the *Apophthegmata*, the very work in which the spirituality of anchoretic monasticism finds its chief expression: " It is a self-evident presupposition in the *Apophthegmata* that a man cannot make himself into a monk, but that he first comes a monastic teacher; this man gives him the monk's robe, and this makes him a monk."[155] But even when one has long exercised oneself in monastic asceticism, the necessity of allowing oneself to be directed still remains. Anthony expresses the idea in this way: " I have known monks who have fallen after long ascetical efforts . . . , because they have placed their trust in their own activity and because, full of blindness, they have not followed the counsel of the one who says: ' ask your father and he will announce it to you ' " (Deut. 32: 7).[156]

It is not our task to describe here the manner in which this direction of souls was carried out.[157] Especially important for us is the emphasis placed by monastic spirituality upon such an attachment to a spiritual father. It is always presupposed that the one who assumes the spiritual direction possesses the needed " spiritual " armor. He must be a man of the spirit who, above all else, is endowed with the charisma of the discernment of spirits.[158] He must have become — to speak in the language of ancient monasticism — an " Abba," usually translated " abbot." The term is not to be understood as signifying a grade in the hierarchy which one receives on the basis of official appointment or sacramental ordination. Nor does old age play a decisive role in this. The decisive factor is simply whether one has the witness of the Holy Spirit for oneself; that is, whether one is outstanding in the discernment of spirits[159] and can help the other on his way to God.

If we glance through the instructions that Ignatius gives about the place and role of the one who gives the Exercises from this point of view, one again sees the obvious necessity of many elements, something that apparently has eluded many interpreters of the

---

155 Heussi, *Ursprung*, p. 198.
156 *Apophthegmata Patrum*, " Antonius," no. 37, in PG 65, 88.
157 See Heussi, *Ursprung*, pp. 195-205.
158 Hausherr, " Direction spirituelle," pp. 180-184, portrays the dilemma into which the beginner in the spiritual life could fall when trying to find the right spiritual father. The correct choice presupposed a spiritual " maturity " that could only be attained through the help of the " spiritual father."
159 Ibid., pp. 17-39; Heussi, *Ursprung*, pp. 164-167.

Exercises (at least in the practical application of them). First this, that the one who gives the Exercises is an essential element of the Exercises as Ignatius conceives them. The days of the Spiritual Exercises, according to the saint's intention, are not only days of fundamental decision but are also a time of increased spiritual danger. It is not without danger to betake oneself " into the desert " and to expose oneself to the influence of the " various spirits." The more one strives for higher things, the greater is the danger that one will be tempted by the devil under the most subtle of disguises. At such times, when either a deceptive euphoria causes the exercitant to lose the secure footing of reason and prudence or when crippling desolation and exhaustion make him despondent, he needs the clear judgment and illuminating words of the spiritual director. Ignatius knew too much about the spiritual life to have sent a man along this road without the protection of an experienced guide. Precisely because he, along with the whole of early Christianity, was convinced that the devil is not a mythical figure or unreal symbol but a threatening reality, it was important to him to offer to the exercitant the necessary protection.[160]

In the same way Ignatius' conception of the function of the one who gives the Exercises can be understood better in the light of monastic spirituality. According to the instructions given in the book of the *Exercises*, his most important and irreplaceable task is most certainly not that of presenting themes for meditation in the way a preacher does.[161] There is scarcely a more dangerous misunderstanding of the proper concern of the Exercises than the one expressed in the formula, " to preach a retreat." Whoever turns the one who gives the Exercises into a preacher misses the entire point of what should be going on in the Spiritual Exercises.[162] The task of the one who gives the Exercises is primarily the " spiritual direction " of the exercitant — and here the word " spiritual " is to be taken in its most complete sense. In continual contact with the exercitant he must determine the direction and the tempo of the Spiritual Exercises and especially must be on hand with his

160 This necessity for a guide through the Exercises can of course be maintained only for the full course of the Exercises, not for the many varied forms of adaptation.
161 See *SpEx*, [2]. The " models " provided by Ignatius himself in the *Spiritual Exercises* prove the same thing by their unadorned sobriety and brevity.
162 This in no way excludes the possibility of occasionally " preaching " the material of the first week.

spiritual experience in order that the exercitant may come through the temptations without danger.

Therefore the most important weapon which the one who gives the Exercises must bring to the task is the ability to discern the spirits. He himself must be a " spiritual man." Such men of the spirit have never been numerous, and even in the days of the early monks we hear many complaints about this lack.[163] No wonder that Ignatius dared say of only a few of his companions that they completely fulfilled the expectations he had for the ideal director of the Exercises.[164] It must seem all the more strange that later times appear to trust practically anyone to have the knowledge to manage this difficult instrument of the Exercises properly.

It is on the basis of the same presuppositions that Ignatius so emphatically warns the one who gives the Exercises to be reserved. Especially indicative of this are the fourteenth and fifteenth Annotations ([14 and 15]). However useful and serviceable it might otherwise be to urge a man to " every manner of perfection " — provided he has the necessary qualifications — still the one who gives the Exercises is to refrain unconditionally from doing this. Rather, " during the Spiritual Exercises, when one is seeking the divine will, it is better and more fitting that the Creator and Lord communicate himself to the soul that is devoted to him, inflaming it to love and praise him, and preparing it for that way of life by which it will be able best to serve him in the future." Behind this there is the firm conviction that at this time God himself is acting in the soul in an ineffable manner and that the only thing that the one who is directing the Exercises can do, as soon as he has made certain of this, is " to keep in equilibrium like a balanced scale, allowing the Creator to deal directly with the creature and the creature with its Creator and Lord."

In all this Ignatius desires that a clear distinction be maintained between the role of the confessor and the role of the one who gives the Exercises.[165] This is the way we are to understand the seventeenth Annotation, according to which " he who gives the Exercises should not wish to inquire into or know the private

---

163 Hausherr, " Direction spirituelle," pp. 178-179.
164 See Bernard, *Essai historique*, p. 105; the only men that Ignatius specifically named as good directors of the Exercises were Pierre Favre, Salmerón, Francisco de Villanueva, and Doménech.
165 In the *Directory* drafted by Ignatius himself, it is expressly stated: " Mejor es, podiendo, que otro le confiese, y no el que le da los exercicios " (*SpEx*MHSJ, p. 779).

thoughts and sins of him who receives them." But he is to be informed "faithfully of the various agitations and thoughts inspired in him by the different spirits."[166] For only thus is he in a position "to give some spiritual exercises fitted to and suitable for the needs of the soul thus agitated." There is hardly a text that expresses more unequivocally the "spiritual" (in a pregnant sense!) character of the Exercises as Ignatius conceived them. We would do well repeatedly to measure our own understanding and practice of the Spiritual Exercises against this norm. Adherence to it is of decisive importance for deriving from this sublime school of sanctity its full worth and import.

Final Considerations

At the end of our study let us be allowed to refer once more to the purpose of this article. As we stressed at the beginning, our intent was not to add another attempt to the many that have already been made to derive the spirituality of the *Exercises* from older sources. Therefore there was not the slightest intention of discussing the "originality" of the spirituality of the *Exercises* or of calling it in question. We wished rather to make two points clear.

The first one was, how deeply the spirituality of the *Exercises* is rooted in the ascetical and mystical tradition of the Church from the very beginning on. Certainly many of the things that Ignatius worked out and offered to other men were new and unusual in their external form. Otherwise those objections of which we spoke in the introduction could never have been made. But he was too much a man of the Church, and his way of thinking was too ecclesial, for him to have gone his spiritual way without consulting the guide posts of tradition. It is certainly correct that he had no conscious contact with this tradition at the start of his own spiritual development. But it cannot be denied that, with a sure instinct, he took the same road as that which early monastic spirituality had marked out. It was that same feeling for the things of the Church that later drove him, once he had begun to study theology, consciously to make sure of this union with tradition.[167]

---

166 Ignatius accordingly demands from the exercitant the same openness and readiness to follow his director that the disciple was to show to his spiritual father in ancient monastic spirituality; see Hausherr, "Direction spirituelle," pp. 152-177.

167 See H. Rahner, "Ignatius und die aszetische Tradition," *ZAM*, XVII (1942), 62-63.

Our study has made clear how essential elements of that spirituality, which had developed in the early monasticism of the East, became concrete in the spirituality of the *Exercises*. We are aware that we have not exhausted this topic. In order to be complete, we would have to speak about the integration of ascetical and mystical elements that is characteristic of both the *Exercises* and ancient monastic spirituality, and also about the teaching, common to both, that progress in the spiritual life is made by degrees. Whoever comes from a study of the old monastic documents and then studies the book of the *Exercises* will receive the impression that Ignatius has summarized as if in a compendium the essential points that, in ancient monasticism, the Abbot disclosed to his disciples during long years of active instruction. The spirituality of the *Exercises* is, both in content and in method, a " concentrate " (if one may use this modern expression) of early monastic spirituality. However, one must be careful not to press this dependence on tradition too far. It must always be kept in mind that early monastic spirituality on its part consciously and vigorously modeled itself on Holy Scripture, and that thus the *Exercises* — quite apart from their direct roots in Scripture — are also indirectly grounded in biblical spirituality.

To speak more precisely, the analysis of the term "*spiritual exercises*" has shown us how Ignatius linked his spirituality to one specific stage in the development of early monastic spirituality; namely, to the stage where the active ascetical aspect was given particular stress, as is made clear if we compare Cassian's use of the term *spirit(u)alis* with that of Evagrius, for example. But a disastrously false inference was made by some who wanted to conclude from this that the spirituality of the Exercises is totally or one-sidedly " ascetical," not to say " ascetistical."[168] Those who spoke in this way did not know that for Cassian also all asceticism is ordered to " contemplation "; that is, it is a preparation for the elevation of man in grace to the higher stages of prayer which God alone can unfold to him. They have also overlooked the fact that the spirituality of the *Exercises*, from the Annotations through the Rules for the Election to the Rules for the Discernment of Spirits, is permeated with the conviction that God manifests himself to a man who gives himself to the Spiritual Exercises with greatness of heart and firmness of purpose. For Ignatius the Exercises are truly

---

168 Henri Bremond shows a special liking for this term in " Notes sur les Exercices," *Vie Spirituelle, Supplement* III (June, 1929), 147-190.

a "spiritual event," a time in which the "various spirits" become operative in the soul; and they can therefore be made to full effect and indeed without danger only when someone is present who can discern the "spirits." Without this "spiritual realism" the *Exercises* of St. Ignatius simply cannot be understood. But it is precisely this realism that clearly proves them to be a link in the one long chain of the tradition of Christian spirituality that stretches unbroken from the very beginnings.

This proof that the *Exercises* are rooted in ascetical and mystical tradition was, indeed, the primary concern of our study. Nevertheless, the second and more practical point which we hoped to make clear in our study should not be overlooked. From the history of the *Exercises* we know that even during the lifetime of St. Ignatius, strong requests came in, asking how one or another point in them was to be understood and, in general, how this "instrument" was to be applied.[169]

To each generation is given anew the task of making what Ignatius has bequeathed to us accessible to its contemporaries. It seems to us that we have too often forgotten that one of the paths leading to this goal leads us by way of the spirituality of ancient monasticism. Only to the superficial observer is this a detour. In reality there is no more trustworthy path into the heart of an intellectual structure than one which investigates its basic sources. For it is at the roots of such a structure that we learn the reason for its existence. Thus it is only in appearance that we have been concerned "merely" with history. In reality our interest was in the present; and today too our duty lies there more than with all that is past and transitory.

---

169 Thus Francisco de Estrada, while at Siena, in 1539, wrote requesting the rules for the first, second, and third weeks of the Exercises, and *otras cosas nuevas*, if any new ones had meanwhile been added: *SpEx*MHSJ, p. 746 (not p. 740 as is mistakenly given in the index, p. 1216); see also H. Bernard, *Essai historique*, p. 92.

THE "EXERCISE WITH THE THREE POWERS OF THE SOUL" IN THE EXERCISES AS A WHOLE

Lambert Classen

CONTEMPLATIVE PRAYER, or as some occasionally prefer to say with a certain amount of emphasis, "meditation," encounters in our day an increased interest. Even in Protestant circles, where contemplative prayer had for a long time been unknown, papers and articles on this exercise, so basic to Catholic tradition, are becoming more numerous. This growing interest is no longer, as it was in the twenties, connected with the questions raised by Henri Bremond about the relationship between contemplation and prayer. The chief concern of the present generation is something else. It is seeking help for the human and religious needs of its life, and it has rediscovered meditation during this search. It has once more been recognized that in meditation we are given a unique opportunity for quickening the life of faith, for penetrating the whole man with the mysteries of revelation. The similarity is stressed between meditative prayer and what Cardinal Newman called "realizing," that saturating of our religious thought with the vivid, the imaginable, and the tangible, so that thereby the concepts of religion become for a man experiential and present realities, become part of his flesh and blood, and determine his thought and activity in everyday life.

Probably nowhere else in the history of Catholic spirituality has meditation been placed so consistently and so extensively at the service of realizing the truths of faith as in the Spiritual Exercises of St. Ignatius of Loyola. Their power, which touches the deepest part of man and transforms him, caused St. Francis de Sales to

Study 8 was translated by Louis W. Roberts.

make the oft-quoted statement that the little book of the *Exercises* has made more men into saints than it contains letters. It is above all the exercise " with the three powers of the soul " that is directed toward penetrating to the depths of the heart of a man and causing his whole life to be permeated by the truths of faith. Yet in the last few decades it was precisely this exercise that was often enough the object of attacks or misunderstandings. Even the commentators on the book of the *Exercises* are not wholly agreed on the meaning of this exercise. Some see in it the alpha and the omega of the *Spiritual Exercises,* and that which is most unique and essential in the Ignatian method. Meditation, as Ignatius teaches it in the *Exercises,* is for them the same thing as the application of the three powers of the soul. The chief proponent of this standpoint was the great restorer of the *Exercises* in the restored Society of Jesus, the general of the order, John Roothaan (1785-1853).[1] In explicit or implicit opposition to Father Roothaan, others stress the fact that in the book of the *Exercises* there are different kinds of meditation, each of which is to be used according to the circumstances and the personal disposition of the exercitant. This view also considers the exercise with the three powers of the soul to be important, indeed quite important, but does not consider it to be the only and not. *the* Ignatian method of meditation.

The great significance of this exercise in the Ignatian Exercises, indeed for the totality of the spiritual life and of apostolic preaching, may justify our examining it more closely in the context of the entire *Exercises.* We will have to discover whether the one group or the other is right — or whether in the end both are, in some sense or other. To do this the exercise with the three powers of the soul must be made clear in itself. We must show what Ignatius meant by it. Then the relationship of this to the other exercises of meditation and prayer given in the *Exercises* must be brought to light. Finally the meaning of this exercise in the

---

1 " According to the mind and doctrine of St. Ignatius, meditation consists in the application of the three powers of the soul: memory, intellect, and will. If they are all rightly applied, the meditation will be good. All three are to be used in each point; so even one point may be sufficient matter for meditation." John Roothaan, S.J., *How to Meditate,* trans. Louis J. Puhl (Westminster: The Newman Bookshop, 1945, p. 17) [However, as De Guibert points out, Roothaan's little treatise was a work of his youth, intended chiefly for beginners (*DeGuiJes,* pp. 469-470.) Translator.]

Exercises as a whole, and further for the whole spiritual life and for all religious activity, must be displayed.[2]

In What Does the Exercise "with the three powers of the soul" Consist?

We read of the three powers of the soul in the First Exercise of the first week (*SpEx*, [45-54]), in language for which the reader has had no preparation. Indeed, this entire exercise is to be an exercise with the three powers. There has been no word to help clarify or introduce the three powers: the memory, understanding, and will (*memoria, intellectus, voluntas*), no word as to why there are three, in what order they operate, or how they are to be applied. The "poor pilgrim" who struggles with his God in prayer in the cave at Manresa (from March 1522 to February 1523) is not writing a book for readers. He is not writing a book at all, but is only making notes for himself in his notebook about that which transpires in his soul and which he thinks could also be of use to others: notes which he completes later while in Alcalá, Salamanca, and Paris by adding further entries up to the year 1535.[3] In order to understand their meaning and to be preserved from misinterpretations, we must ever keep in view that these are the notations of a man who was wholly free from the weight of erudition and book learning, but who was overwhelmed by a lavish abundance of the inspirations and graces of God, who was quite inexperienced in human sciences but greatly experienced in divine things and the ways of God.

A preliminary explanation of the three powers, as well as of their application, presents itself to us when we closely observe what is expected to take place when they are used. This presents itself all the more truly when we are not merely observing but rather, during the course of making the Exercises, preparing ourselves

---

2 [Father Classen notes that he takes the quotations from the *Spiritual Exercises* used in this article from the German translation of Hans Urs von Balthasar (Lucerne, 1946) because "it conforms better than the others to the literary — or rather highly unliterary — style of the original." The present translator has tried to follow the same principle, translating as literally as possible directly from the Spanish text in *Obras Completas*, eds. Ignacio Iparraguirre and Candido de Dalmases (Madrid: BAC, 1963).]

3 Unfortunately this valuable notebook has been lost. All we have is a copy made by one of the saint's religious brethren (Ribadeneyra?) in 1541. However, since Ignatius himself made use of this copy and personally corrected and added various details up to 1548, it is rightly known as the *Autograph.*

actually to perform the exercise, along with the preparatory prayer
and other preliminaries. The little book is not supposed to be read,
but is an instruction for doing.[4] What we are to do, in prayer
before our Creator and Lord, is this: " to apply the memory to the
first sin, which was that of the angels; and then to apply the
understanding to the same by reflecting on it; then the will,
desiring to remember and understand the whole (in the literal Latin
version it runs thus: *trahere memoriam super primum peccatum, quod
fuit Angelorum, et deinde super idem intellectum discurrendo; deinde
voluntatem volendo totum illud memorari et intelligere*), in order to
shame myself the more and to confound myself by comparing my
many sins with the one sin of the angels; and while they have gone
to hell for one sin, how often have I deserved it for so many.
I say, to recall the sin of the angels, how they were created in
grace, yet, not willing to make use of their liberty to help themselves
pay reverence and obedience to their Creator and Lord, but having
fallen into pride, they were transformed from grace into malice, and
hurled from heaven to hell; then to reflect on the matter more
in particular with the understanding, and then to move the affections
still more with the will " ([50]). " To do the same once more,
namely to apply the three powers to the sin of Adam and Eve,
recalling to memory how·for that sin they did such long penance
and such great corruption came upon the human race, so many
people being put on the way to hell. I say to recall to memory
the second sin, that of our first parents; how after Adam had been
created in the plain of Damascus and placed in the terrestrial
Paradise and Eve had been formed out of his rib, having been
forbidden to eat of the tree of knowledge, yet eating of it and thus
sinning, afterwards being clothed in garments made of skins and
driven out of Paradise, they lived without original justice, which
they had lost, all their life long in many labors and much penance;
and accordingly with the understanding to reflect on all this,
making use of the will as has been said before " ([51]). " To do
the same thing once more in like manner in regard to the third
sin, the particular sin of some one person who for one mortal sin
has gone to hell; and many others without number (who have been
condemned) for fewer sins than I have committed. I say, to do the
same with the third, particular sin, recalling to the memory the
gravity and malice of sin committed against one's Creator and Lord;

4 " One must make the Exercises to get to know them, and study them
thoroughly to be able to give them " (Urs von Balthasar in some concluding
remarks to his translation, p. 156).

then to reflect with the understanding how in sinning and acting against the Infinite Goodness, [the sinner] has justly been condemned forever; and to conclude with the will, as has been said " ([52]).

So continually: first the memory, then the understanding, the power of reason, then the will — thus is the exercitant to put the powers of his soul to work. This activation of the powers seems to have been a quite clear and familiar thing to the poor pilgrim. It is less clear to us and, if we have also studied a little psychology, we experience all sorts of difficulties and second thoughts about this threefold division of the life of the soul. In the case of the memory, which is to be applied again and again, perhaps we recall Plato's doctrine of *anamnesis*, according to which all progress in knowledge is a recall to consciousness, a remembrance of things seen earlier which now rest in the dark depths of the soul and can be brought to light again only by " re-minding " in the literal sense of the word. Or we think of the brilliant and penetrating statements of St. Augustine about the " fields and broad palaces of the memory," where the treasures of numberless images are hidden, on those " halls " of the memory, " where heaven and earth and sea, together with everything that I could ever perceive in them, are stored up, with the only exception that which I have forgotten." This forced from him the cry of wonder: " Great, O my God, is the power of the memory, exceedingly great, a broad, immeasurable inner sanctuary. Who has ever plumbed its foundations ? And this is a power of my spirit and belongs to my nature, nor do I myself wholly comprehend what I am...! "[5] However, thoughts of this kind were far from the author of the *Exercises* as he made his entries in his notebook.[6] He did not draw his ideas from books; his " sources " are his interior visions and experiences.[7]

In view of their context in the *Exercises*, no doubt appears possible about the awkward expressions and thus about the prayerful activity in which they seek to instruct us. First we are to picture

5 Augustine, *Confessions*, Bk. X, ch. 8.
6 This is not to say that it would not be proper to investigate the metaphysical depths that lie behind the saint's experiences. This has been done in an unusually informative manner in the valuable book of Johann Lotz, *Meditation. Weg nach innen. Philosophische Klärung und Anweisung zum Vollzug* (Frankfurt am Main, 1954).
7 " It is right to assert, as some have done, that if Iñigo had consulted all the sources that, in all academic seriousness, he has been ' proved ' to have consulted, he must have had, at the time of his sojourn in the cave of Manresa, a stately library of Latin and Spanish authors." H. Rahner, *Spirituality of Ignatius*, p. 23.

to ourselves the divine truth — here the revealed truth about the sin of the angels, about the sin of humanity in its first parents, and about the personal sin of a single man,— and make it as vivid and living as possible. Then we are to consider the truth profoundly and reflectively from all points of view. Finally we are to grasp it to the heart, embrace it, and make it part of our life, with fervent and complete oblation.

It is presupposed that we are acquainted with the truth of faith, or have made ourselves sufficiently acquainted with it (during the preparation for the meditation), that in the meditation itself the truth actually becomes alive for us through the use of the memory, through re-minding. In order that the vivid representation, the reflection, and the embrace by the will may take place in that attitude of reverence due to the Divine Majesty who reveals Himself and addresses the person who is meditating, we should first prepare ourselves and arouse the proper mood in ourselves by means of the remote and proximate preparations, particularly through the preparatory prayer and the preparatory exercises, which are considered to be of great value ([45-49]), and about the proper performance of which the exercitant is to examine himself daily in the sight of God ([90]).

When God, " our Creator and Lord," the " eternal Majesty," the " Lord and Creator of all things," as Ignatius is so fond of saying, speaks to us (and he speaks to us in his creation and in his revelation, in all the realities of nature and of supernature), then the first and most obvious response is that man listen to this word. He does this by calling it to mind in an attitude of holy reverence, reflecting on it with holy earnestness, so that he may then with a holy determination affirm it and order his life accordingly. In our dealings with the Divine Majesty, with the Lord " to whom every will speaks " (from a prayer of the liturgy), the first and most important thing is not what we say to him, but what he says to us. The Creator talks to us to no other purpose than that, inasmuch as he gives existence to us and to all the world, we may listen, that his word may penetrate us and may completely fill our heart and life. And man, in the deepest, most intimate part of his being, in his individual personality, is that which he is (namely *potentia oboedientialis*, a being who can and ought to listen), to no other purpose than that he may listen to the One who speaks to him, and shape his whole life and his whole being into a listening and obeying.

Thus the man who puts his three powers of the soul to work is like the deaf and dumb man who let himself be led by Jesus apart from the crowd to an intimate, personal encounter with him, and who expectantly lifted ears and mouth to him that he might open his hearing and loosen his tongue, whereby " correct speech " was given him (Mark 7: 31-37). In activating the memory and the understanding, we are like the deaf and dumb man on the way to his personal meeting with our Lord. In activating the affections and the will, we begin to be like the man who was healed, who could speak correctly.

In this encounter with God through the application of the three powers there is contained an interior dynamism. What has gone before urges toward what follows, and what follows toward what comes still later. The representation is the gateway and bridge to becoming deeply affected spiritually; and this deep affection in turn is the bridge to divinely inspired action and living. In the representation we listen to our Creator and Lord; when we consider and reflect, this listening becomes attention; and in the embrace of love and in strong-willed affirmation this attention becomes obedience. Between the truth and the reality of God and the heart of man there takes place a reciprocal possessing and being possessed. This mutual self-possession, in which God the Lord has the first and last word, strives after an ever deeper perfection. This deepening encounter is accomplished through a unique *method* (from *methodos*, a following after): the Creator pursues His creature, the intellectual, human person; the creature pursues his Creator. God and the soul approach each other; two abysses call out to one another (" abyss calls to abyss " [Ps. 42: 7]) and find one another: the abyss of the divine fullness and the abyss of human emptiness, the abyss of the giving love of God and the abyss of the receiving love of the human heart.

Accordingly, the exercise with the three powers is in no way something artificial, constructed, forced. It is anything but a random collection of intellectual activities arbitrarily joined together. Rather it is something wholly natural, indeed *the* natural way for man to act before his God and Creator, the way of behaving ontologically proper to man when confronting the truth of the human situation. The activation of these powers, and consequently the " parts " of the exercises, are not placed alongside one another as disparate steps but are phases of one path, the path on which God comes to man and man comes to God; the path on which man, while he comes to God, begins to come to himself, to his truest, deepest, most personal self, since he is " created for the purpose of praising God our Lord, showing Him reverence, and serving Him," as it is put in the first sentence of the Principle and Foundation of the *Exercises* [(25)]. The exercise with the three powers illuminates for us the specific way the human spirit develops, a spirit clothed with the body, living in the world, gradually unfolding and developing itself. It is not an optional path, in place of which one could substitute other ways to the same goal, but *the* path of man to God, following along the path by which God comes to man.

The exercitant must not come to a halt on this path nor wander about aimlessly (the Exercises are not to lead to just any kind of pious life), but must ever keep the goal in view and strive for it. The one who gives the Exercises must especially keep it in view. He is to help the exercitant in making vivid representations (*memoria*), in obtaining a clearer perception and deeper penetration (*intellectus*), and finally in finding God with his entire heart and in his life (*voluntas*). He is to see to it that as much as possible the exercitant travel the way on his own, that he let himself be led and formed and shaped by a personal encounter with his God and Lord. The second prelude already points to this with great emphasis. "He who gives to another the method and order of a meditation or a contemplation ought faithfully to narrate the history of the contemplation or meditation, hurrying through the points however with a short and summary explanation. When the person who contemplates learns the true groundwork of the history so that he can reflect and reason by himself, and thus meets with something that casts some light on the history or causes him to be more affected by it, whether this happens through his own reasoning, or through the enlightenment of his understanding by the power of God — he thereby receives greater contentment and spiritual fruit than if he who gives the Exercises had minutely explained and enlarged upon the meaning of the history; for it is not in knowing much, but in being moved by things and savoring them interiorly, that the soul is filled and satisfied " ([2]).

From this we see that it is contrary to the meaning and nature of the Exercises when the director holds long and extended lectures, when he even lectures at all. The purpose is not an enrichment of the understanding, not exciting entertainment of the spirit, but the complete penetration of the interior man by the divine truth (*sentire et gustare res interne*) becoming one in will with the will of the Creator. The chief concern of the director is to be that he "allow the Creator to work immediately with the creature, and the creature with its Creator and Lord " ([15]). The one and only goal of the Exercises is a living encounter of man with God in knowing and loving, in willing and accomplishing.

So it would be wrong if the one meditating were to let himself be halted along the way. The imaginative representation does not take place for its own sake but for the sake of a deeper knowledge; the deeper knowledge again is only for the sake of a deeper impression on the heart and greater union of will. The entire activity of the one meditating, not only his interior but also his exterior behavior, must be ordered to "that which I seek," "that which I desire," namely the animation of his will and activity by the holy will of God. Therefore the Fourth Addition advises: "To enter into the contemplation at one time kneeling, at another prostrate on the earth, or lying with my face upwards, now seated, now standing, always with the intention of seeking that which I desire. We will take note of two things: first, if kneeling I find that which I want, I will not try any another position (or if prostrate, etc.); secondly, that at the point where I shall find what I desire, there I will remain, without being anxious to proceed to the next point until I have satisfied myself" ([76]). One could, in the process of recalling to memory (*adducere in memoriam*), and especially in the moving back and forth with the understanding (*discurrere per intellectum*), proceed from one point to the next at will; he could ask question after question. Father Roothaan, in his instruction on how to meditate, offers an almost endless string of questions that *could* be considered — for instance, one could undertake a discussion on a whole theology of grace when considering the first verse of the Song of Songs: "Let my beloved kiss me with the kiss of his mouth," somewhat as St. Francis de Sales does at the beginning of his *Treatise on the Love of God* — but this would in no way accord with the concept of contemplative prayer and would not lead nearer to the goal, but would be a hindrance and a distraction. It would not be the way to allow God to possess the heart, to the encounter with God which is to penetrate and fill one's life and for which the Exercises are to be a preparation.

There is a natural sequence in the activity of the three powers — it accords with the sequence found in the personal life of every man: perception, thinking, willing; as expressed in the two scholastic principles: nothing is in the understanding which was not previously perceived (*Nihil est in intellectu, quod non prius fuerit in sensu*) and the will cannot embrace anything which has not been given previously in the understanding (*Nihil volitum nisi praecognitum*). Yet the three powers are meshed together in the surge and flow of the life of the soul and compenetrate one another in the most varied ways. Willing (loving) can bring about a new representation and new considerations; the new representation, on the other hand, can bring new ideas and new acts of the will; the new ideas, again, new willing and new representations; all of this takes place in an intensity of immeasurable richness and in a variety of forms beyond compre-hension. Ignatius points out, right in the meditation on the sin of the angels, how the will, activated by the memory and the under-standing, is for its part to stimulate the activity of memory and understanding — thus, in the text already cited: ". . . and then the will, desiring to remember and understand the whole, in order to shame myself the more and to confound myself by comparing my many sins with the one sin of the angels . . ." ([50]).

The farther the contemplative activity proceeds along this path and the more this activity makes the exercitant familiar with the object of the meditation and with the entire realm of divine truths and makes him feel at home with them, his activity during the meditation turns that much more in the direction of the *sentire et gustare res interne,* from remembering and considering to loving and striving, from meditative to effective and volitive. In other words, the more divine truth — that is, the Lord and Creator who speaks to man in His revelation — is present and the more man *has* comprehended the truth and reality of God, so much the less is there need for the activity of imaginative representation and for efforts at reflective thought. Indeed they would be a hindrance and a distraction. All the more can the one praying now say with St. John of the Cross: " My only business from now on is to love."

To complete this part of the discussion, let one more point be mentioned. Since in the case of the exercise with the three powers it is a question, not of a path chosen arbitrarily, but of *the* path of human encounter with God, not only the sanctification of self but the entire apostolate is ordered to it. The help of souls (*juvare animas*) as a favorite expression of St. Ignatius runs, can only consist in the fact that we aid them to the proper application of their three powers; that we stand helpfully at their side to aid them in forming meaningful images of the truth and reality of God, in reflecting upon these images so as to comprehend them and grasp their full meaning, and to embrace these truths fervently and resolutely. Herein lies the intent and the goal of all religious formation and instruction, all catechesis and preaching, all pastoral care and direction.[8] The care of souls (*juvare animas*) is nothing

---

8 In regard to catechetical instruction, Josef Andreas Jungmann describes how, in the past several decades, the struggle to find the right catechetical " method " has laboriously led to a recognition of this " method of the Exercises " in his *Handing on the Faith. A Manual of Catechetics* (New York: Herder and Herder, 1959). He refers to Otto Willmann, " a leading Catholic pedagogue at the beginning of the century." Willmann gave great

other than the care for that encounter of man with God which is simultaneously the encounter of God with man. It is a service of God that serves man and a service of man that serves God, a glorification of God that sanctifies man and a sanctification of man that glorifies the Divine Majesty.

impetus to the catechetical impetus — not least in that he cleansed the " formal steps " of catechetical instruction from the effects of Herbart's philosophy and returned its attention to the essential lines for true progress. Willmann distinguishes " only three steps, corresponding to the faculties of the soul: memory, understanding, and will. The resulting three steps are as follows: (1) Presentation, a perceptible basis is offered; (2) Explanation, notions are singled out; (3) Application, references to life are established. Looked at from the standpoint of the children they are: (1) Perception, (2) Understanding, (3) Practical application " (ibid., p. 181). Jungmann sees these essential lines of Christian instruction flash forth again and again in different historical eras. " The principles of this new method are actually so clear that it is not surprising that in their essential broad outlines they can also be met with in the past and under circumstances not specifically concerned with children " (ibid., p. 182). It was in the mind of St. Augustine when he admonished catechists to speak in such a way that " he to whom you speak believes when he hears, hopes when he believes, loves when he hopes ": " Quidquid narras, ita narra ut ille, cui loqueris, audiendo credat, credendo speret, sperando amet " (*De catechizandis rudibus*, ch. 4). The " three powers " stand out more clearly in Hugo of St. Victor's *Liber didascalius*. He there " distinguishes three steps in the absorption of intellectual matter: *lectio, meditatio, operatio*, which correspond to the three steps: perception, understanding, application ' (Jungmann, *Handing on the Faith*, p. 183). Jungmann notes that our Redeemer himself followed the same path. Christ " did not, like the Pharisees, take propositions from the Law or from the Prophets in order to rephrase their contents in different words. If the situation did not supply Him with a starting point [a question by one of the disciples, a meeting with Pharisees], He spoke in parables or used examples taken from the world around Him. In these the audience quickly discerned a deeper meaning. He emphasized this meaning which usually concerned the invisible world of God's kingdom and concluded with a challenge: ' Go and do likewise,' ' He who has ears to hear, let him hear ' " (ibid., pp. 182-193).

The uniform German catechism follows the same path in its practical applications (*Lehrstücken*). First there is a representation, in which a divine truth is presented in an example taken from Scripture, the liturgy, or church history. Then follows the clarification, explanation, and mastery of the example. Finally the transposition of this now familiar truth into one's own life is aided by the addition of maxims or prayers.

In regard to preaching, recall the long traditional and well-known division of the sermon taught in homiletics: proposition, explanation, application — which comes to the same thing as the application of the " three powers " as taught in the *Spiritual Exercises*.

So what the poor pilgrim wrote in his notebook in the loneliness of Manresa, on the basis of his personal encounter with God our Lord, so stiffly and with truly touching awkwardness, about the exercise with the three powers of the soul, touches the most profound depths of our human existence. One might call it a sort of illumination of the nature of human existence. In it there lies a light from that light "which illumines every man coming into this world" (John 1:18) and which desires to transform man "from glory to glory" (2 Cor. 3:18), by transforming him more and more into its own eternal glory — if only man will allow it to lay hold of him and transform him, which is precisely the purpose of this exercise and of the entire Spiritual Exercises.

What Is the Relationship between the " exercise with the powers of the soul" and the Other Methods of Prayer and Meditation in the Exercises ?

The specific nature and the significance of the exercise with the powers of the soul become clearer when we consider how it is related to the other exercises explained in the *Spiritual Exercises*.

The author speaks of various methods of prayer and meditation. He knows no narrowness, no set preference for a specific kind of meditation. Anyone who is only slightly familiar with the saint's personality, especially as it is revealed in his instructions and letters, of which some 6,500 are extant, knows how alien, how repugnant to him were all stereotypes and schematizations of the spiritual life. One of his trusted companions, Ribadeneyra, writes of him, " Ignatius was accustomed to blame directors and teachers of others who measure everything according to themselves and who want to impose the same manner of life and way of prayer that has proved useful for themselves. This is dangerous, he used to say, and leads a man astray who does not know the manifold gifts of the grace of God and the varied inspirations of the Holy Spirit and who does not sufficiently understand the way in which the gifts of grace are communicated in one and the same spirit (1 Cor. 12: 4-11). For every man has his own special gift from God; the one so, but the other so " (1 Cor. 7: 7).[9] A man of prayer and a director of souls

---

9 Quoted in Huonder, *Ignatius*, p. 175. Completely in the spirit of the saint and of his Exercises is the spiritual advice of the twentieth-century son of Ignatius, Father Considine: " There are only a few fixed rules in the spiritual life; one is this, pray in the way you like best and which helps you the most." " Forget systems and constricting rules in the spiritual life and give yourself over entirely unto the guidance of God so that

like Ignatius cannot possibly advocate pattern and stereotype, cannot possibly be the man of schematization and of stereotype that he has often been made out to be.

To the superficial reader of the *Exercises* some remarks may seem to be such patterns and schemata for prayer. But, as cannot be stressed enough, the *Exercises* are not to be read but to be made. In the process of making the Exercises they show themselves to be helps and spurs toward a living, personal encounter with " the Lord and Creator of all things," and on man's part, are always an activation of his three powers of the soul; that is, of the life of the spirit proper to human beings.

First we meet with the " application of the senses," a way of meditation in which we are directed to apply the five senses one after another — seeing, hearing, smelling, tasting, feeling — to the subject of the meditation. Certainly a quite unique and, apparently, a very different exercise from meditation with the three powers of the soul. If we look through the commentators, we find that they are divided into two groups in judging and evaluating this exercise. Some hold the opinion that we have here an easier and thus less valuable way of praying, an exercise which is in a certain sense opposed to " genuine " prayer, which considers the subject discursively. But there are others who hold that this calls for an especially high degree of prayer, a special depth of familiarity with the divine truth in question or with the holy mystery upon which one is to meditate; it is a high, indeed mystical kind of prayer. If we see how this exercise fits into the *Exercises* as a whole, and especially if we truly perform this exercise in the proper context, following the direction given, no doubt can remain as to the nature of this exercise.

Right on the first day of the first week we come upon an application of the senses, to the mystery of hell, as the last, the fifth exercise of the day. In the preparation we pray for a remarkable grace; namely for " an interior sense of the punishment which the damned suffer " ([65]). We ask that God our Lord give us the grace to feel as profoundly and vividly as possible how it works, what the eternally rejected must suffer, those who during their lifetime have made a definite break with him, " in order that,

you live every moment in his presence and are ready at any moment to give him what he asks for." " Keep yourself pliant in God's hand and let him sanctify you in his way. Almost always it will be in a way that you did not expect ! " Daniel Considine, *Frohes Gehen zu Gott* (Munich, 1932), pp. 32, 36, 63.

if I through my faults should forget the love of the Eternal Lord, at least the fear of punishment may help me to avoid falling into sin " (ibid.). And then we are urged, as usual, by means of extremely brief remarks, to try to feel and experience this thing interiorly with the five senses. Since hell is a mystery of faith, of divine supernatural revelation, completely inaccessible to our bodily senses and indeed even to the higher senses of our natural power of understanding through reasoning, there can be no question of the physical senses — not even of the imagination nor of the intellectual senses of natural reason, but only of the higher, supernatural senses, the senses of faith and of reason illuminated by faith, for which the bodily senses as well as the higher senses of the natural life of the spirit may be sensible images and models for us. This appears in a few places in the extremely sparse instructions of the text; thus, for example, " to taste with the taste bitter things, such as tears, sadness, and the worm of conscience " ([69]). The application of these senses (of the eyes, ears . . . of faith) is absolutely the only thing that corresponds to the whole meaning and nature of this exercise.

Here then there is question of that interior sense and taste for things (*sentire et gustare res interne*) which we are to strive for according to the Second Annotation ([2]), in all the meditations on the truths and mysteries of God. It is ordered to precisely the same goal toward which reverent imaginative representation (activation of the " memory ") and penetrating consideration and reflection (activation of the " understanding ") are truly the only possible path. Only the one who has grasped it with the spirit of faith is able to apply the senses of his soul to it, in order to receive and make part of his life the special grace for which he has begged the Lord. Accordingly, the application of the senses is the final phase of the application of the three powers of the soul. It is itself an application of these powers of the soul, an intensified and more resolute application of them.

The application of the senses embraces a broad area in the three weeks of meditations on the life of Jesus. As the final exercise of the day, it is to summarize the results of the previous exercises of the day and complete them, thus intensifying and deepening further the profoundly interior knowledge of our Lord Jesus Christ (*intima cognitio Domini nostri Jesu Christi*), the goal of all these exercises. In no way is it merely experiencing the exterior event as vividly as possible, say the journey to Bethlehem or the death of Jesus on the Cross. An infidel, if he is gifted with a strong imagination, could experience most vividly and represent to himself in a most touching manner the exterior event as reported in the Gospels. This would lack the slightest trace of what is the intent and significance of these exercises.

These exercises are intended to be used for the contemplation of the mysteries of the redemptive life of Jesus, those supernatural events which the Triune God has worked on earth for the salvation and sanctification of the human race. The mysteries of the life of our Lord Jesus Christ are realities in space and time, of a definite place in space and a definite moment in the course of time — " at Bethlehem in the land of Juda," " at that time "— but these are not like other spatial and temporal realities; they surpass and include in a mysterious manner all places and all times; they also embrace the here and now. Both I and my life are present to them, and they are present to me in my life today and at all times. I stand before them with a decision; they want to enter into my life and my life ought to enter into them. Separation in space and time, which separates man from man in the natural order, disappears in the mysteries of the life of the Redeemer. That life includes all men of all times and all places and gathers them to itself.

Therefore these exercises also are always to close with a lively conversation with the Redeemer who is present to the exercitant, as we read at the end of the first exercise of the second week (On the Incarnation of the Eternal Word): " At the end a colloquy is to be made, thinking what I should say to the Three Divine Persons or to the Eternal Word Incarnate, or to His Mother and our Lady. According to what each feels in himself, he will ask better to follow and imitate our Lord, thus newly become incarnate " ([109]). The child just born, as it once lay in the crib at Bethlehem, sees me, loves me, his Heart beats for me. I stand before him. My life must be a response to him for the love which he has brought into our human life, and even for me, especially by letting himself be born in such poverty.

By the activation of the senses of faith, our inner man grows familiar with the mystery and makes it part of itself so that from this point on our life becomes a more profound companionship with the Son of God who has come into the world, a more active attendance upon him and a more steadfast cooperation with him. For the mystery which encompasses me not only makes it possible but makes it imperative that I place myself at its service, make it part of my life, and give it a fitting response through the way I live. Thus, for example, in the case of the mystery of the birth of our Lord, I can and should truly " make of myself a poor, unworthy servant " ([114]), who offers his services to the holy persons, to all

251

who share in this in heaven and on earth; and I can truly " hold a conversation " with the Lord " who is present to me on the Cross: how He as Creator came to make Himself a man, and descended from eternal life to a temporal death, and thus to die for my sins. Then to turn my gaze upon myself and consider what I have done for Christ, what I am now doing for Christ, what I ought to do for Christ, and, seeing Him so ill-treated and hanging on the cross, reflect on what may offer itself " ([53]).[10]

Basically it is always the Divine Majesty himself whom we perceive interiorly and taste in the " application of the senses." In all the mysteries of faith and of grace we always perceive and taste his grandeur and majesty, which is ever opening and revealing itself to us; his goodness and condescension communicating itself to us; but above all his mercy on our sinful generation, a mercy that surpasses all human understanding. Even in the Meditation on Hell, and in it in a special manner, it is the eternal God whom we experience and suffer along with the damned; inasmuch as we feel interiorly how bitter and evil it is to have refused to serve his infinite Majesty, to have despised his incomprehensible love. He, " the Lord and Creator of all things," reveals himself in all things, speaks to us in everything and through everything, in the damnation of the damned no less than in the blessedness of the blessed.[11]

---

10 For the theological foundation for this prayerful personal experiencing of the mysteries of Christ's life, see the highly suggestive article of W. Bertrams, " Die Gleichzeitigkeit des betenden Christen mit den Geheimnissen des Lebens Jesu," *GeistLeb*, XXIV (1951), 414-419. [See also the chapter, " Preface to the Contemplations of the Second Week," in David Stanley, *A Modern Scriptural Approach to the Spiritual Exercises* (St. Louis: Institute of Jesuit Sources, 1967), pp. 85-93. Editor.]

11 The " senses " which we are to turn toward the mysteries of faith and to the Lord and Creator contained within them are none other than those of which St. Augustine speaks in a famous passage: " What do I love when I love you [O my God] ? Not beauty of body nor temporal glory; not the splendor of light, so pleasing to the eyes; not the sweet melodies of all the varieties of song; not the sweet odors of flowers, ointments, and spices; not manna and honey; not fair limbs that attract one to embrace them: that is not what I love when I love my God. And yet I love a certain kind of light and sound and odor and nourishment and embrace when I love my God: the light, sound, odor, nourishment, and embrace of the inner man. That is where there shines upon my soul that which no place can contain, there resounds that which no passage of time takes away, there is the fair odor that no wind can blow away, there I taste a flavor that no enjoyment can diminish, there I am united in an embrace of which I can never tire. That is what I love when I love my God " (*Confessions*, Bk. X, ch. 6).

All this shows us the relationship between the application of the three powers of the soul and the application of the senses: the application of the powers of the soul is *already* an application of the senses. This is true all the way from the beginning, the representation formed in the memory, and so on in the entire process up to the interior tasting and feeling (*sentire et gustare res interne*). On the other hand, the application of the senses is *also* application of the powers of the soul — and indeed in a most decisive and intensive manner. Therefore both exercises are not merely related to one another but form a living unity, a logically developing spiritual process. Metaphorically one could say: they are related to one another as flowers which are opening are related to themselves in their later stage of development. Only to a superficial observer, who cannot see beyond the brief clumsy words of the poor pilgrim, are they two different methods. In their inner nature, in their dynamism, they are only one method; namely the method by which man encounters the God and Lord who reveals Himself. It is a pursuit. Man pursues the God who calls him by listening, paying attention, and obeying. Basically it is none other than that pursuit with which the Lord and Creator of all things pursues man in all his self-revelations in order to bring him home to Himself.

At the start of the second week we hear about a particular and — as it may appear at first — distinct way of meditating. We are to become absorbed by means of prayer in the mystery of our redemption through the Incarnation of the eternal Word. After the usual preparatory prayer and the threefold introductory prelude, we are directed to see first the persons involved, then to listen to their words, and finally to consider their actions:

" The first point is to see the persons, the one group and the others: first, those on the face of the earth, so varied in dress and behavior; some white and others black; some in peace and others in war; some weeping and others laughing; some healthy and others sick; some being born, others dying, etc. Secondly, to see and consider the Divine Persons, as on their royal seat or throne of their Divine Majesty — how they view the whole face of the earth and all nations in such blindness and see them die and descend into hell. Thirdly, to see our Lady and the angel who salutes her, and to reflect in order to derive profit from such a sight.

" The second point is to hear what the people on the face of the earth are saying: how they converse with one another, how they swear and blaspheme, etc. In the same way, what the Divine Persons are saying; namely ' Let us work out the redemption of the human race,' etc.; then, what the angel and our Lady are saying. Afterwards to reflect, in order to draw profit from their words.

" The third point is to consider what the people on the face of the earth are doing: how they wound and kill one another, go to hell, etc. In the same way, what the Divine Persons are doing; namely effecting the most holy Incarnation, etc.; and similarly, what the angel and our Lady are doing; namely the angel performing his office of legate, and our Lady humbling herself and giving thanks to the Divine Majesty. Afterwards to reflect, in order to draw profit from each one of these things " ([106-108]).

One who merely reads the little book of the *Exercises* may see in these directions still another, separate method, which seems to stand in distinction to the meditation with the three powers. However, anyone who makes the Exercises and sees how they fit into the whole context, who performs them in effective conformity to the annotations and additions, will have to think otherwise. Here also it is a question of nothing else than the interior feeling and tasting, toward which the activation of the three powers is the naturally given path and the application of the senses the culmination of that path. We should strive to penetrate ever more deeply into the innermost core of the mysteries upon which we are to meditate. This means that, in the case of the mystery of the redemption, we are to penetrate as deeply as possible into the interior of the persons to be redeemed and of the Persons who are redeeming. But we penetrate into the interior of persons only step by step, just so far as personal beings reveal their inner life to our human understanding. And since it is a question of the realities of faith, as always in the exercises of piety, we must see the persons with the eyes of faith, hear their words with the ears of faith, observe their actions in the light of faith, in order thus to penetrate into their hearts.

We receive a first impression of what exists and takes place in the inner life of persons from their appearance, their bearing, their countenance, their look, their expression. How much is expressed merely by the loving look that Jesus turned upon the rich young man (Mark 10: 21) or by the one with which he surprised Peter in the court of the high priest (Luke 22: 61) — if we would only make this look vividly present to ourselves, reverently consider it, and let it penetrate into the heart! The words of the persons, the sound of their voice and what they say, tell us even more of their interior life. What depths of the heart are opened to us, for example, by the word of the Virgin to the angel at the Annunciation (Luke 1: 38) or the word with which Jesus addresses the traitor

on the Mount of Olives (Matt. 26: 50), provided we make such a
word present to us, reflect on it, and let it make an impression
on us! The actions of the persons give us still more profound
information, their attitude and behavior in happy and in difficult
hours. What an abyss opens for us in the action of the eternal
Son of God as He clothes himself in the womb of the Virgin Mary
with our human nature, in order " to die for my sins " ([53]) !

Thus in prayer we gain an affinity with them, learn to understand
them with an intimate knowledge, penetrate with our heart into
their hearts. In ordinary human life hearts find one another in no
other way. The bride will always make her bridegroom present to
herself, his words, his behavior; she will reflect on this and above
all will conduct a loving colloquy with him. Thus through *col-loquium*
(speaking with each other) they find their way to *con-cordia* (union
of hearts), and this con-cord becomes *con-vivium* (living together).
Therefore we find in this exercise once more the same dynamism
at work, that dynamism which will lead the depths of the soul into
the depths of God, the depths of God into the depths of the soul,
the urgent dynamism of the " deep calling to the deep."

It lies in the nature of things that this deep interior compre-
hension and understanding is possible only to the extent that we
have the persons, their words, and their actions present or make
them present to us (through the first of the three powers, the
memory); that we embrace them and penetrate into them with our
minds (through the second power, the intellect); and that we form
an attitude toward them with a sensitive and appreciative heart
(through the third power, the will). The three powers are at work
in this seeing the persons, hearing their words, considering their
actions; indeed, this seeing, hearing, and considering is nothing other
than the activation of them; just as it is also nothing more than
the highest personal activation of the senses which are set in motion
in the application of the senses.

Consequently what may appear to the reader of the *Exercises*
as a separate way of meditating, or method of meditating, shows
itself to the exercitant as a more detailed determination of the
exercise with the three powers, a help toward the *one* method of
human encounter with God, which is fundamentally the method
of the divine visitation of man, a help to the interior sense and
taste for things (*sentire et gustare res interne*).

The result is no different if we consider the exercise with the
three powers in relation to those three types of spiritual exercise
to which Ignatius — without a word of explanation — gives specific
names. Again the three names that occur in the text lead us

to think at first of varied and distinct ways or methods of meditation. There is mention of *meditación*, of *consideración*, and of *contemplación*. German translators are not agreed in their versions of these expressions, especially of the first and the last. Some translate *Betrachtung* as meditation, *Besinnung* as consideration, and *Beschauung* as contemplation. (Thus, for example, Feder.) Przywara has, in place of *Beschauung*, *Anschauung* with no real difference of meaning. Others use *Erwägung* for reflection; and *Besinnung* and *Betrachtung* are used for meditation; but for von Balthasar *Betrachtung* is not a specific but a generic term. It would be rather difficult and would little accord with what took place in the soul of the pilgrim at Manresa if one wanted to define clearly and make sharp distinctions about the meanings of these words. It can certainly be supposed that the man who prayed in that cave had at his disposal, in the tremendous riches of his spiritual experience, a considerable number of ways of praying from which to choose. One could probably indicate the differences toward which the terms seem to point in this direction: Where the discursive activity of the understanding, reflection, and consideration on the divine truth, stands more in the foreground and assumes a larger role in the efforts of the one praying, the exercise is called *meditación*; where the concern is more for the correct understanding of one's own self and one's own behavior before God the Lord, it is called *consideración*; where it is a matter more of a large overview, which calls upon the whole man and his whole life, it is called *contemplación*. At any rate they are all ordered to the one goal of the Exercises, finding God as intensely and comprehensively as possible, actively possessing and being possessed, toward which the application of the three powers of the soul is the path proper to the human spirit.

There is a natural temptation to make the differences into contrasts or at least to consider variations to be distinctions. This has been especially true in regard to the first and the third type, meditation and contemplation, which have been opposed to one another to the extent that there has been a tendency to identify meditation with the exercise with the three powers of the soul; and so some have sought to contrast it, as a discursive exercise, to the contemplative. That this was not the intention of the originator of the Exercises, and in particular is not in accord with their interior dynamism, is clear from the final exercise, which is most decidedly a contemplation, the Contemplation for Obtaining Love. In this the exercitant strives for a comprehensive view, indeed *the* comprehensive view of all the revelations of God and all the gifts of God to man, the active vision and experience of what the Lord and Creator of all things wants to say to us and to be for us by means of the entirety of natural and supernatural reality. This exercise is the summation of the whole of the Exercises; in it we are raised up to that summit toward which we have been on the way in all of them; or rather, toward which the Lord wills to raise us in and through all his works. Everything is divine love: love which gives us all things and benefits us in them all; love, which is close to us in everything; love, which is active in everything and labors for us; love which in all things and through all things wishes to bestow himself and hand himself over to us. Each one of the four points — one could better call them four circles, since the whole universe revolves in them and wants to draw us ever deeper into its revolution — is an activation of the three powers.

" The first point is to *call to mind* the benefits I have received, of creation, redemption, and my personal gifts, pondering with much devotion how much God our Lord has done for me, and how much he has given me of that which he has; and consequently, how much he desires to give me himself, so far as he can according to his divine ordinance. Then *to reflect on myself*, considering with many reasons and much justice, what I, for my part, ought to offer and give to his Divine Majesty; that is, all that I have, and myself with them, as one who makes an offering with great devotion: ' Take, O Lord, and receive all my liberty, my memory, my understanding, and all my will, all I have and possess. You have given it to me; to you, O Lord, I return it. All is yours, dispose of it according to your entire will. Give me your love and grace, for this is enough for me.'

" The second point is *to consider* how God dwells in creatures, in the elements giving them being, in the plants giving them vegetative life, in animals giving them the life of the senses, in men giving them understanding, and so in me: giving me being, life, sensation, and endowing me with understanding; likewise how he makes of me a temple, since I am created in the likeness and image of his Divine Majesty. Again *reflecting on myself* as has been said in the first point, or in any other way that I shall feel to be better. And the same shall be done in each of the following points.

" The third point is *to consider* how God works and labors for me in all created things on the face of the earth; that is, he behaves like one who is laboring. Thus, in the heavens, elements, plants, fruits, herds, etc., giving them being, preserving them, giving them growth and sentient life, etc. Then *to reflect on myself.*

257

" The fourth point is *to see* how all goods and gifts descend from above, as does my limited power from the supreme and infinite power on high; and also our justice, goodness, piety, mercy, etc., just as the rays descend from the sun, waters from the spring, etc. Then to conclude *by reflecting on myself* as has been said. Concluding with a colloquy and an Our Father " ([234-237]).

We must in every point make present to ourselves God's love (which gives us all things, approaches us in everything, labors for us in everything, shares itself with us in everything), reflect upon it, and give ourselves to it. Man's response to this love can be no other than the total offering of the three powers: " Receive my memory, my understanding, and all my will." In handing them over to God, who is love and only love, man activates his freedom, makes use of his freedom, of his very being as a person, in the way which he owes his Creator and Lord — the use most in accord with his nature. In this prayer, which must be lived out, freedom, memory, understanding, and will are not simply four powers which may rank as equals. Rather, freedom is the whole man, the person who is making his decision and election before God; and the three powers of the soul are the activities of this freedom, the activity of the free person before God the Lord. The total offering is the restitution of what is due — which finds expression in the middle of the *Suscipe* — and at the same time is the deepest satisfaction of the human heart, the fulfillment of the most intrinsic destiny of man — that which the final words of the prayer express. God and man have met each other most intimately.

If the activation of the three powers is the path of human encounter with God, then contemplation, in particular its highest and most inclusive form, the Contemplation for Obtaining Love, is the way of walking along that path that presses on toward the ultimate objective and finally arrives at this goal. Deep calls ever to deep, heart to heart, life to life, love to love.

In addition to the foregoing types of spiritual exercises that are named in the body of the *Exercises* and are always explained by a few short remarks, there are still other types that are explained as supplements or substitutes. There are above all the two Examinations of Conscience, the " particular and daily examination " ([24-31]) and the " general examination of conscience to purify oneself and to better one's confessions " ([32-34]), which stand right after the Foundation before the First Week, and the Three Methods of Praying ([238-260]), which we find after the Contemplation for Obtaining Love. These methods of prayer — even the Examinations of Conscience have the form of methods of prayer — might at first produce the impression of being schemes and patterns. They appear, at first, to have only a superficial relationship with the other exercises and with the whole intent of the Spiritual Exercises. Yet they too are nothing other than helps toward the one great concern of the Exercises: the most profound encounter possible between man and his God and Creator, the most complete conformity possible of the human will and its efforts to the divine will. It would be easy to show how they too are activations of the soul, ordered to finding God ardently and totally. Again and again this shines through the sober, stiff words of the pilgrim, in ([240, 252, 254, 258]) and elsewhere.

The *Spiritual Exercises* knows only one manner of human encounter with God which does not grow out of the activation of the three powers. We read about this in the "rules for the purpose of discerning spirits more exactly" ([328]), which are more suited to the second week. There we read of a special divine visitation which is essentially distinct from the way in which God usually visits man: "Only God our Lord can give consolation to the soul without any preceding cause; for it belongs to the Creator alone to enter into, go out of, and move the soul, drawing it entirely to the love of his Divine Majesty. I say without cause, without any previous sensation or perception of any object through which such consolation might come to the soul by means of its own acts of understanding and will" ([330]). As Creator of the soul, God the Lord can go in and out of all its depths in sovereign freedom as in his own house. His entrance is not limited to the way through his external world, nor to the way of his revelation that takes place in the interior world; there is not even any need of the human efforts of the faculties of the soul. Without any effort on our part He can illumine us with his light, pour in his love, move our will, and restore our character and our life. These are mystic graces in the strictest sense of the word, with which Ignatius — as early as the time at Manresa — was so richly endowed. Nothing more is said about them in the *Spiritual Exercises* because they lie quite outside the realm of spiritual exercises, of the activity of the powers of the human soul.

If we review comprehensively all the ways of praying and meditating given in the little book of the *Exercises*, together with the additional instructions and rules, we must then say: This work of Ignatius is at the same time extremely unmethodical and extremely methodical. In its external form and from the first impression it must make on the reader, it presents a wild profusion of methods and schemes, seemingly without any proper order and cohesion —

259

hardly to be called a " book " at all — and there can scarcely be found any other work so unmethodical in the religious literature of the world. But if we enter into the inner meaning of the *Exercises*, if we give ourselves over to their inner dynamism, then the book shows itself to be an extremely methodical work having an inner unity and cohesion such as is scarcely to be found in any other religious work. All the exercises and instructions have always but *one* aim, the living encounter of man with the living God. All the exercises are thus basically just *one* exercise, a training for the true life, for divine love. All the methods of meditation and prayer are just *one* method, man's enthusiastic search for and acceptance of the call of God, of the invitation given by eternal love. They are all a training and activation of human freedom in the presence of the Divine Majesty through the offering of memory, understanding, and will, even unto the whole offering in the *Suscipe* of love. One might call this basic inner method the method of the *mysterium aquae et vini*, the mystery of water and wine, of which the offertory prayer of the Mass speaks.

Ignatius himself does not speak in the little book of methods. We never meet the word. But if one were to ask him which is his method, which is the Ignatian method, and whether he teaches one or more methods, he would surely turn on his usual smile and answer: *iuvare animas*, to help souls, to help them come closer to their Creator and Lord, to help them in any way one can help them. All the apparent methods in the different ways of meditation and prayer are for him a help and nothing more than a help to the one underlying method, which is as he experienced it so marvelously during the visitations of grace at Manresa. Nadal writes of this one method: " The originator of this method of the Exercises was Father Ignatius, by the grace and impulse of God; and indeed from the time when he withdrew to Manresa for the sake of penance and prayer. What he himself at that time experienced and judged helpful for others, he compiled in a notebook. He made use of these Exercises for himself and for others as long as he lived."[12]

The secret of the Exercises lies in the single-mindedness with which this one method is pursued and made the dominant law of the whole. This is the explanation of the profound effect they have — provided only that this method is followed in the spirit of

12 *MonNad*, Ep. 31.

its author. If one were to ask the question in a competitive examination: What can we do in order to be touched as deeply as possible by the individual truths of God, to be moved as strongly as possible ? — one could find no other answer than that which the book of the *Exercises* gives with the exercise of the three powers of the soul: Let one make for himself a vivid representation of the word of God which has taken place (Luke 2:15); let him then consider and reflect upon it with all reverence and zeal; in prayerful colloquy with the Lord let it have its effect upon the heart and let the will be moved and inspired by it ! And if one were to ask: How can we arrive at the point where our life accords as much as and as perfectly as possible with what God plans and proposes for us ? — the answer would be: The path which the *Exercises* take from the Foundation to the Contemplation for Obtaining Love. The Ignatian method consists in nothing other than in the fact that man allows himself to be drawn by the Divine Majesty into its method and to be more and more carried away by it.

After what has been said, it is scarcely necessary to point out that it is a basic misunderstanding of the spirit of the Exercises when one always makes the activation of the three powers in the meditation or the points for meditation the principle for his arrangement of the material. This can be done now and again, as takes place in the book itself in the three points of the first meditation on sin and — less clearly developed — in the four points of the Contemplation for Obtaining Love. This threefold division of powers should be dealt with as is that other threesome: persons, words, and actions. Although this latter threesome is stressed in the models given for all meditations on the life of Jesus at the start of the second week, it is still never found used as the basis for the arrangement of the matter to be considered in all these meditations as sketched briefly at the end of the book. This threefold division is not meant to be given as a pattern but only as a guide to the deeply interior knowledge (*intima cognitio*); and this, to be sure, again and again. Otherwise it would give rise to weariness and confusion, as the official *Directory* remarks: " That which is said in the meditations on the Incarnation and the Nativity about making the contemplation on the persons and their words and actions, should be understood in reference to the arrangement we have mentioned that is placed at the end of the book. That is, they are to be thought of in each one of the points, taking these in their proper order. It is not necessary first to meditate separately on all the persons of the whole mystery, then on all the words of it, and finally on the actions. This would, especially in certain meditations,

261

generate confusion."[13] So also the threefold division of powers is in no way a scheme, but rather a basic law for all human encounter with God.

What Effect Does the Exercise " with the three powers of the soul" Have in One's Daily Life?

From this quality of the exercise as an encounter with God there follow its consequences in a man's life. Only the most important effects will be mentioned briefly. An exhaustive presentation would mean writing a theological anthropology of the Exercises.

The first effect consists in the fact that it makes man alert to God's inspirations, receptive and ready for God's graces and the guidance of his grace. From the very beginning the exercise is an acceptance of the call of God, which is issued to man through all of reality. Throughout the entire course of the exercise, it is a collaboration with the grace of God that calls and guides us.

Only superficial readers could read into the *Exercises* what some have wanted to read into it: voluntarism, activism, asceticism of the will, or even an acrobatics of the will, moralism, asceticism. We do repeatedly meet with the expression: "... that which I desire " (*id quod volo*). It occurs fifteen times, particularly in the final prayer of preparation for the meditation, as in the first exercise of the first week: " To ask of God our Lord what I long for and desire " ([48]). Yet from the context it is perfectly clear that the exercitant does not here present himself self-willed before God, but only inspired by that attitude of will which has become for him a most solemn duty, in his consideration of the Foundation, because of the absolute superiority of the Creator and the infinite glory of the Divine Majesty. He prays for this before each exercise in the first, general preparatory prayer throughout all the weeks; and the Exercises are without exception to be a training for this: " that all my intentions, actions, and operations (*omnes meae intentiones, actiones, et operationes*) may be ordered purely to the service and glorification of his Divine Majesty " ([46]). Before each exercise what we are to ask for in particular (the *id quod volo*) is nothing other than the entire conformity of our will with the divine will as it reveals itself in the mystery being considered. What we will is precisely to overcome and clear away every trace of self-will before God, as is stated in the title of the *Exercises*: " Spiritual Exercises to conquer oneself and to order one's life, without allowing oneself to come to

---

13 *Directory* of 1599, ch. 19, no. 5, in *SpEx*MHSJ, p. 1149.

a determination through any disordered affection " ([21]). One could say that Ignatius knows but one self-will; namely that of having no self-will and letting oneself be led and driven in absolutely everything by God's merciful will.[14]

The *Exercises* are not activism but the very death of activism; not a reliance on one's own will but prayerful acceptance of and conformity to divine grace, the prevenient grace of the Lord which is offered in all things. Of course, in response to this we are to offer the ultimate in good will, inasmuch as we magnanimously make a gift to the Lord of our entire will: " It is very beneficial to him who is receiving the Exercises to enter upon them with magnanimity and liberality towards his Creator and Lord, offering all his desires and liberty to Him, in order that his Divine Majesty may make use of his person and of all he has according to his most holy will " ([5]).

Ignatius is convinced that, by proper activation of the powers of the soul (by prayerfully making vivid representations to ourselves, prayerfully considering and reflecting, prayerfully loving and desiring), we can receive the particular grace in question from the goodness of the Lord. The Lord offers it to us in that revelation, that mystery, to which we turn our attention in the meditation. He is even more inclined to give us this grace than we may be inclined to receive it. We must be ready for it and make ourselves receptive, taking it into our heart and life — which is exactly what happens in the Exercises.

Therefore we should not only pray for this particular grace at the beginning of every exercise, as it says in the very first exercise, which gives directions for all exercises: " To ask of God our Lord what I long for and desire." This petition ought also to be in accordance with the subject matter. Thus, if the contemplation deals with the Resurrection, to ask for joy with Christ rejoicing; if it deals with the Passion, to ask for sorrow, tears, and torment with Christ in torment. Here it will be to ask for shame and confusion at myself, seeing how many have been damned for one mortal sin alone, and how many times I have merited to be condemned forever for my so many sins " ([48]). But also, if the objective is not yet attained, the special grace not yet received or not sufficiently, we should repeat the exercise in question in the same manner until we have received the grace from the Lord.

14 The *id quod volo* is given detailed treatment by Alexandre Brou, *The Ignatian Way to God*, trans. William J. Young (Milwaukee: Bruce, 1952), pp. 36-44.

Even the length of the individual weeks is to differ according to the same principles: " For since it happens that in the first week some are slower to find what they seek; that is, contrition, grief, and tears for their sins; and as some are more diligent than others, and some more agitated and tried by the various spirits, it is necessary sometimes to shorten the first week, and at other times to lengthen it, and so likewise in all weeks following, always seeking to arrange everything according to the subject matter. Yet the Exercises should be completed in thirty days more or less " ([4]).

The Lord grants his grace to the one who prays humbly and makes an honest effort, and indeed to the degree to which he has renounced all self-will and surrendered himself unconditionally to the guidance of God's grace — according to the Ignatian maxim: " There are but a few men who have any idea what God would make of them if they would deny themselves and surrender themselves entirely to the divine Master so that he might form their souls in his hands."

The *Exercises* conform man to grace; they are a " way of preparing the soul and disposing it to cast off all disordered inclinations, and after they have been cast off, to seek and find God's will for the ordering of one's whole life towards the salvation of one's soul " ([1]).[15]

The more a man cooperates with the grace of God — by the proper use of the powers of his soul — the more he comes to live a life of intimate companionship with his Creator and Lord. He becomes in ever increasing measure — like Ignatius — a man of " familiarity with God," a man of " finding God in all things." In making progress along the road of the Exercises, he will somehow exprience what the man who was praying in the cave at Manresa experienced. Looking back afterward, Ignatius could say: " At that time God treated him as a teacher treats a child."[16] God makes him an ever more intimate friend; for through the Exercises he makes it possible for God " that he can silently enter into the soul as into his own house in order to attract her wholly to the love of his divine Majesty " (see [330, 335]); and " that he himself, the Creator and Lord, communicate himself to the soul dedicated to him, embracing it in his love and praise and disposing it for that path upon which it can better serve him in the future " ([15]).

---

15 See an article that has grown out of a profound knowledge of the Exercises: Steger, " Der Primat," *Geist und Leben*, XXI (1948), 94-108.
16 *Autobiog*, 27, in *FN*, I, 400.

While for the man who neglects the proper activation of the powers of the soul, the created world becomes more and more the be-all and end-all, for the exercitant the living God becomes little by little the sum total of all reality, the all in all. He learns the high art of finding God in all things not only with the knowing spirit but also with a relishing and loving heart and with a joyously ready will and activity. It is the same with him as with Ignatius. Ignatius could be moved to tears at the sight of a flower with the thought, " If this flower is already so lovely, how lovely then must be the Lord."[17] His companions said that he was a contemplative in action (*in actione contemplativus*) and that, however contradictory it may sound, he was capable of finding God even when he felt abandoned by God.[18] What the founder of the order required of his spiritual sons, the closest possible union and familiarity with God, not only in prayer but also in all activity,[19] is the natural effect of the activity of the three powers of the soul. For by putting them to prayerful, dedicated use, the soul makes itself " better fitted to approach and come in contact with its Creator

17 This Ignatian art of finding-God-in-all-things is masterfully and strikingly expressed in the poetry and other writings of Gerard Manley Hopkins, S.J. He once wrote in his diary (May 18, 1870): " I do not think I have ever seen anything more beautiful than the bluebell I have been looking at. I know the beauty of our Lord by it"; in W. H. Gardner (ed.), *Gerard Manley Hopkins, a Selection of His Poems and Prose* (Harmondsworth: Penguin Books, 1953), p. 122.

18 Ignatius writes in his *Spiritual Diary* on March 12, 1544: " When Mass was finished, and afterwards in my room, I found myself completely deprived of all help, without being able to receive any consolation from the mediators [Jesus and Mary] or from the Divine Persons. Rather I felt so remote and separated from them as if I had never felt their help and would never feel it again in the future. Thereupon there came to me thoughts against Jesus, then against someone else; and I found myself much confused with conflicting thoughts. . ." (*SpDiar*, [145]). At a later date (April 2), he recognized that this state of feeling abandoned by God was also a proof of God's grace; that is, that he can also find God when in such a state: " In times of greater knowledge and of greater visitations, it seemed to me that I ought to be just as content even when I was not visited with tears and that I should consider to be better whatever God did or whatever pleased Him, whether to visit them upon me or not. . ." (*SpDiar*, [184]).

19 " They should seek God in all things, divesting themselves as much as possible of the love of all creatures in order to bestow all their affection on the Creator of them, loving Him in all creatures and all creatures in Him, according to His most holy and divine will " (*Cons*, [288]). Each individual should be " closely united with God our Lord and intimate with Him in prayer and all his actions " (*Cons*, [723]).

265

and Lord " (*se reddit aptiorem ad appropinquandum Creatori suo ac Domino suo eumque attingendum*); and the more it thus binds itself to him, the more it disposes itself to receive graces and gifts from his Divine and Supreme Goodness " ([20]).[20]

In the course of the prayerful activation of the soul's powers, the man who is progressing in familiarity with God also comes to an ever greater understanding of the incomprehensible greatness of God, the limitlessness of his Divine Majesty and of his Divine Love; and all this enters more profoundly into his heart and life. He becomes a man of the *magis*, the continual striving for " more." This divine call for *magis* rings powerfully throughout the whole of the Exercises, from the beginning, seemingly so prosaic, to the exalted conclusion (e.g. [20, 23, 97, 104, 130]). The Contemplation for Obtaining Love is throughout its entire course an exercise in training ourselves to allow this call to possess us as totally as possible and without any resistance by self-will. In the service of the Most High Majesty, of the infinitely sublime and beneficent Lord, the exercitant experiences more and more what St. Bernard expressed in the maxim: " The right measure in which to love God is to love Him without measure." As the *Exercises* develop, this longing for more grows: the more we know our Creator and Lord, and the more we " touch " ([20]) him and come in contact with him, the more we recognize how little we know him; the more ardently we love him, the more we become conscious of how little we love him; the more zealously we serve him, the more we experience how unworthy of his infinite Majesty and Goodness our poor service is.

From the time of Manresa Ignatius was carried away by this *magis*; and from then on he could only live and act " to the greater glory of God," " to the greater service of God," "to the greater service of the Divine Majesty," " to the greater help of souls "— as the constantly recurring expressions say. Whoever will

---

20 Ignatius expresses a desire that the Duke of Gandía, Francis Borgia, receive this precious fruit of the Exercises and of grace: " When persons go out of themselves . . . they notice and feel with constant attention and consolation how our eternal highest Good is in all created things, giving them all being and preserving them in it with his infinite being and presence. . . Those who love God with their whole soul are helped by all things, and everything aids them to merit more and to be more closely united with their Creator and Lord in intense love " (*EppIgn*, I, 339; *LettersIgn*, p. 84).

In regard to this finding-God-in-all-things, see the article of Josef Stierli earlier in this same book, " Ignatian Prayer."

activate the powers of his soul in the presence of God as he did will experience something similar, will become a man of the perpetual comparative, a man of the love of God who is restlessly aspiring and zealous to do more. He will never, in the service of *this* Lord, be able to sit down and rest; never will he be able to say: there is enough of love, enough of service — that would be to refuse the response owed to his infinite Majesty and infinite Goodness. So however alien and contrary to the nature of the *Exercises* activism is, activity is necessary and natural to them. The prayerful activity of the powers of the soul makes of the exercitant a man of the " ever greater glory of God."

The God-Man Jesus Christ stands at the center of the great vision of God to which the exercitant enters by means of his spiritual activity, supported by grace. All that God announces to us in his revelations is brought together in Him. All creatures endowed with freedom stand before him at the decisive moment of their existence. For all of them, angels and men, he is set for their resurrection or their fall. The damned have shattered against him; the perfect have been perfected by him. In him the infinite Majesty and goodness of God stand in person before us. Therefore: " In colloquy with Christ our Lord, to bring to memory the souls which are in hell, some because they did not believe in his coming, others because despite their belief they did not act according to his commandments; distinguishing three groups: the first, before his coming; the second, during his lifetime; the third, after his life in this world. Then to give thanks that he has not, by ending my life, let me fall into any of these groups. In like manner, how up till now he has always bestowed on me such pity and mercy" ([71]). Thus the reverent, loving attentiveness toward God becomes of itself a loving, obedient attentiveness toward Christ; the activation of the powers of the soul becomes the following of Christ. The more the exercitant turns to him with " memory," " understanding," and " will," the more does he familiarize himself with the " life hidden with Christ in God " (Col. 3: 3) (*vita cum Christo abscondita in Deo*); the more Christ becomes for him the life of his life, and he can confess from the depths of his happiness: " for me to live is Christ " (Phil. 1: 21) (*Mihi vivere Christus est*). The prayerful activity of the soul's powers, accompanied by grace, produces the man of the following of Christ, the man of the Society of Jesus.

The more we accustom ourselves through activity to be companions and followers of Jesus, the more does the Most Holy Trinity shine forth for us in the countenance of Jesus Christ; and we accustom ourselves to live with the interior man the life of the Triune God.

267

The Exercises work by " baptizing." They immerse the soul deeper " in the name " (eis to onoma: Matt. 28:19); that is, into God, the Father and the Son and the Holy Spirit, who reveals himself to us and thus enables us to call upon him and speak to him. They make the exercitant more and more a participant in the divine nature, in the threefold divine life. To the extent that we participate in the life of our Redeemer and imitate it, we become more and more a child of God in the depths of our heart. Together with the Son of God we love the Father in the Holy Spirit and with the Son of God are loved by the Father in the Holy Spirit. With every mystery in which we immerse ourselves and which we make a part of our lives, we become more deeply absorbed in the mystery of all mysteries and assimilate this central mystery of the divinity ever deeper into our lives. The Exercises are a training in unity of life with the Triune God. They make man — if only he responds with the powers of his soul to the call of grace — into the trinitarian man.

Since from the very beginning the life of Jesus is ordered to the Cross, since his coming into our human life is a " descent from eternal life to temporal death (on the Cross) " ([53]), so our following of Christ can only be a fellowship with the Lord carrying the Cross and dying on the Cross. Only by his Cross does Jesus conquer the enemy of human nature, does he effect the salvation of our humanity; only through his Cross is he our savior and redeemer. Love of Jesus becomes love of the Cross. Through the gentle, irresistible power of grace this love forces the exercitant to pray for fellowship with the cross bearing and crucified Jesus: " A colloquy with our Lady that she obtain for me from her Son and Lord the grace to be received under his Standard. And first, in the greatest poverty of spirit, and, if it should please his Divine Majesty, and he should desire to choose and receive me to it, not less in actual poverty. Secondly, in suffering insults and injustices, so that I may better imitate him in these, provided only I can endure them without sin on the part of any person or displeasure to his Divine Majesty; and with this an *Ave Maria*. To ask the same from the Son, that He obtain it for me from the Father; and with this to say an *Anima Christi*. To ask the same from the Father, that He grant it to me; and then to say a *Pater Noster* " ([147]). Whoever is intimately united with Jesus and truly follows him can do nothing else. By an inner necessity the Exercises form a man who loves the Cross and follows the Cross.

Further, since the mysteries of the life and death of Jesus are, in the continuation of the life of Jesus, his Church, a mysterious reality in the world, the following of Christ becomes a life in and with the Church. The *sentire cum Christo*, feeling with Christ, becomes *sentire cum Ecclesia*, an ardent union with the "true bride of Christ our Lord, who is our holy mother, the hierarchical Church" ([353]). Military service under the standard of the Cross of Christ becomes military service in and with the Church militant. The book of the *Exercises* gives us instructions for this in the Rules for Thinking with the Church, which the author has drawn both from mystical and practical experience: "To obtain that true feeling which we should have in the service of the Church, the following rules shall be observed..." ([352-370]). Ignatius and his companions were formed into men of the Church by the Exercises. As Nadal expressed this before his fellow religious: "We must make ourselves thoroughly familiar with the thought that we are all followers of Jesus Christ, who even today still carries his Cross in the Church militant. We follow after him with our cross; for to this purpose the Eternal Father has made us his servants."[21] The exercitant who faithfully follows the impulse of grace with the powers of his soul becomes, by a logic intrinsic to the situation, a man of the Church.

In the battle that is fought within the Church militant, we see under God's illumination the two fronts standing opposed to one another and struggling with one another. As the exercitant progresses steadily on the way of the Exercises, he experiences this recruitment by both sides. He experiences the recruiting of the "good" and of the "evil spirit," and sees himself forced to make a decision. Therefore Ignatius advises: "When he who gives the Exercises observes that no spiritual motions, such as consolations or desolations, take place in the soul of the exercitant, and he is not agitated by various spirits, he should question him much about the Exercises: whether he makes them at the set times, and how; and in the same way about the Additions, if he observes them with diligence. He should make detailed inquiries about each of these things" ([6]). The exercitant learns by faithful, conscientious fulfillment of the Exercises

---

21 *MonNad*, IV, 678. Hugo Rahner sees the following of Christ with which the Exercises are concerned to consist in the community of life and cooperation in the struggle with the Christ who appears to us in his Church. "This, precisely, is the radical distinction between Ignatius and the 'modern devotion' (of the Brothers of the Common Life). Ignatius at Manresa refashioned their rather formless 'Imitation of Jesus,' changing it to the following of Christ present in the Church Militant. The Kingdom of Christ is the Church, and in her all the other mysteries coalesce" *Spirituality of Ignatius*, p. 55).

to discern the spirits; he becomes a man of discernment. To help him in this are the " Rules for in some manner perceiving and recognizing the various motions that are caused in the soul; the good, to admit them; the bad, to reject them " ([313-327]); as well as the " Rules to the same end, with a more exact discernment of spirits " ([328-336]).

To the extent that the exercitant ever more clearly discerns the spirits and takes his position ever more firmly in the camp of Christ and against the camp of Satan, he enters ever more deeply into the great community of the followers of Christ, into the community of the saints. He knows he is more intimately bound to them all by the bonds of grace than brothers and sisters of the same family can be united by the bonds of blood. All are his helpers in the fight, helpers also to an ever deeper union with Christ and union with God. A powerful consciousness of belonging to a community which spans heaven and earth fills him. He knows he is specially united to our Mother and Queen, Mary, more closely than a child is to its own mother, than a noble knight to the exalted lady of his heart. Therefore the threefold colloquy (to Mary, the mediatrix with the mediator; to Jesus, the mediator with the Father, and to the Eternal Father) is close to his heart not only in the case of particularly important decisions; it gradually becomes with time his habit in all situations of life. Yet in addition to the two great mediators, Jesus and Mary, he does not forget or neglect the countless other intercessors in heaven and on earth. He becomes a man of this vast, holy community, the communion of the saints.[22]

---

22 To what an extent this awareness of community had entered into the very lifeblood of Francis Xavier by means of the Exercises is shown in a letter which he wrote to his religious brethren in Europe (January 20, 1548). In it he speaks of the great dangers encountered in a storm at sea on the journey from Malacca to India. As the storm, which raged for three days, reached its high point and all on the ship awaited what seemed to be certain death, he took " for my first intercessors on earth all those belonging to the Company of Jesus, blessed of God, and the friends of the Company." With such help and support, he then commended himself " to the loving prayers of the Spouse of Jesus Christ, Holy Mother the Church." He then commended himself "to all saints in the glory of paradise, beginning with those who here below were of the holy Company of Jesus . . . the angels, praying to them choir by choir, and . . . the patriarchs, prophets, apostles, evangelists, martyrs, confessors, virgins — all the saints of heaven." Then he took "for my protectress the glorious Virgin, our Lady, because in heaven everything she asks of God our Lord is granted. Finally, I put all my trust in the infinite merits of the Passion and Death of Jesus Christ, our Redeemer and Lord." And what does he ask, relying on all

Finally the exercitant becomes a man who has lost his life and, precisely by losing it, has found it: a life lost in Christ, in God, in the Church, in the good of souls; and thus he gains his most profound, most unique, most personal life. He travels the road which the Creator in his boundless goodness plans personally for him in a unique manner, never to be repeated. Every soul has in His grace its own proper name! And he is forced to say in astonishment — as Ignatius did after the days of grace in Manresa: " What kind of a new life is it that now begins ! "

Summarizing all these effects we can say: the proper activation of the three powers of the soul, the recollected, prayerful, faithfully obedient exercise of them in the presence of the Creator and Lord makes of the exercitant a man of ceaseless striving, a man who is possessed by Christ and who possesses Christ, who with the apostle Paul can say: " Not that I have already obtained this, or already have been made perfect, but I press on hoping that I may lay hold of that for which Christ Jesus has laid hold of me. Brethren, I do not consider that I have laid hold of it already. But one thing I do: forgetting what is behind, I strain forward to what is before, I press on towards the goal, to the prize of God's heavenly call in Christ Jesus " (Phil. 3:12-14).

these intercessors ? That the Lord God might save him from the storm only if he would be allowed to endure similar or still greater dangers later, in case that would be to His greater glory — he prayed for a new cross to bear for the sake of Christ and his Church. His awareness of this community led him to shed tears of joy and of consolation when in such great danger of death. This passage of the letter is printed in: *EppXav*, I, 393-394; Brodrick, *Xavier*, pp. 301-302; *CartasXav*, pp. 235-236; Coleridge, *Xavier*, pp. 419-420.

"BE PRUDENT MONEY-CHANGERS":
TOWARD THE HISTORY OF IGNATIUS'
TEACHING ON THE DISCERNMENT OF SPIRITS

Hugo Rahner
Epitomized[1] by *Harold E. Weidman*

THE LIGHT that modern research has thrown on the *Spiritual Exercises* has made it both easier and more necessary to write an historical account of each of their fundamental ideas. We are not concerned here with the immediate literary sources that influenced Ignatius, but with the coherence of his doctrine with the great tradition of patristic and medieval asceticism, a coherence often called " meta-historical." The similarity of his spiritual insights and mystical enlightenment to those of the great spiritual masters of the past resulted in a surprising similarity of thought and expression which goes beyond any mere literary dependence. This enabled the early Jesuits to show that the ascetical teaching of their master was in agreement with the tradition in the Church. Thus, while they were convinced that Ignatius had drawn the basic principles of the *Spiritual Exercises* more from the inspiration of the Holy Spirit and from personal experience than from books, they could meet the charge of illuminism brought against them by showing that their doctrine was fully in line with accepted ascetical tradition.

In this article we shall concentrate on one single point: the Ignatian Rules for the Discernment of Spirits and their use in

---

1 Editor's Note: This essay of Hugo Rahner was first translated by Thomas N. Gallagher, S.J. But since a translation of the article into English later appeared in Hugo Rahner, *Ignatius the Theologian*, translated by Michael Barry (New York: Herder and Herder, 1968), pp. 32-52, it seemed that a digest of the article would be more helpful than another complete translation. Hence Father Harold E. Weidman, who knew and heard Father Hugo Rahner at Innsbruck, prepared the present digest.

making the Election. We shall try to show that these developed within the tradition of the Fathers of the Church. This may show that the teachings, developed out of their experience by Ignatius and the Fathers, have more than a merely historical interrelationship. It may also help the theologians to understand more profoundly the doctrine of Ignatius, which is so often misunderstood. We shall consider two things in this article: (1) the understanding of Ignatius and his companions of the Rules for the Discernment of Spirits and the Election; (2) the appeal to patristic tradition by the early Jesuits in defense of the teaching of Ignatius.

It was felt quite early by Ignatius' companions that his teaching on finding God's will in the Election of the *Exercises* through discerning the movements of the various spirits in the soul was something new and surprising. At the same time, however, they tried to make it clear that it contained some of the best thoughts of the ancient tradition. This was expressed by Everard Mercurian, later general of the Society, when he said that, although the Election in the *Exercises* summarized everything that could be found on the subject in the writings of the doctors and the saints, it nevertheless contained much that was new, especially the observations on the " three times " for making an election (*DirSpEx*, p. 269).

It was also thought that there was nothing more difficult in the Exercises, for both exercitant and director, than the election. Dávila compared it with the time of birth, in which there is much pain and involuntary sadness, and which requires an experienced midwife. St. Ignatius himself realized that during this period, when the retreatant comes face to face with a life-long commitment to the poor and crucified Christ, he will be specially subjected to the movements of the various spirits, and therefore, will have special need of a skillful director.

Ignatius clearly insisted that the election was not to be proposed to every one indiscriminately. Its object is exclusively the " more perfect." Therefore, it is meant for those who have purified their hearts in the first week and who now feel called to realize the " more " of the Foundation through the imitation of the crucified Lord. Ignatius assumed that one entering the dangerous area of election and the movement of the Spirits was inclined towards conformity with the humiliated Christ. This, in practice, meant an inclination to a life of the counsels rather than to a life of the commandments only. Ignatius, nevertheless, maintained that not every one so inclined was actually called to be a religious or to the life of the counsels. In his Directory he says that the matter about which a choice is to be made is: " First, whether the counsels or the commandments; second, if the counsels, whether in a religious order or not; third, if in an order, which one; fourth, when and in what manner. But if it is a choice of the commandments, in which state or way of life [married or single] " (*DirSpEx*, pp. 76-77).

This teaching of the " more perfect " as the object of the Election marks off the sphere in which the movement of the spirits takes place. These limits are always kept in view to guard against floundering about in some mystical vagueness, or falling victim to pure emotionalism. The limits are: (1) every choice is of something that is acceptable within the hierarchical Church; (2) only those are selected for the election whose progress in the course of the Exercises has shown them to be naturally and spiritually fit for the spiritual combat involved; the election, which is made by the aid of the Discernment of Spirits, must at the same time be made and completed by prayerful contemplation of the mysteries of Christ's life on earth.

Of the Three Times in which a good election can be made, Ignatius and his companions made more of the First and Second Times than of the Third. This last was considered a substitute for the other two and a means for checking on them. The First Time was not considered so miraculous among the early Jesuits as it is today. Yet such a call was rather exceptional even in Ignatius' experience, and he considered the Second Time to be of greater importance.

To understand the Second Time rightly, we must keep in mind that Ignatius characterized it as a Time in which the exercitant " experiences " consolation and desolation and recall what he says about the inner relationship between the election made in this Time and the Rules for the Discernment of Spirits. The exercitant must not direct his attention primarily to the experience of consolation and desolation, but rather to his love of God, while he is directly contemplating the mysteries of the life of Christ. Then he notes in which direction he is moved in the experience of consolation and desolation that accompanies his meditation. This is what Polanco means by prayer without " reasoning."

Given the nature of the Second Time, one can understand why Ignatius was so insistent that exercitant and director alike follow the Rules for the Discernment of Spirits, which were meant especially for making an election in this Second Time. He and the early commentators on the *Exercises* were quite aware of the saying of St. Paul that Satan can appear as an angel of light (2 Cor. 11:14). Hence two things are necessary if one is not to be misled in an election made in the Second Time: (1) the ability of discerning the spirits; (2) checking the results by rational understanding in the manner of the Third Time. There is no intention in this of subordinating the results from the Second Time to a " lower " principle. It is rather the prudent realization that, if the evidence is truly from God, it cannot conflict with right reason enlightened by faith.

To meet the first need, Ignatius drew up the Rules for the Discernment of Spirits, especially by giving lists of the contrasting influences of the " good spirit " and the " evil spirit "; for example, interior peace and joy as opposed to disturbance and sadness. Such lists can be found in the *Exercises* [316, 329, 333-335], and in Ignatius' *Directory* (*DirSpEx*, p. 72). From these lists the exercitant can cautiously discern what comes from God and what comes from the devil. If he makes his way prudently through all these interior effects, he will gradually come to a clear recognition of God's will without the ordinary processes of reasoning, provided he does not restrict his attention to mere introspection but devotes himself to the contemplation of the life of Christ and to the total surrender of self to the love of God that inspired these interior movements in the first place. Thus a system of checks and balances is built into the Second Time. The application of the Rules for the Discernment of Spirits guards against emotionalism, and the attention to what one " feels " spiritually guards against excessive rationalism.

Besides these controlling factors inserted into the psychological process of discernment itself, there are others that are more external yet closely linked to the former. Everything must be under the influence of the desire for the " more perfect "; but this can be discovered and tested by experience only through contemplating the life and example of the God-Man. Another means of controlling inner illuminations is the external judgment of the spiritual director enlightened by faith. Then there are the word of God and the magisterium of the Church. The general principle is that there can be no contradiction between the light of reason and the light of faith since both proceed from God.

We have been concentrating on those aspects of the Election which the opponents seized upon to show that the *Exercises* were infected with Illuminism. But these were the very points that the defenders used to show that the *Exercises* were closely linked to the patristic tradition and in full accord with the teaching of the Church.

The suspicion that he belonged to the Alumbrados pursued Ignatius ever since his student days at Alcalá and Salamanca. A statement in the papal approbation of the *Exercises*, found also in

Polanco's Foreword, only increased this suspicion; namely that Ignatius drew his doctrine " not so much from books as from the unction of the Holy Spirit and from his own interior experience " (*ExSp*MHSJ, pp. 216, 218-219). The " prenote " to the *Exercises* [22] was Ignatius' reply to those who accused him of this heresy.

There were two main factions among the Illuminati or Alumbrados of Spain: those who stressed the value of hidden, solitary prayer (*los Recojidos*); and those who emphasized detachment from all self-will to receive immediately from God the communication of his will (*los Dejados*). It is understandable that a hasty reading of Ignatius' direction to ask God to " place in my soul that which I ought to do " (*SpEx*, [180]) could lead to an interpretation equivalent to the exaggerations of the *Dejados*. Melchor Cano considered the Election an attempt to " force " God's grace through " sweetness of heart."

There were holy persons among the Alumbrados, and not everything they said was wrong; but they probably did exaggerate the possibility that a spiritual man could be certain that he had received a direct illumination from God. This helps us to understand why Ignatius placed so many checks and controls in the process of the election. The best example of the attacks on the *Exercises* is a censure written for the Archbishop of Toledo by Fray Tomás Pedroche, O.P. (*PolChron*, III, 503-524). He considers especially heretical the idea that a man can know " certainly and infallibly " that he has received infused charity. In his reply, Nadal says that the immediate " effects " that one " feels " in the soul according to Ignatius are in the realm of the " spiritual senses " — from which the presence of supernatural charity is " inferred." Of course, such feelings can also be a source of deception. That is why they are to be tested through the discernment of spirits.

This brings us back to our starting point: the similarities between the doctrine of Ignatius on discernment of spirits and that of patristic tradition. To point up these similarities, we shall briefly summarize the main points in the history of this idea in earlier tradition.

The idea that all Christians should test the spirits first appears in 1 Thess. 5:21 and 1 John 4:1. The *Didache* shows how serious this problem of discernment was in early Christian communities and expresses for the first time the fundamental principle of discernment: " Not everyone is a prophet who speaks in the name of the Spirit, but only if he lives according to the ways of the Lord " (*Didache*, XI, 8). The *Pastor Hermae* goes a step further by trying to list the signs of the good and of the evil spirits. By speaking of the good and evil spirits in man as two angels, he used an image that was taken up by Origen and thus came to be used throughout monastic asceticism. The author lists the marks by which these two angels can be recognized: The good angel is mild, modest, gentle, peaceful. The bad angel is irascible, bitter, irrational.

An examination of these authors shows that their similarities are due to a similarity of experience that transcends all merely historical dependence on each other. This is likewise true of Diadochus of Photice, whose teaching on the " relish for what is good " and on the purposes of desolation is strikingly " Ignatian." The same is true of the treatment of St. John Climacus' *Ladder of Paradise.*

We shall not follow the continuation of this tradition in the great spiritual writers of the Middle Ages, except to draw attention to the fact that the *Life of Christ* by Ludolph the Carthusian, the book read by Ignatius at Loyola, gives a description of the workings of the evil spirit which stands mid-way between that of the early Fathers and that of Ignatius. Echoes of Ludolph's treatment can be found in the first draft of the *Constitutions* made by Ignatius and his companions (*Life of Christ*, I, 54; *Cons*MHSJ, I, 17).

Throughout the whole of this history of the discernment of spirits, there is one saying that keeps recurring. This is the agraphon (a saying attributed to Christ but not found in Scripture): " Make yourselves into prudent money-changers." Often enough the expression is mentioned in order to determine whether it really should be attributed to Christ. Its significance in the ascetical tradition of the Church still needs examining.

The image of the " prudent money-changers," it seems, first appeared in the writings of Apelles, a disciple of Marcion. There and in the pseudo-Clementine homilies it is found in a somewhat suspect Gnostic context, warning that one must distinguish the " true from the false " when reading Holy Scripture. Origen and Ambrose interpret it as a warning to distinguish the non-canonical from the true gospels. Victor of Capua uses it in a general sense for the discernment one must exercise when interpreting Scripture. After the saying became popular, it was applied also to discretion in matters of dogma. Origen compares truth and error with genuine and counterfeit coins. Athanasius thought that one had to proceed like a shrewd money-changer to distinguish the divine from the human in Christ without separating them. Pamphilus gave the expression an added meaning when he defended Origen against the " snoopers " and " money-changers " who scrutinized Origen's writings to see whether his doctrine came from the Spirit or from his own heart. Dionysius of Alexandria reports a vision in which he received permission from above to read heretical books without danger to himself since this accorded with the words of Christ: "Become prudent money-changers." On the other hand, the *Didascalia* and the *Apostolic Constitutions* say that only the bishops are to judge matters of dogma.

The vision of Dionysius of Alexandria shows that it was easy to make the transition from the use of this discernment in matters of exegesis and dogma to the use of it in ascetical matters. The important question to be answered was already asked in the Gnostic *Pistis Sophia*: How can a man distinguish the activity of the good spirit from that of the evil spirit? Christ there replies with our agraphon. This approach was the reason why the saying is so prominent in the theology of the pioneers of monastic asceticism, Clement of Alexandria and Origen. Clement speaks of the true "Gnostic" who advances by discernment of spirits and thus fulfills the command to be a prudent money-changer. Origen says that the perfect Christian must make the genuine coins secure in his heart and be able to distinguish the messenger of Christ from that of antichrist.

This is already the language of future monastic asceticism and the beginning of the history of the discernment of spirits. Very typical is chapter in the *Vita Syncleticae* (100, in PG 28, 1549). While speaking of the value of Christian asceticism, it says that this can also be inspired by the devil if not controlled by obedience to one's spiritual father. The true mark of Christian asceticism is moderation. All excess is of diabolic origin: "This seems to me the meaning of the words spoken to me by the Savior, 'Become prudent money-changers.' That is to say, look carefully for the royal stamp on the coin."

Although many others made use of this image, it was Cassian who, through his *Collationes*, made it a part of the traditional teaching on the discernment of spirits. His answer to the problem of distinguishing divine thoughts from those that are diabolical is somewhat complex; nevertheless, he clearly makes the humility of complete openness with the spiritual father the touchstone of genuine discretion. In the fourth Collation he also gives a list of the contrasting workings of the various spirits. All of this is expressed in the image of the genuine and counterfeit coins: "All the thoughts which arise in our hearts must be tested through an acute discernment of their causes, by tracing them back to their first authors and causes, so that we may become prudent money-changers as the Lord commanded." It was this passage especially that preserved the image for posterity.

The early Jesuits had two sources for their familiarity with this agraphon: the *Collationes* of Cassian and the writings of Gerson. Of the latter's works two had a special influence: *De probatione spirituum* and *De distinctione verarum visionum a falsis*.

This article, perhaps, has not shed too much light on what Ignatius actually taught about the discernment of spirits and the election. Yet even a glimpse into the history helps us to see that the early Jesuits were probably right when they felt that they had found something original in the spiritual teaching of Ignatius. The theologian now has the sources available to aid his speculations on that teaching. A study along these lines will show that Ignatius was truly one of the great figures in the history of the spiritual life.

THE IGNATIAN PROCESS
FOR DISCOVERING THE WILL OF GOD
IN AN EXISTENTIAL SITUATION

Some Theological Problems in the Rules for Election
and
Discernment of Spirits
in
St. Ignatius' *Spiritual Exercises*

Karl Rahner
Epitomized[1] by *Harold E. Weidman*

THE CLASSIC COMMENTATORS on St. Ignatius' *Spiritual Exercises* may have satisfied the men of their own times; and yet it is not unfair to them to say that we still lack a theology of the Exercises which comes up to what is expected today. Each age must reexamine works such as the *Exercises* from its own point of view. For example, Ignatius placed his meditations on the Three Sins and on the Kingdom in a perspective of the history of redemption. The new emphasis in present-day theology on the history of salvation leads us to see Ignatius' procedure as something deeper than merely

---

1 Editor's Note: This essay was first translated by Louis W. Roberts.

The German title of Father Karl Rahner's essay, when translated with literal precision, is "The Ignatian Logic of Existential Knowledge: Some Theological Problems in the Rules for Making an Election in St. Ignatius' *Spiritual Exercises*." In this highly important theological study the author employs an original approach by applying existential philosophy to the interpretation of the Election and of the discernment of spirits which is utilized in making it. An English translation of the entire long article, made by W. J. O'Hara with the abbreviated title "The Logic of Concrete

a skillful teacher's device for a vivid presentation of truths and ethical principles which would otherwise remain abstract.

Erich Przwara made a good start toward this kind of a theology of the Exercises in his *Deus semper maior*; but much still remains to be done. At the beginning of such an undertaking, the right questions must be asked. Theologians, however, are prone to consider classics of spirituality such as the *Exercises* to be merely edifying and psychologically effective popularizations of what is contained in the textbooks of theology — and therefore to have no particular interest for theologians. Many such simplifying, derivative popularizations do indeed exist. But there is also another kind of spiritual literature, one which precedes theological reflection and expresses the belief of the Church, the word of God, and the activity of the Holy Spirit in a fresher and more authentic way than any theological treatises. The works of this literature possess a creative originality and, like Scripture and the Church's magisterium, they should be considered more as sources of theology than as derivations from it. They are gifts by which the Holy Spirit makes the revelation given long ago in Christ into something better understood in a new era.

To do justice to such works, a theologian must be able to see the difference between a mere recasting of earlier thought and a creatively original expression of that thought. He must also be aware that such creative works, prophetic utterances in their era, tend to be weakened or diluted in subsequent expositions and interpretations.

Individual Knowledge in Ignatius Loyola," is already available in pages 84-170 of Rahner's *The Dynamic Element in the Church* (New York: Herder and Herder, 1964). Therefore it seemed that a digest would be more helpful and welcome to the readers of the present book than another complete translation. Father Rahner himself expressed his agreement with this opinion. Consequently Father Harold E. Weidman, who had often listened to him at Innsbruck, prepared the digest which is offered here. It was submitted to Father Rahner and received his approval. Father James M. Quigley, S.J., also a former student of Father Rahner, gave further valuable help in the final editing of the text.

In *Woodstock Letters* for spring, 1965, Father Avery Dulles wrote an extended appreciation and review of Rahner's original article and suggested several relevant questions where further study and exposition would be very valuable, as is explained more in detail in a second Editor's Note on page 290 below. While this present book was being edited, Father Rahner kindly consented to write for it his clarifying answers and comments which are found below on pages 290-293.

The *Spiritual Exercises* belong to this creative type of spiritual literature. They ought not to be written off as merely an occurrence in the history of Tridentine or Baroque or somewhat later ideas. Rather, they have a fundamental, archetypal quality which will be understood in its depths and have its full influence only in an age yet to come.

That there are different ways of realizing the Christian life, ways which are unique for each individual person and in each historical period, and which are not merely a deduction from general principles or an application of them — that is something which Ignatius "taught" the Church. Yet the awkward or obscure language of the *Exercises* makes it difficult for a theologian to recognize them as a worthy object of theological study, that is, to put theological questions to them in order to expound them by learning from them, instead of thinking in his pride that he can expound them merely by what he knows without them. When we theologians hear the ancient tradition that the *Exercises* resulted from a special inspiration of the Spirit, we scarcely believe it in any serious sense. The real miracle for us is that a man uneducated in theology except for popular works of piety never broke the rules of theology. If we approached the *Exercises* and similar books with questions for which we do not have our own ready-made answers, they would no longer have the appearance of platitude and over-familiarity. This article is an attempt to ask and answer some theological questions of this kind.

I. The Problem of the Election in the Exercises
The Uniquely Personal as the Will of God

It is generally agreed that the *Spiritual Exercises* is not a doctrinal book explaining what *is*, but a set of instructions for something to be *done*: to discover God's will and decide to follow it. Even when the text expounds truths found in any catechism, it does so to help the exercitant toward that goal.

The first question that arises in considering the Election is: Just exactly what is the will of God that we are to discover? Are the Exercises merely a technique to facilitate the difficult work of discovering what is right, although it is *possible* to deduce this from the general principles of Christian living? Or does God normally have a definite will for an individual that goes beyond what can be discovered by a reasoned application of these Christian principles to a concrete or existential situation? Of course, these principles must have a directive function in the search and must never be infringed upon. But are they all that is needed for the full recognition of God's will?

No Catholic can doubt that such an individual will of God does at least sometimes exist, for it is a necessary presupposition of belief in God's free revelation of himself. The Church has always accepted, both in practice and in theory, the possibility of such personal calls — for example, in the cases of St. Catherine of Siena and of St. Margaret Mary, to whom God revealed definite tasks as his will obliging them, which they could not have known without that revelation. We think it clear that Ignatius thought such a personal vocation to be the normal thing for those who are fitted to make the whole of the Spiritual Exercises — and not only for such rare cases of mystics. Furthermore, the fact that the excesses of Illuminism have shown the dangers of misinterpreting this concept is not sufficient reason for denying that Ignatius believed in genuine guidance by the Holy Spirit.

Now the Rules for the Discernment of Spirits are based on the premise that God is guiding an individual toward his personal vocation, and Ignatius thought that these rules were essential to the process which the making of the Exercises is. He took it for granted that the exercitant would normally experience interior movements of consolation and desolation, and he considered absence of such movements a situation to be looked into (*SpEx*, [6]). He could not hold this if he regarded the Third Time of Election ([177]), the state of tranquillity, as the ordinary time for making the election. Even when it is made then, the exercitant is to ask God to confirm the choice ([180, 183, 188]).

What can all this mean except that Ignatius expects the Spirit to guide a man to a choice different from the one he would rationally make on his own? If we do not accept this, we make the heavenly guidance a merely negative one which keeps us from choosing wrongly, rather than a communication of the divine will which could not otherwise be recognized. But this would certainly give a banal meaning to the exalted statement that the Creator is dealing directly with the creature and the creature with the Creator ([15]). For instance, if in the mind of Ignatius choice or rejection of a life of evangelical poverty depends entirely on one's being willing and fit to answer the general invitation of the gospel, why does he have the exercitant offer to follow Christ in such poverty "*if* your most sacred Majesty desires to choose and receive me into such a state of life" ([98]) ? This poverty of the counsels obviously includes something beyond that poverty of spirit which the gospels recommend to all Christians. If one says that a call to such poverty requires a special grace of vocation, then the experience of this grace clearly belongs to the Second Time of Election.

283

We might remark parenthetically that this Ignatian theory of vocation in no way contradicts the thesis which was propounded especially by J. Lahitton (*La vocation sacerdotale*, Paris, 1914), to the effect that the signs of a vocation to the clerical or religious state are suitability, right intention, and freedom from impediments, — and that an " inspiration " from above is not necessary. First of all, Lahitton's rules are intended above all for the use of religious authorities in determining whether to admit some particular person to orders or vows. Furthermore, no one can deny that vocations have been and continue to be discovered not by rational methods alone but by methods similar to Ignatius', even if less systematic. Finally, Ignatius' rules are aimed at helping one to find his own fitness for his choice of a religious or other vocation, and in what sense this fitness can be regarded as the will of God.

The Ignatian approach avoids the dangers of unverified mysticism and uncontrolled Illuminism, by requiring in advance that the object of choice must be in accord with the teachings and the practice of the Church. Besides, consolations and desolations are experienced as related to conceptions rationally constructed. What is done in the Second Time of Election necessarily contains the activities of the Third; and this latter is to be considered an imperfect form of the Second which aims at being re-integrated into it as a part into the whole. Furthermore, since the instruction on the Election is intended primarily for the spiritual director, and he does not experience the movements himself, he must judge the movements of the spirits according to their effects, their objective suitability. It is thus not false to say that the third method must always be applied, at least by the director.

II. The Ignatian Logic of the Perception of Religiously Important Concrete Particulars: The Method of Election

The most important practical question to be asked here is just how an individual can discover God's will for him, precisely what God wants him to do. The full importance of the *Exercises* for theology is most important here. Especially in the Rules for the Discernment of Spirits, they are an attempt to provide a systematic method for discovering the particular will of God for the individual. The originality of the Ignatian rules for the discernment of spirits is shown by the consistent lack of understanding evidenced in commentaries on the Exercises. If these rules were merely the repetition of what was well established in tradition (where rules for the discernment of spirits were not much used for making an election), the commentators would not have erred so commonly by considering the Third Time as the ordinary one.

a. Are There Immediate Divine Impulses in the Soul, and Are They Recognizable as Such?

The first thing that strikes one in the Rules for the Discernment of Spirits is that Ignatius expects that there will be inner experiences which come from God and can be recognized as such, and also can be recognized as different from the impulsions of Providence which are necessary for every good work. The problem is not to distinguish between good and evil objects of choice, but to discover which possible choice is inspired by God and is thus his will. The divine origin of the impulse is a criterion.

Modern man, with his knowledge of psychology, is tempted to consider the thesis that good or evil spirits can inspire particular thoughts or moods as an attempt of medieval theologians to explain psychological events for which they could find no other explanation. Even if one should concede that such interior movements arising from the spirits are possible but hold that the only practical way of distinguishing them is by seeing whether the objects to which they lead are good or evil, this would be no solution to the problem presented us by Ignatius. He holds that the objects can be evaluated precisely by the origin of the impulses toward them. Perhaps this reflects the experience of a man who was once pushed to the brink of suicide by compulsive thoughts.

It is often said that, if God speaks to an individual, he will do it in such a way that the hearer will be certain that God spoke, with the kind of certitude the prophets must have had. However, we can hardly suppose that the miraculous gifts given to those who had such an important place in the history of salvation will also be the means chosen by God to call an individual to his personal vocation. What we are looking for here should not exceed the bounds of what is ordinary in Christian life. Besides, subjective certainty is not all we are seeking. There must be some quality in the experience that provides an evidence that it has come to the individual " from outside." Perhaps the prophets themselves needed the external wonders that convinced others of the truth of their inspiration, in order to be certain themselves that the revelation they received came from God.

b. The Doctrine of the Exercises on the Divine Impulses and How They Can Be Recognized

Do Ignatius' Rules for the Discernment of Spirits maintain that there are mental movements whose origin from God is certain?

The first principles of logic make the other rules of logic possible; and these rules are, in fact, an application of the principles. Do Ignatius' Rules for the Discernment of Spirits presuppose some first principle or certainty which does for them pretty much what the first principles of logic do for it ? Yes, in the " consolation without a previous cause " of the Rules for the second week ([330, 336]). The problem is that Ignatius' description is a masterpiece of brevity, but not of clarity. He calls it a " consolation without previous cause," one " without any previous perception or knowledge of any object by which such a consolation might come through the mediation of acts of understanding and will." What does this mean ?

The only interpretation of " without cause," in the definition which Ignatius gives of it, is that there is no object or objective basis that is recognized as the source of the consolation, no conceptual knowledge of which the thought would cause peace of soul or its opposite, desolation. This is further specified by a positive aspect, " drawing the soul entirely into the love of His Divine Majesty." One experiences God himself, not any conceptual representation of him. It is an experiencing of the complete openness of the soul to all being, the limitless capacity of the mind to know all things knowable, its " transcendence " or ability to go beyond any particular, limited object, as now directed toward its limitless limit, God himself. If, like Suarez in his commentary on this passage, one makes no distinction between " being known " and " being an object of knowledge," this interpretation is impossible. Yet the self-awareness that accompanies every knowledge of an object is just such a non-conceptual knowledge; it is different from the conceptual knowledge of the " I " which comes when one reflects back upon this self-awareness. Furthermore, Ignatius emphasizes that one should distinguish the consolation itself from the " discourse " which follows, that is, from that activity of the mind which uses conceptual objects. The " suddenness " of the consolation is not a sufficient criterion of its divine origin, since sudden changes of mood are and may arise from natural or even subconscious causes, common in Ignatius' day as well as today.

Why then, in the mind of Ignatius, is such a " consolation without a previous cause " certainly divine in its origin ? He gives an indication in [330]: " For it belongs to the Creator [alone] to enter, depart, and cause a movement in the soul, by drawing it entirely into the love of his Divine Majesty." Note that he does not say that it belongs to God to do this " at will," as many interpret it. What is proper to God is to come and go unaccompanied by any object, to cause *that kind* of consolation which draws one *entirely* into love for Him. It is not a question of a conceptual image of God, for that would be as susceptible to error as any other of our conceptual thoughts. God Himself is not the object, for that would already be the beatific vision. It is the " awareness-become-conscious " of one's complete openness, and *in it* of God as the term of this openness; and this not merely as an act of the intellect but also as a dynamic act of the will opening itself and affirming that term — in other words, an awareness and act of freedom and love. Such a complete openness cannot deceive, because it contains no concept or judgment that might falsely limit God, and also because it is the experience of the fundamental, self-evident, unlimited condition of the possibility of all knowledge.

This view is supported if we give full force to the words Ignatius himself wrote as a commentary on these Rules of Discernment of Spirits for the Second Week, in a letter of June 18, 1536, to Sister Teresa Rejadella (*EppIgn*, I, 105; *Letters Ign*, p. 22): " It often happens that our Lord moves and constrains our soul to one activity or another, by opening up our soul; that is, by speaking within it without any sound of words, by raising it entirely to his divine love, and raising us to an awareness (*sentido*) of himself, such that, even if we wished, we could not resist. This feeling of Him . . . is necessarily a conforming of ourselves with the commandments, the precepts of the Church, and an obedience to our superiors; and it is filled with a deep humility, since the same divine Spirit is in everything. Nevertheless we can sometimes be deceived, because after such consolation or inspiration, while the soul remains joyful, the enemy creeps in with joyful appearance, to bring us to add to what we have felt from God our Lord, and to throw us into disorder and confusion."

Here we have a completely certain experience, with error possible only after the experience itself is over. Not its suddenness but the experience itself shows that it comes from God. It is " wordless," that is, without concepts or objects. It is the experience of being constantly and completely open to God, which Ignatius wished to carry over from the election to everyday life. This openness to God, too, could be one explanation as to why Ignatius could " find God in all things." And so our theory harmonizes well with his spiritual doctrine as a whole.

There are many details still lacking for a full development of this thesis. For instance, there are such questions as describing the many different degrees in which this sort of consolation could exist and to what extent concepts could also be present in the mind without invalidating this object-less kind of consolation.

c. Divine Consolation as a Criterion for
Recognizing God's Will for the Individual

The Rules for the Discernment of Spirits are means of determining which consolations come from God, and thus lead one to make the right choice, and which from other sources, which may lead us either towards or away from the will of God. Two things must be noted in this regard: (1) the object of choice is a means to God, not God himself, and is thus distinct from the fundamental consolation; (2) this fundamental consolation must be the basic criterion and the origin of the correct choice.

If the above is correct, then the process of making an election according to the Second Time must consist in one's bringing this fundamental consolation and the possible object of choice into juxtaposition or confrontation, while observing whether they are in harmony or not. If such a confrontation preserves or strengthens the experience of complete openness to God, thus bringing peace and joy, the proposed object of choice is a good one. If the confrontation weakens this basic consolation, bringing disturbance and confusion, then something is wrong. It is a process of experiment and trial, to see whether the direction in which the possible choice leads the exercitant can be synthesized with his fundamental religious experience of complete openness to God. This introduction of an object makes the actual time of choice a case of the "subsequent time" (*segundo tiempo*, [336]). So it will require considerable time to see whether the two things actually are in harmony.

It is further to be noted that consolation and desolation caused by angels or men are probably combinations of the basic divine consolation with our attitudes toward possible objects of choice. In this "subsequent time" of [336] the divine consolation is still effective, but overlaid by impulses toward finite objects. And conversely, it is only in this "subsequent time" that an election can be made (if we disregard the First Time, which requires revelation in the strict sense). For, in contrast to the time of pure consolation, only here do we have both a finite object and the principle of choice which is the exercitant's experienced orientation to God.

Since it is the purely divine consolation which is the real principle of the discernment of spirits and of the process of election, it is not absolutely necessary to be sure about the origin of other consolations and desolations. The medieval tradition was more prone than we to see good and evil spirits at work. Even if we consider the movements of these spirits as rather in the line of mythological personification, the Ignatian logic of election remains valid. For it is just as clear today as it ever was that the fundamental consolation can come only from God.

This raises another question. Our theory that the Second Time of Election is the normal one supposes that God's will for the individual is existentially unique: It includes God's general will regarding essential natures but goes beyond it and cannot be recognized by mere rational or conceptual thought. How can this be, since most men make their choices, their " elections," without any concern for such a will ? Or can we use the Third Time to seek a differently structured will of God ?

The reply is that, first of all, people often make moral decisions in ignorance of relevant factors. But besides that, *what* one chooses is very often a matter of indifference; *how* one handles it is more important. Finally it can be said that most good people make important decisions pretty much by using the Ignatian logic, only less co.isciously and with a greater possibility of error. They choose, not on purely rational and objective ground, but according to what is suitable to them, what fits in with their basic feeling about themselves, what corresponds to their fundamental personal orientation. In particular, many a person is certain about his religious vocation without being able to give a completely reasoned account of how he reached this certainty. Thus his process seems to be simply an instinctive use of Ignatius' logic.

What can we say of one who is fit for the Exercises yet experiences no movements that enable him to make his election according to the Second Time, and who thus must proceed to the Third Time ? Since God has authorized him to proceed according to the Third Time by not giving him the consolation that is necessary to choose in the Second Time, it may be that he is showing the man that the object of choice is indifferent in his case. Or perhaps God wills that the exercitant remain in a state of uncertainty, of experimentation. Besides, since the Third Time of Election is one of " tranquillity a⁻d quiet "— the similarity of terminology with that which describes the consolation of the Second Time is inescapable — perhaps God is leading him according to the Second Time even though he thinks that he is making his choice by considering his situation calmly and rationally and without any movements of the spirits.

This essay as a whole, then, should have made it clear that Ignatius' logic for the discovery of God's will in regard to a concrete existential cases raises many questions which have not yet been sufficiently treated in moral and spiritual theology. The Church and her theologians have not yet fully understood all that this holy teacher has to tell them.

COMMENTS BY KARL RAHNER
ON QUESTIONS RAISED BY AVERY DULLES

Translated by James M. Quigley, S.J.

I have been requested to supplement my previous essay by making a few brief remarks in answer to the questions about existential knowledge which Father Avery Dulles put to me in *Woodstock Letters*, CXIV (1965), 139-152, even though it is not possible to give here an extensive and thorough answer.[2]

I

When I speak [in my previous study mentioned just above] of the experience of transcendence, within which the choice of a definite categorical object takes place, naturally I always mean a transcendence and an experience of transcendence which is elevated

---

2 Editor's Note: In "Finding God's Will: Rahner's Interpretation of the Ignatian Election," an article which appeared in *Woodstock Letters*, CXIV (1965), 139-152, Father Avery Dulles, S.J., gave a summary and analysis of Karl Rahner's "The Logic of Concrete Individual Knowledge." He regarded this as "a brilliant essay" and "a major break-through in the theology of the *Spiritual Exercises*," opening the field for an immense program of future work. For example, the article stimulates theologians to investigate these questions which it has treated insufficiently:

1. The maxim that pure transcendence is self-authenticating is chiefly philosophical and seemingly needs to be supplemented by theology, since Ignatius' viewpoint was chiefly one of faith. Also, is there such a thing as "natural mysticism"? And would it be sufficient to explain the experience of openness to God in the "consolation without a cause"?

2. This essay does not sufficiently accentuate the Christological element of the Ignatian election, which ordinarily occurs amid exercises on the events of Christ's life and with reference to him as the living norm.

3. This leads us into ecclesiology, too. For the right decision is the one which will best enable the exercitant to reenact Christ's own decisions within his body, which is the Church.

Father Karl Rahner graciously accepted the editor's invitation to use the present book as a vehicle for comment on the issues raised by Father Dulles. That comment is now presented here.

through God's supernatural self-communication and cannot be experienced in any other way. I start with a supposition which is certainly permissible theologically, namely that man's natural transcendentality is always elevated by the supernatural free gift (or at least offer) of God's self-communication, because even after the fall, God wills that all men be saved. This does not mean, of course, that man always uses his freedom to accept God's offer and be justified. Neither does it mean that men are thematically aware of, reflect upon, and formulate sentences about this real supernatural dynamism of man's transcendentality towards God's immediacy. But it is always there, and it is within this horizon that man makes his concrete choice.

And so it is my opinion that there is no purely natural mysticism. What is called by that name is simply the "basis in nature" aspect of man's total constitution, and it is this constitution which (through the "supernatural existential") puts to man the inescapable question whether he will accept in immediacy to God the fact that he is ordered to him, or will fail to do so, and how he will mediate this YES or NO to the supernatural finalization of his existence through the categorical objects of his choices. "Consolation," therefore, consists in this supernatural dynamism's remaining open to the immediacy of God without being distorted by a particular object of choice.

Naturally most men in most situations will not have a reflex awareness that this logic of the existential decision is the norm of their choices any more than they are explicitly aware of Aristotelian logic in everyday reasoning, even though they use it. But just as it is useful or necessary to subject the more difficult situations of ordinary secular life to the norms of a reflex logic, if we wish to be sure of succeeding, so we should use the "logic of existential decisions" in the business of salvation. I still think that in this respect Ignatius of Loyola is as important for the Church as Aristotle is in the field of secular logic. In the secular field Aristotelian logic has always been used, even before Aristotle's time; and even before Ignatius' time people used a logic of existential decisions without reflecting upon it, but in the light of grace, that is, under the graced finality of man's transcendentality, which is real even if we are not reflectively aware of it. It was only through Aristotle and Ignatius that these logics came into explicit awareness, the one becoming the science of the philosophers concerning their own method, the other becoming the science of the saints concerning Christian existence. This is not to deny that the science of the saints developed by Ignatius had forerunners in the doctrine

291

of " the discernment of spirits " and so forth. Nor do I deny that what Ignatius raised to the level of a science was afterwards understood only poorly and little developed.

II

Dulles asks also: What is the Christological dimension of this theology of choice? It has this dimension, of course. And it is clearly given and applied by Ignatius in the *Exercises* throughout the contemplations on the life of Jesus, in the meditation on the Two Standards, and so forth. It is true that my own studies said little or nothing about it, that there is a lacuna here — just as the ordinary treatises on grace unfortunately fail to bring out its Christological dimension explicitly. But this dimension is there. For one thing, all grace, under the most diverse aspects, which I am not going to treat now, is the grace of Christ, and therefore the grace which in the form of " consolation " stamps and determines the business of election must be thought of under all these respects as the grace of Christ. Secondly, if this grace were not thought of as the grace of Christ, the *Exercises* as a whole would be unintelligible, since on the one hand they present themselves as one grand choice and on the other they consist almost entirely of meditations on the life of Jesus.

The Christological dimension of the Election and of its logic can be seen most clearly, perhaps, if we take a particular aspect. A person can choose or reject a particular object only if he has, by the grace of God, freed himself from an immediate attachment to this object and has thus achieved openness to immediacy to God as the sole focus of his existence. This detachment, not merely theoretical but existential, from a particular finite value, from a good in the existential realm, is in all truth, whether one reflects on it or not, a participation in Christ's death. Only Christ, crucified and risen, guarantees that such a dying is possible and that it is not after all merely the descent into the void of absurdity. The only one who can really choose freely is the person who by the grace of God (which is that of Christ crucified) has been liberated from the enslaving tyranny of intramundane " principalities and powers," that is, from the unbelieving illusion that, in order to exist, man must absolutize something in the world of existential experience. The death of this illusion, this " dying," which is a basic element in every Christian choice, takes place in the grace of Christ together with Christ, whether we explicitly know it or not. It reaches its climax and perfect victory in real death, if one dies " in the Lord," just as it got its start in one's being baptized " into the death of Christ."

III

It would take too long to treat adequately here of the ecclesiological dimension of the Election. For Ignatius it is obvious that every election of which he treats must take place in the context of the hierarchically constituted Church, if the question of its rightness is going to be raised at all. The Church as a historical reality is for him at least a " negative norm " for every choice that has anything to do with salvation. Ignatius' own life gives evidence that he did not expect the individual existence to find its place in the Church without pain or conflict. Rather, he was the kind of man who, even in the Church, was always ready to defend himself against ecclesiastical authorities, and who freely admitted that all the bones in his body had trembled when he heard of the election of Paul IV.

On the other hand, for Ignatius it is also obvious that the individual cannot simply deduce from the doctrines and institutions of the Church any concrete imperative for the decisions of his own Christian life. Otherwise Ignatius' Rules for an Election, which put the individual on his own before God, would make no sense and have no area where they could be applied. The charismatic imperative which must be taken up only by the individual in the election process is not, on the other hand, anti-ecclesial. For the charismatic element, which escapes the control of the institutional Church, belongs to the nature of the Church, inasmuch as the latter is inconceivable except as subject to the sovereign disposition of her Lord.

I agree with Dulles, of course, when he stresses that in the concrete the three different Times for an election do not occur in complete separation from one another but rather signify aspects of a single election, in which all three aspects appear, though in very different intensities.

ABBREVIATIONS

used in the footnotes

AHSJ — *Archivum historicum Societatis Jesu*
Autobiog — *The Autobiography of St. Ignatius* (dictated to Da Câmara)
Cartas — *Cartas de san Ignacio de Loyola.* 6 vols. Madrid: 1874-1889
Cons — *The Constitutions of the Society of Jesus,* in any edition
*Cons*MHSJ — *Constitutiones Societatis Iesu* in the series of critically edited texts of the Monumenta historica Societatis Iesu. See MHSJ, MI, Series III
ConsSJComm — *The Constitutions of the Society of Jesus.* Translated, with an Introduction and a Commentary, by G. E. Ganss, S.J.
DeGuiJes — De Guibert, *The Jesuits: Their Spiritual Doctrine and Practice*
DirSpEx — *Directoria Exercitiorum Spiritualium* (1540-1590). See s.v. MHSJ
EppIgn — *S. Ignatii Epistolae.* See s.v. MHSJ
EppMixt — *Epistolae Mixtae.* See s.v. MHSJ
EppXav — *Epistolae S. Francisci Xaverii.* See s.v. MHSJ
Exam — *The General Examen* or *Examen Generale*
FN — *Fontes narrativi de Sancto Ignatio.* See s.v. MHSJ
InstSJ — *Institutum Societatis Iesu.* 3 vols. Florence, 1892-1893
LettersIgn — *Letters of St. Ignatius,* translated by W. J. Young
LitQuad — *Litterae Quadrimestres.* See s.v. MHSJ

MHSJ — MONUMENTA HISTORICA SOCIETATIS JESU, the Historical Records or Sources of the Society of Jesus in critically edited texts.

This scholarly series which now contains 100 volumes, was begun in Madrid in 1894. The project was transferred to Rome in 1929. Most of the manuscripts on which these volumes are based are in the Archives of the Society of Jesus in Rome. The series is being continued by its publisher, the *Institutum Historicum Societatis Iesu,* Via dei Penitenzieri 20, 00193, Rome.
MI — Monumenta Ignatiana. The writings of St. Ignatius of Loyola.

Series I
EppIgn — *S. Ignatii . . . Epistolae et Instructiones.* [Edd. M Lecina,

V. Agusti, F. Cervós, D. Restrepo.] 12 vols., Madrid, 1903-1911. The letters and instructions of St. Ignatius.

Series II

*SpEx*MHSJ — *Exercitia Spiritualia S. Ignatii . . . et eorum Directoria.* [Ed. A. Codina.] 1 vol. Madrid, 1919. The critical text of the *Spiritual Exercises* and of the *Directories* for conducting them.

New Series II. A revision

*SpEx*MHSJ*Te* — Vol. I. *Sti. Ignatii de Loyola Exercitia Spiritualia. Textuum antiquissimorum nova editio. Lexicon textus hispani.* Edd. J. Calveras et C. de Dalmases. Rome, 1969. A revision of *SpEx*MHSJ.

DirSpEx — Vol. II. *Directoria Exercitiorum Spiritualium* (1540-1599). Ed. I. Iparraguirre. 1 vol. Rome, 1955. This is a more complete edition of the *Directories* than the earlier one of 1919 in *SpEx*MHSJ.

Series III

*Cons*MHSJ — *Constitutiones et Regulae Societatis Iesu.* 4 vols. The critically edited texts of the *Constitutions* and *Rules* of the Society of Jesus, along with copious introductions and notes.

*Cons*MHSJ, I — Vol. I. *Monumenta Constitutionum praevia.* [Ed. A. Codina.] Rome, 1934. Sources and records previous to the texts of the *Constitutions.* Historical introductions.

*Cons*MHSJ, II — Vol. II. *Textus hispanus.* [Ed A. Codina.] Rome, 1936. Critical texts of the four chief and successive texts of the Spanish original.

*Cons*MHSJ, III — Vol. III. *Textus latinus.* [Ed A. Codina.] Rome, 1938. The critical text of the Latin translation which was approved by the First General Congregation of the Society in 1558 .

*Cons*MHSJ, IV—Vol. IV. *Regulae Societatis Jesu.* Ed. D. F. Zapico. Rome, 1948. Ancient drafts of rules or directives.

MHSJ — continued

Series IV

SdeSI— *Scripta de Sancto Ignatio.* [Edd. L. M. Ortiz, V. Agusti, M. Lecina, A. Macía, A. Codina, D. Fernández, D. Restrepo.] 2 vols. Madrid, 1904, 1918. Writings about St. Ignatius by his contemporaries.

Series IV, revised

FN — Fontes narrativi de S. Ignatio de Loyola et de Societatis Iesu initiis. Edd. D. Fernández Zapico, C. de Dalmases, P. Leturia. 4 vols. Rome, 1943-1960.
Vol. I — 1523-1556
Vol. II — 1557-1574
Vol. III — 1574-1599
Vol. IV — Ribadeneyra's *Vita Ignatii Loyolae* (1572)
Narrative sources, that is, writings about Ignatius by his contemporaries. An improved edition of the documents contained in *SdeSI.*
Fontes documentales de S. Ignatio. [In preparation.]

Primary Sources from Ignatius' Contemporaries

EppMixt — Epistolae Mixtae ex variis Europae locis, 1537-1556. [Ed. V. Agusti.] 5 vols. Madrid, 1898-1901. Chiefly letters to Ignatius.

LittQuad — Litterae Quadrimestres. [Edd. M. Lecina, D. F. Zapico.] 7 vols. Madrid and Rome, 1894-1932. Quarterly reports to the central government of the Society in Rome. 1546-1562.

MonBobad — Bobadillae Monumenta. [Ed. D. Restrepo.] Madrid, 1913. 1 vol. Letters of Ignatius' companion, Nicolás Bobadilla.

MonBorg — Sanctus Franciscus Borgia. [Edd. I. Rodríguez, V. Agusti, F. Cervós.] 5 vols. Madrid, 1894-1911. Letters, diaries, and instructions of St. Francis Borgia.

MonBroet — Epistolae PP. Paschasii Broet, Claudii Jaji, Joannis Codurii et Simonis Rodericii S.J. [Ed. F. Cervós.] 1 vol. Madrid, 1903. Letters of Ignatius' companions, Paschase Broët, Claude Jay, Jean Codure, and Simão Rodrigues.

MonFabri — Fabri Monumenta. [Ed. F. Lirola.] 1 vol. Madrid, 1914. Letters and diaries of Ignatius' companion, Pierre Favre.

MonLain — Lainii Monumenta. [Ed. E. Astudillo.] 8 vols. Madrid, 1912-1917. Letters of Ignatius' companion, Diego Laynez.

MonNad — Epistolae P. Hieronymi Nadal. 6 vols. Vols. I-IV, ed. F. Cervós, 1898-19 05. Vols. V, *Commentarii de Instituti S.I.,* 1962, and VI, *Orationis observationes,* 1964, ed. M. Nicolau. Letters and instructions of Ignatius' companion, Jerônimo Nadal.

MonPaed — Monumenta paedagogica. [Edd. C. Rodeles, M. Lecina, V. Augusti, F. Cervós, A. Ortiz.] 1 vol. Madrid, 1901. Pedagogical documents which antedated the first *Plan of Studies* (*Ratio Studiorum*) of 1586. A revision of this volume is now in progress and will have probably four volumes.

MonPaed (1965)— *Monumenta paedagogica Societatis Iesu, I* (1540-1556). Ed L. Lukács. Rome, 1965.

MonRib — *Ribadeneira.* [Ed. D. Restrepo, J. Vilar.] 2 vols. Madrid, 1920, 1923. Letters and notes of Ignatius' contemporary, Pedro de Ribadeneyra.

MonSalm — *Epistolae P. Alphonsi Salmeronis.* [Edd. R. Vidaurre, F. Cervós.] 2 vols. Madrid, 1906-1907. Letters of Ignatius' companion, Alonso Salmerón.

MonXav — *Monumenta Xaveriana.* [Edd. M. Lecina, D. Restrepo.] 2 vols. Madrid, 1899, 1912. Writings, chiefly letters, of St. Francis Xavier.

PolChron — *Chronicon Societatis Iesu, auctore Joanne Alphonso de Polanco, S.J.* [Edd. J. M. Velez, V. Agusti.] 6 vols. Madrid, 1894-1898. Early history of the Society by Ignatius' secretary, Juan Alonso de Polanco.

PolCompl — *Polanci Complementa.* [Edd. D. Restrepo, D. F. Zapico.] 2 vols. Madrid, 1918-197. Letters and notes by Ignatius' secretary.

MONUMENTA MISSIONUM

1. *Missiones Orientales.* (Missions Eastward from Rome.)

EppXav — *Epistolae S. Francisci Xaveri* [Edd. G. Schurhammer, J. Wicki.] 2 vols. Rome, 1944-1945. An enlarged and improved edition of the *Monumenta Xaveriana* of 1899.

Many other volumes exist in this series but it is not necessary to list them in detail here.

MonBobad, or *MonBorg,* etc. See above s.v. MHSJ.

NCathEnc — *The New Catholic Encyclopedia*

PG — Patrologia Graeca, ed. Migne

PL — Patrologia Latina, ed. Migne

PolChron — Polanco's *Chronicon Societatis Iesu,* See s.v. MHSJ

PolCompl — *Polanci Complementa.* See s.v. MHSJ

RAM — *Revue d'ascétique et de mystique*

RazFel — *Razón y Fe*

RevRe — *Review for Religious*

SdeSI — *Scripta de Sancto Ignatio.* See s.v. MHSJ

SMV — Sommervogel, *Bibliothèque de la Compagnie de Jésus*

SpDiar — The *Spiritual Diary of St. Ignatius* (1544-1545)

SpEx — The *Spiritual Exercises of* St. Ignatius or his *Exercitia Spiritualia,* in any edition

SpExMHSJ — *Exercitia Spiritualia* in the critical edition of MHSJ. See s.v. MHSJ

ST — *Summa theologiae* of St. Thomas Aquinas

WL — *Woodstock Letters*

ZAM — *Zeitschrift für Aszese und Mystik*